DRIVEN FROM HOME

SERIES EDITORS

Stephen Berry
University of Georgia

Amy Murrell Taylor
University of Kentucky

ADVISORY BOARD

Edward L. Ayers
University of Richmond

Catherine Clinton
University of Texas at San Antonio

J. Matthew Gallman
University of Florida

Elizabeth Leonard
Colby College

James Marten
Marquette University

Scott Nelson
College of William & Mary

Daniel E. Sutherland
University of Arkansas

Elizabeth Varon
University of Virginia

Driven from Home
North Carolina's Civil War Refugee Crisis

DAVID SILKENAT

The University of Georgia Press *Athens*

Paperback edition, 2018
© 2016 by the University of Georgia Press
Athens, Georgia 30602
www.ugapress.org
All rights reserved
Set in Berthold Baskerville by Graphic Compostion, Inc.

Most University of Georgia Press titles are
available from popular e-book vendors.

Printed digitally

The Library of Congress has cataloged the hardcover
edition of this book as follows:
Names: Silkenat, David, author.
Title: Driven from Home : North Carolina's Civil War
Refugee Crisis / David Silkenat.
Description: Athens : The University of Georgia Press, 2016.
Identifiers: LCCN 2016001702 | ISBN 9780820349466 (hardcover : alk. paper) |
ISBN 9780820349473 (ebook)
Subjects: LCSH: Refugees—North Carolina—History—19th century. |
Refugees—Confederate States of America—History. |
North Carolina—History—Civil War, 1861–1865—Refugees. |
United States—History—Civil War, 1861–1865—Refugees. |
North Carolina—Social conditions—19th century. |
Confederate States of America—Social conditions.
Classification: LCC E573.S55 2016 | DDC 973.7'13—dc23
LC record available at https://lccn.loc.gov/2016001702

Paperback ISBN 978-0-8203-5473-6

CONTENTS

Acknowledgments   vii

Introduction   1

Chapter 1. Gwine to Liberty   11

Chapter 2. Crowded with Refugees   55

Chapter 3. Driven into Exile   100

Chapter 4. Confederacy of Refugees   128

Chapter 5. In Good Hands, in a Safe Place   160

Chapter 6. A Home for the Rest of the War   184

Epilogue   217

Notes   233

Bibliography   261

Index   285

ACKNOWLEDGMENTS

I began this book in 2010 at my dining room table in Fargo, North Dakota, when I was teaching at North Dakota State University. The blizzards and subzero temperatures outside my window presented a very different picture than the somewhat more temperate North Carolina environ I was trying to re-create on the page. I finished revising this book in 2015 in my office in Edinburgh, Scotland, an even greater remove from the Tar Heel State. The distances, both physical and metaphorical, between those locales helped me to empathize, at least in a small way, with many of the individuals I was writing about. Although I've been lucky enough never to have been a refugee, I did manage to live a somewhat peripatetic life while writing this book.

I have benefited from a number of generous grants that allowed me to do the archival work that made this book possible. An Archie K. Davis Fellowship from the North Caroliniana Society, a Guion Griffis Johnson Visiting Scholar Grant from the University of North Carolina's Southern Historical Collection, and a Hendrickson Faculty Development Award from North Dakota State University allowed me to spend two summers in North Carolina archives. An Andrew W. Mellon Fellowship from the Huntington Library allowed me to spend a restful month researching and writing. As with most historical works, the archivists are the unsung heroes who make the research possible. For special praise, I wanted to single out the robust help of Laura Clark Brown and Matt Turi at UNC's Southern Historical Collection and Chris Meekins at the North Carolina State Archives.

This book has benefited from innumerable conversations with friends and colleagues. A radically incomplete list of those whose thoughts and comments have helped me along the way include Bruce Baker, David Blight, Judkin Browning, Karl Campbell, Catherine Clinton, Frank Cogliano, John Cox, Adam Domby, Owen Dudley Edwards, Susan-Mary Grant, Hilary Green, Matt Harper, Mark Harvey, Fabian Hilfrich, Michael Hill, Tom Isern, Anya Jabour, Suzzanne Kelley, Kelly Kennington, Bill Link, Robert Mason, Cecelia Moore, Barton Myers, Megan Kate Nelson, Larry Peterson, Paul Quigley, Angela Smith, John David Smith, Diane Miller Sommerville, Harry Watson, and Tim Williams. I owe a particular debt to Fitz

Brundage, who has continued to provide sage counsel long after I left graduate school. Steve Berry has been a constant supporter of my work and has been invaluable in transforming my often inchoate thoughts into something worth reading.

My family has been more indulgent with me than I deserve during the writing of this book. My father and my parents-in-law have been, as always, very supportive of me and my work. My darling wife, Ida, has not only given me her unconditional love and the time and space to research and write this book but also carefully read the manuscript, catching many poor turns of phrase. My most significant regret in writing this book is that time I spent working on it could have been spent with her and our children, Chamberlain, Dawson, and Thessaly. This book is dedicated to them.

DRIVEN FROM HOME

Introduction

On May 7, 1864, the *Mercury*, a Raleigh, North Carolina, weekly magazine, published the first part of a novelette titled "The Refugee's Niece." The author, William D. Herrington, a soldier in the Third North Carolina Cavalry, claimed that his story was "Founded on Real Incidents of the War in North Carolina." Herrington would later publish three other novelettes in the *Mercury*, two of which, "The Captain's Bride" and "The Deserter's Daughter," would eventually also be published as freestanding volumes. The titular refugee in Herrington's story was "Mr. Holmes, a respectable citizen, and a true southerner at heart, who at the fall of Newbern [North Carolina] had taken refuge here within the Confederate lines to avoid that inhuman brutality that the enemy were in the habit of inflicting upon such non-combatants as were so unfortunate as to fall within their jurisdiction." Holmes had moved to the North Carolina Piedmont with his orphaned nineteen-year-old niece Annie, who possessed "a sylph-like form, with raven black hair, dark eyes, and rosey cheeks." The plot of "The Refugee's Niece" centered on a love triangle involving Annie and two Confederate soldiers who vied for her affection. Unfortunately, the issue of the *Mercury* that contained the concluding half of "The Refugee's Niece" has not survived, so we do not know how Annie Holmes's romance resolved itself. Although the plot was hackneyed, the prose awkward, and the spelling and grammar poor, "The Refugee's Niece" was a popular success, making Herrington a minor Confederate literary phenomenon. Both set and published in the North Carolina Piedmont, "The Refugee's Niece" reverberated with readers because so many of them saw themselves in its pages. By March 1864 thousands of refugees had descended on the Piedmont, not only from New Bern and eastern North Carolina, then under Union control, but from across the Confederacy. Located in the Confederate interior, the Piedmont offered the promise of isolation, situated at the spot farthest from Union armies.[1]

Exactly one hundred years after the publication of Herrington's "The Refugee's Niece," historian Mary Elizabeth Massey published her study of Confederate refugees, *Refugee Life in the Confederacy*. Born in 1915, Massey was one of the most prominent female Civil War historians of her generation. After receiving her doctorate at the University of North Carolina, Massey taught for more than two decades at Winthrop College in Rock Hill, South Carolina. Massey had the distinctions of being the only woman to serve on the Advisory Council for the Civil War Centennial Commission and, in 1972, becoming the third woman president of the Southern Historical Association. Over the course of her scholarly career, Massey published ten articles and three books, among which *Refugee Life* has had the most significant and lasting influence. Massey published *Refugee Life* in 1964, at the height of the Civil War centennial observations. The product of more than ten summers of research, Massey's original manuscript ran to 664 pages, too long even by the standards of the day, which seemed to embrace Civil War tomes. After being prodded by her editor at Louisiana State University Press, Massey pruned the text to 370 pages. According to her preface, Massey's original intention was to examine "all groups uprooted by the war—Confederate and Union sympathizers, Negroes, Indians, and whites." However, Massey was advised "by several authorities, whose opinions I value and respect," that such a project would prove unwieldy, and she therefore restricted her study to "Confederate sympathizers who spent the war years trying to stay within the contracting Confederacy." If her acknowledgments provide any clue, those authorities who urged Massey to restrict her study to white Confederates included some of the most notable Civil War historians of the era, including Bell I. Wiley, Fletcher Green, T. Harry Williams, and David Donald. Although Massey attempted to include the experiences of Confederate refugees from a variety of social backgrounds, she admitted that her sources biased her study toward the upper-class refugee experience.[2]

The refugees who populated Massey's book consisted primarily of elite women, including Varina Davis (wife of Confederate president Jefferson Davis), Katherine Polk Gale (daughter of Confederate general Leonidas Polk), and Mary Boykin Chesnut (wife of Confederate general and former South Carolina senator James Chesnut). In Massey's narrative the prototypical Confederate refugee was not unlike the titular character in William Herrington's novelette, figures such as Mary Norcott Bryan, a wealthy refugee from New Bern who fled to the North Carolina Piedmont. While Massey's focus on these women and others from similar backgrounds illuminated one facet of refugee life, she largely ignored the experience of nonelite refugees, Unionists, and African Americans. Although Massey's elite refugees experienced some mild hardships, about which they complained bitterly in their diaries and correspondence, they managed to get through the Civil War with their lives relatively intact, an experience few other refugees shared.

In the fifty years since the publication of Massey's *Refugee Life*, historians have focused on another segment of the Confederate refugee population, examining how hundreds of thousands of African Americans fled slavery during the Civil War. Starting in 1976, the Freedmen and Southern Society Project at the University of Maryland has documented their experiences, drawing from materials in the National Archives to produce a series of volumes that chronicle the formation of contraband (refugee) camps, often in the shadow of the Union army, where fugitive slaves began the transition from slavery to freedom. Many historians (several of them veterans of the Freedmen and Southern Society Project) have over the past two decades deepened our understanding of the black refugee experience, including insightful work done by Thavolia Glymph, Steven Hahn, Leslie Schwalm, Yael Sternhell, and Jim Downs, among others. As a consequence of this important scholarship, we have a much greater understanding of the significant role that African Americans played in pushing the federal government into adopting emancipation, of the origins of free black labor in the South, and of the black military experience during the Civil War. The picture that emerges from this scholarship on refugee life differs dramatically from what Massey presented. Whereas Massey's elite white refugees left their homes to maintain their lives with as little disturbance as possible, black refugees who fled to Union lines sought to radically transform their lives, escaping bondage in the hopes of establishing a new life in freedom. In doing so, they reconstructed separated families, pursued educations denied to them in slavery, and established social and political institutions to defend their freedom. They also experienced enormous hardship and suffering, struggled with inadequate food and shelter, and died from epidemic disease. For federal officials and relief workers, the formation of the refugee camps served as a device to manage and control refugees, providing sites where they could be counted, categorized, and drawn up for necessary labor. For black refugees, the camps became places of cultural formation and political mobilization. Because of this remarkable body of scholarship, we know far more about how some African Americans experienced the transition from slavery to freedom.

This scholarship on black refugees, however, does not situate fugitive slaves' experiences within the broader Civil War refugee crisis. While a great deal of scholarly attention has been paid to black refugees who fled to Union lines, far less attention has been paid to the thousands of enslaved African Americans forcibly removed by their owners into the Confederate interior to distance them from Union armies and to prevent them from running away. Because those historians who have examined black refugees have been primarily interested in the transition from slavery to freedom, they have overlooked how many black Southerners experienced forced migration during the Civil War to maintain their enslavement. Existing studies of black refugees also often fail to compare their experiences with those of the thousands of white Unionists who joined them in fleeing to Union lines.[3]

This book endeavors to fulfill Massey's original intention by recognizing that one of the most important and distinctive features of the Confederate refugee crisis was its diversity, as Southerners of all races, genders, classes, and political alliances chose or were forced to move as a consequence of the Civil War. It argues that understanding the diversity of refugee movements illuminates dynamics between them that have remained invisible when looking at them individually. Throughout the Confederacy, black and white Southerners fled away from and toward Union lines. Recognizing the scope and diversity of these migrations should force us to reconsider how we understand the Confederate home front when so many Southerners experienced the war away from home.[4] As Yael Sternhell has recently observed, the journeys of refugees and soldiers amounted to a "gargantuan wave of motion that swept through the Confederacy," the erosive power of which remade the South's social landscape.[5] Refugeeing formed a critical part of the wartime friction and abrasion that wore away at slavery and the institutions that supported it.

North Carolina provides a particularly fruitful venue for studying the Southern refugee crisis. While Virginia, Louisiana, and Tennessee may have had more refugees, the refugee crisis manifested its complexity most fully in North Carolina. First, because of its location in the Confederate interior and because it was one of the last sites to be occupied by Union armies, North Carolina became a destination site for refugees from across the Confederacy. Second, the refugee crisis in North Carolina lasted for the duration of the conflict, beginning before the first shots were fired at Fort Sumter and lasting well after the Confederate surrender at Bennett Place. In the process, refugees forged communities that created or enlarged urban spaces. Refugee camps near New Bern had more than eighty-five hundred residents, a population greater than any antebellum North Carolina city except Wilmington. The influx of refugees caused cities such as Raleigh and Charlotte to double in population. Third, and probably most significantly, North Carolina's refugee crisis included the entire spectrum of refugee experiences, ranging from wealthy plantation owners who fled from Union armies to safety in the Piedmont and Blue Ridge Mountains to the fugitive slaves who fled toward Union armies in the east, hoping for freedom. While these disparate refugee experiences are worthy of investigation individually, they share certain fundamental features. Refugees, regardless of class, race, status, or gender, were forced to cope with the practical difficulties of finding housing, food, and other necessities far from home, all of which were in short supply. They also all dealt with psychological ramifications common among refugees, including depression, anxiety, and homesickness.

For the refugees themselves, however, their differences were far more significant than their similarities. Indeed, Civil War–era North Carolinians employed a vocabulary that distinguished between different segments of the refugee population. The term "refugee" itself was used almost exclusively to refer to pro-Confederate whites, especially wealthy slaveholding whites. Slaves who fled to Union lines are referred to in Confederate sources as "fugitives," while Union sources describe them as "contraband" and, after 1863, as "freedmen." Whites who fled to Union lines were generally referred to as "Buffaloes," a term whose origins remain unclear. No universally adopted term was used to describe enslaved African Americans who were forcibly relocated by their owners to the interior, although slave owners often described this movement as "removing" their slaves. This linguistic segmentation of Civil War refugees continued until the end of the war and manifested itself in the official title of the Freedmen's Bureau–the Bureau of Refugees, Freedmen, and Abandoned Lands–which distinguished between freedmen and (white) refugees. This racialized distinction between different classes of refugees also appeared in the bureau's first circular issued in North Carolina, which proclaimed its jurisdiction over "all subjects relating to Refugees and Freedmen in the State."[6]

This book explores five distinct elements within the refugee population in Civil War North Carolina. The first and largest group was composed of the thousands of African Americans who fled from slavery to freedom, seeking liberty under the protection of the Union army in eastern North Carolina. The second group, smaller, but no less significant, was the thousands of white Unionists who also fled to Union lines in eastern North Carolina. While both white Unionists and fugitive slaves sought refuge within the shadow of the Union flag, as we shall see, their experiences as refugees were radically different. A third refugee population consisted of pro-Confederate whites from across the South who sought safety within the Confederate interior, placing as much distance between themselves and Union armies as possible. Fourth, white Confederate refugees often brought their slaves with them to central and western North Carolina, in part to work, but mainly to prevent their slaves from running away, thus securing their most valuable form for property. The removal of slaves to the Confederate interior created unforeseen problems for slave owners, undermined slave discipline, and dramatically expanded slave hiring. Finally, while schools and colleges across the Confederacy closed during the war, girls' boarding schools in central North Carolina flourished, as concerned parents sent their refugee daughters to the most secure location in the South. Proud to call themselves refugees, these schoolgirls viewed the war from a unique perspective, one that would shape how they would remember and commemorate it for decades afterward.

Each of these five categories represented a distinct refugee experience. However, in curious ways, these refugee movements reinforced each other. For instance, slaves responded to the possibility of removal by running away in increasing numbers to Union lines. While planters often attempted to prevent slaves from knowing about their imminent forced migration, rumors of relocation pushed irresolute slaves to take the opportunity while it was available. Thus the voluntary migration of slaves to Union lines and the involuntary migration of slaves to the Confederate interior reinforced each other, pushing North Carolina's enslaved black population east and west, toward freedom and slavery. With each passing month, as some slaves escaped to freedom, slave owners removed others to keep them from running away.

From the perspective of 1861, few Americans anticipated that the impending conflict would generate a refugee crisis of the scale, complexity, and duration that developed. The historical antecedents that Americans drew on, notably the American Revolution and War of 1812, suggested that refugee problems would be localized, be of brief duration, and encompass no more than a few thousand people. During the Revolution, the British occupation of Boston and New York prompted thousands of civilians to relocate, with Loyalists fleeing toward the British standard and Patriots seeking shelter elsewhere. During both the Revolution and the War of 1812, enslaved African Americans, especially in the Chesapeake, used the chaos created by war to make a break for freedom. Although immensely significant for those dislocated, these earlier refugee migrations on American soil offered only hints of the crisis that emerged during the Civil War. Those who looked across the Atlantic, however, may have seen the potential for modern warfare to create mass refugee crises, as the Crimean War made hundreds of thousands of Orthodox Bulgarian peasants and Crimean Tartars into refugees. There is little evidence to suggest, however, that the political and military leaders of the Union and the Confederacy gave serious thought to the impact that a highly mobile Southern population would have on the war. While many observers correctly predicted that the outbreak of war would dramatically increase the number of slaves running away, they never grasped the consequences of hundreds of thousands of white and black Southerners being on the move.[7]

This failure of either Union officials on North Carolina's coast or Confederate officials in the North Carolina Piedmont and mountains to anticipate the magnitude of voluntary and forced relocations made the refugee problem into a refugee crisis. I use the term "crisis" not only to reflect the number of refugees and the difficulty of their circumstances but also because the response of governmental and charitable organizations was often woefully inadequate. For Union officials, efforts to help refugees were hampered by racial and regional prejudices, by conflicts between civilian and military oversight, and by fears of fostering dependence on the federal government.[8] For Confederates, the failure to provide meaningful aid for refugees derived primarily from the financial problems that plagued the Confederacy after 1863, coupled with relief aid structures that favored local residents over refugees. The failure of both the Union and the Confederacy to adequately respond to the refugee crisis reflected not only their inadequate planning and scant resources but also shifting attitudes toward the role of government in helping people in times of disaster. The formation of the Freedmen's Bureau in the war's final months reflected the culmination of the failure to adequately address the refugee crisis.

We do not know how many Southerners became refugees during the Civil War. Mary Elizabeth Massey refrained from making an estimate, undoubtedly daunted by the prospect of clearly delineating refugees from other civilians. Historian George Rable has estimated that 250,000 white Southerners became refugees. Many historians have tried to estimate the number of enslaved African Americans who ran away to Union lines during the Civil War, with estimates ranging from five hundred thousand to one million. The roundness of these figures suggests the extent to which the available evidence makes it impossible to accurately assess how many Southern civilians were forced or chose to leave home during the conflict. While the sum total of Southern refugees may prove elusive, even the more conservative estimates suggest that the Civil War generated one of the largest refugee crises in American history, comparable to the forced relocation of Native Americans during the Jacksonian era, Plains farmers during the Dust Bowl, Japanese Americans during World War II, and most recently, the roughly one million people displaced due to Hurricane Katrina. Indeed, the refugee population of the South exceeded the number of men who fought in Confederate gray. Understanding their experiences should force us to reconsider how we understand the Confederate home front and indeed the entire Confederate experiment.[9]

This book has been inspired and informed in part by the experiences of contemporary refugees. Like many Americans, I have been moved by the struggles of refugees and internally displaced people from Syria, Palestine, Iraq, Congo, and Sudan (among other localities). Conversations with refugees and with aid workers have shaped the questions I have asked about the refugee experience during the Civil War. In particular, these conversations and the growing scholarship on refugees have pushed me to give greater consideration to how refugee communities are formed and maintained. They have also pushed me to examine the role of government and aid agencies in responding to the suffering of refugees. Today, humanitarian crises across the globe can prompt the international community to respond in the form of aid from the United Nations High Commission on Refugees, the Red Cross, Doctors without Borders, and similar organizations, and international law prescribes protections for refugees, internally displaced people, and asylum seekers. Although the international responses to refugee crises today are often woefully inadequate, they exist within a framework in which providing aid to refugees has been institutionalized. None of these structures existed during the nineteenth century, and the obligation of governments to protect refugees did not become an established part of the laws of war until nearly one hundred years in the future. Finally, we are only beginning to understand the significant emotional and psychological toll that refugees pay. Recent scholarship has suggested that refugees suffer from many of the same lasting psychological scars as soldiers on the front lines.[10] If my conversations with refugees and aid workers have taught me anything, it is to appreciate the diversity of their experiences. Each refugee had his or her own story to tell of homesickness, grief, and perseverance.

Figure 1. Coastal North Carolina. *Harper's Weekly*, October 5, 1861.

ONE
Gwine to Liberty

In February 1862 a band of fifteen to twenty slaves fled from their plantation along the Chowan River in northeastern North Carolina, boarded a small boat, and floated downriver toward the Albemarle Sound. The group, which consisted of men, women, and children, had heard about the Union occupation of Roanoke Island only days earlier. Union forces under the command of Gen. Ambrose Burnside had overwhelmed the nominal Confederate defenses, establishing a base from which they could move against the North Carolina mainland. The fugitive slaves also knew that slave owners in the region were beginning to remove their human property inland to isolate them from the threat posed by the presence of Union soldiers.

Their departure did not go unnoticed, as their owners chased them along the riverbank with dogs and unsuccessfully fired at them. In the pouring rain, they made their way to the Federal encampment on Roanoke Island. Met there by Union soldiers, most of whom came from New England and some of whom professed abolitionist sentiments, the "happy party rejoic[ed] at their escape from slavery and danger, and at the hearty welcome which was at once extended to them." Cold and dripping wet, the women and children in the party were offered shelter by Vincent Colyer, a civilian representing the U.S. Christian Commission, who volunteered his tent.[1]

The fugitive slaves sheltering in Vincent Colyer's tent represented the first wave of thousands of refugees in eastern North Carolina during the Civil War. The Burnside invasion of 1862 created several distinct streams of refugees. The first and the largest was composed of the thousands of

African Americans who escaped from slavery to the potential and promise of freedom under the banner of the Union army. The second stream, almost as large as the first, consisted of pro-Confederate civilians who moved into the North Carolina interior in advance of the Union invasion. Many of these pro-Confederate refugees brought their slaves with them to central and western North Carolina in order to place as much distance between them and Union armies as possible. Finally, a smaller third stream of white Unionists fled from their homes in Confederate-controlled territory into Union-occupied towns.

The following chapters highlight three themes about the refugee experience in eastern North Carolina. First, refugees dealt with significant material and physical hardships. Housing and food shortages, overcrowding, and disease were chronic problems in eastern North Carolina throughout the Civil War, and these problems grew more significant as the refugee population increased. Second, the contested status of slavery and loyalty shaped the nature of the refugee experience. The first black refugees arrived inside Union lines when that did not necessarily entail freedom, a freedom that remained contested for the duration of the war. White refugees entering Union lines had to demonstrate and perform their fidelity to the Union cause, constantly under the suspicion of disloyalty. Third, both white and black refugees had to work with and against military officials, soldiers, and Northern aid workers, many of whom had their own priorities and prejudices concerning refugees. Each of these themes contributes to a deeper understanding of the refugee experience and the formation of refugee communities.

In eastern North Carolina, refugee communities were formed within the confines and context of refugee camps. The refugee camps established in early 1862 matured over the next three years, becoming increasingly overcrowded, polluted, and disease-ridden. Historian Jim Downs has recently described black refugee camps as "holding grounds" created by the federal government to contain fugitive slaves until they could "re-create the plantation labor force," with the federal government taking "over the role of slaveholders." According to Downs, "contraband camps performed a similar function to antebellum slave pens where auctioneers held people before they were sold on the market."[2] Although Downs has identified a thread of paternalism that informed the creation of refugee camps, his characterization obscures and distorts much more complex processes at work. As Downs points out, for black and white refugees, living in refugee camps meant dangerously overcrowded conditions, poor sanitation that promoted epidemic disease, and federal officials who often did not sympathize or understand what refugees wanted or needed. However, camps were also sites where refugees raised (and rebuilt) families, established churches, schools, and fraternal organizations, and crafted new identities. They were the birthplace of Southern free labor and black politics. Their construction and development were the result of a complex and often contentious partnership between the federal government (especially the army), relief workers, and the refugees themselves. They were neither purely places of oppression nor sites of liberation, but oftentimes both.

Compared to the white refugees who fled to the Piedmont, who left voluminous records of their experiences in diaries and letters, black refugees on North Carolina's coast left few written accounts, especially during their early months in New Bern. Evidence of their experiences must be read primarily through the words of white Union soldiers and relief workers like Vincent Colyer. The windows that they provide into the black refugee experience are both revealing and limited. Even sympathetic whites, like the abolitionist Vincent Colyer, brought with them decades of prejudices and misconceptions that blinded them to black refugees' priorities, hopes, and needs. Most white Union soldiers held racist assumptions about African Africans that colored their accounts of black refugees. Reconstructing the lived experience of black refugees, therefore, requires reading these sources carefully, recognizing that much of what transpired within the refugee camps remained invisible to white eyes.

In March 1862 New Bern became the heart of the Union occupation in eastern North Carolina and the locus for both the black and white refugee migrations. Founded in 1710, New Bern served as the colonial capital of North Carolina. With a population of 5,432 in 1860, New Bern was the second-largest city in the state, after Wilmington, and slightly larger than the capital, Raleigh. The town's antiquity, history, and Federal architecture gave it a regal bearing, leading to its reputation as "The Athens of North Carolina." New Bern's antebellum economic importance and its Civil War strategic significance rested in its location at the confluence of the Neuse and Trent Rivers. Running through the center of town, the Atlantic and North Carolina Railroad linked New Bern to Morehead City on the coast and to Goldsboro in the west. On the eve of the Civil War, New Bern featured two hotels, a courthouse, several churches, an academy, and wharfs and warehouses lining the rivers.[3]

Despite its antebellum prosperity, the town that greeted Union soldiers on March 14, 1862, paled in comparison, as the preceding months had transformed New Bern into a shell of its former self. New Bern residents had been expecting and dreading the Union invasion for months. When rumors about a potential attack began circulating in September 1861, a few of the region's white residents decided that refugeeing themselves to the North Carolina interior would be prudent. The vast majority, however, waited and watched for the planned invasion. A January 1862 newspaper editorial complained that invasion rumors had resulted in a "cruel and unnecessary panic now raging in our town, crushing up furniture and driving crowds of people from their homes." Fearing that Confederate currency would become worthless in the aftermath of a Union occupation, the Bank of New Bern stopped accepting it in February 1862.[4] On the evening of March 13, the day before the invasion, most of the white population nervously remained in New Bern, fearful of the immediate future.

Most New Bern residents correctly assessed that the thinly spread Confederate forces were unlikely to repulse a Union attack. Writing in her diary in late January 1862, Clarrisa Phelps Hanks, a New Bern resident, observed, "We have no naval force to meet them on water[;] they have every advantage of us in that respect and unless God fight for us we must be defeated." In the days leading up to the expected attack, many white New Bern residents, especially women and children, fled the city, taking trains and boats bound for the interior. One resident observed that since New Bern was "in an exposed position, it was thought best for as many women and children as could leave to do so." Despite the preinvasion exodus, however, many white New Bern residents remained in the city until it became clear that Union forces would be entering the city within hours, creating "a perfect panic and stampede, women, children, nurses, and baggage getting to the depot any way they could." Retreating with the rest of his unit, William Curtis, a Confederate soldier from Cherokee County, came across dozens of fleeing soldiers and civilians on the road from New Bern to Kinston. "We found a perfect stampede," he wrote. "The panic stricken crowd consisted of a heterogeneous mixture of soldiers, citizens,—men, women, children, and negroes leaving the town in the utmost confusion." Curtis found the road littered with debris—"trunks, boxes, and household plunder"—as fleeing civilians abandoned their treasured possessions to stay ahead of the Union advance. "It was an affecting sight to see ladies, both young and old, many of whom appeared unaccustomed to hardships and toil, trudging along the road in mud and water, on foot, carrying immense loads of their household articles, perhaps those most highly prized, and with tears, beseeching for some mode of conveyance to enable them to escape from the ruthless invader."⁵

This last-minute exodus of all but approximately two hundred of the town's white residents left the streets littered with baggage and furniture that could not be loaded onto railroad cars and ferries. To deprive Union soldiers of the benefits of holding New Bern, retreating Confederate soldiers set fire to the town. One Union soldier noted that "only for the prompt efforts of the troops crossing into the city, and aid furnished by the colored people, New Berne would have been destroyed." Refugees fleeing along the Kinston road could see their homes go up in flames. William Curtis observed that many of the refugees fleeing New Bern were wealthy young women, who "now turned their backs sadly upon homes, that a short time before were pleasant and happy, and perhaps could now, for the first time in life, cast a lingering glance back, only to be met by the lurid glare of the fiery element consuming the home.... Their agonizing cries of grief, and anxious entreaties for assistance, were heard on all sides, amid the din and clatter ... and the panic stricken-rabble."⁶

Shortly after their victory at New Bern, Union forces occupied the towns of Washington, Beaufort, Morehead City, and Plymouth. Together with New Bern, Roanoke, and the Outer Banks island of Hatteras (occupied by Union forces in August 1861), these towns formed the heart of the Union occupation of eastern North Carolina that would last the duration of war. As in New Bern, a significant proportion of the white population refugeed themselves inland in advance of the Union occupation. When Union soldiers marched into the town of Washington, a Northern journalist noted that "some two thirds" of Washington's twenty-five hundred inhabitants "have seen fit to leave for the interior." Similarly, in Plymouth, Union forces discovered that "the most rabid of the secessionists here all left the city, including all the ministers of the gospel, except the Baptist."⁷

In the months to come, as Union soldiers established control over northeastern North Carolina, slaves took every available opportunity to seize their own freedom. Even before they had established firm control over the region, Union officials found themselves inundated by fugitive slaves. Indeed, in many locations, fugitive slaves occupied coastal towns after the white residents had fled and before Union soldiers marched in.⁸ Rev. Horace James, serving as chaplain for the Massachusetts Twenty-Fifth Volunteers, observed that when Union soldiers marched into New Bern on March 14, 1862, "one class of the population gave us a hearty welcome, viz: the negroes. They stood in lines along the street as we advanced, and showed their ivory in the most remarkable manner.... They seemed too happy for expression, and were actually wild with delight." On the next day, one Massachusetts soldier noted that the "Negroes are coming in by the hundreds." A few days later, Gen. Ambrose Burnside observed that New Bern was "overrun with fugitives from the surrounding towns and plantations." Burnside regarded these fugitives as "a source of very great anxiety" but concluded that "it would be utterly impossible if we were so disposed to keep them outside of our lines, as they find their way to us through the woods and swamps from every side." One of Burnside's soldiers agreed with his assessment of the situation in New Bern, noting that "every expedition to the interior, securing a passage safe from rebel pursuit over all the space between our troops and New Berne, was the sign for great numbers [of fugitive slaves] to come in." Burnside's personal secretary observed in March 1862 that fugitive slaves were "stealing in from every direction by land & sea—in squads from 6 to 30 each—they come and dump themselves by the side of the fence and 'wait for order from Mr. Burnside.'" Although she was only a small child at the time of the invasion, the slave Hattie Rogers remembered that "all who could swim the [White Oak] river [in Onslow County] and get to the Yankees were free." Dr. R. R. Clarke of the Thirty-Sixth Massachusetts observed in April 1862 that fugitive slaves were "continually coming in, in squads from one to a dozen—wending their way through the swamps at night, avoiding pickets—they at last reach our lines."[9]

Although most of the fugitive slaves arriving in New Bern came from eastern North Carolina, some black refugees had traveled much farther. According to Vincent Colyer, two runaway slaves came from northern Alabama, having spent the previous year hidden in the woods and having trekked for three months "through the woods and bye-paths, avoiding white men all the way" to New Bern, a distance of 750 miles. Two other slaves arrived in New Bern in 1862 from South Carolina, where they had fled to the woods shortly after the fall of Fort Sumter. The *New York Times* reported in June 1862 that one literate slave arriving in New Bern had traveled some five hundred miles to reach Union lines, having written himself passes to facilitate his journey.[10]

In making the decision to run to Union lines, slaves drew on decades of experience with clandestine travel. Most slaves in eastern North Carolina knew, either directly or indirectly, how to leave their plantations undetected, how to evade slave patrols, and how to navigate the woods and swamps, at least in their immediate vicinity. They used this knowledge to covertly visit friends and relatives on neighboring plantations, to seek a temporary respite from the brutality of slavery by taking refuge in the wild, and, on rare occasions, to escape slavery entirely. Born a slave in Chowan County between 1835 and 1840, Allen Parker noted that "in spite of the danger of being caught the slaves were often out nights without passes." Parker admitted that he often left the plantation at night, usually to steal and butcher hogs, "for the night was the slaves' holiday." While Parker usually returned before daybreak, on one occasion he ran away for two weeks, living in the woods. In August 1862, six months after Union forces had invaded eastern North Carolina and established a permanent foothold in the state, Allen Parker met with slaves from neighboring plantations to plan their escape. After some deliberation, Parker and his associates, "finding that lots of the slaves from the neighboring plantation were running away we concluded that we would take our chance, as soon as we could get any." After seeing a Union gunboat positioned on the Chowan River, Parker plotted with three other slaves to escape that night. Waiting until the dead of night, they eluded slave patrols, making their way to the river, where they unchained a dugout canoe and rowed to the Union gunboat.[11]

Many African Americans in coastal North Carolina, both free and enslaved, worked as boatmen and brought information about the broader world to slaves on plantations, including information about Union and Confederate troop movements, slave patrols, and routes to freedom. In 1862 Sutton Davis, an enslaved boatbuilder and carpenter living in Carteret County, rowed a small boat to deliver himself and his family across Jarrett Bay to the outskirts of New Bern and Union lines. In March 1862 Union soldiers from Massachusetts preparing to leave Roanoke for the impeding invasion of New Bern were confronted by a little schooner carrying twenty-four fugitive slaves. Several months later, slave families sailed into Beaufort via Bogue Sound. In August 1863 a Beaufort resident wrote in his diary that "about fifteen negroes—men, women, and children—arrived here today by sea in a small open boat, from Snead's Ferry in Onslow County. They are fugitives in search of freedom."[12]

Fugitive slaves' determination to reach Union lines manifested itself during the siege of Washington, North Carolina. Captured by Union forces shortly after the occupation of New Bern in March 1862, Washington had served as an important Union base in Beaufort County. In March 1863 Confederate forces under Gen. D. H. Hill began a lengthy siege of the town, erecting batteries on the Pamlico River, effectively cutting the town off from resupply or reinforcement by water. Confederate brigades stationed between Chockowinity crossroads and Blount's Creek prevented reinforcement by land, leaving the town cut off from the outside world. In the midst of the siege, seventeen fugitive slaves managed to pass through the Confederate blockade. Led by an enslaved preacher named "Big Bob," they had traveled fifty miles the previous night, evading Confederate patrols on both land and water.[13]

Some fugitive slaves arriving in Union lines were experienced refugees. Union territory in northeastern North Carolina abutted the Great Dismal Swamp, a vast wilderness that straddled the border of North Carolina and Virginia. More than a thousand square miles in area, the Great Dismal Swamp had been a refuge for fugitive slaves for more than a century, sheltering one of the largest maroon communities in the United States. Although the number of fugitive slaves living in the swamp at the time of the Civil War is impossible to estimate with any degree of certainty, its population must have run into the hundreds, if not thousands. During the Burnside invasion of 1862 most Dismal Swamp refugees joined the flood of fugitive slaves converging on New Bern and other Union-held sites. In his postaction report to Secretary of War Edwin Stanton, Burnside reported in March 1862 that among the fugitive slaves arriving in New Bern were two men "who have been in the swamps for five years." William Kinnegy, a fugitive slave who later worked as a Union scout, had lived in the swamp since February 1857. Kinnegy described the swamp as "a close jungle, so thick that you could not penetrate it, except with an axe." During his years in the swamp, Kinnegy lived in a hut constructed from tree branches and killed cattle and hogs that grazed on the edge of the swamp. Although Kinnegy used the swamp as a refuge, he was not entirely cut off from the surrounding communities. He continued to visit his enslaved wife during brief clandestine nighttime rendezvous, occasionally traded with poor whites, and evaded slave patrols that periodically visited the swamp.[14]

In May 1862 a company of the Ninth New York Volunteer Regiment was assigned to patrol the Dismal Swamp Canal. Constructed in 1805, the canal ran along the eastern edge of the swamp, connecting New Bern to Norfolk. While on patrol, they were confronted by five fugitive slaves who had been living in the Dismal Swamp. One soldier remembered that they "presented themselves fearlessly and asked to be permitted to join the party. There was no hesitation or distrust. They had evidently received full information regarding the situation by that unexplained and mysterious system used for spreading information, known only to them and which no white man has yet been able to discover." One of these five men informed the commanding officer that he had escaped in 1855 and had been living in the swamp during the seven years since.[15]

Free African Americans also fled to Union lines. Vincent Colyer noted that two free African Americans from Onslow County arrived in New Bern in 1862 "to escape being drafted to work on the enemy's fortifications," presumably at Fort Fisher near Wilmington. They had spent more than a year in the woods avoiding Confederate conscription agents and slave patrols before they successfully made their way to New Bern. Emily Pailin, a free black woman from Elizabeth City, moved to New Bern with her nine-year-old son, hoping that there would be more opportunities there, far from the threat of Confederate attack.[16]

Native Americans living in eastern North Carolina, most prominently the Lumbee of Robeson County, also joined the flood of refugees fleeing to Union lines. In June 1861 a trainload of white refugees from Wilmington en route to Laurinburg stopped at "a Station called Scuffletown" (now Pembroke), where they saw "a collection of [the] most singular-looking mulattoes, who inhabited that neighborhood, and had come in crowds both men and women, to see that novel sight to them, an engine with a train of cars attached." From aboard the train, one white refugee marveled at the Lumbees' "reddish yellow color" and "long straight black hair," which the women wore in "long thin braids," all of which seemed not to fit within the white refugee's neat racial classifications. She speculated that they were of Portuguese origin but "also had Indian and negro blood in their veins." Staring at each other as the train refueled, the Lumbees at the station and the white refugees aboard the train must have wondered at the strange places and people the war, then only a few months old, had brought into their lives.

Although the Lumbee would have preferred to sit out the war in Scuffletown, many of the forces that drove white and black North Carolinians to become refugees also impinged on the Lumbee. Like free blacks and enslaved African Americans, the Lumbee were subject to Confederate conscription. Hundreds of Lumbees were compelled to labor in the construction of Fort Fisher near Wilmington, where many died from yellow fever. To avoid conscription, many Lumbees fled to the swamps along the Lumber River. One of the white refugees on board the train to Laurinburg later commented that Lumbees "knew every hiding place in the swamps around & very exceedingly cunning, like their Indian fore-fathers, in concealing themselves." Many Lumbees would remain in the wilds of Robeson County for the duration of the war, with some participating in guerrilla warfare against Confederate forces, culminating in the Lowry War, a conflict between the Lumbee and local whites that lasted well into Reconstruction. Although most Lumbees remained in Robeson County, at least some Lumbees made their way to Union-occupied territory. Mary Barbour, a runaway slave who had escaped with her parents from McDowell County, lived in the refugee camp on Roanoke Island, where she remembered that the residents included an "ole Indian Witch 'oman." Some of the refugees whom white Union soldiers classified as mulattoes may have been Lumbees.[17]

Most of the earliest slaves to flee to Union lines were young men. Enslaved men in their teens and twenties had always been the most likely to run away prior to the Civil War. Fugitive slave ads suggest that four out of every five runaway slaves were male and a similar proportion were described as young, between the ages of thirteen and twenty-nine. In Civil War North Carolina this propensity for young men to run away was exacerbated, as young men were the most likely to be removed by their owners to the interior, in large measure because they were the most liable to run away and because they were the most valuable slaves. Furthermore, slave women may have been frightened by the prospect of entering a military camp, home to hundreds of soldiers and potentially dangerous places for women and children.[18]

Having made their way within Union lines, some refugee men returned to Confederate territory to help their families escape. In February 1862 a group of black men on Roanoke Island left the protection of the Union army to return to the mainland. They explained to a disingenuous Union officer that "We'se wives and chillern in slavery. We can't leave them. Bress de Lord, de day ob jubilee is come. We'se all to be free now. We must go back and get our wives and chillern." As the number of fugitive slaves entering Union lines grew, so too did the demographic diversity of the refugee slave population. After the initial wave, the vast majority of fugitives arrived in family groups, including very young children, the elderly, and the disabled. Two weeks after the battle of New Bern, one Massachusetts soldier noted that "there are swarms of negroes here. They are of all sexes, ages, sizes and conditions." On Roanoke Island, the refugee population included many infants and an elderly slave who claimed to be 102 years old. In New Bern, Massachusetts soldier Henry Clapp met several fugitive slaves who claimed to remember the Revolution, including one who said she was 107 years old. In December 1862 a Beaufort resident claimed that the "town is crowded with runaway negroes. Not only the able bodied, but the lame, the halt, the blind and crazy." A Massachusetts soldier noted that "the contrabands in our vicinity of all ages, sizes and colors, and of both sexes, paid us daily visits in great numbers."[19]

Every Union expedition into Confederate territory brought more refugee slaves into Union lines. In June 1862 a Union scouting party along the Neuse River encountered four slave women on the Latham plantation who asked if "they might go with us to Newbern." They knew that the presence of Union soldiers meant safe passage to freedom. When the women departed with the Union soldiers, Mrs. Latham "came running down the lawn, shouting after them at the top of her voice, 'Here, Kitty, Peggy, Rosa, Dinah, where are you going with those horrid men? Come back here right this minute!' The women, looking back over their shoulders and showing immense rows of ivory, replied to her, 'Goo-bye, missus, goo-bye! spec we'es gwine ober to Newbern.'" Later that summer, as the unit marched through Martin County, a soldier observed that "the contrabands flocked in droves to our standard." At the end of their expedition, he claimed that among their spoils were "upwards of 1000 negroes." Similarly, a Massachusetts soldier noted that after one scouting expedition in late 1862 "Negroes by the hundreds followed us into Plymouth." In December 1862 another Massachusetts soldier noted that "one of the unlooked-for results of the expedition was the bringing back with the soldiers a large number of ex-slaves, who, putting their entire possessions in a bundle, larger or smaller, as the case might be, added themselves to the column, and to the number of 500 or more came into Newbern with the army." On a mission in early 1863, "negroes by hundreds followed us on our return march to Winton, with little bundles tied up and swung on sticks over their shoulders, shouting 'We's gwine to liberty, hi-yah, gwine to liberty!' The negroes would stop work in the fields, gaze at the Yankee column a few minutes, drop hoe or axe, and fling up their old hats and shout 'Gwine to liberty.'" In November 1862 a Massachusetts soldier noted that "a day or two after our return from the mud-march to Trenton, some of the results of that raid came straggling through our camp, a hundred or more contrabands, escaped from slavery." Sometimes the column of black refugees following Union soldiers into camp resembled a parade. One soldier observed that "another feature of the return march is a procession of 'contrabands,' men, women, and children, in [the] strangest medley of rags, but with a kind of earnest and solemn joy on their faces, that make them look sublime.... They followed the flag and saw its bright folds streaming over them, red with the flames of their morning, Freedom's star leading them on."[20]

Not all slaves encountered by Union soldiers during their ventures into the interior accompanied them on their return to New Bern. One elderly slave in Trenton told Massachusetts soldiers that his owner had gone "up country." When they asked him if he would return with them, he "said he wanted his freedom, but he wanted to go 'clar,' meaning that he wanted to take his whole family with him, four of his children were at home, but he had five still in slavery." Presumably, these five enslaved children had been removed by their owner during his retreat "up country." At other times, Union soldiers saw slaves who desired to secure their freedom but refused to help them. One Massachusetts soldier on a Union gunboat en route to New Bern witnessed "some 40 or 50 negroes came running down to the shore and begged to be taken aboard." Although his unit had recently liberated "upwards of 1000 negroes," they had no room aboard ship for these additional passengers. Describing them as "the most forlorn and wretched looking beings I had ever seen," clothed in "little else than rags, scarcely covering their nakedness," the Massachusetts soldier watched them as they followed the boat downriver for nearly a mile, "begging piteously to be taken aboard."[21]

Slave owners in eastern North Carolina tried to dissuade their slaves from running away. One black refugee indicated that his owner had told him "that the yankees will harness them to their carts & if they don't draw they will bayonet them—that they will sell them in Cuba." The slave evidently saw through the lie, claiming, "I said *yes sir* at the same time I was making preparations to leave him.... I Knowed that you [the Union soldiers] was our friends because they told such stories about you." Slaves inherently distrusted what their owners told them. After being told the horrors that awaited them among Union soldiers, one fugitive slave revealed, "We knowed dey lied—we'd be praying to de Lord dat you Yankees might come." After the occupation of New Bern, a Massachusetts soldier observed that "the slaves did not appear to be afraid of the [Union] soldiers, although they had been taught to fear us."[22]

Not all slaves who fled the plantation for Union lines reached their destination. Slaveholders in eastern North Carolina increased slave patrols starting in 1861 in an effort to dissuade slaves from running away and to capture them if they did. Slave patrols worked in conjunction with the Home Guard and the Confederate army in eastern North Carolina to monitor slaves, creating a powerful disincentive for slaves contemplating escape. According to one North Carolina slaveholder, increased patrols in Duplin County had been "of great service in preventing the escape of slaves." A corps of twenty patrollers had been hired, accompanied by hounds ("at heavy cost"), as "we are not distant from Yankee lines."[23]

In their efforts to prevent the exodus of slaves to Federal-controlled territory, slaveholders authorized patrollers to use lethal violence. In contrast to antebellum practice, which emphasized capturing runaway slaves unharmed, wartime slave patrols and Confederate pickets adopted a more militant approach. When Amos Homans, a slave on Riley Murray's plantation in Hyde County, fled towards New Bern in 1862, he was mercilessly pursued by Confederate soldiers, who shot him in both legs before capturing him. Planters also authorized overseers to use lethal violence to prevent slaves from running away. An overseer reported in September 1862 that "I had a dificulty withe old Pompey ... heay broke and run [so] I shot him withe my pistol."[24]

Maps of the Burnside invasion of eastern North Carolina, including those produced by the army during the war, often overstated the extent of Union control in the region. In truth, Union authority fell over only a handful of coastal towns, such as New Bern, Beaufort, and Morehead City, and the sandy Outer Banks islands. While Union boats patrolled the coast and made regular sorties upriver, and scouting missions frequently probed the interior, the territory safely under Union control stopped somewhere short of the picket lines established around each town. All of the land beyond the picket lines was effectively a no-man's land, under neither Union nor Confederate control. The territory where black and white refugees could find protection under the Union army, therefore, was small. Like midday shadows, refugees in eastern North Carolina stuck close to fortified Union enclaves. According to one relief worker, "We control, indeed, a broad area of navigable waters, ... but have scarcely room enough on land to spread our tents upon."[25]

Much of this no-man's land between Union and Confederate lines quickly became depopulated by a mass exodus, as pro-Confederate whites removed themselves and their slaves west to the interior and fugitive slaves and Unionist whites fled eastward. One Union soldier described this region where "wide fields remained uncultivated, and in not a few cases ripened crops were left to perish unharvested. Vast barns and granaries were left entirely empty. On the most extensive plantations but few signs of life were visible. A few aged negroes, too old to run away and too valueless to be removed, were loitering about, bewildered by the sudden and inexplicable change."²⁶

Approaching Union lines could also be fatal for fugitive slaves. Expecting a Confederate attack, Union soldiers on picket duty often mistook refugee slaves for Confederate soldiers. A New York soldier stationed on Roanoke Island in 1862 described the danger that fugitive slaves faced when approaching the island:

> Nearly every night one or more boat-loads of slaves landed on the beach and were taken in charge by the guard. This was an extremely dangerous proceeding for escaping slaves, and would have been considered heroic bravery had they been white men. No sooner had the danger of pursuit and capture by wrathful owners abated, and the peril of the watery journey been overcome, than a new danger, demanding the greatest caution, presented itself. They were obliged to approach a strange shore in the darkness of night, where the sentinels were keenly alert for the approach of an enemy, especially by water. The flapping of sails or the sound of oars from the water was naturally accepted by the picket guard to denote an attempted night attack and surprise, and their faculties were doubly keen, and they were ready to at once fire in the direction of the sound. . . . In their efforts to gain their freedom they had risked death at the hands of the very men from whom they sought protection.

In April 1862 a half dozen runaway slaves approaching New Bern were surprised by a picket, who fired on them, the bullet "wizzing by old darkie's head." The frightened refugees were spared a second shot when they called out and the pickets recognized their distinctive accent.²⁷

Rowland Hall, a Union officer stationed in New Bern, wrote to his father in May 1863 that "a poor negro was shot dead in the middle of the night by our picquets [sic]." The next day another fugitive slave arrived in camp, who revealed that the two men had escaped from Danville, Virginia, three weeks earlier. They had trekked more than two hundred miles, evading slave patrols and Confederate soldiers and living in the woods. "They knew not where they were, only knew that they were seeking our lines. They had nothing to eat in three days, not one mouthful of any kind," Hall wrote. "The survivor was naked except the remains of a pair of cotton drawers, torn with briers, bleeding all over, emaciated, haggard, such an object as you have no idea of. No wolf ever looked more frightful."²⁸

The Burnside expedition of March 1862 occurred against the backdrop of evolving federal policy on fugitive slaves. In May 1861 Gen. Benjamin F. Butler, stationed at Fort Monroe, Virginia, argued that the use of slave labor by the Confederacy transformed slaves from private property to implements of war, and he could therefore prohibit the return of refugee slaves on the grounds that they were "contrabands of war." In August 1861 the First Confiscation Act made Butler's reasoning into national policy, authorizing the confiscation of all property used in support of the rebellion. As historian James Oakes has recently observed, in theory, the First Confiscation Act freed only those slaves used in the Confederate war effort, but in practice, the act effectively emancipated all slaves entering Union lines from disloyal states. On March 13, 1862, the day before Burnside's attack on New Bern, Congress enacted legislation prohibiting Union soldiers from returning fugitive slaves to their owners, effectively repealing one of the key provisions of the Fugitive Slave Act of 1850.[29]

In authorizing the assault on North Carolina, General-in-Chief George McClellan advised Burnside to avoid linking the invasion to emancipation. A vocal critic of the recent changes in federal policy, McClellan wrote to Burnside that "I would urge great caution in regard to proclamation ... say as little as possible about politics or the negro. Merely state that the true issue for which we are fighting is the preservation of the Union and upholding the laws of the General Government, and stating that all who conduct themselves properly will as far as possible be protected in their persons and property." Unwilling to disobey a directive from his military superior, Ambrose Burnside ordered his men to "protect the persons and property of the loyal and peaceable citizens of this State," and in a February 1862 "Proclamation made to the People of North Carolina" indicated that he had no intention "to interfere with your laws constitutionally established, your institutions of any kind whatever, your property of any sort, or your usages in any respect." Furthermore, he assured them that rumors that he intended to "liberate your slaves" were "not only ridiculous, but utterly and willfully false."[30]

Although Burnside pledged not to interfere with slavery, his actions immediately after the invasion indicate the opposite. Shortly after the occupation of New Bern, Burnside wrote to Secretary of War Edwin Stanton that "in the absence of definite instructions upon the subject of fugitive slaves," he had adopted a policy to "allow all slave who come to my lines to enter" and "to give them employment as far as possible, and to exercise toward old and young a judicious charity." He also pledged to "deliver none to their owners under any circumstance."[31] As James Oakes has recently observed, Burnside's actions mirror the decisions made only a few months earlier by Gen. Thomas W. Sherman in the Sea Islands. Both generals issued conservative proclamations about their intentions regarding slavery prior to invasion, only to pursue a more liberal track afterward. Cognizant of the shifting federal policy on black refugees, Burnside followed the model established by Butler in Virginia and Sherman in South Carolina and outlined in the First Confiscation Act. He allowed fugitive slaves to enter Union lines, refused to return them to their former owners, and authorized their employment as manual laborers.

Like Butler, Burnside saw fugitive slaves largely in terms of the labor they could perform for the Union army. Col. Rush C. Hawkins of the Ninth New York, whom Burnside had left in command of Roanoke Island before the invasion of New Bern, arranged for fugitive slaves to work as cooks, laundresses, teamsters, woodcutters, and porters. By mid-March 1862, Hawkins informed General Burnside that 130 former slaves were now working on Roanoke Island, building a storehouse and, when proper tools arrived, a wharf. Hawkins also outlined a payment schema for fugitive slaves working for the Union army—men would receive ten dollars per month plus rations and "a soldier's allowance of clothing," while women would receive four dollars per month plus rations and an "allowance of money equal to an[d] in lieu of a soldier's allowance of clothing." In addition to providing for wages for fugitive slaves in the employ of the army, Hawkins's General Order No. 2 also created a broader framework for free labor on Roanoke, mandating that fugitive slaves privately employed would receive at minimum the same wages and benefits afforded to those working for the army. Hawkins's General Order No. 2 marked the birth of free labor in North Carolina, but it also marked a turning point in the relationship between the black family and the federal government. It authorized black children under the age of twelve to also receive a ration and specified that they would "remain with their parents," providing one of the earliest legal claims that black parents had for their children. Unlike their parents, these black refugee children were not expected to work for their rations. Hawkins concluded that "in all cases they [fugitive slaves] will be treated with great care and humanity. It is to be hope[d] that their helpless and dependent condition will protect them against injustice and imposition." In effect, Hawkins situated the army and the government as the fugitive slaves' protectors. While he had neither the power nor the authority to emancipate the fugitive slaves on Roanoke Island, General Order No. 2 effectively created a framework for de facto emancipation and free labor.[32]

Neither Burnside nor Hawkins saw himself as an abolitionist or the emancipation of black refugees as a critical aspect of their mission in North Carolina. Nonetheless, the presence of the U.S. army under their command quickly and dramatically undermined slavery in eastern North Carolina. By May 1862, William H. Doherty, an Irish-born college professor who had established a school in New Bern, claimed in a letter to President Lincoln that "it is sufficiently evident to every unprejudiced man dwelling in or visiting the South, that the victories of the U.S. troops, & the occupation of the country by Northern armies, have, unintentionally perhaps, but necessarily, overthrown the whole fabric of society, founded as it was, on the Institution of Negro Slavery." From what Doherty could see on the ground in New Bern, the Burnside invasion had almost instantaneously ended slavery within the occupied portion of North Carolina. The social changes brought about by military emancipation, according to Doherty, were permanent, as "it is perfectly futile to hope, that the slaves now practically emancipated, will ever return to their former condition, or that they can be forced, any longer, to labor for their former owners." What remained unclear, however, was how black refugees, "now practically emancipated," would rebuild their lives in Union-occupied North Carolina.[33]

By the end of March 1862, Burnside reported to Secretary of War Edwin Stanton that "the negroes continue to come in [to New Bern] and I am employing them to the best possible advantage."[34] Fearing that the influx of fugitive slaves would overwhelm his time and resources, Burnside appointed Vincent Colyer as the superintendent of the poor on March 30, 1862, to coordinate fugitive slave policy in eastern North Carolina. Born in Bloomington, New York, in 1825, Colyer had studied painting at the National Academy in New York City. A devoted Quaker, Colyer had involved himself in a number of philanthropic organizations, especially the Young Men's Christian Association (YMCA). Starting in April 1861, Colyer spent three months visiting military encampments around New York, holding "meetings for prayer, singing, and exhortation, distributing tracts, Testaments, [and] hymn-books." After the battle of Bull Run in July 1861, Colyer traveled to Washington to tend to soldiers in hospitals and assist chaplains in camps. Working tirelessly among soldiers in Washington for six months, Colyer saw the need for a more orchestrated civilian relief effort. Corresponding with other YMCA workers, Colyer became one of the founding leaders of the U.S. Christian Commission, an organization formally established in November 1861.[35]

After the formation of the Christian Commission, Colyer decided to eschew a leadership position in the organization in favor of continuing his relief work in the field. In February 1862 he attached himself to Burnside's expedition as a civilian representative of the Christian Commission, where he assisted the regimental chaplain in tending to the sick and wounded after the battle of Roanoke Island. Soon thereafter a boatload of refugee slaves arrived in Roanoke, about which Colyer later wrote, "Commenced my work with the freed people of color, in North Carolina." In March 1862 Colyer accompanied Burnside's soldiers during the invasion of New Bern.[36]

Colyer's appointment created an uneasy partnership between civilian relief workers and military officers that would last for the duration of the war. Colyer and other relief workers felt their mission in North Carolina was primarily to care for the spiritual and physical needs of soldiers and civilians in a combat zone. "Gen. Burnside," Colyer wrote, was "by no means an abolitionist." Instead, from Colyer's perspective, Burnside saw fugitive African Americans primarily as a source of potential labor. The first order that Colyer received from Burnside was to "employ as many negro men as I could . . . to work on the building of forts." Burnside authorized Colyer to recruit as many as five thousand African American men, offering them eight dollars per month, along with "one ration and clothes."[37] Left to his own devices, Colyer probably would have prioritized his time differently.

Under Vincent Colyer's supervision, refugee slaves were put to work during the spring and early summer of 1862 building fortifications at New Bern, Roanoke, and Washington. He also organized refugees to work as stevedores and as manual laborers in the Quartermaster, Commissary, and Ordinance Offices. Skilled black refugees were put to work as carpenters, blacksmiths, and coopers, building wooden hospital cots, a railroad bridge across the Trent River in New Bern, and docks on Roanoke Island. One Union soldier noted in April 1862, one month after the occupation of New Bern, that over seven hundred fugitive slaves had arrived in town, eager to work in whatever capacity would support the Union cause. "They all find employment," he wrote. "Some work on fortifications, some unloading ships."[38]

Vincent Colyer also supervised a volunteer corps of more than fifty fugitive slaves who worked as spies, scouts, and guides in 1862. Prohibited from officially enlisting in the Union army, fugitive slaves volunteered in these extra-military roles. According to Colyer, these spies "frequently went from thirty to three hundred miles within the enemy lines; visiting his principal camps and most important posts, and bringing us back important and reliable information." Reporting on Confederate forces in Kinston, Goldsboro, Trenton, Onslow, Swansboro, and Tarboro, fugitive slaves became the eyes and ears of the Union army. Colyer was repeatedly impressed by their bravery. One scout, a teenager named Charley, made three separate trips from New Bern to Kinston, a distance of forty-five miles, most of it in Confederate hands. Home to Fort Campbell and Fort Johnston, Kinston had the largest concentration of Confederate soldiers in eastern North Carolina, with approximately four thousand men under arms. During his third expedition, Charley, this time accompanied by another fugitive slave turned spy, was nearly captured by a Confederate sentry on horseback who was tracking them with bloodhounds. Hiding in the woods, they managed to ambush the sentry, shooting his horse and two of the dogs with revolvers. To evade capture, the two young men split up, taking to swamps and woods while Confederate scouts took chase. Over a thirty-six-mile sojourn, they "came home as fast as they could run, throwing off coats, pants, caps, and everything but their shirts, drawers, and revolvers, finally reaching our lines in safety, completely exhausted." Simon H. Mix, a soldier with the Second New York Cavalry, claimed that white Union soldiers relied heavily on the local knowledge that black scouts provided, noting that "in all our expeditions in North Carolina we have depended upon the negroes for our guides, for without them we could not have moved with any safety."[39]

Refugee slaves working as spies and scouts risked their lives not only to aid the Union war effort but also, and probably primarily, to rescue family members still enslaved. Shortly after his arrival in New Bern, William Kinnegy heard, presumably from other refugee slaves, that "my wife's owner has run away, and she and the children are up in the country alone." He asked Vincent Colyer for a pass to bring them to New Bern. Colyer told Kinnegy that he would pay Kinnegy if he would, "while after his wife, ... go a little further, up to Kingston and thereabout, and take a good look at the rebel encampments, make a careful note on his memory of their number and situation, inquire of the negroes in their cabins all about the enemy, and bring this information, with his wife and children on his return."[40]

Union officers ignored the advice proffered by fugitive slaves at their peril. In 1862 the fugitive slave William Henry Singleton was called into General Burnside's headquarters in New Bern in preparation for the Union assault on Wise Forks (which Singleton referred to as "Wives Forks"), near Kinston. Singleton recalled that "I laid the route out for them the best I knew how, but said that if I were going to command the expedition I would give them a flank movement by way of the Trent river, which was five miles farther from Wives Forks than the Neuse river." General Burnside, however, did not heed Singleton's advice, "with the result that they were repulsed."[41]

Confederate North Carolinians, slaveholding and nonslaveholding alike, were amazed and horrified at the number of slaves escaping to Union lines. In March 1862 Pvt. William Loftin wrote to his mother that "a good many negroes are running away and are going to the Yankees everyday. All of mine are going to them. From the oldest to the youngest left as soon as they herd [sic] that New Bern had fallen." Living in Union-occupied Beaufort, Confederate sympathizer and slave owner James Rumley had a firsthand perspective on the influx of black refugees into Union lines. In May 1862 Rumley wrote in his diary that "slaves are now deserting in scores from all the parts of the country, and our worst fears on this subject are likely to be realized." Stationed in Goldsboro, Confederate general Thomas Clingman wrote to D. H. Hill in August 1862 that "negroes are escaping rapidly, probably a million dollars' worth weekly in all." In December 1863 overseer Henry Jones wrote to planter John R. Donnell that "something like 100 [slaves had] gone off in past month," including 35 in a single night.[42]

For Union soldiers who had only experienced slavery in the abstract, the arrival of hundreds of refugee slaves challenged their ideas about race and slavery. Coming primarily from Massachusetts and New York, most of the soldiers on the Burnside expedition knew slavery only through reading Harriet Beecher Stowe's *Uncle Tom's Cabin* or through newspaper accounts. One Massachusetts soldier noted in April 1862 that although he had "always been a very stiff advocate for southern rights," his experience with fugitive slaves in New Bern had transformed his view of slavery, such that "I have become so far 'educated up,'" that now there was only a "little strip of land between Charles Sumner's views and mine." His understanding of slavery was galvanized by a conversation with a five-year-old fugitive boy. He had asked the boy why he and his family had fled slavery, "not thinking that the little fellow could realize anything." To the soldier's surprise, the boy quickly responded, "Kase I don't want to be a slave—I'se want to be free."[43]

Even those soldiers who had considered themselves abolitionists were transformed by the sight of fugitive slaves. Speaking at the New England

Anti-Slavery Convention, Lt. Thomas Earle of the Twenty-Fifth Massachusetts revealed that he "had listened from his boyhood to anti-slavery lectures but only after his enlistment as a private in this war had he realized what it was to be an antislavery man." His regiment's experience with fugitive slaves had "abolitionized the young men." Some of the soldiers had "been proslavery from Worcester [Massachusetts] to Hatteras, but their eyes were opened on that island." Henry Clapp, also from Massachusetts, wrote to his family in February 1863 that the sight of refugee slaves who "flocked into Plymouth ... to the tune of two hundred or so" moved him. He noted that, time permitting, he was "going to let myself out on the subject of emancipation and the negro-race. I feel strongly enough on the subjects and am much more decided in my anti-slavery ideas that I ever was before."[44]

Although their experiences with fugitive slaves caused many soldiers to reconsider their views on slavery, they did not erase Union soldiers' ideas about black racial inferiority. James Emmerton of the Twenty-Third Massachusetts claimed that fugitive slaves' "mental development was, as a rule, in direct ratio to the proportion of white blood." However, he was surprised to see that the slaves were more civilized and less savage than he had expected, such that "the brutishness of the black field-hand of the Gulf States was rare in our part of North Carolina." A New York soldier claimed that the "negroes hardly appear like human beings. You would be surprised to see such uncouth ragged miserable savages landed direct from the coast of Africa."[45]

Many Northern soldiers marveled at black refugees' appearance. A Massachusetts soldier stationed in New Bern observed that "we no longer wondered where the minstrels at the north procured their absurd costumes; here was material for an endless variety. It was better than any play simply to walk about and examine the different styles of dress." Expecting slaves to embody the traits seen in minstrel shows, soldiers often demanded that black refugees dance and sing for them. A Massachusetts soldier recalled that when his regiment arrived in Washington, North Carolina, in 1862, "squads were sent out to pick up negroes and bring them to the quarters, where they were made to show their agility in dancing." Not all refugee slaves were willing to play along. One demurred, claiming that he was unable to dance because "I'se got de rheumatiz," only to be told by the soldiers to "never mind, you must dance." Another fugitive slave refused to dance on religious grounds, while a third "was brought in, struggling violently with the soldiers ... then making a sudden spring he broke through the crowd and ran like a deer." The abusive treatment that black refugees faced at the hands of white Union soldiers revealed not only the racist attitudes that most Union soldiers held but also how piecemeal the transition was from slavery to freedom in refugee camps.[46]

Fugitive slaves were not the only refugees to seek asylum behind Union lines. White Unionists by the thousands also fled to Union encampments in coastal North Carolina, creating a second distinct refugee population in the shadow of the federal army. In late 1862 a Massachusetts soldier observed the twin streams of refugees flowing into Union lines: "Many people came into Plymouth while we were there, coming down the river in dugouts.... These people were both whites and blacks, and were seeking protection under the starry flag." While the motivation to attain freedom within Union lines united African American refugees in eastern North Carolina, white refugees who sought asylum did so for a variety of reasons. As Barton Myers has recently argued, North Carolina's Unionists were a heterogeneous lot that incorporated a spectrum of political opinions. Their number included unconditional Unionists, whose support for the federal government remained unwavering during the secession crisis and afterward, but also many white Southerners who grew dissatisfied with Confederate policies, especially conscription. The first wave of white Unionists to arrive as refugees in eastern North Carolina consisted primarily of the former variety, committed Unionists who had never supported the Confederacy. In February 1862, shortly after the battle of Roanoke Island, eight white men arrived via boat on the island. Their spokesman, a well-dressed, gray-haired gentleman, saluted the Union flag, proclaiming that "we come to you as citizens of North Carolina, and, in the name of God, in the name of the Constitution to which we are loyal, *we claim protection of that flag!*" With a cheer from the surrounding soldiers, the commanding officer granted them refuge. A Massachusetts soldier stationed in Plymouth observed that "refugees kept coming down the river, some from a distance of fifty miles, in their dugouts. Some of these boats were quite large; one, I remember, contained three men, three women and six children, with all their household effects. Most of these people were going to New Berne, having been driven from their homes on account of their Union sentiments."[47]

The second wave of white refugees to arrive in Union-occupied eastern North Carolina were distinguished less by their embrace of a Union identity than by their rejection of Confederate conscription. The institution of the Confederate draft in April 1862 pushed many reluctant Confederates to pass into Union lines, some alone, others bringing their families with them. In September 1862 Bertie County planter and Confederate John Pool worried that "the attempted execution of the [military conscription] law has driven many [men] of not very reliable character to the enemy at Plymouth." Because the 1862 draft exempted planters, many nonslaveholding whites in eastern North Carolina became disaffected with the Confederate war effort and sought refuge in federally occupied towns. Pool pleaded with Confederate officials to exempt the county from conscription because "any further attempt at executing the law ... would run recruits to the enemy." Pool's statement reveals the growing distrust between affluent and poor white North Carolinians in the eastern coastal plain. In February 1862 Washington County planter Charles Pettigrew argued that "the low whites are not to be trusted at all. They would betray or murder any gentleman."[48]

Other white refugees, seeking to avoid being caught in the no-man's land between Confederate and Union armies, acted pragmatically, assuming that they would be safer in Union-held territory. As noted earlier, much of the land between Union-occupied New Bern and Confederate-occupied Goldsboro became deserted, and many of its few remaining residents experienced significant hardships. A Massachusetts soldier noted that after the Union occupation of Kinston in December 1862, "many of the poorer class came rambling through the Union camp, begging bread of the soldiers, and eagerly picking up the fragments which our surfeited troops had thrown away." Still other white refugees saw the war as an opportunity to escape a bad situation. For instance, in September 1861 two white apprentices fled to Hatteras Island, then the only Federally occupied territory in North Carolina, in order to escape their indenture to a planter on Roanoke Island. Like black refugees, they provided valuable military information about Confederate troop strength that paved the way for the upcoming invasion.[49]

Some white refugees did not linger long within Union lines but proceeded on to the North. Teacher William Eddins told a Union provost marshal in Newport that he "came in these lines because I became tired of being hemmed in so narrowly in rebeldom.... I wish to go North, to go into business."[50] In February 1864, fourteen refugee Quakers from Guilford County in central North Carolina arrived in New York City. They had successfully avoided conscription because of a religious exemption, until 1864, when they were ordered to join the Confederate ranks. Hiding in the woods during the day and traveling at night, they managed to make their way to New Bern, two hundred miles distant, "where they were joined by other escaped conscripts and some negroes." Not lingering in New Bern, they boarded a ship bound for New York.[51] The vast majority of white refugees, however, remained in eastern North Carolina. Longing to return home, they had no inclination to go elsewhere. Further, most white refugees could not afford the passage to New York or Boston and had no social connections there.

Union soldiers presumed that white civilians were secessionists unless they demonstrated otherwise. Whereas African American refugees were generally assumed to be dedicated to the Union cause, white refugees arriving in Union lines were not given the benefit of the doubt, and the association in the minds of many Federal soldiers between white Southerners and the Confederacy made them inherently suspect. White refugees, therefore, had to regularly prove their Unionist bona fides. While African American refugees usually received only a cursory examination upon their arrival in New Bern, Washington, Beaufort, or other Union-occupied towns, white refugees bore much more close examination.

The passport system reflected some of the significant differences in the Union treatment of white and black refugees in eastern North Carolina. According to one Union soldier in New Bern, "All civilians were obliged to prove identity before the provost-marshall, and no one allowed to move about the city without a pass, except officers in uniform and the colored people." The soldier noted that "there was not the least demonstration of loyalty or Union sentiment with the whites, but a sullen moroseness, indicative of intense disloyalty." For black refugees, a passport system that required whites to carry documents to travel while permitting blacks to move freely without documentation marked a significant role reversal, as slaves traditionally had to carry passes issued by their owners in order to travel beyond their plantation. A black refugee in New Bern told a Union soldier, "'Bress de Lord an Massa Lincoln! Hallelujer! Dat dis yer ole nigger should lib to see dis happy time, when white folks mus hab a pass to go bout, and dis nigger wid the officer can go whar him pleas widout one! Bress de Lord!" Conversely, white refugees bristled at the passport system, believing that it effectively demarked them as slaves.[52]

Even after admission into Union lines, white refugees remained a suspect commodity. One Massachusetts soldier in New Bern noted in the fall of 1862 that "all the white hereabouts are of doubtful loyalty and have to be watched all the time." Another Massachusetts solider noted that "many white residents, professedly Union, are believed to be playing possum." Even sympathetic Union soldiers regarded white refugees with suspicion. Giles Ward, a first lieutenant in the Twelfth New York Cavalry Regiment, remarked in a letter home that "I know the truth of the reports of famine among them; day after day, men, women, and children come to our lines to get into New-Bern to buy bread, and beg to be allowed to enter the lines; the women weeping and children crying for food." Although he sympathized with their plight, Ward approved of severe restrictions on white refugees, as "many of them are spies, and we can not sacrifice our cause to alleviate the suffering." Some Union soldiers believed that as many as two-thirds of the "men that passes our lines were rebs with citizens' clothes."[53]

Union soldiers' fear of espionage by white refugees was not unwarranted. Several white refugees in New Bern passed information and goods to Confederate scouts stationed outside of the town. Probably the best known of the Confederate spies in Union-occupied North Carolina was Emmeline Pigott. Born to a prosperous coastal family, Pigott had fled New Bern in 1862 aboard the final train to leave the town after the invasion. After working for several months as a nurse in Kinston, tending to wounded Confederate soldiers, Pigott relocated to Concord, a town in Cabarrus County just north of Charlotte. While in Concord, Pigott learned of the death of her beau at Gettysburg and rededicated her commitment to the Confederate cause. According to a memorial recorded after her death, Pigott befriended a "Mrs. Brent," the widow of a Union chaplain, in Concord. Traveling together, the two women moved from Concord to Union-occupied Morehead City by "means of ox carts, on foot and rail, back to the little farm on Calico Creek." Pigott's choice of traveling companion probably eased her entry into Union territory, as did her youthful, innocent-looking visage. Once within the Federal zone, Pigott quickly developed a smuggling and intelligence network in New Bern, Morehead City, and Beaufort, gathering information from fishermen about the comings and goings of Federal vessels. According to her diary, Pigott "often met the Confederate scouts & often carried the scouts their meals in the woods. They had places to hide. Some times Yankeys would be in the house while the Confederates were both fed from the same table." Like many female smugglers, Pigott concealed her wares beneath her voluminous hoopskirts. When she was arrested in February 1865, Pigott's hoops bore dozens of items intended for Confederate soldiers, including boots, shirts, gloves, candy, and "several letters addressed to rebels denouncing the federals ... and giving information about supposed movement of federal troops."[54]

Pigott was not alone in smuggling goods and intelligence to Confederate scouts. In New Bern alone, at least five women actively participated as Confederate couriers. Throughout their occupation of coastal North Carolina, Union officials suspected that white refugees were smuggling across the lines but struggled to apprehend those responsible. Not only did fears of espionage temper much of the sympathy that Union soldiers might have felt for poor refugees, but many white refugees proudly displayed their Confederate sympathies. While white men risked arrest if they exhibited any pro-Confederate feeling, white women felt empowered to vocalize their support for the Confederate cause. Dr. William Smith, a surgeon in the Eighty-Fifth New York Volunteer Infantry, arranged to board at a house in New Bern and observed that "my hostess & her fair daughter are intensely 'secesh'–they set a good table, however, and are courteous and kind. ... Mrs. Allen, with whom I board, is an elderly lady with very motherly ways, except when her Rebel proclivities are displayed. She has a very pretty daughter of some 20 years, 'Miss Susie,' who is very charming, so long as the 'secesh' in her is not roused. She has one or two brothers in the service of the Rebellion."[55]

Union soldiers generally had a low opinion of white North Carolinians. One Massachusetts soldier observed, "We saw some of the native whites here, 'the poor white trash.' ... They all, as far as I have seen them, look inferior to the negroes, in intelligence, energy, and everything else that makes up a noble character. They are horribly sallow, pale, and all have the shakes. The women are frightful and are chewers of clay and snuff-dippers." The habit of snuff-dipping among white refugee women disgusted many Union soldiers, who frequently commented on it in their letters home. One Massachusetts soldier described his revulsion with white North Carolina women, noting that

> most of the females were so coarse and unfeminine in habits, as to degrade their sex. The leaded eye, sallow skin, swaggering gait and uncouth slang were too much for the Northern man, and made him devoutly thankful he descended from a nobler lineage. A lady's evening call (they never speak of afternoon) would be incomplete without snuff, and to omit to offer it to a caller was unpardonable. After the seating of the guests, the hostess was expected to pass saucers, twigs, and a bladder of snuff, with which the visitors regaled themselves during the call. Some were so addicted to the

habit of snuff-dipping, as to indulge in it upon the streets, regardless of their disgusting appearance.

Refugee men also received the soldiers' scorn. A Massachusetts soldier noted that "the alleged loyal North Carolinians, whom the soldiers denominate 'buffaloes,' do not stand very high in the minds of the men from Massachusetts. Seemingly they are more observant of calls for rations than for work of any kind."[56]

During the summer of 1862, Vincent Colyer grew concerned about the emergent humanitarian crisis among white and black refugees within Union lines. Most African Americans fled to Union lines with few material possessions. For fugitive slaves whose flight had required hiding in the woods or swamps, their clothes were often reduced to rags. According to Colyer, slaves entering Union lines at New Bern "were immediately provided with food and hot coffee, which they relished highly for they were usually both hungry and tired from their oftentimes long journeys and fastings."[57] While Colyer could provide this modest repast when fugitives entered camp, he had neither the resources nor the authority to distribute food to hungry refugees on a more permanent basis.

Even if he had been granted the ability to distribute food more generously, it is unlikely that Colyer would have done so. Like most Northern aid workers, Colyer espoused the "free labor" ethic, a central tenet in Republican thought. Such thinking held that the problems of poverty could not be resolved through charity alone but rather required the creation of opportunities for individual advancement. Charity in isolation, Colyer believed, created dependence, a form of enslavement. Part of a coherent Northern philanthropist ideology, this aversion to dependence had deep roots and fundamentally shaped much of Colyer's (and later others') approach to the refugee crisis in North Carolina.[58] Significantly, Colyer titled his account of his work with black refugees in North Carolina *Report of the Services Rendered by the Freed People to the United States Army in North Carolina*. By emphasizing the productive work of black refugees on behalf of the Union war effort, Colyer was indicating that they were not dependent on the generosity of the federal government, but rather that the army depended heavily on the labor of freed slaves in North Carolina. Indeed, Colyer labeled one of the first sections in his report "Negroes Not a Burthen."[59]

Especially during the spring of 1862, in the immediate aftermath of the occupation of New Bern, most fugitive slaves arrived in camp empty-handed.

However, some fugitive slaves, especially those from plantations near Union-occupied towns, were able to abscond with some of their personal possessions. Those whose owners had fled in advance of the Union invasion often appropriated whatever material goods they believed necessary, limited by what they could reasonably transport. Vincent Colyer noted that some fugitive slaves arrived in New Bern with "the women carrying their pickaninnies and the men huge bundles of clothing, occasionally with a cart or old wagon, with a mule drawing their household possessions."[60] Even these few fugitive slaves who did arrive bearing clothing, blankets, and other household items could bring only enough food to sustain themselves during their escape. Once inside Union lines, they needed to find a new source of sustenance.

The material poverty of black refugees manifested itself in July 1862, when General Burnside was ordered to take part of his force north to support McClellan during the Peninsula Campaign. Burnside ordered several regiments to pack quickly, and, as they were unable to take with them the material goods ("mattress, tables, chairs, Dutch ovens, etc.") they had accumulated over several months, soldiers left them in camp. As the soldiers boarded their ships, "crowds of negroes pounced upon the household goods which we had been enjoying."[61]

The employment of adult men did little to alleviate the deepening humanitarian crisis. Working as manual laborers or scouts, men were provided with clothing, a soldier's ration, and a small income. However, an informal census taken by Vincent Colyer during the summer of 1862 revealed that only one out of every four black refugees was an adult male. With the exception of a handful of black women who worked as hospital nurses (earning four dollars per month), the majority of the refugee population, women and children, were left to fend for themselves. From the very beginning of the Union occupation of eastern North Carolina, black women found themselves excluded from Union labor policies that empowered black men. While black refugee men gained government employment as spies, scouts, and manual labors (and eventually as soldiers), no equivalent positions existed for black refugee women, who found themselves excluded from the federal bounty. Some fugitive women offered Union soldiers their services as cooks and laundresses. One soldier noted that "the Negro women are round every day selling gingerbread[,] cakes[,] pies[,] and other things." Another New Bern soldier noted that with the exception of bread, meat, and coffee, the majority of foodstuffs consumed by soldiers in his unit were "bought of negresses, who come up here by scores to sell their stuff," including apple and sweet potato pies and yams. When army rations proved unpalatable, he and a dozen of his company evaded the guard patrolling the town to have "supper at the little low house of a negro woman, famous for her skill in cookery," where they dined on "a stunning ham, boiled sweet potatoes, tea, coffee, and oysters and tripe." A Massachusetts soldier noted that "there are lots of 'contrabands' around; from sunrise to sunset they are in the camp with almost everything in the eating line: gingerbread, pies, oysters, plenty of cookies, sweet potatoes, fried fish, etc." Teenage boys not old enough to work on fortifications hired themselves to Union officers as servants. One soldier noted that "the black boys want to hire out as servants, and at such low rates that many of the men in the ranks have one to run errands, draw water, [and] wash their tin dishes." A tent of Massachusetts soldiers hired "a darkey boy (about 16 years old) to wash dishes[,] black our shoes and do our errands. He is a treasure and a character."[62]

Desperate for employment, fugitive slaves took whatever positions were available to them, which at times included tolerating abuse by Union soldiers. Writing to his family from New Bern in June 1862, Union officer Rowland Hall described Richard Butler, a fugitive teenage slave from Warrenton whom Hall had charged with the maintenance of his horse. Although Hall praised Butler for his diligence and expertise with horses, he derided his intelligence, noting that he had "a forehead less than an inch high." Coming from a wealthy New York family, Hall instinctively treated Butler as his inferior, claiming that he was "just as much my slave as if I owned him. I am obliged to govern him in this way because he can understand no other. I sometimes threaten to have him tied up, & always to good effect." Richard Butler's experience suggests that his employment options were limited. One Massachusetts soldier dismissively compared black children to pets, noting that "we picked up at Plymouth, as soldiers will, many pets—a curious lot—squirrels, owls, raccoons, birds, and little darkies, the latter quite useful in blacking shoes and such odd jobs."[63] As the population of refugee black women and children within Union lines grew to approximately seventy-five hundred by July 1862, finding employment became increasingly difficult.

The material condition of white refugees in eastern North Carolina in the spring and summer of 1862 did not differ significantly from that of African American refugees. Most arrived with little more than the clothes on their backs, especially those men fleeing Confederate conscription. According to one solider in Washington, "Every [white] family coming into our lines required immediate attention ... not less than one family daily, and often as many as half a dozen families in one day, the duty falling upon the Provost-Marshal to procure a tenement for each, supply them with some kind of furniture, and make provisions for rations until they could manage for themselves." However, as both housing and furniture were in short supply, "it was often necessary to rob Peter to pay Paul, the result being that both were left poverty-stricken.... Many poor women with children, were forced to live in small rooms, without bed, table or chairs, subsisting on the meager rations furnished by the government." Unlike black refugees, white refugees had no immediate employment opportunities devolving from the Union military occupation. Distrusted by Union officers and enlisted men, white refugees were not hired to work on fortifications by the Union army or by Union officers as servants. White refugees were also unwilling to work for the low wages that black refugees accepted. One soldier noted that while black refugees were "very intelligent and charge reasonable prices," white refugees "ask four times what they are worth."[64]

Unable or unwilling to find work, white refugees turned to the federal government to provide food. Vincent Colyer reported that four hundred white refugee families, some eighteen hundred individuals, received food from the army commissary. Colyer noted that "some of these families had a few months before been in affluence, [and] many children and ladies of refinement came for food." For white refugees accustomed to luxury, such dependence on the beneficence of strangers proved humbling. A white refugee identified only as "Miss Mary —" pleaded to Vincent Colyer that "necessity compels me to come and ask you for provisions, although it is very galling.... We have been raised in affluence, but we are poor now.... Our rents are all stopped and our servants have left us. We must now have something to live on."[65]

To prevent starvation, some white and black refugees received handouts of food. In March 1862 General Burnside authorized Vincent Colyer to distribute whatever supplies he deemed necessary to the poor from the Depot Commissary in New Bern. Colyer's records indicate that white refugees were more much dependent on aid than black refugees, such that the eighteen hundred white refugees demanded far more food and supplies than the seventy-five hundred black refugees. While the far more numerous black refugees received only 19 pounds of fresh beef, 16½ barrels of pork, and 27½ pounds of candles, white refugees received 169 pounds of fresh beef, 29½ barrels of pork, and 379 pounds of candles.

Indeed, the only items that African Americans received in parity to their numbers were beans, peas, and soap.⁶⁶

The most significant problem confronting Colyer in the spring of 1862 was where to house the rapidly growing refugee population. The earliest black refugees took possession of homes vacated by whites who had fled inland. Describing the situation in New Bern, one Massachusetts soldier noted that "the white citizens had fled . . . as to leave the negroes practically in possession of all their leavings." Another Massachusetts soldier observed that "seven railroad trains loaded with men, women, and children, left New Berne on the day of the battle, and so, . . . only about two hundred out of . . . seven or eight thousand white, remained in their homes. . . . The colored people received the troops with the wildest manifestations of joy. . . . Somehow, without proclamation or general orders, it came to be generally understood that slavery expired wherever the Federal army advanced." Similarly, in Plymouth, a Union soldier noted that "the negroes who have lately flocked into the town from the surrounding country . . . are quartered in huts and houses that their master and other inhabitants of Plymouth have kindly and considerably left them." On Roanoke Island, the earliest black refugees were housed in deserted Confederate army barracks, some of which had suffered fire damage during the Union invasion.⁶⁷

In assuming control over abandoned property, black refugees had to compete with Union soldiers, who occupied the most prime real estate in New Bern and other Union-occupied towns. One Massachusetts soldier in New Bern noted that "all the whites are gone, and their houses occupied by our troops." Another Massachusetts soldier observed shortly after the battle of New Bern that "we are nicely settled in the fine mansions of the lordly fugitives, who but yesterday ruled these spacious homes and paced the pictured halls. What strange infatuation, bordering on insanity, must have possessed these people, to bring this terrible calamity of war upon themselves, thus becoming voluntary exiles and strangers from their homes and property."⁶⁸ In all of the Union-occupied towns in eastern North Carolina, the Union army claimed the best properties, relegating black refugees to the periphery.

It did not take long, however, before the refugee slave population exceeded the available housing. By July 1862, less than six months after the Union invasion, ten thousand black refugees had fled bondage. According to an informal census conducted by Vincent Colyer, this figure included seventy-five hundred in and around New Bern, one thousand on Roanoke Island, and fifteen hundred in other Union-occupied sites, including Washington, Hatteras, Carolina City, and Beaufort. The influx of so many black refugees in such a short time created some of the largest and most densely populated areas in the state.[69]

Overcrowding was most pronounced in New Bern. By July 1862, New Bern was home not only to seventy-five hundred fugitive slaves but also to more than ten thousand Union soldiers, many of whom occupied civilian housing in the town. New Bern's white civilian population in mid-1862 is difficult to estimate. While a majority of the white residents had fled prior to the invasion, not all of them had the means or ability to leave their homes. One Union soldier estimated that approximately two hundred white residents of New Bern were still in the town when Union soldiers marched in. During the white refugee exodus from New Bern, many of the elderly and the poor elected to remain. Others stayed in an effort to protect their homes or property, especially nonslaveholders who had little moveable property and who believed they had less to fear from Union occupation than their slaveholding neighbors. Merchants with connections to the North also were more likely to stay, believing they could use those relationships to curry favor with Union officials.[70] Although arriving in smaller numbers than black refugees, white refugees, many of them committed Unionists, were also pouring into New Bern. From his headquarters in New Bern, Colyer could observe that the overcrowded residences could not sustain the growing population and the daily arrival of additional white and black refugees only made the problem worse.

While Vincent Colyer was primarily concerned about the humanitarian consequences of such dramatic overcrowding, military officials had other concerns. Living in close quarters in occupied towns, soldiers and refugees interacted in ways that distressed many officers, who feared that it would harm morale and impede combat effectiveness. Some soldiers resented the presence of refugee African Americans, with one soldier noting that he was "sick, tired, and disgusted with the sight" of refugee slaves and hoped "to be transported to a place where niggers are unknown." Furthermore, the rampant overcrowding had turned the streets of New Bern into open sewers, and many officers worried that poor sanitation endangered the soldiers' health. In March 1862 an African American man in New Bern developed smallpox, a highly contagious disease. Unable to find a military or civilian doctor willing to treat him, Colyer arranged for the man to be cared for by an elderly black woman who had had smallpox and was therefore immune. He was relocated "to a hut on the outskirts of the town, some distance from our office." To prevent a more general outbreak, General Burnside authorized Colyer to vaccinate more than one thousand refugee slaves against smallpox and to open a hospital to treat refugees.[71]

In the midst of the overcrowding and confusion in Union-occupied eastern North Carolina, nascent black refugee communities emerged. Arriving in New Bern, Roanoke, Washington, and other Union-occupied sites as individuals, as families, and in larger groups, black refugees began in the spring and summer of 1862 to establish social organizations to help them survive the ordeal of living without stable residences, regular employment, or a guarantee that their temporary freedom would become permanent. These refugee communities were not purely extensions of the social and cultural networks established in slavery. Rather, within Union lines, fugitive slaves created new social networks shaped by their status as refugees.

Black refugees quickly established churches in Union-held territory. In New Bern, the existing black Methodist church continued to hold services. With Vincent Colyer's assistance, refugee slaves established a Baptist congregation in a church that appeared to have been abandoned for some time. Within weeks of Union occupation, both black churches were filled to capacity, with congregants spilling out of the pews into the aisles and galleries. Black churches also quickly formed in Washington, where one Union solider noted that they were "extremely fervent in their prayers for the success of the Northern cause, and rightly attribute their enlarged liberty to the presence of our soldiers." Lacking an established church to occupy, black refugees on Roanoke Island built one. Vincent Colyer noted their dedication as they "constructed a spacious bower, cutting down long, straight pine trees and placing them parallel lengthwise for seats, with space enough between for their knees." Using whatever materials were available to aid in construction, fugitive slaves built the pulpit out of discarded quartermaster's boxes and roofed the edifice with pine branches. By the end of February 1862, less than a month after the battle of Roanoke Island, a second black church opened on the island.[72]

White soldiers often visited black churches in New Bern and other occupied cities. Alfred Roe, a Massachusetts soldier, visited a black church in New Bern in November 1862 with eleven of his fellow soldiers. He noted that "the people seemed to be earnest and deeply engaged. They sing old-fashioned tunes, whose words the minister lines for them." Raised in the confining dictates of the New England Congregational and Unitarian churches, many soldiers marveled at how different the particulars of black religious expression were. One Massachusetts soldier wrote,

> A novel and interesting service to us Northern boys was that held in the Contraband Methodist Church.... The galleries reserved for visitors were filled, principally by soldiers drawn thither by curiosity. The body of the church was filled by colored people, the men on one side of the aisle and the women on the other. They were of all shades of color from light yellow to inky black. The leader, an intelligent looking colored man, occupied a chair in front of the pulpit.... Our expectations regarding the beautiful singing of the colored people were dashed to the ground. The tunes were screamed forth from the cracked throats of the old and the shrill voices of the young, all singing the air and all pitched in a different key. There was no harmony, only a babel of sound.[73]

While most soldiers were more charitable with their musical assessment, their accounts of visiting black churches universally praised the devotion and enthusiasm of the congregants.

James Glazier, a soldier with the Twenty-Third Massachusetts Volunteers who would be ordained after the war, took a particular interest in black refugees' religious expression. Shortly after the battle of New Bern, Glazier "spent the evening in singing and conversation with the contrabands, there being many with us. I found that all but one of them were pious." Assigned police duty in New Bern, Glazier found himself drawn to a black church an hour before sunrise by "the wild musical voices of those happy freemen [which] went up in hymns of praise to Jesus the Great Emancipator." Although regulations dictated that he should not enter the building except when making an arrest, Glazier felt compelled to go in after hearing "a fervent prayer ... to the *lover of the lowly*, in which the 'dear Union soldiers' were remembered, then followed another song of Zion." Glazier followed a middle-aged man into the sanctuary, and "when the singing was ended made a few remarks. I told them the voice of prayer and singing drew me into their midst, spoke a few feeble words of encouragement, and then told them I must leave them to serve the Lord, while I must be about my street duties." Glazier expressed amazement at the choral singing, completely unlike any he had ever experienced. "I wish I could give you an idea of these melodies and their manner of singing," he wrote home. "No instrument, or combination of them can equal them in beauty or sound. And to look at their happy faces while they sing and witness the earnestness and devotion pictured there is enough to make one sorry he is not in one of their black skins."[74]

Despite their interest in the religious expression of black refugees, Northern soldiers often expressed bafflement at some of the more unusual elements of black spirituality. A Massachusetts soldier noted that "the negroes here honor the Hibernian custom of 'waking' their dead. On occasions of this sort, they sometimes render night so hideous by their songs and shoutings that the guard is attracted to the scene of their spiritual orgies, to enforce order. At midnight, the revelers solemnly refresh themselves with coffee, and then resume their howling, reciting and chanting simple hymns, line by line."[75] Union soldiers also expressed confusion at the local custom of Jonkonnu. Importing the Christmastime ritual from Jamaica, slaves in eastern North Carolina had observed Jonkonnu since at least 1824. Performing in troupes, black men danced and sang wearing calico robes and white masks, enacting a racial role reversal in which black dances in whiteface demanded rewards of money or alcohol from white audiences.[76]

Black refugees in eastern North Carolina also created schools to signify their freedom. As in most of the South, North Carolina law prohibited slaves from learning to read, fearing that such knowledge would undermine white authority and potentially foment slave rebellions. While most schools for African Americans were opened by white missionaries, the first school in North Carolina appears to have been opened by a literate fugitive slave. In February 1862 Martha Culling, "a bright smart mulatto girl," opened a school near Union headquarters on Roanoke Island. Observing fugitive slaves' passion for spelling primers and readers, Vincent Colyer opened two schools in New Bern in mid-April 1862, with classes held at the two black churches. The larger of the two, with more than eight hundred students, was for the illiterate, while the smaller school provided instruction for the approximately two hundred literate fugitive slaves. Opened with the approval of Union general John Foster, the schools in New Bern operated with the aid of more than thirty soldiers from the Twenty-Fifth Massachusetts Volunteers serving as teachers. By comparison, the white refugee communities developed more slowly, in large part because of the white refugee population's fragmentation and smaller size. At the same time that he facilitated the opening of schools for black refugees, Vincent Colyer helped to open a school for seventy white refugee children in New Bern, engaging a young woman as a teacher.[77] With the white churches filled every Sunday with Union soldiers, most white refugees refrained from attending.

In May 1862, two months after the occupation of New Bern, Abraham Lincoln appointed Edward Stanly as military governor of eastern North

Carolina. The Burnside invasion in the spring of 1862 created a stable Union enclave in northeastern North Carolina, and Stanly's appointment was intended to mark a return to civilian leadership in the region. Fifty-two years old at the time of his appointment, Stanly had been born in New Bern to a prominent slaveholding family and had served five terms in Congress as a Whig. In 1853 he had declined to run for a sixth term, deciding instead to move to California, where he ran unsuccessfully for governor as a Republican in 1857. In February 1862, believing that North Carolina had been coerced into secession and that he could rally Union sentiment, Stanly offered his services to Secretary of State William H. Seward. Two months later, Stanly received a telegram from Secretary of War Edwin Stanton summoning him to Washington from California. On May 19, 1862, Stanly received his commission from President Lincoln to "exercise and perform" the office of military governor of North Carolina "until the loyal inhabitants of that State shall organize a civil government in conformity with the Constitution of the United States." Commission in hand, Stanly took the next available steamer for New Bern, arriving in the pouring rain on May 26, 1862, when General Burnside handed over civil and political jurisdiction to Stanly, promising him military support for his efforts.[78]

In the same month that Governor Stanly arrived in New Bern, President Lincoln authorized the formation of regiments of loyal white North Carolinians. The soldiers recruited into the First and Second North Carolina Union Volunteers primarily consisted of refugees who had fled from conscription or deserted the Confederate army. Nicknamed Buffaloes, the recruits came almost exclusively from the nonslaveholding class. As with his appointment of Edward Stanly as military governor, Lincoln's decision to authorize Union regiments among the loyal population grew out his persistent belief in the Unionist sentiment in eastern North Carolina. A recruitment poster for the regiment informed white refugees that any man "willing to enlist under the 'Old Flag,' will be paid, clothed, and fed, by the United States." As a further enticement, the poster informed prospective soldiers that "this regiment is intended for the protection of loyal citizens . . . and will not be called upon to leave the State." The poster also warned that men of fighting age who did not enlist and "stand aloof from this movement" should not "expect that the Government will protect those who make no effort to aid themselves."[79]

Some Union officers were disappointed that more white refugees did not enlist. John Hedrick expressed disappointment in the unenthusiastic response of white refugees to recruiting efforts. He noted in July 1862 that "the people about here are so so. They profess to be Union, but are not fighting Union men." Some of the white refugees, he observed, had taken the oath of loyalty, while others had taken an oath of neutrality, and many refused to take any oath at all.

Others, however, were more sympathetic, noting that if captured by the Confederates, white refugees in Federal uniforms would be treated as deserters and executed. One Massachusetts soldier sympathized with a Buffalo he met in Plymouth in February 1863. According to his diary, "John Fenno, a unionist, was drafted into the rebel service, deserted, ran to our lines, and joined the native cavalry regiment (Buffaloes), and consequently is in a bad predicament. He will have to fight to the death; for if he is taken the rebels will hang him." Fenno had fled to Plymouth with his family and lived in fear of a Confederate raid on the town.[80]

Stanly's commission from Washington was silent on the subject of African Americans, a silence that Stanly read as granting him wide discretion respecting fugitive slaves. Stanly interpreted his instructions to return North Carolina to civilian government as a dictate to uphold antebellum laws regarding slavery. Stanly claimed that he "did not profess to agree with, or defend the political opinions of the President, or his Cabinet, nor those of the present Congress" and that he would take any legal measure possible to protect slavery in North Carolina. Stanly said he would provide "protection to any loyal citizen, who, with his neighbors, would take his negroes home." Stanly later claimed that Stanton had assured him that he had the autonomy of a "dictator" and "could do what I pleased."[81]

With such an overwhelming sense of his authority and discretion as governor, Stanly immediately undertook to dismantle the nascent black refugee community in New Bern and across Union-occupied eastern North Carolina. In his "first administrative act," Stanly ordered Vincent Colyer to close the two black schools in New Bern, arguing that he "had been sent to restore the old order of things." Stanly informed Colyer that "the laws of North Carolina forbade slaves to be taught to read and write." Furthermore, Stanly argued that the black schools undermined the growth of white Unionism in eastern North Carolina, which Stanly valued far more highly than the welfare of black refugees.[82] Proud of the progress in black education over the previous six weeks, Colyer protested Stanly's order to General Burnside and other military officials, who informed him that they were powerless to countermand the order.

Dejected, Colyer went to the larger of the two schools, then meeting at the Methodist church on Hancock Street in New Bern, interrupting classes in session. He informed the refugee students that "these schools are now to be closed, not by the officer of the army, under whose sanction they have been commenced, but by the necessity laid upon me by Governor Stanley [sic], who has informed me that it is a criminal offence, under the laws of North Carolina, to teach the blacks to read." A *New York Times* reporter who accompanied Colyer on his journey to the school indicated that "the old people dropped their heads upon their breasts and wept in silence; the young looked at each other with mute surprise and grief at this sudden termination of their bright hopes. It was a sad and impressive spectacle." Having informed the students at the Methodist church about the closing of their school, Colyer made his way to the Baptist church, "where the more advanced scholars were placed," where he delivered the news a second time.[83]

The closing of black schools signaled to white North Carolinians that Stanly was no abolitionist. Within days of taking office, Stanly received petitions from local whites for what a *New York Times* reporter described as the "restoration of their fugitive property who have sought protection from the tyranny of the plantation within our lines." One of these petitioners, Nicholas Bray, a farmer who lived two miles from New Bern, asserted his ownership of two female slaves. After Bray promised to take the oath of allegiance, a promise that he never fulfilled, Stanly authorized Bray to reclaim his fugitive property. Armed with Stanly's order, Bray proceeded to the nearby New Bern Academy, now functioning as a hospital, where he found the older of the two fugitive women "lying sick abed." Bray then proceeded to drag "her forth and drove away with her to the plantation."[84]

The sight of a slave owner forcibly recapturing a refugee slave in the heart of Union-occupied New Bern with the authorization of the new military governor terrified the city's black refugees. They turned to Vincent Colyer, the superintendent of the poor, to defend their freedom after the forced removal of Bray's slave. Arriving at his office, Colyer "found the place filled with affrighted negroes, crying and wailing terribly." Among the dozens of fugitive slaves amassed in the courtyard in front of Colyer's office was the second slave Bray had come for, the younger sister of the woman who had just been dragged back into bondage. The frightened young woman, named Harriet, told Colyer that she feared that she would be sold inland, as Bray had been offered $1,500 for her. While Colyer had begrudgingly accepted Stanly's authority to close the schools for black refugees, he refused to believe that Stanly would countenance slave owners reclaiming their property. Colyer "went to the Governor and asked how these things were? He said he knew the man very well. I asked if he had taken the oath—not presumptuously, but because I had heard of the man before. He said No, but he had promised to, and he had given him authority to take his property."

Disgusted with Stanly's response, Colyer told Harriet to hide. When General Foster told Colyer that he had no authority to overturn the governor's decision, Colyer offered to resign. Foster advised him to forestall his resignation, and Colyer prepared to protest Stanly's actions through official channels. He hurried home to pack for the next available steamer to the Washington, where he hoped that Seward, Stanton, or Lincoln would rein in Stanly, stop the return of fugitive slaves, and allow the schools to reopen. Within a week, at least four other fugitive slaves were forcibly returned to their owners. Stanly's actions led to a wave of terror among black refugees in eastern North Carolina. According to a *New York Times* reporter, "The slaves express the greatest horror at the prospect of being sent back to their old homes, and say that they will be unmercifully 'cut up' for having absconded. One old man of sixty told me to-day that he would rather be placed before a cannon and blown to pieces than go back. Multitudes say they would rather die." Stanly's policy on refugee slaves created a "stampede in all directions." One observer noted that, "frightened at this turn of affairs, a number of the slaves who have congregated in the town had scattered like a flock of frightened birds. Some have taken to the swamps, and others have concealed themselves in out-of-the-way places. A perfect panic prevails among them. The greater part who were employed on the fortifications are so much alarmed at the prospect of being returned to their enraged masters, and being punished, that they are of little use as laborers."[85]

Most Union soldiers rejected Stanly's refugee policy, as his administration fell on them "like a wet blanket." Rowland Hall expressed the disdain that many Union soldiers held for Edward Stanly: "To see a Pro-Slavery, nigger-hunting, hound sent here to a town, redeemed by the blood of Massachusetts troops." A *New York Times* reporter indicated that "prominent officers, from colonels and quartermasters down to the humblest soldiers in the ranks, speak in terms of the most vehement indignation of the course which the new Governor is pursuing." Daniel Reed Larned, Burnside's aide, wrote to his sister that Stanly's policies had undermined the piecemeal progress that black refugees had made toward freedom. "It seems as if all we had accomplished was being undone," he wrote. "What the effect will be on the blacks I cannot tell." John Hedrick was also disdainful of the new governor. When Governor Stanly visited Beaufort, he "made only one appointment when he was here. He called him Harbor Master but he has none of the duties of a Harbor Master to perform. Negro Searcher would be a more appropriate title for him. He has to examine the vessels as they leave to see that no 'niggs' are aboard." Although Hedrick was disgusted at Stanly's fugitive slave policy, he concluded that "it don't amount to much: for anybody disposed to take them away, can easily box them up, till they get to sea. When the 4th Rhode Island Regiment left here, they took about a dozen, some barreled up, others boxed, and others concealed among the vessels['] cargo." Stanly also ordered the harbormaster in New Bern to "search all vessels leaving the port for negroes." He was rebuked by the soldier, who told the governor, "I am a New Yorker. Do you suppose that I have come down here to hunt niggers? I'll see you in H—ll first!"[86]

While most Union soldiers rejected Stanly's efforts and some actively undermined them, a few Union soldiers welcomed the change in policy. In late June 1862, Capt. William W. Hammill of the Ninth New York Volunteer Regiment helped a slave owner recover two runaway slaves in Plymouth. According to one soldier, the slave owner bound them by the wrists, "leading them through the streets by the other end [of the rope], as a farmer might lead cattle to market." As the coffle passed by the regimental guardhouse, a sympathetic soldier cut the rope with his pocketknife, telling the fugitive slaves to run. Captain Hammill ordered their recapture and reduced the soldier in rank for aiding them.[87]

Unable to work with Governor Stanly, Vincent Colyer sought redress in Washington. News of Stanly's refugee policy had reached Northern newspapers and had incited widespread protests. Accompanied by Massachusetts senator Charles Sumner, Colyer visited President Lincoln to protest Stanly's refugee policy on June 5, 1862. In Colyer's account of their meeting, Lincoln indicated that Stanly was misinformed about his mandate. Lincoln was particularly incensed about Stanly's returning fugitive slaves, telling Colyer that his policy was that "no slave who once comes within our lines a fugitive from a rebel, shall ever be returned to his master." Lincoln did not explicitly prohibit the return of slaves to proclaimed Unionists, although in light of Lincoln's issuance of the preliminary Emancipation Proclamation in September 1862, Colyer later

Figure 2. African American refugees entering New Bern. *Harper's Weekly*, February 21, 1862.

concluded that his meeting with Lincoln foreshadowed and potentially influenced Lincoln's thinking at a critical juncture. Sumner concluded that Lincoln had repudiated Stanly "in his absurd wickedness, closing the schools, nor again in his other act of turning our camps into a hunting ground for slaves. He repudiates both—positively." On the day after their meeting with Lincoln, Sumner introduced a congressional resolution censuring Stanly.[88]

When he returned to North Carolina in late June 1862, Colyer met with Governor Stanly. Stanly told him that he had "misunderstood him; that he never intended to enforce those [antebellum slavery] laws, and that with regard to interfering with my schools for colored people, or the return of fugitive slaves to their masters," he was expecting instructions from Washington. Two months later, with no directives forthcoming from the Lincoln administration, Stanly traveled to Washington to confer on black refugee policy, as he "could learn more by talking with the President two hours than by writing a week." Stanly arrived in Washington shortly after the Union victory at Antietam and Lincoln's declaration of the preliminary Emancipation Proclamation. Horrified at the prospect of emancipation, Stanly offered to resign. Committed to the idea of local Unionist government, Lincoln attempted to mollify Stanly. Some soldiers objected

Figure 3. Refugee relief in New Bern. *Frank Leslie's Illustrated,* June 14, 1862.

to any compromise with Stanly about the status of refugee slaves within Union lines. A Massachusetts soldier wrote home that "our principle business now is to assist the —, I mean his excellency Governor Stanley [sic] in protecting rebel property and feeding the poor snuff-dipping, dirt-eating, union-defying, yellow skinned North Carolinians, nine-tenths of whom will stab us the moment they get a chance."[89]

While Stanly awaited orders from Washington, the situation for black refugees in eastern North Carolina remained in limbo. Military developments in Virginia, however, led to a reorganization of the military forces in North Carolina. In July 1862, after Gen. George McClellan's defeat at the Seven Days and subsequent retreat, President Lincoln ordered Gen. Ambrose Burnside to reinforce Union forces on the peninsula. Taking seven thousand soldiers with him, Burnside left Gen. John G. Foster with over nine thousand troops to defend the federal enclave in eastern North Carolina. Fearing that a momentous battle between Confederate and Union forces was imminent and that his services would be needed tending to injured soldiers, Vincent Colyer accompanied Burnside's forces north. After he arrived in Virginia, Colyer discovered that

INDUSTRY OF THE WOMEN AND CHILDREN.

Figure 4. Refugees in New Bern. Vincent Colyer, *Report of Services Rendered by the Freed People to the United States Army, in North Carolina* (1864), 33.

representatives from the Sanitary Commission and Christian Commission were in ample supply in McClellan's army. Exhausted after a year of intense labor, Colyer decided to go home to New York rather than return to North Carolina.

Colyer's absence created a vacuum in the relationship between the refugees and the federal government. Shortly after his return to New York, Colyer received a letter from Amos Yorke, a black refugee living in New Bern who had served as Colyer's assistant. Yorke informed Colyer that "there are great inquiries for you by the people of color in Newbern;

Figure 5. Refugees in New Bern. *Harper's Weekly*, June 9, 1866.

they are much at a loss for they have no one now to apply to for comfort or satisfaction; no one that sympathizes with them as you did." During the four months between Colyer's departure and the appointment of a successor, black refugees in Union-occupied North Carolina remained without an advocate within the occupying authority. The status of their freedom was as unclear as it had been in March 1862 when Union troops first entered New Bern.[90]

TWO
Crowded with Refugees

In the years to come, black refugees in eastern North Carolina would celebrate the first of January as the anniversary of the day Abraham Lincoln signed the Emancipation Proclamation. In 1864 black refugees in Beaufort celebrated the "anniversary of our existence as citizens of the United States," thanking God "for hearing our cry when in the house of bondage, and for opening to us the door of escape."[1] In 1865 the *Old North State*, a recently commenced Unionist newspaper in Beaufort, described the "numerous celebrations ... commemorative of the Emancipation Proclamation." The largest celebration in North Carolina occurred in New Bern, where "the second anniversary of the Proclamation was enthusiastically celebrated by several thousand colored people." Organized by African Americans under the auspices of the newly formed National Equal Rights League, the celebration included the presentation of a regimental flag to the First North Carolina Colored Heavy Artillery, a parade through the streets of New Bern, and speeches by the city's most prominent black leaders, including Abraham Galloway and Rev. James Walker Hood. Black students from eight schools in New Bern participated alongside U.S. Colored Troops soldiers in the parade, signifying the conjunction of education, military service, and citizenship among the city's black refugees. The onlookers included approximately four thousand black refugees, including a number from Roanoke and the Outer Banks who traveled to New Bern to participate in the celebration, the vast majority of whom had been slaves only a few years earlier. The *Old North State* noted that "thousands of white people looked upon the scene with mingled emotions of pleasure and astonishment—pleasure that this old seat of the effete Pro-Slavery

Aristocracy at last resounded with the welcome shouts of freedom, and astonishment, that the Proclamation within two years had extended such a powerful moral and political influence." The newspaper also observed that "we did not see a colored person drunk during the whole day. Wish we could say as much for the whites."[2]

Despite the importance and ceremony that they later attached to the date, black refugees in New Bern did not celebrate the Emancipation Proclamation on the first of January 1863. No parades or public festivities distinguished that day from any other. More than seven months after Edward Stanly had been appointed governor over Union-occupied eastern North Carolina, black refugees had little to celebrate. Under his authority, the schools remained closed and the social and legal status of black refugees remained nebulous. The only public recognition of the day's significance occurred in the town's churches, where the proclamation was read aloud. At Andrews Chapel, New Bern's largest black church, Rev. Horace James, a chaplain with the Twenty-Fifth Massachusetts, read the president's statement to the gathered crowd. After explaining the proclamation's ramifications, James noted that the "slaves generally begin to understand, and dare to believe that they are free." The proclamation remained "the prominent topic of their conversation" for weeks afterward, as black refugees sought to make sense of how to reconcile the finality of President Lincoln's statement that they were "then, thenceforward, and forever free" with their recent experiences under Governor Stanly, which suggested that their claims to freedom were tenuous at best.[3]

Despite its inconspicuous passing, the first of January 1863 marked a significant turning point in the lives of both white and black refugees in eastern North Carolina. Unlike many occupied areas in the Confederacy, the Union enclave in eastern North Carolina was not exempted from the Emancipation Proclamation's provisions because it had not yet sent a duly elected representative to Congress.[4] One soldier in New Bern noted that black refugees "were quite well informed upon the President's proclamation, at least the portion relating to their own freedom." Another soldier agreed, observing that they "are considerably interested in the President's proclamation, which many of them understand very well." In February 1863 Henry Clapp talked with a mulatto woman in New Bern. Although "she had been free for many years," she had "very clear ideas on the subject of slavery. We talked about the emancipation proclamation and what was to become of the blacks, after they were freed. On all these subjects she had something to say and her mind seemed to me very clear and vigorous." Other soldiers indicated that the Emancipation Proclamation was not universally known or understood among black refugees. A Massachusetts soldier noted that "some of the colored people knew of their good fortune, while others were as ignorant as ever."[5]

Coming primarily from New England and including a significant number of prewar abolitionists, most soldiers in Union-occupied North Carolina embraced the Emancipation Proclamation. As one Massachusetts soldier noted, "It did not take men from the Bay State a great while to enter into the spirit of President Lincoln's Proclamation." A soldier stationed in Plymouth noted in February 1863 that "the town was crowded with fugitive *negroes* (not *slaves* now, thank Heaven!)." Although most Union soldiers in North Carolina favored freedom for black refugees, some soldiers expressed apprehension about enlisting African Americans into the Union army. In March 1863 a cavalry officer from New York noted that "the President's emancipation proclamation, and more particularly the Bill for arming the negroes which is supposed by this time to have become law, is very freely discussed in the army, finds but very few supporters, and if enforced here will no doubt cause numerous resignations among the officers and a great deal of discontent in the ranks." Other soldiers, however, saw the palpable hatred that black refugees expressed for slavery and recognized the military advantages that arming black men would provide. Three weeks after the Emancipation Proclamation took effect, William Willoughby, a soldier in the Tenth Connecticut, wrote to his wife that "I think there could be here in Newbern One thousand who formerly were slaves but who are now free, enlisted into the Union Army, who would fight like *Tigers* to defend their rights as they now enjoy them." Willoughby believed not only that arming black men would crush the Confederacy but that "the first day of January 1863 should be classed with the fourth day of July 1776 as commencing a new Era."[6]

The first of January also marked the first day of work for Vincent Colyer's replacement. In November 1862 General Foster appointed Rev. James Means, a Massachusetts chaplain, as "Superintendent of Blacks" in North Carolina, or as the *New York Times* described it, "Superintendent of Contrabands."[7] The change in title from Colyer's "Superintendent of the Poor" to Means's "Superintendent of Blacks" marked a shift in thinking among Union officers in North Carolina. Whereas Colyer's title encompassed both white and black refugees, Means's responsibilities encompassed only black refugees. Means's more constrained title reflected the size of the black refugee population: by November 1862, the time of Means's appointment, more than ten thousand refugee slaves lived in the shadow of Union-occupied towns. This semantic shift also expanded and foreshadowed the Union policy of segregating white and black refugees.

Fifty years old at the time of his appointment, although many thought he looked older, with a long, "patriarchal beard of pure white," Means was "an enthusiast with regard to the negro race and treated the blacks as if they were all honest and faithful." Frail and thin, Means preached at the black Methodist church in New Bern and cultivated the admiration of black refugees, who respected his Christian piety and charity. When Means took office on the first of January 1863, black refugees in eastern North Carolina had lived without direct federal support or supervision for nearly five months, an oversight that one observer attributed to "Gov. Stanley [sic], who was an oppressor of the negroes."[8]

Governor Stanly himself militantly opposed Lincoln's Emancipation Proclamation. Persistent in his faith in white Unionist sentiment in North Carolina, Stanly concluded that the Emancipation Proclamation "put to flight all hope of peace by any measure of reconciliation." He was particularly perturbed by the news that in Elizabeth City there were "250 negroes armed and daily drilled by officers of the Army of the United States." In a letter to General Foster, Stanly worried that black soldiers would engage in wanton "pillage and robbery" and incite a "servile war." Unable to reconcile his position on black refugees to that espoused in the Emancipation Proclamation, Governor Edward Stanly submitted his resignation on January 15, 1863. President Lincoln accepted his resignation letter six weeks later. Although Daniel Reeves Goodloe, a North Carolina abolitionist then serving as a commissioner to supervise emancipation in the District of Columbia, was briefly floated as a replacement military governor, the post was never filled after Stanly's resignation.[9]

After Stanly's departure, the black schools in New Bern reopened. As before their closure, the schools quickly filled with refugee African Americans. Within days, the school on Hancock Street had more than five hundred students. In March 1863 a white teacher who had come from Boston to New Bern marveled at the enthusiasm black refugees manifested for education, noting, "I never knew anything like the craving the contrabands have to learn. There was notice given that there would be a class at such a time in the Methodist church, and more than 300 scholars presented themselves!"[10]

In the weeks and months to come, the black refugee population flourished, buoyed by the legal recognition of their freedom and the departure of Governor Stanly. However, the increasing black refugee population and continuing lack of resources expanded the humanitarian crisis, as black refugees struggled to find adequate food and shelter in overcrowded refugee camps. A Union soldier from Massachusetts stationed in New Bern captured the conflicting sense of excitement and despair among black refugees in the immediate aftermath of emancipation, writing,

> On our right are the humble homes of our colored people, the refugees who have come into Union lines. A little farther on is the large camp, or settlement of freedmen, freedmen now, not contrabands, as the Emancipation Proclamation went into effect on the first of January. Their rough-log huts generally have but one room, with the usual 'stick and clay' chimney and fire-place at the gable end. Many of the able-bodied among them have found opportunity for labor in the Government employ, yet the conditions of life among them are such as to touch one's heart, for the helpless creatures are 'sheep having no shepherd,' and that passing hour was born the revolve to do something to make their freedom indeed a boon to these freedmen.[11]

One of Reverend Means's highest priorities after he assumed his post as superintendent of blacks was to assess the size of the black refugee population. Although Union officials had attempted to regulate the admission of black refugees into Union lines, their efforts had been inconsistent. Means enlisted four Union soldiers to aid him in conducting his census, including Henry Clapp, who chronicled the experience in his letters home. Clapp and his three associates moved into Means's house in the center of New Bern. Clapp noted that their opportunity "to learn the African character is a rare and indeed an extraordinary one." During the day they went from door to door, collecting names, and at night they compiled their data around a wooden table in Means's house. Their task was complicated by a constant influx of new black refugees, the high black mobility within New Bern, and fugitive slaves' lack of consistent last names, as "they change their surnames ... according to the names of their employers or when ever they take a fancy to," forcing the census takers to catalog the refugee population by first names. While the vast majority of refugees were illiterate, Clapp was surprised to find that "one in fifteen of the men, women, and children could read. We find that many learned or began to learn before they were freed by our army—taking their instruction mostly 'on the sly' and indeed in the face of considerable danger." In addition to recording the names, sexes, ages, occupations, and literacy of African American refugees, census takers also recorded their skin color in four grades: black, dark, light, and very light.[12]

By late March 1863, after a month of diligent labor, Henry Clapp and his associates had made good progress on their census of black refugees in New Bern. They had "'taken' all the town including its immediate outskirts ... and have only three negro camps left ... about twenty-five hundred souls." The growth of these outlying camps reflected the overcrowded refugee population within New Bern itself. As more and more black refugees arrived in Union-occupied New Bern, a policy was established in late 1862 in which "the colored refugees who could not find quarters among their friends in town were placed in camps or settlements a little out of town." While some black refugees might have been glad to avoid the overcrowded and unsanitary conditions in New Bern, they may have feared for their safety. Within New Bern, black refugees were protected by Union soldiers. Two of the three outlying camps, however, were located "a mile or two outside of interior lines of fortifications," and the third was across the Trent River from New Bern, placing black refugees in a precarious position, vulnerable to Confederate attack. Fugitive slaves in Washington manifested a similar anxiety about their vulnerability. A Massachusetts soldier indicated in March 1863 that "the colored population here [is] quite fearful of an attack, and many of them with their effects packed up preparatory to a hurried removal to boats."[13]

In May 1863 Clapp and his three associates finished their census of black refugees in New Bern. Unfortunately, their detailed records, including the names, ages, occupations, and literacy of the town's black refugee population, have been lost. Their final total, however, survives: after three months of work, they concluded that New Bern (including the outlying camps) had more than eighty-five hundred black refugees. Reverend Means himself did not live to see the conclusion of the census, as he succumbed to typhoid fever in April 1863, after several weeks of illness.[14]

While black refugees quietly recognized the signing of the Emancipation Proclamation, January 1863 also marked a significant transition for white refugees in eastern North Carolina. Union military officials began requiring white refugees to take the oath of allegiance. Although earlier efforts had been made to obligate white refugees to take the oath, they had been frequently undermined or countermanded by Governor Stanly. In a series of ultimatums, General Foster required white residents within Union-held North Carolina to positively affirm their loyalty to the United States or leave the region. The loyalty oath presented the most visible and contentious marker of the distrust that Union soldiers harbored for white refugees.[15] The simultaneous imposition of the loyalty oath on white refugees and the Emancipation Proclamation freeing black refugees further delineated the racially differentiated treatment of the refugee population. The earliest imposition of loyalty oaths came in New Bern in late October 1862. According to one Union soldier, "The white people of this city have had their choice—to take the Oath, or leave. . . . This leaves us with none but loyal whites & negros [sic]." Those who refused the oath were escorted to Confederate lines on transport vessels.[16] Viewing the loyalty oath as an unjust military imposition on civilians, many white refugees complained to Governor Stanly, who had previously condoned the presence of white refugees who had taken an oath of neutrality and even of many white refugees who refused to take any oath whatsoever. By January 1863, however, Stanly was in the process of resigning his post to protest the Emancipation Proclamation. On January 9, 1863, the commanding officer in Elizabeth City posted a notice that all white men over the age of sixteen were required to take the oath of allegiance or leave the city, giving them four days to make the decision. Within weeks, similar notices were posted in Edenton, Washington, and Beaufort. In May 1863, according to a report filed by Confederate general D. H. Hill to the secretary of war, Union officials expelled from New Bern and Washington "the citizens who have hitherto furnished information," suggesting that at least some of the white refugees acted as spies.[17] A Union soldier stationed at Washington noted "a great exodus of its citizens who would not take the oath of allegiance to the United States. For according to an order from Gen. Foster, they had to do one thing or the other."[18] Although most white refugees who refused to take the oath left voluntarily after General Foster's ultimatum, when necessary, Union military officials escorted civilians unwilling to take the oath out of Union lines. In June 1863 a Union soldier in New Bern wrote to his girlfriend that he "went up to the river on a steam boat with a flag of truce to take some of the families who refuse to take the oath of allegiance," delivering them to Confederate pickets on the Neuse River near Kinston.[19]

In the months after the Emancipation Proclamation, African Americans eagerly awaited the creation of black regiments in eastern North Carolina. Black refugees had anticipated the creation of black regiments for months, creating their own militia companies to prepare. During the summer of 1862, not long after the battle of New Bern, William Henry Singleton, a black refugee who had fled from Kinston, organized one of the first black militias. After working for the Union army as a scout, Singleton "commenced to recruit a regiment of colored men. I secured the thousand men and they appointed me as their colonel and I drilled them with cornstalks for guns. We had no way, of course, of getting guns and equipment. We drilled once a week. I supported myself by whatever I could get to do and my men did likewise." When he offered his regiment to General Burnside in July 1862, however, Burnside refused Singleton's offer, citing Federal policy against enlisting black soldiers. Undeterred, Singleton and his men continued to drill, and similar black militias formed in Plymouth, Washington, and Beaufort.[20]

Working as scouts and spies, black refugees had functioned as soldiers from the beginning of the Burnside invasion. Scouts were routinely issued weapons and occasionally uniforms. Some local military officials in North Carolina took President Lincoln's proclamation as grounds to start enlisting black soldiers immediately and without authorization from their commanding officers. By mid-January 1863, Governor Stanly had been hearing complaints from "residents of Elizabeth City" that "about 250 negroes" were "armed and daily drilled by officers of the Army of the United States." In a letter of protest to General Foster, Stanly questioned whether "every subordinate officer at every post can receive negroes in the service without some regulations from headquarters." At the same time that Governor Stanly was hearing about refugee slaves being armed in Elizabeth City, William Loftin, a Confederate soldier and slave owner, visited Kinston under a flag of truce. There he was surprised when "my boy Tony came up with the Yankees in full uniform saying he was a U.S. soldier."[21]

While working on Reverend Means's census of black refugees, Henry Clapp received palpable evidence that many black refugees were eager to join the Union army. In April 1863 he met a former cavalry sergeant who had been appointed as "overseer of blacks" in Elizabeth City. He believed he

> could easily raise a company of [black] cavalry there and that he knew they would make splendid soldiers. . . . About fifty of them are now put on here as a sort of night-picket in half defiance of the directions from head-quarters, and perform their duties splendidly. It is absolutely impossible for any one to get either in or out of their lines, when they are on guard. They are in respect models of courage, vigilance, and trustworthiness, and the bands of rebel guerillas who infest the out skirts and who caused almost constant alarms by night, before these men were put on, stand in the greatest dread of them. They all know every forest path and have eyesight like cats so that at night while

their color will let them be perfectly hid in the shadow of a tree they themselves see everything. They exhibit great eagerness to fight and at one time were formed into companies and made admirable progress in drill.[22]

Two appointments in April 1863 transformed black refugee life in eastern North Carolina. The first was Gen. John G. Foster's appointment of Rev. Horace James to fill the position of superintendent of Negro affairs vacated by Means's death. A graduate of Andover and Yale, James hailed from abolitionist roots, had preached against slavery since at least 1846, and had applied a month earlier to be a chaplain of one of Massachusetts's newly formed black regiments. James had been serving as the chaplain of the Twenty-Fifth Massachusetts Volunteer Regiment since November 1861 and had been present during the Burnside invasion of February and March 1862. James inherited the office with more than a year of experience in eastern North Carolina, including a period when he assisted Vincent Colyer in his schools. He had recognized the centrality of the African American experience in the conflict from the beginning, telling his soldiers in a sermon in New Bern on the Fourth of July 1862, "We have not introduced the negro into this war. But he is in it, and in every part of it, and can no more be expelled from it than leaven can be removed from the loaf that has begun to ferment." James had long advocated emancipation and embraced Lincoln's Emancipation Proclamation. Viewing the war in moral terms, James saw no middle ground between loyalty and treason. In a sermon to Massachusetts soldiers in March 1863, Chaplain James said "there could be no such thing as neutrality; a man must be one thing or the other, and those who do not declare for the government, should be treated as its enemies."[23]

At the same time that Horace James assumed responsibility for black refugees, President Lincoln authorized Gen. Edward Augustus Wild to raise four black regiments in North Carolina. A Harvard graduate, a surgeon, and a committed abolitionist, Wild had volunteered in May 1861 and fought at Bull Run. Wild received serious wounds at both the battle of Seven Pines and South Mountain; his right hand was permanently shattered by a bullet at the former and he lost his left arm to an exploding shell at the latter. Together with the Fifth-Fifth Massachusetts (Colored) Volunteers, the regiments raised among black refugees in North Carolina would form Wild's "African Brigade."[24]

Despite their enthusiasm for enlisting, black refugees demanded that recruiting agents treat them fairly. By early 1863, Abraham Galloway had emerged as the most prominent and militant voice among black refugees. Born in Smithville, a small fishing village near Wilmington, in 1837, Galloway had escaped from slavery by stowing away aboard a ship bound for Philadelphia in 1857. After obtaining his freedom, Galloway traveled extensively in the free North, including Kingston, Ontario, a hotbed of black political activism; Massachusetts, where he met the abolitionist William Lloyd Garrison; and Ohio, where Galloway gave antislavery speeches to hostile crowds. In January 1861 Galloway had traveled to Haiti with a contingent of radical abolitionists and black militants to explore the possibility of establishing a colony for American blacks on the island. Returning to the United States only two weeks before the firing on Fort Sumter, Galloway, an intellectual descendant of David Walker, had become committed to the most militant strand of abolitionist thinking. Recruited into the Union spy service by allies in Massachusetts, Galloway served under Gen. Benjamin Butler in Virginia, Louisiana, and Mississippi. Captured by Confederate forces near Vicksburg in the summer of 1862, Galloway managed to escape, making his way to New Bern. While the details of his service as a spy and of his capture and escape remain a mystery, when Galloway returned to North Carolina for the first time since he escaped slavery in 1857, he did so with a profound commitment to black freedom and equality and with a militant understanding of the steps that would need to be taken to achieve them.[25]

In New Bern, Galloway persuaded black refugees to refrain from enlisting until they could be guaranteed pay equal to that of white soldiers and equitable treatment for their families. Galloway's sway over the black refugee population was immediately apparent to Edward Kinsley, an abolitionist tasked by Massachusetts governor John Andrew with recruiting in New Bern for Wild's brigade. Arriving in May 1863, Kinsley had expected that recruiting black soldiers in New Bern would be easy, only to discover that "blacks did not come forward to enlist." He quickly attributed black refugees' hesitation to Galloway's injunction. In Kinsley's estimation, Galloway was "a man of more than ordinary ability.... So great was his influence among the colored people that all matters of importance concerning them were left to his decision." On several occasions, Kinsley unsuccessfully attempted to persuade Galloway to change his mind. Like many prominent Massachusetts abolitionists, Kinsley dined at the house of Mary Ann Starkey, a former slave. Starkey's residence served simultaneously as a reading school for black refugees, a boardinghouse, and a locus for political and military intrigue. Reportedly the best cook in the region, she became known as the "Delmonico of New Bern," after the famous New York restaurant. Presumably impressed by Kinsley's commitment to raising a black regiment, Mary Ann Starkey approached him, informing him that if he would return to her house at midnight, she would arrange a meeting with "a couple of friends from the rebel lines." Arriving in the dead of night, Kinsley was blindfolded and led into an attic room, and "when the bandage was removed he could see, by the dim light of the candle, that the room was nearly filled with blacks." Before him stood Abraham Galloway, armed with a revolver and flanked by John A. Randolph Jr. and Rev. Isaac K. Felton, both prominent leaders in New Bern's black refugee community. Galloway told Kinsley that "they could raise a regiment of able-bodied colored men in a few days," but only on the condition that they received equal pay, clothing, and rations as white soldiers and that housing, food, and education be provided for soldiers' families, stipulations to which a terrified Kinsley quickly agreed. The night's longest and most contentious conversation concerned the treatment of captured black soldiers. Galloway and other black leaders in New Bern knew that the Davis administration had declared that any black man captured in a Union uniform would not be treated as a prisoner of war but returned to slavery or executed for participating in a slave rebellion. They demanded that Kinsley pledge that the Lincoln administration would pressure Confederates to treat captured white and black soldiers equally, a pledge that presumably everyone involved knew that Kinsley was powerless to enact. After five grueling hours of interrogation, Galloway placed a Bible in Kinsley's hands, while Galloway's associates pointed pistols at either side of Kinsley's head. Galloway administered "a solemn oath," in which Kinsley pledged that "any colored man enlisted in North Carolina should have the same pay as their colored brethren in Massachusetts; their families should be provided for; their children should be taught to read; and if they should be taken prisoners, the government should see to it that they were treated as prisoners of war." Appeased, Galloway endorsed black enlistment and told Kinsley that he would have his soldiers within a week. Four days later, Galloway, Felton, and Randolph marched into New Bern at the head of a column of four thousand black refugees, recruited from nearby plantations still under Confederate control on the promise that they would be able to serve in the Union army.[26]

With Galloway's endorsement, black refugees flooded recruiting offices. A soldier in Washington, North Carolina, observed that "our black recruits are industriously drilling in marching and the manual.... Our colored recruits are already winning golden opinions for the soldierly qualities. Our most bitter negropholists [sic] admit that they will *fight*, and one of the sincere haters has been detailed to officer them. Some of the poor fellows lie behind the breastworks with a spelling book in one hand and a musket in the other." He also noted that "we have no such enthusiastic soldiers in the department as they. They begged the privilege of having guns placed in their hands, and almost quarreled for preference. They swear they will sell their lives as dearly as possible." A month later, a soldier in New Bern observed that "recruiting for the African brigade is progressing lively and enthusiastically.... Four thousand colored soldiers are counted upon in this department." A soldier from Massachusetts expressed his admiration for the newly enlisted soldiers in June 1863, noting that "Wild's Brigade of negroes at Newbern is nearly organized. It would do you good to see the sense of importance of the soldiers, the pride they take in saluting the Officers, & in blackening their shoes."[27]

General Wild's arrival in mid-June 1863 created a cause for celebration among black refugees in New Bern. A Massachusetts soldier recorded in his diary that "General Wild arrived this morning for the purpose of enlisting contrabands. He is a tall, slim man with a reddish beard. He has lost his left arm and the empty sleeve dangles at his side. The darkeys are very ready to become soldiers and they have been enlisting all day." A black soldier in the Fifty-Fifth Massachusetts who had come to North Carolina with General Wild expressed his admiration for the abilities of his new comrades, noting that "I never saw a regiment, white or black, drill better, and they have been organized only since the 1st of May. Many may wonder that this North Carolina regiment is so well drilled. They take more pains to learn, and go through with every movement as though their very lives depended on the manner in which it is executed." A white Massachusetts soldier expressed a similar admiration for the newly constituted regiment encamped along the Neuse River, observing that "the problem of whether these newly enfranchised freedmen could be converted into serviceable recruits was speedily solved. The National uniform was as a magic robe to them and they straightened up and stood erect in it, at once men and soldiers. The touch of the rifle as their hands clasped it seemed to fill their veins with electric life."[28]

The enlistment of almost all of the military-age black refugees into the Union army radically transformed the refugee camps' demographics. Within a few short weeks, almost all of the healthy young men had left with General Wild, "leaving only the old and decrepit." On July 30, 1863, less than a month after forming his "African Brigade," General Wild left with more than four thousand black soldiers, bound for South Carolina, where they would take part in the sustained campaign against Charleston. Horace James's wife, Helen, described the population remaining in the refugee camps as the "infirm of both sexes, and aged,–women and children."[29] Refugee camps that had contained a healthy gender balance, including many intact nuclear and extended families, now consisted of almost exclusively of women, children, and men too old or sick to fight.

By the time that Horace James assumed his post, the refugee crisis in eastern North Carolina was more than a year old. The recently completed census indicated that the black refugee population of New Bern was almost twice its entire antebellum population. With new white and black refugees arriving daily into the city, James knew that the chaotic arrangement of refugees created the potential for a significant humanitarian crisis, the challenges of which changed with every new wave of refugees. He observed that "what with confederate troops, guerillas, small pox and yellow fever, the negroes (and poor whites as well) have been tossed upon a sea of troubles, and our care of them has assumed a new phase almost every month."[30]

Building on the Union policies crafted by Gen. Benjamin Butler and others, and working with military officials such as Gen. Edward Augustus Wild, Horace James worked to establish organized refugee camps at New Bern, Plymouth, Washington, Carolina City, Beaufort, and Roanoke, the last of which was envisioned by some Union officials as a permanent resettlement location. With the end of the conflict nowhere in sight, James sought to bring order to the haphazardly arranged refugee camps. The establishment of organized refugee camps in 1863 exacerbated the influx of black refugees into New Bern and other Union-occupied communities in eastern North Carolina. One Massachusetts soldier claimed in May 1863 that "there is perhaps not a slave in North Carolina who does not know he can find freedom in New Bern, and thus New Bern may be the Mecca of a thousand noble aspirations."[31] Throughout the year, black refugees continued to pour into New Bern and other Union-occupied towns. In December 1863 Horace James's wife, Helen, reported that between seventeen thousand and nineteen thousand freedmen and freedwomen fell under her husband's care, including nine thousand at New Bern and three thousand each at Beaufort and Washington. "The number of freedmen is constantly increasing–I am unable to say at what rate," she wrote with alarm. She worried not only that the number of refugees would continue to overwhelm the overcrowded refugee camps but that the more recent arrivals required more aid, as "more women and children, with aged people, come in than formerly. These are utterly destitute."[32]

The most significant new policy adopted by Horace James was the creation of a permanent refugee colony on Roanoke Island. James's vision for the Roanoke colony grew out of his desire to free black refugees from their dependence on the federal government. The colony, James wrote, would not only "locate them in places of safety" but also "teach them, in their ignorance, how to live and support themselves." Like Vincent Colyer, James believed that the transition to free labor would come quickly were black refugees provided with land and the tools to till it, "thus stimulating their exertions by making them proprietors of the soil, and by directing their labor into such channels as promise to be remunerative and self-supporting." Working through Northern relief agencies, James lobbied for public donations to help get the colony running. The most urgent needs were for farm equipment, followed by "clothing of all descriptions, particularly for women and children," and educational material. James also hoped to acquire a steam engine "to saw our own lumber, and grind our own corn," thereby making the colony truly self-sufficient.[33]

The plan for the "African town" consisted of three main avenues, bearing the names Lincoln, Roanoke, and Burnside. Fifty feet wide and twelve hundred feet apart, these avenues were intersected by twenty-six streets at intervals of four hundred feet, creating a grid of blocks four hundred feet by twelve hundred feet. According to the plan established by Horace James, each block would be subdivided into twelve lots, each two hundred feet square. Slightly less than an acre each, these lots were to provide homesteads to refugee slave families.[34]

The ambitious plan for a refugee community on Roanoke Island helped to entice black men to enlist. Hesitant to separate themselves from their wives and children, potential enlistees saw the colony as a potential safe haven for their families. In June 1863, shortly after Wild's arrival in North Carolina, Joseph Williams, a soldier in Wild's brigade, wrote to the *Christian Recorder*, a popular black newspaper based in Philadelphia, that "Gen. E. A. Wild has surveyed and examined Roanoke Island, and established a colony there for the support of the wives of the soldiers in his brigade, and also homes for the old and the young and those who are not fit for service. He will establish and erect churches and schoolhouses for the use of the colony; and also a number of vessels of all sizes, such as schooners and small sail boats that are lying along the island, which have been captured from the rebels, will be turned over for the use of the colony."[35] For Williams and thousands of other soldiers, the promise of a new home for their families, a home that might continue after the war ended, proved persuasive.

The planned community on Roanoke Island that James envisioned would take time to implement, however, and the pressing need for housing led to interim solutions. The first homes on Roanoke Island for many black refugee families were two military barracks, originally constructed to house Confederate soldiers and later used by Union soldiers after their occupation of the island. By the summer of 1863, the barracks had been filled to capacity.

In December 1863 Elizabeth James, Rev. Horace James's cousin and a Massachusetts schoolteacher working with the American Missionary Association, described the significant housing crisis on Roanoke Island, observing that "two barracks, built long ago, are FILLED, and another is in the process of construction; but the heavens and the earth are visible through them in almost every direction." In the meantime, "those who are escaping from bondage are pressing in all directions. From one to two hundred arrive every few days, and it is a matter of no small moment to know where to shelter them. . . . Where to shelter them is a problem which remains to be solved in a camp where every nook and cranny is already crowded to excess." Nine months later, the situation on Roanoke Island had not improved significantly. In September 1864 Sarah Freeman, a relief worker with the National Freedmen's Relief Association, noted that "many are dying in consequence of suffering from last winter's cold and exposure; and there are many more who must die unless protected against the cold rains of autumn, which will soon be here."[36]

While the refugee colony on Roanoke struggled to establish itself, other refugee camps closed because of Confederate attacks. Under the command of Gen. George E. Pickett, thirteen thousand Confederate soldiers marched on New Bern in February 1864 in an effort to recapture the city. Dividing his forces into three columns, Pickett hoped to coordinate his attack. While the assault on New Bern failed miserably (one historian called Pickett's handling of it "bungled"), Confederate forces did manage to get within one mile of the city, overrunning two black refugee camps located east of the city and outside Union pickets. These outlying camps housed more than eighteen hundred black refugees, and, "every man, woman, and child from these camps came rushing wildly into town, struck with fear, and feeling as keen a sense of danger as if they had been actually returned by force to their old masters." An army nurse in Morehead City noted that shortly after the attack, "the negroes began to flock in; they came by hundreds, such frightened beings, leaving everything except their children behind them.... Such a scurrying time you never saw ... the terrified negroes constantly arriving." According to Horace James, the early morning attack sent "the poor negroes, fleeing for dear life ... flocking into town from every quarter, driven off the farms and plantations they had occupied and made again vagabonds on the earth." According to Elizabeth James, "They land at 'headquarters,' about three miles south of the camps, and walk up bringing their children and parents (the aged are not forgotten,) and goods and effects, when they have been so fortunate as to bring anything with them; but there are many who escape literally 'with the skin of their teeth,' and need friendly eyes to look after them and friendly hands to aid." Not all of the black refugees living in the outlying camps made it safely into New Bern; according to Horace James's account, an untold number were killed and captured within two miles of the city. In the aftermath of the Confederate attack, disparate black refugee settlements in New Bern were merged into the Trent River settlement, across the river from the city proper.[37]

Nearly three months later, the Trent River settlement's population swelled again, as the camp absorbed nearly three thousand refugees from Plymouth and Washington. Assuming control over Confederate forces in eastern North Carolina after Pickett's failed attack on New Bern, Gen. Robert F. Hoke launched an assault on Union-occupied Plymouth in April 1864. Located at the mouth of the Roanoke River, Plymouth had served as an important supply port for Union forces in the region and hosted more than three hundred white refugees and one thousand black refugees, most of whom were women and children. A Massachusetts soldier described the town as "a general rendezvous for fugitive negroes, who came into our lines by families, while escaping from conscription [impressment] or persecution, and for rebel deserters, who had become lean, hungry, ragged, and dissatisfied with fighting against the Union." Many of the white refugees fled to Morehead City, where a nurse noted that "we are full of refugees; three hundred and fifty women and children came here ... and since then Bedlam has been let loose.... They occupy two big barracks; some of them have not a change of clothes. They had only an hour's notice to quit Washington. You cannot know anything of squalor till you see these people." Armed with the ironclad ram *Albemarle*, Hoke's forces bombarded the city, such that "the shot and shell shrieked through the town, crushing through the walls and roofs of the houses and shanties. On the side of the houses towards the river were ... groups of negro men, women, and children, who had gathered in the rear of their frail shanties, as if vainly hoping they might prove a protection against the iron messengers of death. They made a preposterous noise, in which were mingled religious exclamations, prayer and supplication, with shrieks and lamentations." While Confederate forces sieged the town from both land and water, a Union steamer ferried wounded soldiers, black and white refugees, and other civilians to Roanoke under the cover of night, evacuating approximately six hundred refugees, roughly half of those in the town, to safety.[38]

After a three-day siege, the overwhelmed Union forces at Plymouth, whose defenders included two companies from the Second North Carolina Volunteers and eighty black recruits, surrendered. Fearful of being executed as deserters, many Buffaloes in the Second North Carolina Volunteers fled to the swamps, as did most of the black refugees, who feared being returned to slavery. Confederate forces offered no quarter to those fleeing the town. According to one Confederate soldier, "About 800 [blacks] made a break ... and tried to reach the thickly wooded swampy ground in the direction of Little Washington.... Few reached the swamp alive. Those who were successful in gaining refuge there, were afterward killed or died of starvation.... For three weeks after the place was captured negro bodies were seen floating out of the swamp into the river. The sight was sickening." An anonymous civilian in Plymouth wrote to the *Daily Confederate* that "a large body, perhaps six hundred negroes and buffaloes ... made for the nearest point of Peacock swamp. Three companies of cavalry and one of infantry were hunting them there all day, and nearly all were killed. I suppose no prisoners were taken." Those fleeing to the swamps included not only soldiers but also many refugee women and children. Another account, also published by the *Daily Confederate*, spoke of the "negroes, buffaloes, and deserters, who are scattered in the swamps, and whom our cavalry are hourly shooting or bringing into town. Three or four hundred negro women and children have already given themselves up." Warren Lee Goss, a white Massachusetts soldier captured at Plymouth, noted that apprehended civilians were marched out of the town "like so many cattle, [the] whole population of Plymouth" into an open field. There "little children at the breast,–white, yellow, and black,–

old women and young, were all huddled together in an open field, preparatory to—they knew not what." Many of the black soldiers captured at Plymouth faced summary execution at the hands of Confederate soldiers. According to Goss, black soldiers "who surrendered in good faith were drawn up in lines, and shot down . . . like dogs. Every negro found with United States equipments, or uniforms, was . . . shot without mercy."[39]

One of the black soldiers at Plymouth narrowly escaped execution. Helping to recruit a black regiment in Plymouth, Samuel Johnson recognized that the Union surrender of the town imperiled his life. He quickly stripped off his uniform and replaced it with a "a suit of citizen's clothes . . . and when captured I was supposed and believed by the rebels to be a citizen." He remembered that "upon the capture of Plymouth by the rebel forces all the negroes found in blue uniform . . . was killed. I saw some taken into the woods and hung. Others I saw stripped of all their clothing and then stood upon the bank of the river with their faces riverward and there they were stop. Still others were killed by having their brains beaten out by the butt end of the muskets in the hands of the rebels." Confederate soldiers forced Johnson to work for two weeks in Plymouth before he was relocated to Weldon, Raleigh, and finally Richmond. Assigned as a servant to a Confederate officer, Johnson escaped near Hanover Junction.[40]

The Confederate capture of Plymouth necessitated the evacuation of nearby Washington, where only months earlier a sizeable refugee camp had been established. According to Jesse Harrison, a solider in the First North Carolina Union Volunteers stationed at Washington, "the poor negroes," fearing that they would be captured by Confederate soldiers during the haphazard evacuation, "are flying for protection in every direction." Terrified white and black refugees from Washington and Plymouth fled to New Bern, Beaufort, and Roanoke, seeking sanctuary. According to the *North Carolina Times*, "The capture of Plymouth by the Rebels and the evacuation of Washington has filled our town [New Bern] with women and children, most of whom, if not all, are entirely destitute. Distress and suffering is painfully apparent among this unfortunate class whenever met. Many of them doubtless are widows and orphans from the recent barbarous butchery of husbands and fathers at Plymouth." More than two thousand refugees from Plymouth and Washington "are suffering for want of clothing and bedding. A very large number of these refugees are women and children who need comforts." Returning to New Bern in 1864 after spending a year in Virginia, one Massachusetts soldier observed that his regiment's old camp had been overrun with "negro shanties," presumably occupied by refugees from Plymouth and Washington. In Beaufort, John Hedrick noted that "our town is still filled with women and children from Plymouth & Washington. Quite a number of them are stopping at the hospital and the Baptist and colored Churches are crowded with them. A great many of them are soldiers' wives and their immediate connections." According to Horace James, refugees from Plymouth and Washington followed the "troops to New Berne and Beaufort" where they were housed in tents until rudimentary housing could be constructed out of "shakes," irregular, hand-split pieces of lumber four to five feet in length. James noted that while white refugees from Washington and Plymouth came into New Bern depressed and dejected, "the negro is always jolly, and when driven out of one home, he will 'tote' his small inventory of household stuff upon his head, until he finds a place in which to establish another."[41]

The influx of black refugees in the spring of 1864 dramatically increased the population of the Trent River settlement, located on a small peninsula across the Trent River from New Bern. Bounded by the Trent River on the north and west, the Neuse River on the east, and Scott's Creek to the south, the peninsular community occupied a scant thirty acres, a tiny area in which to house its nearly four thousand residents. According to the *North Carolina Times*, "The contrabands on the Southside of the Trent river ... are building up quite a city," which the *Times* predicted would soon become larger than New Bern. The newspaper noted that the settlement had "some eight hundred cabins full of little darkies and big darkies, old darkies and young darkies, and a miscellaneous assortment. They have also started a graveyard."[42]

The presence of a graveyard in the Trent River settlement suggests that black refugees had begun the process of establishing a permanent community. Archaeological excavations conducted on the site of the refugee settlement indicate that its earliest residents relied on a single well for their water supply. Located near the middle of the crowded settlement, the solitary well probably served as a social hub, a location where black refugees could meet their new neighbors, trade, and exchange news and gossip. Although the well may have served a useful social function, it probably provided an inadequate supply of water for a community of that size. Indeed, the excavations suggest that the Trent River settlement suffered from significant overcrowding and deep poverty. On lots measuring sixty by fifty feet, refugees lived in three-room cabins, with one family occupying each room. Built from shakes, the cabins provided at best a rudimentary shelter and probably were of lower quality than many of the slave cabins that black refugees had fled from. Excavations reveal an absence of postholes in the construction of these cabins, suggesting that they were constructed in haste. When large numbers of black refugees arrived simultaneously, such as after the evacuation of Plymouth, they were housed in discarded army tents until more permanent housing could be constructed. Adjacent to the cabins, most black refugees farmed small gardens. Growing squash, collards, string and pole beans, onions, okra, potatoes, and corn, black refugees struggled to produce a subsistence crop on undersized plots and in poor soil. Much of the choice produce was sold to Union soldiers across the river in New Bern, leaving many of the residents of the Trent River settlement chronically undernourished. By the summer of 1864 the streets had become open sewers. When a sanitary inspector from the Freedmen's Bureau visited the settlement two years later, he ordered more than one hundred of the shanties razed, claiming that the entire settlement was overcrowded, with inadequate water and inhumane sanitation.[43]

Black refugees were not the only new arrivals in Union-occupied North Carolina during 1863 and 1864, as dozens of Northern aid workers also arrived to help the growing refugee population. Coming primarily from Massachusetts, they represented an array of nongovernmental agencies, including the Christian Commission, the New England Freedmen's Aid Society, the American Missionary Association, and the National Freedmen's Relief Association. According to Horace James, the vast majority of aid workers were white women who came as teachers. By the end of 1864, white aid workers had opened nineteen day and eight evening schools for black refugees.[44] Although the tremendous growth in educational opportunities for black refugees heralded the beginning of a new age, their material conditions in refugee camps continued to languish.

The priority that aid workers gave to education over the more pressing material needs of black refugees reflected a long-standing aversion among Northern philanthropists to providing charity to those able to work, fearing that even temporary aid would create a class dependent on charity. The subtext of many of the proclamations made by aid workers and later by the Freedmen's Bureau was that freedom from slavery precluded dependence on charity. This premise informed a distinction between legitimate charity in the form of education and illegitimate charity in the form of handouts of clothing and food. Although aid workers labored relentlessly to provide for young children, the elderly, and the disabled, they rejected outright the idea that those able to work were entitled to any kind of material aid, fearing that doing so would promote vagrancy and idleness. Throughout his tenure as superintendent of Negro affairs, Horace James believed that among his primary obligations was preventing black refugees from becoming dependent on the federal government. Like most Republicans, James feared that government- or philanthropic-sponsored charity would undermine the growth of a free labor ethic among black refugees. James proudly noted that the rations given to refugees were smaller and less expensive than those given to soldiers, "furnished with 'necessary sustenance,' in such quantities as they absolutely require." Whenever possible, James believed that black refugees should pay for what they received, noting that "philanthropy can do no better thing for people in such a condition, than to furnish them the necessities of life, and to some extent its comforts, not as a gift, but by purchase, at low rates." To this end, James helped to create a "cheap store for the colored people" in New Bern. Stocked with clothing and other goods donated through Northern aid agencies, the store provided necessities without charge to "the refugees newly arrived, the sick, the infirm, and ... orphans," while charging modest prices (compared to those charged by sutlers) to refugees who had "a little money in their purses."[45]

In his 1864 annual report, James praised the extent to which black refugees had created economic opportunities for themselves in freedom. He observed that in New Bern, black refugees had found work as "carpenters, caulkers, shipwrights, blacksmiths, masons, shoemakers, coopers, millwrights, engineers, carriage-makers, painters, barbers, tailors, draymen, grocers, cooks, hucksters, butchers, gardeners, fishermen, oyster-men, sailors, and boatmen" and that "some of these people are becoming rich.... They evince a capacity for business, and exhibit a degree of thrift and shrewdness." To demonstrate black refugees' entrepreneurial spirit, James conducted a survey of black refugees not employed by the government. He found more than three hundred men privately employed, a few of whom had earned a considerable income in the past year. James listed the names and incomes of the eighteen wealthiest African Americans in New Bern, most of whom derived their income from the manufacture and sale of turpentine, a traditional industry in the region near New Bern. James noted that the respondents to his survey were "nearly all males," thereby excluding the majority of New Bern's black refugee population, which by 1864 was overwhelmingly female.[46]

James's efforts to cultivate economic independence among black refugees were hampered and the suffering of the refugees themselves increased by significant delays in payments owed to black workers by the government. James noted that the wages of more than two thousand black refugees working for quartermasters or engineers had not been paid in six months. According to James, the workers had "waited so long for their dues, as almost to have lost faith in the intentions and honesty of the government." While the workers received rations, "their wives and children had nothing to eat, and nothing with which to buy food."[47] Furthermore, many of the black men who had enlisted in the Union army in 1863 experienced significant delays in receiving their wages, leaving their families in New Bern, Roanoke, and other refugee sites without support.

Horace James also attempted to institute political self-government in refugee camps. James believed that to fully exercise their freedom, black refugees had to take political responsibility for their communities. On Roanoke Island, he established a "Board of Councilors" in January 1864. According to James, this board of fifteen men was "to act somewhat like a Board of Selectmen in a New England town," to assist in the colony's management and to form "the germ of a self-government." Although the initial board was appointed, James intended that their successors would be elected. However, after several months, James effectively disbanded the board as "the 'councilors' were too ignorant to keep records, or make and receive written communications, were jealous of one another, and too little raised in culture above the common people to command their respect."[48]

Although Horace James believed his efforts to create self-government among black refugees had failed, autochthonous political organizing experienced tremendous growth, with the development of an independent political culture within black refugee camps. Among the earliest manifestations of local political organization was the formation of the Colored Ladies Relief Association. Led by Mary Ann Starkey, the association solicited money for refugee families in New Bern and Roanoke from Northern philanthropic organizations such as the New England Freedmen's Aid Society and distributed money and clothing to needy refugee families. The association also raised money locally within New Bern to purchase a regimental flag for the First North Carolina Colored Regiment. When it was presented to the regiment in July 1863, a reporter for the *New York Times* observed that the "flag was procured by the contributions of the negroes in this place, and certainly they are entitled to great credit, for, with their limited means, they did nobly." Designed by Harriett Beecher Stowe, whose brother James C. Beecher had accompanied Edward Kinsley to New Bern, the flag depicted the Goddess of Liberty on one side and a rising sun on the other, symbolizing the illuminating power of freedom.[49]

While the Colored Ladies Relief Association sought to mediate the suffering of refugee families and rally support for black soldiers, a more militant and confrontational form of political organizing developed within black refugee camps. In 1864, figures such as Abraham Galloway and John Randolph Jr. shifted their attention away from recruiting black soldiers. They recognized that the promise of freedom would be limited without legal equality and the power of the ballot. They hoped to use the black military experience to persuade reluctant white Republicans, including President Lincoln, to support full citizenship for black refugees.

In late April 1864, a delegation of six of the most radical black political leaders from North Carolina presented their case to President Lincoln in the White House. The delegation included both Abraham Galloway and Rev. Isaac Felton, who had interrogated Edward Kinsley at gunpoint about the recruitment of black soldiers nearly a year earlier; Clinton Pierson, a former slave who worked as a barber, carpenter, and grocer and a close associate of Abraham Galloway; and Edward Hill, a black refugee who served as the president of Greenwood Cemetery in New Bern. Although President Lincoln had met with Northern black leaders, his meeting with the delegation from North Carolina appears to have been his first with black Southerners in the White House. Politely received by the president, the delegation expressed their appreciation for the transformative effect of the Emancipation Proclamation but impressed on him that freedom alone meant little without suffrage. Although they failed to extract any promises from Lincoln, Galloway and the others considered the meeting a success.[50]

The leaders of this organic political culture included not only local African Americans, such as Mary Ann Starkey, Abraham Galloway, Rev. Isaac Felton, and John Randolph Jr., but also representatives of Northern black churches, who descended on New Bern. The most important of these was Rev. James Walker Hood. Born in Pennsylvania in 1831, Hood arrived in New Bern in late January 1864 as a missionary with the A.M.E. Zion Church, a black Methodist denomination based in New York. Hood was not alone; the rival Philadelphia-based A.M.E. Church also sent delegations to New Bern, as did the Congregationalist Church, each attempting to develop a foothold among the black refugee population. The great prize was Andrews Chapel, the largest black congregation in New Bern. Four days after arriving in New Bern, Reverend Hood met with Andrews Chapel members, who agreed "to unite with the A. M. E. Zion Church, and receive Elder Hood as their pastor." Their decision threw Reverend Hood into conflict with the white Methodist bishop who "claimed ecclesiastical authority over that military department with a right to supply all Methodist churches with pastors, regardless of the wish of the people." Reverend Hood took their dispute to both Gen. Benjamin Butler, who had recently assumed control over Union forces in North Carolina, and Secretary of War Edwin Stanton. With their endorsement, Reverend Hood assumed the pulpit at Andrews Chapel, which he later rechristened St. Peter's A.M.E. Zion Church.[51]

Black refugee political organizing during the summer of 1864 culminated in the election of a delegation to the National Convention of Colored Men, to be held in October 1864 in Syracuse, New York. Called by the black abolitionist Rev. Henry Highland Garnet, the convention came at a critical juncture in African American political thought, when the agenda for the postslavery world would be written. When news of the convention reached New Bern, a mass meeting was hastily arranged in Andrews Chapel. Opened with a prayer led by Rev. James Walker Hood, the meeting elected Clinton Pierson to orchestrate a North Carolina delegation to the Syracuse conference. In the series of meetings that followed over the course of the summer, black refugees from across Union-occupied eastern North Carolina, including sizeable parties from Roanoke, Washington, Beaufort, and Morehead City, met in New Bern to finalize the list of the state's representatives at the Syracuse conference. After lengthy and contentious debates, typical in many ways of nineteenth-century political conventions, three delegates were elected: Clinton Pierson, John Randolph Jr., and John Good, the last of whom had been a free black in New Bern prior to the Burnside invasion.[52]

The election of newly freed African Americans by other African Americans represented a significant milestone in the development of independent black political action and the beginning of a rising black political class. All three men elected would go on to extensive political careers. Clinton Pierson would later serve as a delegate to the 1868 North Carolina Constitutional Convention, representing Craven County. John Randolph Jr. remained a powerful voice in New Bern, serving as a representative to the state's Freedmen's Convention in October 1865 and as secretary of the state's Equal Rights League. John Good would serve as a justice of the peace in New Bern and as Craven County's representative in the North Carolina House of Representatives in 1874–75. Their election in August 1864 also exposed a political rift within the black refugee community. For reasons that remain unclear, Rev. James Walker Hood left the meeting disenchanted with political processes. Possibly, Hood believed that he was better qualified to represent black North Carolinians than his less well-educated and less well-spoken rivals. In an effort to reconcile the growing political factionalism among black refugees, Pierson, Randolph, and Good resigned their appointments just prior to the Syracuse convention, allowing Abraham Galloway to be elected as a compromise candidate. Galloway appears to have been away from New Bern during the contentious meetings, allowing him to serve as an honest broker between the Pierson and Hood factions.[53]

Although it did not keep pace with the growing black refugee population, the white refugee population also continued to grow significantly during 1863 and 1864, swelling whenever Confederate conscription agents appeared in eastern North Carolina. Edward N. Boots, a Union soldier from Pennsylvania, observed in October 1863 that "A body of rebel troops are within a few miles of us putting in force the rebel conscription act. The result of it is, that we are crowded with refugees coming within our lines to escape it." Like many Northern soldiers, Boots denigrated white refugees, claiming that "I have seen numbers of the white refugees & I can hardly say that I have seen a good looking man among them. The majority have dark hair, sallow complexions, high cheek bones, long visages, a treacherous looking eye, a shuffling sort of walk & almost any other ugly look that you can think of." Despite his misgivings about their appearance, Boots admitted that "I am glad that we are able to afford them protection from the rebel despotism." In September 1864 the *North Carolina Times*, a newspaper printed by Union soldiers in New Bern, reported that "a continued stream of [white] refugees are constantly pouring into the 'Yankee wigwam at New Berne.' There is evidently a deep seated feeling of enmity to the Confederates, or the swelling tide of refugees would cease." White refugees almost universally cited the "sweeping conscription" as their reason for fleeing to New Bern. James Rumley, a closeted Confederate sympathizer living in Beaufort, was less compassionate. In December 1864 he noted in his diary that "our town is crowded with refugees from various parts of the state—chiefly from the lower counties. Most of them are young men who have fled from the conscription. They scout the idea of Southern independence, speak very contemptuously of 'Old Jeff' and the 'rebel Confederacy,' and seem to be Yankees in heart and soul. If they think they can abandon their country in this manner, in her hour of trial, and affiliate with her enemies, and not be remembered hereafter as deserters and traitors, we think they are mistaken."[54]

On those few occasions when Confederates captured Buffaloes, as white refugees were often called, James Rumley's pronouncement that they would be treated as "deserters and traitors" rang true. During the Confederate assault on New Bern in February 1864, rebel troops captured almost the entire roster of Company F of the Second North Carolina Union Volunteers. The company had been formed in Beaufort only a few months earlier from white refugees who had recently arrived in the city. Many of the soldiers had previously served in Nethercutt's Battalion in the Confederate army, enlisting on the promise that they would only fight in North Carolina, but had deserted in October 1863 when ordered to Virginia. Like most refugees, they arrived in Union-occupied territory with few material possessions. Promised bounties of $100 to $300 (many of which were never paid), they enlisted in the Second North Carolina Union Volunteers, often with the aid of overzealous recruiting agents. According to one Union general, some recruiting agents sought to "enlist all the men they can possibly persuade, without the slightest regard to their capacity, mental or physical." Agents occasionally used "threats of deeds of violence . . . to compel men to enlist who preferred not to." They also enlisted men clearly unfit for service, including "mere boys, children, some of them weak puny, scrofulous" and "old men, eaten by disease or utterly incapacitated by old age and general infirmity." Among those enlisted at Beaufort and later captured by Pickett's soldiers, was Elijah Kellum, whom a friend described as "a man of deformed body and broken constitution," rejected by Confederate mustering officers as unfit for service. Of the fifty-three soldiers captured, twenty-two were convicted of desertion in a Confederate court-martial, executed by hanging, and buried in a mass grave at Kinston, not far from where many of the soldiers had lived prior to the war. The rest of those captured were sent to prison camps at Richmond and Andersonville, where most of them died of disease within the next four months.[55]

The events at Kinston radically transformed the willingness of white refugees to fight in the Union army. Prior to Kinston, white refugees routinely volunteered after their arrival in New Bern. According to John Hedrick, "pretty nearly all the [white] refugees join the army." He noted that "a great many things [were] brought to bear upon them to induce them to join the army," including their "destitute condition." Promised "large bounties" and "a place for their families to live in and an outfit of clothing," white refugees volunteered primarily because of the financial benefits of enlisting rather than an abstract sense of patriotism. Hedrick observed that the army served as a "place of refuge" where white refugees were socialized into a new community, such that when a white refugee arrived, "all the Buffaloes get after him and before he knows what is about he has joined the regiment." The Kinston executions, however, put a dramatic halt to white refugee enlistment. Shortly thereafter, John Hedrick wrote to his brother that "these refugees do not seem much disposed to join the army. Most of them have come into our lines to keep out the Rebel Army, and not to fight for their country."[56]

In the aftermath of the Kinston executions, an anonymous officer in the Second North Carolina Union Volunteers lamented their deaths and the fate that awaited their families in a letter printed in the *New York Times*. The men of his regiment, like those at Kinston, "fight with a halter around their neck ... because many of them are refugees from the rebel conscription." In order to reach Union lines, they had hidden "for months in swamps and thickets, ... gaunt with hunger and clad in rags." Given their sacrifices and hardships in reaching Union lines, fighting for the Union flag, and dying at the end of a noose, the author bewailed that the soldiers' families received no support either from the military or from charitable organizations. He noted that many of the soldiers had "large and helpless families dependent upon them" who were "left to suffer" after their deaths. Yeoman farmers who had been poor before the war enlisted as much for the economic benefits to their families as their commitment to the Union, such that "when the North Carolina refugee and his family arrive within Union lines, without a crust of bread or a change of garments, the father enlists and receives the Government ration for himself and his family." After a soldier's death, his family would find itself destitute. Unlike black refugees, who found support from Northern relief agencies, "in North Carolina there is no 'Freedman's Aid Society' to foster the destitute families of the 'poor white man,' who ... [d]espite the threat of the gallows, takes up arms for the Union."[57]

The influx of white refugees into New Bern pushed Union officials to establish refugee aid organizations parallel to those already in place for black refugees. While responsibility for black refugees was shared between the military and private organizations, care for white refugees became almost exclusively the burden of the federal government. In May 1864 Dr. D. W. Hand, the medical director for the region, solicited contributions to aid indigent white refugees. While military officials were able to provide meager rations, most white refugees arrived without adequate clothing or bedding. In Beaufort, John Hedrick observed in May 1864 that while white refugees who had recently arrived from Plymouth and Washington received "rations from the Commissary and in some cases the Provost Marshal has compelled citizens to take them into their houses," government efforts to meet their basic needs were inadequate.[58] Dr. Hand pleaded with soldiers and more fortunate civilian residents of Union-occupied eastern North Carolina to contribute, urging them to "remember these poor people, and also remember that the 'liberal soul shall be made fat.'"[59]

In June 1864 General Innis N. Palmer appointed Dr. J. W. Page to the post of superintendent of white refugees. A native of Maine, Page had briefly taught in North Carolina more than a decade earlier and had volunteered for the U.S. Sanitary Commission in 1861. A Massachusetts soldier described Page as "short and rather slightly built and wears a wig and full beard.... He lived in North Carolina sometime before the rebellion, but is a Northern man with strong Northern principles." Rather than integrate white refugees into already established black refugee encampments, Union officials established separate white refugee camps, often adjacent to black refugee camps. Several thousand white refugees were herded into a tent village located in a live oak grove on the shore of Core Sound, just north of Beaufort. Their number included at least two thousand who came en masse from Plymouth and Washington in May 1864, most of whom were the wives and children of white North Carolinians who had enlisted in Union regiments. Despite the efforts of Dr. Hand and Dr. Page, most of the white refugees did not have adequate housing, food, or access to sanitation or medical facilities. According to the local newspaper, the influx of so many white refugees strained federal resources. While "the military authorities are doing what they can to mitigate their misfortunes[,] much remains to be done even to make them comfortable."[60]

Building refugee camps segregated white and black refugees not only from each other but also from military officials who occupied most of the permanent structures in New Bern, Beaufort, and other Union-held towns. Some federal officials believed placing refugees in camps outside of town would make them less of a drag on military operations and would facilitate relief efforts by congregating refugees in particular locations. By minimizing fraternization between Union soldiers and refugees, Union officers also hoped to stop the spread of disease, which they perceived to be rampant among refugees. As historian Gretchen Long has observed, many white Northern soldiers and aid workers equated Southern society with filth, disorder, and uncleanliness. Black bodies received particular condemnation as disease vectors, best isolated away from Union soldiers.[61]

Some federal officials also believed that refugees were more likely to become self-sufficient if removed from town. Many Northerners feared that refugees would become dependent on government largesse, a condition that they believed would destroy the "industrious habits" necessary for success in a free society. John Hedrick argued that the government should remove white refugees "to some such plantation and make them work." In an effort to make white refugees somewhat self-sufficient, the provost marshal in New Bern established a thirty-acre farm on the edge of town in January 1864. Named the "U.S. House of Refuge," the farm was intended to "house and support widows, orphans, and other indigents." By July 1864 the local newspaper declared the experiment "a decided success," with white refugees producing "golden squashes, nice palatable green corn, beets, beans, peas, and potatoes.... Many a poor weary refugee has found a warm and congenial home."[62]

Despite efforts by federal officials to segregate white and black refugees, the two populations did come into conflict over space. After the Confederate capture of Plymouth in April 1864, at least five hundred white and black refugees fled under military escort to Roanoke, the site of one of the largest black refugee camps. While the black refugees integrated themselves into the existing black refugee population, white refugees, consisting primarily of the families of soldiers in the First and Second North Carolina Union Regiments, occupied a hospital and two churches, displacing freedmen's schools that had been using those facilities as schoolhouses. Without alterative locations to meet, the colony's schools effectively closed for several months.[63]

Many Union officials and Northern relief workers claimed that white refugees remained more dependent on government handouts than black refugees. Horace James observed that in Beaufort, white refugees received four times as much in food rations as the equally numerous black refugees. James attributed their dependence in part to their psychological state upon entering Union lines. While black refugees rejoiced when they arrived in New Bern, celebrating their freedom, white refugees arrived desperate and dejected; "so helpless were they, so totally unable to rally from the depression of spirits consequent upon their sudden change of life and their great deprivations. They have been dependent upon charity from that day to this." Most other commenters were less charitable in their assessments of white refugees, claiming that their dependence arose simply from inherent laziness. A journalist for the *Anti-Slavery Reporter* claimed that white refugees in New Bern were "a thriftless people.... The Government has not only to find food, but also to provide shelter. They have been used to but little work. Too proud and idle to cultivate this fertile soil." Dr. Page argued that "the 'piney woods' people, the 'clay eaters,' or whatever name be given to the poor whites of the South, are a more helpless and spiritless race than the negroes of the same section, and indeed, naturally inferior to them. They have more pride, but less activity; they make more pretensions, but possess fewer mental resources."[64]

Homer A. Cooke, a Union quartermaster based in New Bern, saw clear differences between white and black refugees entering the city. "In the fall of 1863," he observed, "there was a good deal of scarcity in the country around, and consequently there were a great many persons coming, both white and black." As quartermaster, Cooke hired many of the black refugees, finding them diligent, zealous workers when engaged in difficult manual labor. By contrast, "the whites did not desire to work to so great an extent. These whites were called loyal refugees. Their loyalty consisted in the fact that they had nothing to eat where they were, and came to Newbern to get something to eat." Cooke also hired a handful of white refugees but "found a decided disinclination on their part to labor."[65]

Despite government assistance, most white refugees remained desperately poor. Distrusted and despised by many Northern soldiers, poor white refugees, many of them women, fell at the bottom of the socioeconomic ladder. Most Union soldiers preferred to hire black refugee women to cook their meals and do their laundry, leaving white refugee women with few options. When one white refugee attempted to buy fish for his family in New Bern, he was confronted by a Union soldier who told him to "stand back, soldiers first, negroes next, and rebels last."[66]

Some white refugee women turned to prostitution to relieve their poverty.[67] Dr. William Smith, an army surgeon from New York stationed in Plymouth, routinely treated Union soldiers for venereal diseases that he believed they acquired from refugee women. For instance, in April 1863 he treated Wallace Hinkley, a young officer, for gonorrhea, which Smith concluded he had "contracted of some abandoned woman of the town." Less than three weeks later, Dr. Smith was called on "to visit a sick woman in a house occupied by some females of notoriously bad reputation." The house, located within eyesight of Dr. Smith's own, was well known to the Union soldiers and sailors, as Dr. Smith claimed to have "frequently seen ten or 12 sailors & soldiers of that low & debased class, that have no shame, waiting around the house for their turn to be served by the wretched females within." Finding the sick woman alone in the house, Dr. Smith was repulsed by her destitution, "for the stench quite turned my stomach, as it was. I have seen much squalid poverty & wretchedness and I have seen many filthy places occupied by human beings, but never in my experience one that equaled this." In his diary, Dr. Smith did not specify whether she suffered from a venereal disease or from yellow fever, then rampant in Plymouth. However, shortly thereafter he did treat a soldier with "syphilitic vegetations" that he had contracted from "his connexions with abandoned women." Under Dr. Smith's supervision, a nurse visited the poor woman almost daily for the next month, when Dr. Smith made a second visit to her house. He observed that her condition had not improved at all, noting that "on a miserable apology for a bed, one dirty sheet covering a dilapidated remnant of what was once a feather bed, constituting all the bed or bedclothing. On this, the poor creature lay, without pillows, a dirty and worn out dress rolled up for a pillow and for a covering, one torn and much worn soldier's blanket was all the house afforded. She was suffering greatly. For five days, she had taken no nourishment. The rations which the government allowed her, as it does all loyal & destitute persons, were not as such as she could use." The next day Dr. Smith brought the provost marshal to visit the sick woman. With his assistance, Smith arranged for a black nurse to attend to the woman and for a bed and clean clothing to be brought from the hospital. Despite this effort, Dr. Smith knew that her condition was perilous, and a couple of days later she died of her illness.

After her death, Dr. Smith talked with the woman's younger sister, who looked about sixteen years old to Smith, describing her as the "most desolate-looking, frail, feeble, worn-faced child I have ever seen." She came to Dr. Smith hoping that he could help her "to secure a place where she could be cared for and earn an 'honest living.'" She explained that her family was very poor, her father had died when she was very young, and her mother was an invalid. At the start of the war, her older brother had brought them from Gatesville to Plymouth, a distance of more than sixty miles. During a Confederate raid on the town, her brother had been seized and compelled to join the Confederate army, her mother dying soon after from grief. In the aftermath of her brother's capture and her mother's death, the young woman told Dr. Smith, she and her older sister had no support, "except as they earned it themselves," and had turned to prostitution. Although Dr. Smith sympathized with her plight and "would gladly save her from a continued life of abandonment and prostitution," he felt unable to provide her any meaningful assistance.[68]

Smith was not alone in observing how many white refugees resorted to prostitution in order to support themselves. In Washington, North Carolina, a white resident observed that "across the street from us ... was a small house occupied after the town was garrisoned by a class of women whom I blush to name. They sat on the porch day and night, and always some soldiers were with them. So offensive was their proximity that we kept the windows closed next to them and passed the street by another way." In April 1865 a Union soldier stationed in Beaufort noted in his diary that "last night disorderly soldiers in the streets kept the patrols trotting all the time. Houses containing certain classes of women were surrounded by large gangs which had to be continually dispersed."[69]

Charged with patrolling the streets of New Bern, William Creasey of the Twenty-Third Massachusetts often had to arrest intoxicated Union soldiers, many of whom visited prostitutes. In June 1862 he broke up a riot at the notorious Baltimore House. He arrived at the scene to find three drunken soldiers attempting to break down the door after the proprietor, a woman named Em Frenchie, had fired three shots from a revolver into the crowd outside the establishment. If Creasey ever learned the cause of the dispute between the soldiers and the women inside, he did not record it in his diary. After dispersing the soldiers, Creasey arrested Frenchie and the other women of the house. After a brief trial, Frenchie was expelled from Union lines, while "the rest of the girls not having anything to do with it, were discharged and returned to the house again." Creasey's diary indicates that black women also ran houses of ill repute. Two weeks before the incident at Baltimore House, he "made upwards of 40 arrests; committed quite a number to jail, stop[ped] three fights and arrested all parties." According to his diary, the arrests resulted from a dispute at the Crow's Nest, a "Fancy colored Ladies establishment," where "some "soldiers got into a row; smashed in the windows and broke the whiskey bottles." According to one Massachusetts soldier in New Bern in May 1863, "Some of the more festive of the line officers in this department have recently assisted in a variegated affair called a nigger ball, which transpired in the house of Black Lovinia, one of the Skittletop sisterhood. . . .

The assemblage occupied two stories of the building, the lower rooms being partly devoted to dancing; but some of the movements were not recognized in any of the modern schottisches, waltzes, or polka-redowas. It was a marbled crowd, the upper stratum being described as yellow and white, the lower one pure black and white."[70]

Black refugee women often experienced sexual assault by Union soldiers.[71] Viewing black women as sexually available, some white Union soldiers took advantage of freedwomen's vulnerability in overwhelmingly female refugee camps. Esther Hawks, a physician working with refugees in the nearby Sea Islands, complained in 1862 that "no colored woman or girl was safe from the brutal lusts of the [white] soldiers—and by soldiers I mean both officers and men. . . . Mothers were brutally treated for trying to protect their daughters, and there are now several women in our little hospital who have been shot by soldiers for resisting their vile demands." Prosecutions of soldiers for raping black women were rare and punishments were often reduced. For instance, in December 1863 a New Bern hospital steward, Eugene Hannel, was convicted of raping a black washerwoman. Originally sentenced to two years of hard labor, Hannel eventually had his sentence reduced to three months in the brig.[72]

With a civilian population exceeding twelve thousand people, almost entirely refugee women and children, New Bern (including the adjacent Trent River settlement) had the largest civilian population of any community in North Carolina. Overcrowding and inadequate sanitation there and at other refugee sites provided fertile soil for epidemic disease that preyed on the refugee population. Cramped living conditions and open sewers created ideal conditions for the spread of pathogens and carriers. A Massachusetts soldier complained that the entire city was plagued with rats, which "seemed to thrive on the unsanitary ways of housekeeping that obtained. They grew quite unconcerned over the presence of human beings, and the latter sometimes had their slumbers disturbed by the rodents running across their faces." Another noted in May 1863 that "vermin grow very rampant indeed though here we see them rather in its disagreeable than in its dangerous shapes. Rats & mice run over our floors at all hours of the night—and day, too, I might add. . . . We suffer no pangs except from the torments inflicted by flies." A third soldier noted simply that the onset of summer in New Bern brought "house flies [which] swarm like the locusts of Egypt." An army nurse observed that the slow-flowing Neuse and Trent Rivers that bounded New Bern brought "dead hogs and dogs and other animals . . . into an eddy at the piers; there they lie, putrid, till they finally melt away." Visiting New Bern in 1864, Union general Benjamin Butler remarked that "when I got within two miles of the place I met an awful stench, one of the unclean and uncovered filth of camps." Without a sanitation infrastructure capable of supporting the military and refugee population, Butler found the "smell of human excrement . . . pervaded all of Newbern," with open sewers and latrines throughout New Bern proper and the nearby Trent River settlement.[73]

In recent years, historians have played greater attention to the role of disease in the Civil War and emancipation. Jim Downs has argued that emancipation brought about an African American health crisis, a crisis in which the response of the federal government was often inadequate and at time callous to the sufferings of African Americans. Downs argues that women, children, the elderly, and the disabled bore the brunt of epidemic disease, as the federal government prioritized health care for able-bodied men. Gretchen Long also attributes some blame to the federal government for the black health crisis, noting that white doctors and military officials were predisposed to see black bodies as disease vectors. While government inaction contributed in part to the high rates of illness and mortality in refugee camps, it was not the only factor and indeed was probably not the primary reason why so many refugees died from disease. Many of the Northern-born Union soldiers in New Bern suffered from many of the same diseases that plagued refugees. Historian Kathryn Shively Meier argues that Civil War soldiers were less healthy than commonly assumed. Official medical reports, she argues, dramatically undercount the number of soldiers suffering from illness, as soldiers often preferred self-care for chronic diarrhea and lice to formal medical treatment. However, while the Northern-born Union soldiers in New Bern experienced significant outbreaks of disease throughout their tenure in North Carolina, much the same as their refugee neighbors did, they died less often and recovered more quickly, due in part to greater access to medical care, but also because of environmental and immunological factors. As Margaret Humphries has pointed out, many white Union soldiers, especially those who grew up in urban areas, had been exposed as children to diseases like measles, typhoid fever, and cholera, exposure that granted them some acquired immunity. Most black refugees, by comparison, grew up in rural environments and would have been less likely to develop acquired immunity. Furthermore, after many of the healthy adult male refugees enlisted in the Union army, refugee camps became disproportionately populated by children, the elderly, and the sick, all of whom were likely to have immature or compromised immune system. All of these factors, paired with the overcrowding that grew progressively worse over the course of the war, contributed to the heightened disease susceptibility and death toll among refugees.[74]

Contagious disease appeared among refugees soon after the Union occupation of New Bern. According to an 1862 letter from a U.S. treasury official, John A. Hedrick, "Small-pox is quite prevalent in Newbern, especially among the negroes."[75] Hedrick later reported epidemics of measles and yellow fever among refugee African Americans in New Bern, noting that the death toll from yellow fever alone numbered more than one thousand. George W. Harris, a refugee slave, later recalled that in New Bern, "de smallpox and yaller fever caught us dere and killed us by the hundreds." With each passing month, as more refugees arrived in New Bern, the incidence and threat from contagious disease grew. In December 1863 Elizabeth James reported that "the small pox is prevailing to an alarming extent in Newbern; the clothes which they have on must of course be burned, and other clothing given them when they emerge from the hospital." That same month, her cousin Helen James concurred with her assessment about the threat of disease, noting that "small pox prevails [among black refugees] to a fearful extent, and is increasing." Although efforts had been made to vaccinate refugees in New Bern, the measures had been ineffective and more than two hundred refugees were currently housed in quarantine. In order to stop the spread of the disease, "all the clothing and bedding of these patients are destroyed, and in most instances, their houses torn down and burned."[76] With most of the refugees living in tents or hastily constructed shelters, they had little refuge from the incessant mosquitoes, a vector for both malaria and yellow fever. The cramped living conditions facilitated the spread of contagious diseases such as smallpox, and poor sanitation enabled the spread of typhoid.

The most deadly disease outbreak occurred at New Bern in September and October 1864, when yellow fever killed more than one thousand white and black refugees.[77] While many Union soldiers died, the yellow fever epidemic preyed most heavily on the refugee population. Accord to one soldier, "The disease made sad havoc among the citizens, they died off like sheep." In September 1864 a Massachusetts soldier noted that "the scourge of yellow fever . . . has broken out in Newbern, and is raging to a great extent, 30 or 40 dying daily. It has not yet reached the [soldiers'] camps outside the city, and hopes are entertained that it will not." A Connecticut soldier noted that "between the 1st and 15th of October the plague reached it[s] highest destructive limit. A terrible gloom hung over the wretched city. Funeral escorts were constantly in the streets, and there were hardly well men enough to attend the ill." A soldier in New Bern observed that "the people died in such numbers that it was almost impossible to bury them. Thirteen hundred died in six weeks.... During the prevalence of this disease in New Bern many sad cases came to our knowledge; in one instance a house was broken up by the police and a whole family found dead; yet many of the sick recovered. The disease was accounted for by the filthy condition of the town." A New York soldier whose regiment arrived in New Bern at the height of the epidemic found that "the stores and houses were all closed. Most of the windows had tight shutters." Walking around the apparently deserted city, he found a "factory making nothing but pine coffins" in which to bury the dead. The yellow fever epidemic also exacted a toll on refugee aid workers. Four of Horace James's clerks died from the disease. James himself contracted the disease in late October 1864, lingering near death for four days. Tended to by Joseph Fowle, a black merchant from the Trent River settlement, James recovered, although it took several months before he resumed his full vitality.[78]

In an effort to control the epidemic, a Union soldier observed in September 1864 that two buildings were ordered to be burned "as possible plague spots and other methods adopted to check the disease." These other methods included keeping "bonfires burning on all the principal street corners, and large numbers of barrels of turpentine in its crude state were consumed," under the belief that the smoke would clear out the miasma causing the disease. Although the effects of the yellow fever epidemic were felt throughout the refugee population, many soldiers observed that white refugees experienced a higher mortality rate, as "it was remarked that the colored people seemed to be proof against its attacks. The greatest loss was among the poor [white] refugees who had sought shelter and protection in New Berne, but found instead, in many instances an unmarked grave."[79] A nurse treating yellow fever patients in Morehead City remarked, "Isn't it singular that black people do not take the fever? Some yellow ones have had it; but not one black. The poor [white] refugees die with it on short notice. Those all-suffering people had had more than their share,–measles, small-pox, worms, and now fever; not many will be left to tell the tale of suffering by the time winter is over. What can the poor things do, so broken now, in their crowded tents,–God help them!"[80]

Black refugees did much of the work of fighting the yellow fever epidemic in New Bern. Roland F. Lewis, a soldier in the Seventeenth Massachusetts, was assigned to head a sanitation force and placed in "charge of a force of four hundred and fifty colored men, with orders to clean up the city and restore it to a sanitary condition." Lewis later wrote that the black men under his command "distributed some two hundred carloads of lime about the yards of the houses in and about the city, cut down the trees, and at night burned over two hundred barrels of turpentine and about five hundred cords of wood. My instructions were to keep the city enveloped in smoke in order to destroy the germs of the fever."[81] The smoke from the turpentine fires shrouded the city in a noxious cloud, coating the buildings with ash and dust.

The suffering of white and black refugees during the 1864 yellow fever epidemic and other similar outbreaks was exacerbated by an unwillingness of many army doctors to treat civilian patients. One surgeon in charge of a military hospital in New Bern observed that white "citizens and contrabands are not admitted to its wards. The citizens have no claim on the attention of the surgeon of hospital, beyond that which humanity dictates." While he did treat civilians on occasion, at times of greatest need, he devoted his full attention to sick soldiers and refused to treat dying refugees. Without professional medical assistance, many sick refugees relied on black folk medicine to cope with the yellow fever epidemic, where the preferred treatment for fevers was the application of herbal poultices.[82]

Although New Bern suffered the greatest loses during the yellow fever epidemic, 1864 seems to have been a deadly year in other refugee communities in eastern North Carolina as well. James Rumley, a Confederate sympathizer living in Union-occupied Beaufort, noted in his diary in April 1864 that after the evacuation of Plymouth and Washington, "squalid and destitute women and children are flocking to Beaufort as their last place of refuge." With housing already at a premium in Beaufort, most of the three to four hundred refugees were housed in the Atlantic Hotel, a structure that was intended to house no more than a few dozen guests and which had already been partially converted into a hospital. A month later, he noted that "a frightful mortality prevails among the unfortunate women and children who fled to this place on the evacuation of Washington." According to Rumley, at least seventy refugees died within a two-week period, primarily from measles and pneumonia. By October Beaufort was suffering from the same yellow fever epidemic as New Bern, some forty miles distant. According to Rumley, more than 150 people died during the first week of October 1864. "Arrows of death fly thick through the air," he wrote in his diary. "Our town is crowded with refugees and negroes to its utmost capacity.... The war news is bad, but men talk little of that now while death in a form more terrible than the battlefield is among them."[83]

The devastation wrought by the yellow fever epidemic tempered but did not extinguish black political organizing in Union-occupied North Carolina. Abraham Galloway returned to New Bern from the National Convention of Colored Men in Syracuse just as the epidemic was ending and its final toll becoming apparent. The Syracuse convention had concluded with the founding of the National Equal Rights League, and Galloway returned to his native state charged with establishing local chapters. In early November Galloway helped to establish the North Carolina state chapter of the National Equal Rights League. Within a month, local auxiliary chapters had been established in New Bern, Roanoke, Morehead City, Beaufort, and Washington, each with approximately two hundred members. In large mass meetings held in December 1864 and January 1865, the latter held to celebrate the anniversary of the Emancipation Proclamation, black refugees from across eastern North Carolina came together as a political body to demand equality before the law.[84] The vitality of these meetings, held when many black refugee families were mourning their lost friends and relatives, speaks to the robust political culture that had developed in the refugee camps since 1862.

Black refugees continued to pour into New Bern during the final months of the war. In January 1865 a New York soldier noted in his diary that "last night another squad of darkies came in. They say the country is getting so stripped of food they can't get food to eat." Loading about twenty women and children aboard a boat, he rowed them across the river to be registered. He expressed relief when they disembarked, as "the odour was not good and their clothing looked greasy." Refugee slaves arriving within Union lines in early 1865 manifested the same joy and enthusiasm that their predecessors had three years earlier. Samuel Duncan, a white colonel with the Fourth Regiment U.S. Colored Troops, described the exuberance of some black refugees in February 1865 in a letter to his brother in New Hampshire. Black men "came jumping & dancing, along the street and shouting 'I'se broke my chain; I'se broke my chain,' while the women were bowing & scraping and tossing their arms in the air and crying, 'Bress de Lord; Bress de Lord. De year of jubilie hab come."[85]

New black refugees contributed to the overcrowding in New Bern and other refugee camps. In New Bern in February 1865, military officials ordered a prohibition on "the erection of shanties by the colored people within city limits," hoping that such a prohibition would encourage black refugees to settle at the Trent River settlement. The Trent River settlement also experienced significant overcrowding. A Union soldier who visited that refugee camp in February 1865 noted, "The houses are built in rows forming streets but not fences. Each house contains but one room, no rooms above." The boards used to build the houses were roughly cut, leaving drafty crevices. On Roanoke Island, a relief worker lamented in February 1865 that "the need and suffering here has been so great that everything else had to yield to that." Working with insufficient supplies, they struggled to "meet the wants of some destitute ones filled with misery in their bones."[86]

White refugees also continued to enter Union lines. A Union soldier who visited a white refugee camp in January 1865 noted that "a more wretched, squalid set of whites never came under our observation." Like most Northern soldiers, he attributed their distress to the degraded condition of poor white Southerners, as "most of their poverty arises from their own thriftlessness and want of industrious habits." An army nurse in Morehead City marveled at their poverty, writing a friend that "they are scattered about in tents and shanties and live not half so good as pigs." She came across one family—a grandmother, mother, and daughter—living "under a quilt spread over a pole." Finding the grandmother lying on a bare mat resting on the sand, the nurse discovered that she had been "driven from a good home, where she had been born and expected to die. She had a nice farm, well stocked; but would be Union and so had to fly for her life."[87]

Gen. William Tecumseh Sherman's arrival compounded the refugee crisis in coastal North Carolina. In March 1865 Sherman ordered that refugees be excised from his army near Fayetteville. Sherman described the black and white refugees following his army as "twenty to thirty thousand useless mouths" and "a dead weight."[88] According to one Union officer, at least twenty-five thousand refugees had attached themselves to Sherman's army since they had marched north from Savannah, the majority of whom were "negroes, chiefly women and children." Like Sherman, he saw these "twenty-five thousand [as] useless, helpless human beings, devouring food, and clogging every step onward."[89] While the majority of refugees excised from Sherman's army were black, there were also at least four thousand white refugees, many of whom had attached themselves to Sherman's army after the burning of Columbia. For some of these refugees, their journey from Columbia to Fayetteville represented only the final stage of four years of refugee life, as many coastal white South Carolinians, including a few plantation owners, had relocated to Columbia, believing that the inland state capitol would provide security.

Sherman ordered that the refugees be escorted east, away from his intended marching route, dividing them into two streams, one headed toward New Bern and the other toward the recently liberated Wilmington. Horace James noted that "ten thousand entered Wilmington, five thousand New Berne, and in large numbers they came down to other places on the coast." The *North Carolina Times* noted in late March 1865 that "refugees are pouring into New Berne at a fearful rate. Every train from Goldsboro brings multitudes of these poor creatures." In Wilmington, Gen. Joseph R. Hawley reported that Sherman "sent down 6,000 or 7,000 miserably destitute refugees, white and black." Arriving on foot and on steamers sent down the Cape Fear River, the refugees from Sherman's army arrived in the city at the same time as nearly nine thousand Union prisoners of war, many of whom had been liberated from Andersonville Prison in Georgia. That same month, the city also experienced an influx of deserters from the Confederate army, including more than two hundred soldiers taking the Union oath of allegiance on the same day that the first refugees from Sherman's army arrived.[90]

Overwhelmed by the sudden arrival of so many impoverished refugees and others, Hawley sent urgent messages to the American Missionary Association for clothing and food. Cognizant of the potential public health consequences, Hawley also "organized a battalion of refugees and freed slaves to clean Wilmington's streets, wharves and hospitals." Hawley ordered that refugees be issued rations but remained adamant that it was a temporary measure. The Union officer in charge of the commissary distributing refugee rations noted that "it is not the intention of the government to allow this class of persons to live in luxury and idleness, but merely to sustain life till such time as they can help themselves." With Wilmington's population now exceeding two and half times its antebellum levels, severe overcrowding, malnutrition, and disease caused a humanitarian crisis in late March 1865. With forty to fifty deaths per day in the city, most of them among refugees and former prisoners of war, Union officials ordered a closed carpentry shop reopened to produce coffins.[91]

Desperate to relieve the overcrowding in Wilmington, General Hawley settled thousands of black refugees on abandoned plantations in New Hanover County. By late April Hawley had successfully relocated the majority of refugees outside of the city limits, including to new refugee camps on Smith Island (now Bald Head Island) and at Fort Anderson, near Old Brunswick. Many of the black refugees sent to Fort Anderson arrived sick, with illnesses compounded by multiple relocations. According to Horace James, the refugees were in "extreme need of blankets and clothing, and also of axes, light and heavy hoes, shovels, hammers and nails, with which to construct their cabins and till the soil." Urging Northern charities to send aid, James noted that their short- and long-term survival depended on immediate intervention.

During the final two weeks of March, approximately two thousand black refugees died, roughly thirty per day. An army surgeon at Fort Anderson reported that "it is impossible to account of the cause or causes of this terrible mortality, as no record was ever kept of the camp, nor any report made of the sickness or death. There was no hospital accommodation at this camp."[92]

When black refugees from Sherman's train arrived in New Bern, teacher Anne P. Merriman claimed that "our streets are literally thronged with colored refugees. They come in by the hundreds,–men, women, and children ... frequently seen in a family. The father ahead, bearing all his effects in a bag thrown over his shoulder, the mother behind, 'toting' the baby, and the ragged children in the rear ... in a state of appalling destitution." Horace James wrote of this final wave of black refugees, saying a "dark tide of population rolled into the sea-board towns." Having attached themselves to Sherman's army during its trek through Georgia and South Carolina, the black refugees bore the signs of miles under their feet. A chaplain with Sherman's army noted the suffering of the "poor women and children on foot." He was particularly drawn to "one poor, old, and blind colored woman, led by a frail girl, both bearing heavy burdens, and sinking into the soft earth at every step, and a little child not more than three years old, tugging to get through the mud, while the mother carried her babe in her arms." Horace James wrote, "Pitiable was the condition of many of them, when they entered our lines. Footsore and weary, ragged and dusty from travel, mostly without covering for either their feet or heads, some of them emaciated and already marked as victims of death, afflicted with hoarse, hollow coughs, with measles, with malarial chills, it seemed like anything but a land of promise into which they had come. But they were happy, and did not complain."[93]

Faced with this sudden and unexpected influx of refugees into New Bern in March 1865, relief workers and military officials knew that the refugee crisis in eastern North Carolina would escalate from its already critical condition. In an article entitled "WHAT SHALL BE DONE WITH THE REFUGEES," the *North Carolina Times*, a newspaper produced by soldiers in New Bern, explored both short- and long-term solutions to the city's refugee crisis. Written at the height of the exodus of refugees from Sherman's army, the article argued that relief should be immediately be offered, as "a large number of refugee families from various parts of the State are daily arriving in New Berne, whose condition is pitiable. Homeless, houseless, destitute of sufficient bedding and clothing, and illy supplied with money, they are certainly objects of charity." Although the army had been issuing rations to arriving refugees, insufficient supplies and an inadequate distribution network led to long lines and significant delays. The newspaper noted that earlier in the week, more than one hundred refugees had been "sitting about the depot for twelve hours without food" after their arrival in New Bern. Without permanent housing available, refugees were given tents cast off from the Union army as temporary shelters. While the newspaper lamented the current suffering of refugees, it also worried about their long-term status, noting that without action, "a dreary prospect is in store for them." It proposed dividing abandoned lands near New Bern into small farms of ten to twenty acres and distributing them to refugees. "Let the authorities assist these destitute creatures," the paper argued, "until the crops commence maturing, when further assistance will be unnecessary."[94]

As with earlier waves of refugees into New Bern, much of the responsibility for providing aid to the destitute fell to the refugee community. In April 1865 Mary Ann Starkey wrote to Edward Kinsley that her "time is mostly occupied now in endeavoring to care for the refugees. There is much suffering among them. We want to buy everything we can get for them." Starkey hoped that Kinsley, then in Boston, would be able to orchestrate relief shipments to New Bern. In the meantime, she informed Kinsley that she, along with other black leaders in New Bern, had formed a committee of twelve to provide aid to impoverished refugees from Sherman's army. They had divided New Bern, presumably including the nearby refugee camps, into wards, collecting donations from the more established refugees to distribute to the recent arrivals. Despite their efforts, Starkey wrote Kinsley that "the suffering is not nearly relieved yet."[95]

Sherman's decision in March 1865 to expel black and white refugees from his army coincided with the passage of the Freedmen's Bureau Act, a measure that marked a sea change in federal policy toward refugees. Before the creation of the Freedmen's Bureau, the responsibility for refugees' welfare largely fell to sympathetic relief workers and chaplains, such as Vincent Colyer and Horace James, and on Union generals, some of whom took an active interest in refugees' welfare, but most of whom, like Burnside and Sherman, saw refugees primarily as a burden. Officially titled the Bureau of Refugees, Freedmen, and Abandoned Lands, the Freedmen's Bureau created a centralized federal agency tasked with easing the transition from wartime to peacetime and from slave labor to free labor for millions of refugees across the South.[96]

In May 1865 President Johnson appointed Gen. O. O. Howard to head the Freedmen's Bureau. A graduate of Bowdoin College and West Point, Howard had served in the Union army since the beginning of the conflict, spending the last two years of the war on Sherman's staff. Like many Union officers, Howard distinguished between white and black refugees. In his autobiography, Howard described the two distinct populations served by the bureau. The first were "four millions of negro slaves" who had "left their places of work and abode and had become indeed nomadic, wandering wherever want drove or untutored inclination enticed them. They had drifted into nooks and corners like debris in slough and eddies; and were very soon to be found in varied, ill-conditioned masses." The second were "the 'poor whites'" who were also "scattered to the four winds." "To these two classes, negroes and whites," Howard argued, "were usually given the names of freedmen and refugees." Howard's distinction reflected the language of the Freedmen's Bureau Act, which granted the bureau "control of all subjects relating to refugees and freedmen."[97]

Howard initially appointed Horace James to fill the post of assistant commissioner for North Carolina. For James, the post essentially continued the work that he had done for nearly two and a half years as superintendent of Negro affairs. Citing poor health and overwork, James resigned the post after a few months. Eliphalet Whittlesey, a former professor at Bowdoin College who had served under General Howard, assumed the position in June 1865. With insufficient support from Washington and inadequate local military resources, Whittlesey faced an actively hostile white population. Without the work of the bureau, Whittlesey told a congressional committee, whites in North Carolina "would re-establish slavery just as it was before." Hearing reports of widespread violence by whites against freedpeople, Whittlesey did comparatively little to aid destitute white refugees. Although superintendents in other states interpreted the law differently, Whittlesey read the Freedmen's Bureau Act as limiting his authority to freedmen and "loyal white refugees," excluding white refugees who had not demonstrated loyalty to the United States during the war. He noted that "there are many cases of great destitution among whites, which I should be glad to relieve; but as they are not 'loyal refugees,' they do not come within my jurisdiction." Even those white refugee families in New Bern or Beaufort whose men enlisted in Union regiments received little attention from the Freedmen's Bureau. Whittlesey noted that upon its formation the bureau aided "many white [Unionist] refugees," most of whom were "found in a wretched condition." After a few months, Whittlesey proudly observed that "very few of this class now remain under our control."[98]

Like Vincent Colyer and Horace James, Whittlesey sought to prevent black refugees from becoming dependent on the federal government, claiming that the highest priority of the bureau in North Carolina was not to engage in humanitarian relief but "to aid the destitute, yet in such a way as not to encourage dependence." In this respect, Whittlesey was not unlike many Freedmen's Bureau agents. As historian Amy Dru Stanley has noted, the Freedmen's Bureau agents often tried to dispel the notion that the bureau provided charity, sending the sometimes contradictory message that served as "an affirmation of the former slaves' right to liberty and a warning that freedom barred dependence." Real freedom, they argued, could only be exercised within the context of self-supporting wage labor. Whittlesey consistently endeavored to reduce the number of freedmen receiving rations from the bureau. In his first quarterly report to General Howard, dated October 15, 1865, Whittlesey noted that he had successfully eliminated the distribution of rations to all but five thousand black refugees, almost all of whom lived in "large communities of blacks who have been gathering during the entire war on the coast—places of refuge from the interior—where they came within our lines. At those points the men have enlisted in the army, and left a large number of women and children dependent upon the government for support."[99]

Working with Horace James, Whittlesey endeavored to end the dependence of black refugees at the Trent River settlement by converting it into a bona fide town, establishing a tax code and municipal government. With the legal title to the land on which the settlement was built unclear, Whittlesey orchestrated an arrangement for the settlement's residents to purchase the land so that "they may not lose what has been expended." James appointed Rev. E. S. Fitz, a local black minister, to act as the town's superintendent, responsible for most of the community's civic services, including a hospital and street sweepers. Assisting Fitz were twelve black councilors, who decided to rename the community James City in Horace James's honor.[100]

Not all black refugees shared in the laudatory feelings toward Horace James. Indeed, many black refugees felt that they had been abandoned by the federal government. In the effort to quickly transition African Americans into fully independent members of society, the Freedmen's Bureau and its agents had neglected to recognize the humanitarian crisis still raging in many black refugee communities. In a June 1865 letter, members of the Thirty-Sixth Colored Infantry, a regiment that began as the Second North Carolina, complained to General Howard that they felt betrayed by how their families had been treated by the Freedmen's Bureau. When they had enlisted, they had been promised that their families, most of whom lived on Roanoke Island, would receive rations. Reductions in rations had resulted in starvation, with many families going without food three or four of every ten days. The commissary agent on the island "kicks our wives and children out of the ration house or commissary, he takes no notice of their actual suffering and sells the rations and allows it to be sold, and our family's suffer for something to eat." Complaints to Horace James about their families' suffering had been fruitless, as he had "been told of these facts and has taken no notice of them." Furthermore, they claimed that James not only ignored the humanitarian crisis on Roanoke but contributed to it by not compensating black refugees for their work, such that "the cause of much suffering is that Captn James has not paid the Colored people for their work for near a year and at the same time cuts the ration's off to one half so the people have neither provisions or money to buy it with."[101]

For both white and black refugees in eastern North Carolina, the summer of 1865 brought both peace and uncertainty. White North Carolinians who had fled westward in 1862 slowly returned to New Bern, Washington, Beaufort, and other communities that had long been under the Union flag to find their homes and lands occupied by refugees. Thousands of discharged Confederate soldiers also gradually trickled back to communities that many of them had not seen in years. For black and white refugees who had sought sanctuary under the Union flag, the return of many local residents who had sympathized with or fought for the Confederacy brought understandable apprehension, as the postwar social order made and remade itself in their streets and neighborhoods.

THREE

Driven into Exile

Mary Bryan spent the morning of March 14, 1862, supervising slaves in the kitchen rather than preparing for her next three years as a refugee. Like many residents of New Bern, Bryan expected that Confederate defenders would be able to repulse the expected Union attack on the town and wanted to prepare extra dinners, hoping to feed the triumphant Confederate soldiers after the battle. Bryan had celebrated her twenty-first birthday only three days earlier. Married in 1859 to Henry Ravenscroft Bryan, a planter and lawyer, Mary Bryan had her first child, a son named Norcott, in 1860 and had recently discovered that her second child was on the way. Although many of the young men in New Bern had enlisted in the Confederate army, her husband had been prevented from joining up by a persistent physical malady. Both Mary and Henry Bryan were children of planters and had inherited or acquired nearly fifty slaves, most of whom worked on their plantation outside of town, though at least three house slaves lived with them in New Bern, attired in white caps and aprons. Although the exact menu they prepared that morning remains unclear, Mary Bryan later recalled that a proper feast would not be complete without "large turkeys, old hams, home-made pickles, mince pies, syllabub and calf foot jelly, [and] sweet potatoes."

While Mary Bryan eagerly prepared for a Confederate victory, her husband was less optimistic. Henry Bryan had concluded that a Union invasion of the North Carolina coast was likely and therefore it would be "useless to make a crop for another year." In January 1862 he sent some of their field slaves to his father's plantation in Wake County near Raleigh, surmising that they would be safer in the interior. While they contemplated moving themselves to the interior, Mary Bryan was reluctant to leave their stately New Bern home. She had recently sold her childhood pony to buy a "very handsome bookcase" and the house was "nicely furnished, a year's provisions in the smokehouse, in the pantry all sorts of Jellies, pickles, catsups, cordials."

When the Confederate center broke just before noon, soldiers fled chaotically through the town, burning the Trent River Bridge in their retreat. Most soldiers headed to the westbound train that had been kept at full steam in preparation for a mass exodus. When the Bryans and other civilians still in New Bern witnessed the soldiers fleeing through the streets, they joined the evacuation, forming "a perfect panic and stampede, women, children, nurses, and baggage getting to the depot any way they could. Our home and hundreds of others were left with the dinners cooking, doors open and everything to give our Northern friends a royal feast, which I understand they thoroughly enjoyed." The Bryans only had time to pack a few trunks before they left New Bern. As Mary Bryan left her house, she envisioned its fate when Union soldiers, "in their mad rage," occupied the town. She also knew that their plantation outside of town would share a similar fate, later recalling that when the Union army invaded New Bern, "we lost everything. The negroes were freed, the houses burnt, the brick house, which was built of bricks brought from England, pulled down, trees cut down, and the plantation left a barren wilderness."

Accompanied by their domestic slaves and Mary Bryan's mother, the Bryans were lucky to make it to the train before its departure. Many refugees fleeing New Bern in advance of the Union army were forced to walk, either because they were turned away from the overcrowded train or because they tarried too long before heading to the depot. Another New Bern refugee remembered that she "left on the cars with my babies and their nurses. There was panic, women and children fleeing for their lives." Overburdened by its civilian and military passengers, the train pulled slowly out of the New Bern depot, more slowly than many of its passengers would have liked. Huddled with her family, Mary Bryan did not know where she and her family would live when they disembarked. The overcrowding on the train made the air difficult to breathe. Young Norcott, sitting with his enslaved nanny, Mammy Ria, squirmed during their long journey inland.

After switching trains at Goldsboro, the Bryans disembarked at Company Shops, now called Burlington, a railroad town halfway between Hillsborough and Greensboro. There they were able to rent two small rooms in a house adjacent to the railroad tracks, cramming into tight quarters, "our excess baggage stored elsewhere." Shortly after arriving at Company Shops, Mary Bryan's mother, always in poor health, took ill, as did young Norcott, "who took the whooping cough on the [railroad] cars, which was followed by measles and then slow fever." In July 8, 1862, less than four months after fleeing New Bern, Norcott died from his illnesses. Mary and Henry Bryan buried their son in a corner of a graveyard in Greensboro. After the war, Mary Bryan was unable to find his grave, as there was "so much burying there during the war." She concluded that "I consider his death as much due to the war as if [he] had been killed by Yankee bullets."

Shortly after Norcott's death, Mary Bryan gave birth to a daughter, Fannie. When the family was well enough to move, they relocated briefly to Lexington, North Carolina. Located just south of Greensboro, Lexington, like Company Shops, was along the North Carolina Railroad, providing the family with the opportunity to return east when and if the opportunity presented itself. Apparently they did not receive a warm welcome in Lexington, leading Mary Bryan to observe that "the refugees in some instances were not cordially received by the up-country people, and had it not been for the yellow fever, which was so fatal in New Berne in 1863, it would have been better for us to have remained at home." After several unpleasant months in Lexington, they decided to move to Wake County. They hoped to move to Raleigh, but the city had become saturated with refugees from eastern North Carolina and Virginia, and it proved impossible to rent a house, so they settled for a log cabin owned by Henry Bryan's father in Wake Forest, a distinctly modest abode compared to their residence in New Bern. Here they were reunited with the slaves that Henry Bryan had removed to Wake County prior to the New Bern invasion. As they were overcrowded and temporarily impoverished, Mary's mother suggested that they sell some of their slaves to buy more land and supplies, but Henry Bryan refused. Although he was physically unable to fight for the Confederacy, he was "heart and soul" with the cause and believed that selling his slaves would run contrary to the ideals of the new nation, "feeling we should risk all" in its defense.

More than one hundred miles from the nearest Union army, the Bryans felt secure in their Wake County refuge. Their stay, however, was not without incident. Late one night in early 1863, Mary Bryan was woken by her mother, who said she heard noises in the yard. Alarmed, Mary and Henry peered out of a small four-pane window into the yard, where "a great many negroes were singing and playing around the fire with many demonstrations of joy." Swinging their arms as they danced, the slaves sang, "Hurrah, hurrah, we are free, we are free!" Glancing at Fannie, still asleep in her crib, Mary worried that "perhaps in a few hours the last of my race would be gone ... perhaps before morning each one of us would be massacred." Although they kept constant vigil during that "night of horrors," by morning the threat had passed, with no evidence of "the terrible mental agony we passed through." When Henry Bryan questioned his slaves about the events of the previous evening, he learned that "our negroes were having an unusual time with some neighboring negroes." While it remains unclear what prompted the Bryans' slaves to celebrate, they possibly had heard news of the Emancipation Proclamation. Although they had been removed to the Confederate interior to isolate them from the destructive effects of the war, when news of a future freedom reached them, they rejoiced, even when that freedom lay two years in the future.[1]

Sometime during her stay in Wake County, Mary Bryan glued a fifty-two-line poem published in the newspaper into her scrapbook. Written by another eastern North Carolina refugee who had sought safety in the North Carolina Piedmont, the poem was entitled "The Refugee," and Mary Bryan returned to it over and over again during her time in Wake County and in later years when she reflected on her experience as a refugee. Like the poem's titular character, Bryan had been "doomed to roam, away from my beloved home," a home now "occupied by foes, who rudely scoff at all our woes." In the poem's central image, the refugee stands on the banks of the Neuse River in the Piedmont, imagining how a leaf entering the flow here would eventually flow past her home in New Bern. The similarity between the poem and her own circumstances resonated deeply with Mary Bryan, who saw herself "removed from all I love."[2]

The story of Mary Bryan, her family, and their slaves resembled those of many other refugees who fled to the North Carolina Piedmont during the Civil War. Because of its location in the Confederate interior, the North Carolina Piedmont was among the preferred destinations for many white refugees. Until the final days of the Civil War, the Piedmont was effectively isolated from the threat of Union invasion. The nearest Federal army was in New Bern, more than one hundred miles to the east of the Piedmont, and rarely appeared interested in advancing into the interior. To the north, the Piedmont was protected by heavily defended Virginia, to the south by South Carolina and Georgia, and to the west by the Appalachian Mountains.

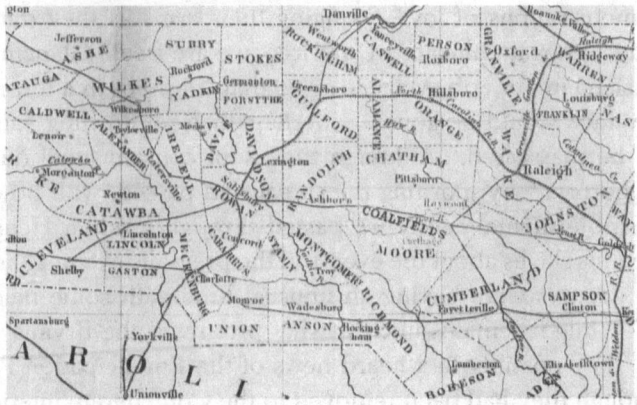

Figure 6. The North Carolina Piedmont. Compiled and drawn by G. Schroeter, from *A North Carolinian's Hints on the Internal Improvement of North Carolina* (1854).

White refugees in the North Carolina Piedmont expected to find a sanctuary where they could continue their lives unencumbered by the effects of war. Anticipating that their geographic isolation from the front lines would permit them to create new homes in which they could mirror their lives before the war, white refugees flocked to the hills of central North Carolina. They discovered, however, that even in the Confederate interior, war exacted a heavy toll. The influx of refugees into the North Carolina Piedmont created significant housing and food shortages, leading many wealthy refugees to shelter in modest dwellings and feast on meager fare, while poorer refugees struggled with homelessness and starvation. Overcrowding and increased mobility in towns set the stage for contagious disease to spread through refugee communities. Far from home, white refugees struggled with homesickness and isolation, discovering that the North Carolina Piedmont was as much a prison as a sanctuary.

The North Carolina Piedmont had a particular attraction to slave owners. In December 1862 Wake County resident Giles Underhill wrote to his children in Mississippi that they should bring "your negroes to North Carolina ... [as] they would be safer here than there for a while. There has been a great many negroes brought up from the eastern part of this state, to the middle and western counties."[3] While the removal of thousands of enslaved African Americans to the North Carolina Piedmont may have extended the term of their bondage, it simultaneously transformed the nature of their enslavement. A fuller understanding of the experiences of these slaves and slave owners should complicate our understanding of the effect of the Civil War on slavery and of the transition from slavery to freedom. While slave owners hoped that removal would enable them to perpetuate slavery in wartime, it fundamentally weakened owners' authority over their slaves. Removal also fragmented established slave communities, as slave owners frequently divided their holdings.[4]

Slavery's economic impact shaped important political and cultural differences between the eastern slaveholding regions of North Carolina and the Piedmont counties where slave owners removed their slaves. Sometimes referred to as the Quaker Belt because of significant Quaker settlement during the colonial period, the central Piedmont counties of North Carolina contained significant Unionist sentiment during the secession crisis and during the war itself. The Heroes of America, a secret Unionist organization, had a substantial base in the Piedmont, and prominent Unionists such as Bryan Tyson and Hinton Rowan Helper came from the area. Furthermore, many residents of central North Carolina who were not Unionists manifested a hostility toward Confederate and state policy during the war due to high taxes and conscription, resulting in some of the highest rates of desertion and draft evasion in the Confederacy. Therefore, when slave owners from eastern North Carolina and across the South removed their slaves to central North Carolina, they were taking them to a region in which anti-Confederate and antislavery sentiments were among the strongest in the Confederacy.[5]

Some white residents of coastal North Carolina quickly recognized the threat posed by the proximity of the Union army and made arrangements to remove themselves to the interior. In early September 1861, one week after the Union invasion of Hatteras Island, twelve-year-old Susie Mallett in Hillsborough wrote to her father, then serving with the Confederate army, that his sister had arrived in town. She wrote, "Aunt Mary arrived here from Newbern last week. The Yankee droved her from it. I suppose you heard that the Yankee had taked Fort Hatrass near Newbern. And all the people thought it wasn't safe to stay." In September 1861 lawyer David Schenck was among the first to note the removal of slaves to the interior, writing in his diary that trainloads of white refugees were arriving daily in Raleigh from coastal North Carolina and that "negroes too are being sent off in numbers to the west for security."[6] While a few slave owners began to remove their slaves from vulnerable parts of the Confederacy early in the war, and meticulously planned the removal of their slaves, most slave owners waited until the last minute to relocate their slaves and themselves from homes under threat from Union forces.

The refugee crisis in the North Carolina Piedmont began in earnest during the spring of 1862, after three events gave slaves and slaveholders reasons to hope and to despair. The first was the Union occupation of the North Carolina coast, with the capture of Roanoke Island in February and of New Bern a month later. White residents of New Bern, Beaufort, Washington, and other eastern towns fled en masse during the Union invasion. Most refugees, like Mary Bryan, left precipitously, taking little with them except what they could carry. The routes of most white refugees followed the railroad lines west from New Bern, through Goldsboro, Raleigh, Hillsborough, Greensboro, Lexington, Salisbury, and Charlotte, forming a crescent of refugee communities.[7]

For enslaved African Americans in the coastal plain, the Union occupation of coastal counties proved an irresistible lure. For slaveholders, the threat posed by Union occupation of eastern North Carolina caused many of them to forcibly remove their human property to locations they felt were more secure, beginning a mass forced exodus of slaves from the eastern third of the state to the North Carolina Piedmont. One planter estimated that "not fewer than two thousand negroes" were removed from Washington and Tyrell County to the interior during a ten-day period in October 1862. In October 1862 Cushing Hassell, a merchant and Primitive Baptist clergyman from Williamston, noted in his diary that there was "a constant stream of emigration from the lower counties to the upper Counties, especially a great many negroes being carried up." Historian Bell I. Wiley observes that "travelers on the highways often met great droves of slaves moving from the coast."[8]

A second impetus for the refugee crisis in the North Carolina Piedmont was the Peninsula Campaign during the spring and summer of 1862. With Union forces threatening Richmond and much of eastern Virginia, white refugees fled to Hillsborough, Raleigh, and Greensboro in hopes of finding a sanctuary from violence, and slaveholders sent thousands of slaves to central North Carolina, where they believed they would be secure. Among the thousands who fled Richmond that summer was Confederate president Jefferson Davis's young wife, Varina, who fled the city with their four children, at least three servants, and $12,000 in Confederate currency. Safely ensconced in Raleigh's prestigious Yarborough House, Varina Davis received both public and private denunciations for leaving her husband. She was accused of cowardice and harboring Yankee sympathies, with one newspaper comparing her to Marie Antoinette. While Varina Davis received unusual criticism because of her decision to leave, she was far from alone in deciding to flee Richmond for the safety of Raleigh, as the city became overcrowded with refugees. One Raleigh resident noted that "there are many here whose homes are threatened, and they have sought refuge here, and there are many who have no homes."[9]

The overcrowding in Raleigh and other Piedmont communities increased throughout the summer of 1862. An outbreak of yellow fever in Wilmington in August 1862 caused many of its residents to flee the city for the North Carolina interior. Although many of Wilmington's most prominent and wealthy residents had already left the city in March during Burnside's invasion, at least nine thousand residents remained when yellow fever arrived aboard the blockade runner *Kate*, carrying "bacon and other supplies" from Nassau.[10] According to the *Wilmington Journal*, more than half of the city's population left for the North Carolina interior during the epidemic. Of the 4,000 who remained, 650 died of the disease. In his diary, Wilmington resident Nicholas Schenck described "a panic to get away—citizens and family—going in all directions. . . . Every body—who could get away—left town." Another Wilmington resident noted in September 1862 that "the fever is much worse here and getting worse every hour. . . . Everyone that can get off are leaving." When Schenck briefly visited at the height of the epidemic, he was shocked "to find almost a deserted town . . . every house on Front Street—closed and shut-up—did not met or see a soul." William Calder, a Confederate soldier from Wilmington stationed in his hometown, wrote to his mother that "the physicians advise families to leave town, and all who can are doing so." Frightened by the Union invasion of New Bern months earlier, Phila Calder had already left Wilmington for Warrenton, where both she and her sons felt she would be safer. In April 1862 William Calder had written her that "you can't imagine the joy we feel that you have at last secured a place of refuge, and one that promises to be so pleasant. We could never content ourselves as long as you remained in Wilmington liable to be left alone and unprotected at any moment."[11]

Many inland communities worried that refugees would bring yellow fever with them. How yellow fever spread remained a mystery, and medical authorities debated whether it could be contracted from infected patients.[12] When Nicolas Schenck fled the city for Warsaw, some sixty miles to the north, he found "every hotel quarantined against us—coming from Wilmington." In a September 1862 meeting, Fayetteville's mayor and city council declared that "yellow fever exists in the town of Wilmington in a most malignant form, and a general apprehension having seized upon the inhabitants of this town that the disease may be communicated by continued intercourse between the two places." To prevent its spread, they ordered that "all intercourse between the town of Wilmington and Fayetteville be and is hereby suspended," requiring that refugees from Wilmington remain outside of the city limits and imposing a forty-eight-hour quarantine and medical inspection for all vessels that had passed through Wilmington. Recently elected governor Zebulon Vance also worried that refugees would bring yellow fever to the interior. In a letter to his wife, Vance warned her that "the yellow fever is raging so at Wilmington that some fears are entertained it may spread. The fugitives have already carried it to Fayetteville & there is one case reported here [Raleigh], though it is supposed it will hardly be communicated in that way." Vance warned his wife, then in Buncombe County, not to come to Raleigh until later in the year, when winter cold would lessen the risk of yellow fever.[13]

News of the deaths in Wilmington reached refugees who had fled the city. Along with many others fleeing the city, the Cronly family settled in Laurinburg, more than one hundred miles to the west. Safe from both the direct effects of the war and the disease, they nonetheless experienced the epidemic vicariously, as "every day the train brought the small sized bulletin containing little but the list of the sick and the dead, and always among the latter the name of some familiar face that should never be seen among us again." Eliza Hill, a refugee from Wilmington who had fled during Burnside's invasion, contrasted her new home in Chapel Hill with the news she received daily from the coast, writing in her diary that "everything looks so bright & cheerful today that I can scarcely realize the melancholy truth, that hundreds are down in my native town with yellow fever. . . . [By] last accounts, Wilmington was said to be one vast Hospital." Not all civilians were able to leave Wilmington before becoming infected. Marie Reston, married nine months earlier and with a newborn baby, was among the first people in Wilmington infected. During her illness, which lasted several weeks, many of her close associates also became infected, including her baby, who succumbed to the disease. Only after she was well enough did she travel to Hillsborough, where the colder weather was believed to be healthier.[14]

Many of the white refugees fleeing the yellow fever epidemic in Wilmington left their slaves behind. When the DeRosset family fled the outbreak, they left their home under the care of a few slaves, allowing them to rent out their time during the day. At the height of the epidemic, Eliza DeRosset, safely ensconced in Hillsborough, received a letter from William Henry, one of their slaves whom they had left in Wilmington. He informed her that "i hav bin sick all this week But ar gitting Better." He warned them that several of their other slaves had "Bin vey Sick with the yeller fever for sevel days pass" and that one of them had been required to work by the family who had rented her despite her illness, such that "she is all mos wurk to Death By them." William Henry's letter also included a note from another sick slave, Bella, who noted that "provisions are very scarce here & nearly all the stores are shut up. The town looks lonesome most all the people has left." Bella asked Eliza DeRosset about those slaves she had taken with her to Hillsborough and asked her to "give our love . . . to Marriah & Fanny & Peggy & tell them if I never see them in this world a gain I hope to meet them in heaven where parting will be no more." When Eliza DeRosset wrote to her daughter in Charlotte about the suffering that William Henry and Bella described in their letters, she reassured her that "I have heard that the fever seldom proved fatal to negroes."[15]

Despite the threat posed by Union forces and disease, many eastern North Carolina slave owners needed to be persuaded that removal was necessary. They received some of the earliest admonitions to remove their slaves from friends and family members. In December 1861 Alice DeRosset advised her sister that "as to your servants . . . you had better take every one of them up with you, away from the Coast." Captain John Benbury, serving with the First North Carolina regiment in Virginia, repeatedly urged his wife in late 1861 and early 1862 to relocate herself, their infant daughter, and their slaves from their plantation near Edenton. Harriet Benbury ignored his advice until Union gunboats under Gen. Ambrose Burnside appeared near Edenton, when she relented and moved the family and slaves to the interior.[16] Harriet Yellowley wrote to her brother about the propriety of keeping his slaves near sites of Union incursions in eastern North Carolina. "I feel very uneasy about our servants at home," she wrote in September 1862. "I wish they were all away from there." After her brother ignored her suggestion, she reiterated it a month later. "There are a great many Negroes being sent up from the lower countrys [sic]," she wrote. "Do you not think it would be advisable for you to have yours brought up after housing your crop?"[17]

After the Union invasion of eastern North Carolina in early 1862, newspapers joined the chorus of voices imploring eastern slave owners to relocate their slaves to the interior. In May 1862, three months after Union occupation of Roanoke Island, the *North Carolina Standard* "urged upon our

Eastern planters, who may be thrown near the enemy's lines ... to remove their force as soon as possible to the up-country.... This is a matter of the greatest importance, and true patriotism should prompt them to do so." Appealing to planters' material self-interest, the paper argued that removed slaves could profitably harvest fields in the upcountry vacated by farmers now in the Confederate army. Three months later, the paper continued to urge eastern slave owners to remove their slaves. In August 1862 it claimed that "thousands of negroes have been lost or ruined, and the information we have from the Eastern Countries especially beyond Roanoke, is alarming. Every negro east of Kinston, Tarborough, Hamilton, Windsor, Murfreesboro, &c, should be removed, if possible, from that section."[18]

Although many Confederate officials initially opposed the removal of slaves to the Confederate interior, after the Emancipation Proclamation and the enlistment of African Americans into the Union army, Confederate officials at both the state and national levels strongly advocated removal. A letter from Col. William Holland Thomas in November 1862 may have persuaded Governor Vance to reconsider his initial opposition to removal. Famous for leading a regiment of "Indians and mountaineers," Thomas recommended that Vance should order "able bodied negro men belonging to the counties in reach of the enemy [be] transferred from their present positions to work on the extension of the [Western North Carolina] railroad." Removing slaves, Thomas argued, had two main benefits. First, it would protect the institution of slavery from the threat posed by the presence of Union armies in the area. Second, "every able bodied negro kept out of the hands of the enemy would lessen the number of troops we have to raise in defence," a savings, Thomas estimated, of $10,000. Therefore, not only would removing slaves prevent them from running away, but it would also facilitate a much needed railroad connection, resulting in a substantial savings for the state and slaveholder alike. In 1863 Governor Zebulon Vance issued a proclamation, declaring "it the duty of all slaveowners immediately to remove their slaves able to bear arms." Vance's stance on removal mirrored that presented by Confederate officials in Richmond, who, in March 1863, told planters in coastal Florida, Georgia, and the Carolinas to remove their slaves to the interior, "since they were liable to be lost at any moment."[19]

Despite the pleading of friends, the press, and government officials to remove slaves, some slave owners resisted. For some, removal suggested retreat and submission, and they therefore stayed with their slaves in vulnerable areas of the Confederacy despite the threat posed by Union armies. According to his diary (which he wrote in the third person), Cushing Hassell had "made up his mind & so told them [his slaves] in the commencement of the war that he would keep them at home [in Williamston, North Carolina], not hire them out, or send them up the country or sell them." Hassell believed that God would protect him and his human property from possible harm. His decision not to remove his slaves had decidedly mixed results. Almost all of his neighbors fled Williamston, which was visited by Union forces on several occasions, "leaving H. [Hassell] & his family almost entirely alone." At the start of the Civil War, Hassell owned twelve slaves; by February 1865 he had lost three men, who had run to Union lines, and one woman, who had "behaved so badly that he was compelled to get clear of her & consequentially sent her & her child to Greensboro & sold her, supposed even that to be better for her than to send her to the Yankees."[20]

Other slave owners were reluctant to remove their slaves because of the logistical difficulties involved. After a dinner with friends from Raleigh in October 1862, Catherine Edmondston confided in her diary that "the negroes they were urgent for us to remove, but where to carry them?–that is the question. How to support them, how to house them, all questions easier put than answered." For large slaveholders, slave removal was an expensive proposition. Removing slaves might make it more difficult for them to run away to Union armies, but it also removed their productive labor from the plantation. Slave owners intuitively knew that while they might be able to find employment for their slaves in the upcountry, it was unlikely to be as profitable as that same labor on their home plantation. Further, slave owners recognized that finding housing and sufficient provisions for their slaves would be expensive and difficult, if not impossible, given wartime shortages. Finally, slave owners worried that transportation would be prohibitively expensive. Writing to his friend James C. Johnston, William Pettigrew estimated that it would cost approximately $2,500 for Johnston to remove his nearly three hundred slaves from Edenton to Rowan County by rail. Pettigrew himself, who had already successfully removed his slaves from Washington to Chatham County, debated the merits of taking them farther west to Davie County in order to place a greater distance between them and Union armies. In Pettigrew's mind, the most significant barrier to a second removal was that "the cost would be very considerable."[21]

Given these difficulties, few slave owners removed their slaves en masse. Instead, they adopted a piecemeal removal plan that prioritized some segments of the slave population. Deciding which slaves to remove often proved contentious in slaveholding families. Catherine Edmondston described in her diary a conference held between her husband, father, and brother in October 1862 concerning the removal of the family's slaves. Her husband "advocates the removal of all the hands—women & children—leaving on the aged, the decrepit, and weakly. Father & brother oppose it—say the cost of feeding them is too great—impossible to build houses for them, etc.!" The men, she noted, after much deliberation "counted & assorted the negroes, so many to go, so many to stay."[22]

Most slave owners placed the highest priority on removing their healthy male slaves. Not only were they the most valuable form of slave property, but they were also the most likely to run away to Union lines. Although he was only five years old, William Sykes vividly remembered the day that he and his father were informed that they would be removed to the interior. With approximately one hundred other slaves, Sykes and his father were marched from Tyrell County "straight ter de Blue Ridge mountains," where their owner believed "dar won't be no trouble, case dey [Union soldiers] won't dar atter us." In a decision that was not uncommon, Sykes's owner decided to remove his only male slaves to Buncombe County, leaving female slaves at home, including Sykes's mother and female cousins.[23]

Slave owners also prioritized the removal of domestic servants, especially those charged with childcare. When William Blount Rodman, a Beaufort County politician and lawyer, relocated his family to Greensboro while he served in the Confederate army, he arranged for only seven of his more than fifty slaves to accompany them. One of the Blount children later recalled that five of the seven were house slaves, and his mother rented the two others to work on the Piedmont Railroad. Tristim Skinner, away serving as an officer in the Confederate army, advised his wife, Eliza, to take only a handful of slaves from their Chowan County plantations, including a cook named Priss and a carpenter named Thomas "with part of his tools & soon make you all the tables, benches, & many other bulky articles you would want & let only compactly packing articles be brought from home."[24]

Elderly and infirm slaves were the least likely to be removed. Not only would it be difficult for them to make the trip inland, but slave owners recognized that it would be impossible to find employment for elderly slaves in the interior. Indeed, some planters left their property in the hands of trusted elderly slaves. When Union soldiers made sallies into northeastern North Carolina in 1862 and 1863, they often found elderly slaves in charge of plantations, the owners having removed themselves and their most valuable slaves into the interior. Because of the cost involved in removing slaves, some slave owners were unable to relocate even their most valuable property. Alabama slave owner Sarah Espy recorded in her diary that her neighbor had sold much of his personal property prior taking his slaves "to N. C. to avoid the Yankees." Espy herself believed that she could not afford the expense, staying in her Alabama home despite the threat posed to herself and her slaves by the approaching Union army.[25]

Slave removal could be a perilous business. The examples provided by the Pettigrew brothers illustrate how slaves actively resisted removal. Two of the wealthiest planters in Washington County and the elder brothers of Confederate general James Johnston Pettigrew, Charles and William Pettigrew owned 254 slaves between them on three plantations. While both brothers remained paragons of the planter class, William proved luckier in politics and finance than Charles, his senior by two years. While William Pettigrew was elected in 1861 to represent Washington County in the North Carolina Secession Convention, Charles Pettigrew made a series of bad investments in the 1850s, requiring him to borrow money from his younger brothers.

Like many planters, Charles Pettigrew decided to remove his adult male slaves first, "leaving the women & children for the present." However, when they discovered that they would be separated from their wives and children, all but two of his male slaves "took to the woods." Pettigrew coerced the fugitive slaves to return by temporarily cutting off food rations to the women and children and decided to forestall removal for the time being. Charles Pettigrew's brother William, probably in an effort to avoid the same circumstances, kept his slaves ignorant of his plans to remove them to the interior and, on the night of the removal, arranged for twenty-five soldiers to surprise his slaves in their quarters and escort "every man, woman & child to Chatham [County]." Given the practical difficulties of slave removal, some slave owners hired others to transport their slaves inland. In May 1862 George Reel, a Craven County slave owner, hired James Beckwith to take a slave woman and her two children "up the country to a place of safety, beyond the reach of our Yankee invaders." In payment, Reel agreed to give Beckwith the slave woman's older child "as a compensation for his services and trouble."[26]

As the Pettigrew brothers' cases suggest, most slaves opposed relocation, not only because it took them farther away from freedom but because it often resulted in broken families. William Henry Thurber, one of the slaves that the DeRosset family left in charge of their Wilmington property, wrote frequently to his owners, safely ensconced in Hillsborough, asking them to "give my Love to my mother," whom the DeRossets had taken with them. Forced removal was particularly devastating to cross-plantation marriages, as enslaved husbands and wives were refugeed to geographically disparate locations.[27] When Lucilla Mosely's owner took her with him to Hillsborough from Wilmington, he separated her from her husband, an enslaved carpenter named Joseph Hall. Both slaves eventually escaped from their owners, reuniting at the black refugee camp in Hampton Roads, "where the lovers met again and were happily [legally] married."[28]

Slaves responded to the possibility of removal by running away in increasing numbers to Union lines. While planters often attempted to prevent slaves from knowing about their imminent forced migration, rumors of relocation pushed slaves who were on the fence about making an attempt to reach Union lines to take the opportunity while it was available. In her diary Catherine Edmondston described a conversation with a friend from Elizabeth City whose "negroes had refused to come with them, how their Coachmen stole their best horse & started to run away in the night but fortunately was overtaken & sent back in irons to them." Similarly, Rowan County lawyer David Schenck observed in his diary that "slaves unanimously refuse to be removed and if it is insisted on, they flee to the swamps. They are fully aware of the causes of the invasion and know that it involves their freedom."[29] Thus the voluntary migration of slaves to Union lines and the involuntary migration of slaves to the Confederate interior reinforced each other, pushing North Carolina's enslaved black population east and west, toward freedom and slavery. With each passing month, as some slaves escaped to freedom, slave owners removed others to keep them from running away.

Refugee planters who fled an unexpected Union advance often brought little with them except their slaves when they relocated to central and western North Carolina. Cornelia Phillips Spencer described the refugees in Orange County as "the best and most highly cultivated of our Southern aristocracy" who had "fled hither stripped of all their earthly possessions, except a few of their negroes." In February 1862 Catherine Edmondston, while herself preparing to evacuate her Halifax County plantation, visited her father's plantation, where she was surprised to find the dining room crowded with refugees "to the number of nineteen whites and seventy negroes, all homeless & houseless." After talking with the refugees, she discovered that the head of this extended family had gone out "to endeavor to rent a place where he could put his negroes," but until then, they were crowded into the space that Edmondston's father had allotted them.[30]

The threat from Union armies was not the only reason why most slaveholders in eastern North Carolina relocated their slaves; they also feared that their slaves would be impressed as manual laborers by the Confederate military. Many planters assumed that the Confederate military would be more likely to impress slaves from coastal counties to construct coastal fortifications. An 1862 law authorized the governor to impress slaves and free African Americans for war-related projects. One Washington County planter who refused to remove his slaves to the interior described the effect of these twin perils: "The valuable portion of my slaves left and went to the Yankees, the Confederates came and took the remainder that had proved faithful to me." Slave owners worried about dangerous conditions on coastal fortifications and about the proximity of such work to Union forces. Furthermore, although slave impressments were supposed to be for a limited duration, many planters discovered that while Confederate officials were quick to seize their slaves to work on Fort Fisher and other sites, they were loath to return them.[31]

For both white and black refugees, the journey inland proved difficult. Like Mary Bryan, many white refugees fled via the railroad. Overcrowded and overburdened, railroads in North Carolina and across the Confederacy suffered from frequent breakdowns and long delays. An anonymous Virginia refugee captured the experience of railroad travel through North Carolina in an 1864 poem. He had fled coastal Virginia in the winter of 1862–63, leaving his home under the control of the "negro Yankee." Like many refugees, he believed that he could find affordable accommodations in the Piedmont as "in the up country I thought, things might be bought / At living rates by a refugee." When he arrived at the railroad depot, he was callously treated by the crew, as "the masters of the cars were as rough as grizzly bears, to this fugitive refugee." The conductor instructed him sit on the only available spot on the floor of the passenger car, where he huddled with other refugees. Many of the windows in the car were broken, and the winter snow made the journey unbearably cold, an antique stove in the car providing minimal relief. As the train lumbered slowly southward, the refugees on board endured "with nothing to eat, or warm our feet."

As the trainload of refugees crossed from Virginia into North Carolina, one of the railcars derailed. While some refugees worked to return the car to the rails, others huddled together around a fire. Fortunately no one was killed in the accident. However, railroad accidents such as this one were common in Civil War North Carolina. Wartime traffic overtaxed the railroad infrastructure, leaving both tracks and rolling stock subject to failure and causing many North Carolinians to become wary of railroad travel. In January 1863 A. W. Mangum warned his sister about the perils of riding on railroads in the North Carolina Piedmont. Not only were the trains overcrowded, making it "exceedingly disagreeable travelling on railroads now," but "it is also very dangerous." He warned her that "everyone now looks on the Central Road [North Carolina Railroad] as unreliable & badly managed. Scarcely a day passes without an accident of some kind between here [Goldsboro] & Charlotte causing delay." Once righted, the refugee-poet's train continued toward Charlotte, punctuating its journey with frequent stops for coal and water. Hungry and tired after his long journey, he expressed his joy at no longer being crammed aboard a railcar: "At last we had got to the town of Charlotte, In good time to be left all alone."[32]

In addition to the overcrowded and frequently perilous conditions, travel via railroad had other significant limitations. Railroad passage was expensive, beyond the reach of many less affluent refugees. Railroads also significantly limited the amount of personal possessions that refugees could take with them into the interior. This limitation was particularly acute during the mass exodus from New Bern, when, in order to make room on the train for additional passengers, refugees were forced to leave trunks of valuable personal possessions behind at the depot to be seized by the imminently arriving Union soldiers. When railcars became filled to capacity, some refugees clung to the exterior of the car.[33]

Refugee families often used wagons to transport themselves and their dearest possessions. Unlike railroads or stagecoaches, wagons allowed refugees to bring many of their household goods with them. Refugees who diligently prepared for removal usually selected a mixture of practical household goods, including clothing, bedding, and cooking utensils, along with an assortment of family heirlooms and keepsakes. Usually these keepsakes amounted to tokens of home and family: a daguerreotype of a son or husband in the army, a grandmother's jewelry, or a family Bible. In February 1862, after the capture of Roanoke Island and in advance of the battle of New Bern, Catherine Edmondston wrote in her diary that the "roads are crowded with Refugees in vehicles of every description, endeavoring to move what of their property they can to save it from the grasp of the invader." A newspaper noted that the refugees "came across the country in carriages, wagons and in any way they could."[34]

Overburdened wagons frequently broke down, as the weight strained the wheels and axles. The wagons also frequently found themselves mired in the deep ruts of eastern North Carolina's muddy wagon roads. After a breakdown, wagons had to be unloaded before they could be repaired, and heavy items were often discarded. One refugee described the chaos on the roads thronged with refugees, wagons, and draft horses: "We were constantly in the sight of, and often jostled by moving crowds of people and vehicles. . . . Fugitives of every grade and degree of misery were toiling on, on foot, or in any kind of broken-down vehicle. Sick men, hungry men, and women with crowds of children, all hurrying on."[35]

The migration into the Confederate interior placed many white women in unfamiliar positions. Particularly for younger adult women, whose husbands had gone off to fight, refugeeing required them to step outside of prescribed gender roles. Social custom in the antebellum South significantly limited white women's ability to navigate the public sphere alone. Respectable women needed a male escort to travel to church or school or to visit relatives. The social proscription on respectable white women traveling alone grew out of a deep-seated belief in women's fragility and the need to protect their sexual purity. With the Union invasion of the North Carolina coast, however, many white women believed that the menacing presence of Federal soldiers posed a much more significant threat to their sexual purity than traveling without a chaperone did. In the flight from New Bern, many respectable women had to travel unaccompanied for the first time, navigating the novel circumstances of buying their own train tickets, shouldering their own luggage, and eventually finding and managing a new household. For slaveholding women, refugeeing with their human property magnified these difficulties. Although plantation mistresses had long played a significant, if underappreciated, role in slave management, the particular demands of relocating themselves, their children, and their slaves to the interior proved daunting.[36]

White women of more modest means, accustomed to the difficulties of living and working in the public sphere, had an easier time navigating and adjusting to the novel social demands presented by refugeeing.[37] However, poorer white women faced significant challenges meeting the financial and material problems posed by leaving home. For poor women, the most significant initial decision was how to depart in the face of Union occupation. Rail travel proved prohibitively expensive for most poor white women. Rural poor women in eastern North Carolina usually loaded whatever material possessions they had onto a wagon before embarking on their journey westward. Poor women living in New Bern and other towns usually had to flee on foot, bringing with them only what they could carry.

Many less affluent women in eastern North Carolina came to the conclusion that even if they could escape Union occupation, the demands of refugeeing outweighed the benefits. Many yeomen families, owning little moveable property, reasoned that they could not abandon their homes, even for a short time, without impoverishing themselves. For many yeomen, the need to protect their immoveable property outweighed the desirability of removing themselves from the sphere of Yankee influence. While almost the entire eastern North Carolina planter class refugeed themselves to the interior, common whites had to balance their desire to live outside of Federal control with the practical difficulties of refugeeing. When common whites did decide to leave home, they were much more likely than their planter neighbors to select a nearby refuge, one that allowed them to return home as soon as possible. Many common whites living in the no-man's land between Union-occupied New Bern and Confederate forces in Goldsboro established temporary refuges within close proximity of their homes, often taking to the woods when Union soldiers approached, only to return home when the threat had passed.[38]

For many white refugees, the decision about where to live proved just as challenging as the decision about whether to leave in the first place. For those who fled at the last minute, like Mary Bryan's family, the decision about where to stay initially was almost made for them. Having escaped New Bern via train, their initial refuge was along the railroad in Company Shops, a town built around the rail yard. Indeed, most refugees settled along the corridor created by the North Carolina Railroad. Completed in 1854, the North Carolina Railroad ran from Goldsboro through Raleigh, Hillsborough, Greensboro, and Charlotte, each of which hosted hundreds of white refugees, many of whom brought slaves with them. White refugees who fled to the interior well in advance of the Union invasion of the North Carolina coast also preferred urban areas along the railroad, believing that these communities would offer greater access to telegraphs, newspapers, and mail, all vitally important conduits of news and commodities during wartime. Many refugees also believed, incorrectly, that urban areas would have available housing. For many refugees, however, the most important factor in deciding where to settle in the North Carolina Piedmont was where their friends and relatives were, and many refugees settled near other refugees from home. Hillsborough, for instance, was the preferred destination for refugees from Washington County, while nearby Chapel Hill hosted several refugee families from Edenton. Consequently, cities and towns in central North Carolina swelled in population as refugees from across the Confederacy sought sanctuary.[39]

Almost all refugees struggled to find adequate housing in the North Carolina Piedmont. The demand for housing in Raleigh, Greensboro, Charlotte, and other large towns led to an immediate and significant increase in prices. Cornelia Phillips Spencer noted that in Chapel Hill "every vacant room was crowded at one time by refugee families from the eastern part of the State, from Norfolk, and latterly from Petersburg. And this was the case with every town in the interior of the State." In May 1862 the *Raleigh Register* lamented, "This city is at present crowded to repletion with refugees from Virginia and different parts of the State. On Thursday night several ladies were compelled to sleep on the floor of the parlor of the Yarborough House [a popular hotel], and one party of ladies were obliged to sit up the whole night for the want of beds to lie upon." The hotel's most famous refugee-guest, Varina Davis, complained to her husband in May 1862 about the conditions at the hotel, noting that "the house is full to overflowing here, and the fare dreadful." She found the rooms "terribly crowded, and very rough" with "everything in rags." While she regretted the relative poverty of her situation, Varina Davis struggled most with the cost, telling her husband that she "could get well on but for the exorbitant charges."[40] After an uncomfortable month at the Yarborough House, Varina Davis moved her family to St. Mary's School, an Episcopal girls' boarding school in Raleigh, where they stayed until it was safe to return to Richmond.[41] In October 1862 one refugee claimed that there was "not a house for rent in Raleigh." In May 1862 the *Western Democrat* observed that "the population of Charlotte has been considerably increased within the last week or two, caused by the evacuation of Norfolk and Portsmouth and other places. The town is about filled up, and it is almost impossible to accommodate more." The newspaper encouraged refugees to find homes outside of the city, noting that "houses can be obtained in Lincolnton, Davidson College, and other interior villages, pleasant places and living much cheaper than in Charlotte." The paper also encouraged rural residents to take in refugees, asking, "Could not the farmers through the country take a few boarders? Eatables are hard to get in towns at this season."[42]

As white refugees had occupied all of the available housing, slaveholding refugees found housing their human property almost impossible. Eliza

DeRosset complained to her sister that while she had found an appropriate rental property for her family in Hillsborough, it had "no place of the servants." In late 1862 planter Paul Cameron noted that "the poor refugees who have brought their slaves up the Country find it impossible to provide a home.... Those who hold them in large numbers must provide by purchase both homes & food! It is indeed a hard time on the slave holder and we can hardly escape ruin."[43]

With urban housing in short supply, many refugees reluctantly settled in less accessible areas. Mary Bayard Clarke desperately wanted to live in Raleigh, where she could be close to family. Her husband, then serving in the Confederate army, counseled her against it, arguing that he had "great misgivings about the plan of your living in Raleigh," as "the towns are filled with refugees." Instead, he hoped that she would "find some good country family" to live with. He suggested that she consider living with a distant relative in Randolph County, as "living may be cheap there, as it is an abundant country and not very convenient to market, consequently the people would have more for home consumption." While her husband saw the isolation in rural Randolph County as an asset, Mary Bayard Clarke felt that she needed to stay near family and communication lines and remained in Raleigh for the remainder of the war.[44]

Hoping to attract refugees unable to secure housing in urban areas, rural landowners advertised available property as an alternative. In a June 1862 advertisement titled "TO REFUGEES AND OTHERS!" a hotel in Graham advertised in a Raleigh newspaper that it had vacant rooms for "transient and permanent boarders." Contrasting its rates with the high prices in Raleigh, the hotel noted that it had moderate prices and "10 or 12 refugees can be accommodated if early application is made." Knowing that many refugees in Raleigh would be unfamiliar with the smaller Piedmont communities, the advertisement informed them that "Graham is in Alamance County, on the N.C. Railroad, and about 50 miles above Raleigh." By noting its proximity to the railroad, the hotel's proprietors hoped to entice refugees who might be concerned about living in rural areas. The advertisement concluded by noting that "the country is healthy and pleasant in the warm season."[45]

Within a short time, however, even rural property in the Piedmont was in short supply because of the demand created by refugees. In October 1864 the *Raleigh Daily Confederate* ran an advertisement headlined "ATTENTION REFUGEES! Valuable Property for Sale." Among the assets of the two-hundred-acre property in Granville County were its relative proximity to railroads (twenty miles from both the Raleigh & Gaston Railroad and the North Carolina Railroad) and its location "in a healthy section of the county, and entirely safe from raids from the enemy." The site also included ten slave cabins, which must have been very attractive to slaveholding refugees. The most remarkable aspect of this advertisement, however, is that the *Daily Confederate* chose to highlight it on a separate page in the newspaper, noting that "'Attention Refugees' is well worth the attention of all wishing to purchase valuable property. In these days it is scarcely possible to purchase such."[46]

Some refugees claimed that they were being gouged by property owners. In April 1862, when the city was overwhelmed with refugees from eastern North Carolina and Virginia, the *Raleigh Biblical Recorder* opined that "there are three national sins in the Bible: the oppression of the widow, the fatherless, and the stranger. No people should ever oppress the stranger—When refugees come from the lower part of the State, board, house-rent, and provision should be afforded on moderate terms." A month later the *Salisbury Watchman* expressed a similar sentiment, arguing that "the hospitality of the people of Western Carolina is likely to be called forth this spring and summer, by our refugee friends of the East, who have been driven from their comfortable, well-furnished homes by the ruthless invaders of our soil.... In their condition, we would desire, and could appreciate, an act of kindness and hospitality; and there should be some pains taken, therefore, and some self-denial made, for their accommodation. They will need boarding houses, or houses to live in." The *Raleigh Christian Advocate* concurred that Piedmont residents had a moral obligation to extend a hand and open a door for refugees, placing treatment of refugees within the framework of nationalism and religious obligation. According to the paper, "Surely a generous and patriotic people will not endeavor to place whose who have been driven into exile by a cruel and vindictive foe; but will ... relieve as far as possible, by delicate and courteous acts, their pressing necessities." The newspaper urged its readers to empathize with refugees, so that "the refugees scattered throughout the uninvaded portions of our Confederacy would meet with a much more cordial hospitality, and be the recipients of a much more bounteous generosity than many of them have hitherto been favored with." The paper particularly targeted farmers, who, many refugees believed, unnecessarily raised their prices and limited their supply. Farmers, the paper argued, "should bear it in mind that it is no fault of the refugee that he is enduring the sad pangs of banishment, but that he is unwillingly constrained to occupy the present position. The refugee must have fuel, and food, and it is your duty to contribute as far as you can to his comfort. Let him have of your surpluses at such moderate rates that he may live as well as you; and be sure to supply with wood and other necessaries, but without endeavoring to relieve him of all his money at once."[47] Despite the efforts of newspaper editors to engender hospitality and generosity, many refugees believed that Piedmont property owners and merchants took advantage of their situation.

D. W. Bagley, a refugee from Williamston, complained that his landlord in Rocky Mount was "an unprincipled scoundrel, and did everything in his power to make life unpleasant for the refugees whose dependence upon him for supplies placed them almost entirely at his mercy." After a year in Rocky Mount, during which he claimed to have been "swindled out of $400 or $500 by his landlord," Bagley moved his family to a house outside of the city, which he shared with his two daughters' families, some twenty-nine people in total. Not only was their new home significantly overcrowded, compromising any expectation of privacy, but their remote location made it difficult to communicate with his son, then in Confederate service, and to secure provisions. According to Bagley, after 1863, "the difficulty of getting provisions now becomes a serious manner." His son-in-law "often travels day after day, over rough road, through rain and all kinds of weather, without being able to buy anything whatever. They have a certificate of need from a government agent, but it does not avail;–they, the refugees, are turned away empty-handed, while others can buy." In June 1864 the *Raleigh Daily Confederate* published a letter from "A Refugee" from New Bern who complained about the "poor shelters we have been able to crowd together in, and what we eat, for which we pay enough, I am sure. We do not expect or wish the citizens to feed us or give us shelter–we only ask them not to abuse us."[48]

Prominent North Carolinians often received letters from refugees in search of housing. Former governor and senator William A. Graham received frequent inquiries about the availability of housing in Hillsborough. In October 1862 Evelyn Perkins, the wife of a Confederate congressman from Louisiana, wrote to Graham that she wanted to relocate the family to Orange County. "Our object," she wrote, "is to find a home during the war, & while we wish it comfortable, we do not expect anything on a very large scale. The neighborhood of Hillsboro we thought desirable, as affording Church and School opportunities, with pleasant society, & at the same time, as being remote from any probable incursions of the enemy."⁴⁹ Another former North Carolina governor, David L. Swain, also received frequent requests to procure housing for refugees. In August 1864 he received a letter from Lloyd Beall, the commandant of the Confederate Marine Corps, asking for Swain's assistance in finding housing for his family in Chapel Hill "either at a boarding house or at the Hotel." Beall was reluctant to impose on Swain, then serving as the president of the University of North Carolina, but he knew of no one better positioned to help him find a safe place for his family. "Let the state of things engendered by the war be my apology," he noted. His wife and two teenaged children were currently living in Pendleton, South Carolina, but Beall felt "compelled by circumstances to remove them in early October" to a safer location. Aware that housing in the North Carolina Piedmont was at a premium, Beall wrote that his family would require only two rooms. Not only would Chapel Hill provide safety for his family, Beall wrote, but also "my children could have the advantages of education that place affords."⁵⁰

From the very beginning of the refugee crisis in 1862, refugees struggled with the quest to find housing that was both safe and affordable. The experience of two North Carolina women, Harriet Yellowley and Mary Lacy, reveals the challenges of finding a good home. Both women began their lives as refugees in 1862, hoping to escape the horrors of war by living in the safety of the North Carolina Piedmont. Harriet Yellowley left her home in Greenville in September 1862, moving to Oak Grove in Nash County, between Rocky Mount and Wilson. The unmarried forty-seven-year-old had lived with her unmarried younger brother, a prominent lawyer, in a stately house on Fourth Street in Greenville, set on 180 acres. Between them, they owned fourteen slaves and employed an overseer to manage their estate. In late 1861 her brother had raised a company of soldiers and received a captain's commission. When his unit was sent east to defend Roanoke Island, Harriet Yellowley was left alone in their home. Like many of Greenville's white residents, she decided during the summer of 1862 to relocate to Nash County, fifty miles to the west. On her own for the first time in her life and in a strange place, she felt an immediate sense of homesickness. "Oh! How I missed my home," she wrote in a letter to her brother shortly after arriving in Nash County. "I have never half appreciated it until now. Should I ever have another home or return to that dear one I will never leave it unless I am driven away again."⁵¹

Like many refugees, Harriet Yellowley did not plan to stay away from home for long and anticipated returning to Greenville as soon as the threat had passed. By November 1862, however, she had concluded that she would not be returning home anytime soon. Over the past two months, she had persuaded her brother to remove their slaves to Nash County, since "a great many [Greenville slaves] had gone to the Yankees." The decision proved fortuitous for her, as she had recently heard from other refugees that Union soldiers had visited Greenville and "gave a general invitation to all the negroes to go with them." Few slaves in Greenville took the soldiers up on their offer, although Yellowley heard that "the negroes were all well pleased at the sight of the Yankees" and were "unmanageable for several days after there [sic] departure." In the aftermath of the Union incursion, Greenville slave owners scrambled to remove their remaining slaves inland. Harriet Yellowley met several slave owners from Greenville who had arrived in Nash County after losing a significant number of their slaves, including a friend who had lost more than thirty slaves. The result of the exodus from Greenville to Nash County, she wrote her brother, was that "the neighborhood is crowded with Refugees and negroes. A great many people have left Greenville and are still moving. What is to become of us all I know not."[52]

For slave owners like Harriet Yellowley, the influx of white refugees and their slaves into Nash County created significant housing and food shortages. In a series of letters to her brother in November and December 1862, she complained about her difficulties in feeding and housing their slaves. All of their slaves, she wrote to her brother, had been safely removed to Nash County, but "I haven't yet been able to get homes for them" as "the Neighborhood is filled with refugee negroes." A week later she reiterated her dilemma: "The negroes are all here. I haven't yet been able to get any of them homes and I fear I shan't be able to do so, unless you pay very high for keeping them, provisions are very scarce and high." Although she lamented having to trouble her brother while he was on the front lines, Harriet Yellowley could not see a viable living arrangement for herself and their slaves and begged him for whatever advice and support he could offer. She desperately wanted to procure proper housing for their slaves, but "the whole country is stocked with negroes and white people.... They are crowded and piled together."[53]

Mary Lacy shared many of Harriet Yellowley's difficulties in finding a home that fulfilled her need for security at a price her family could afford. In July 1862 Mary Lacy wrote to her stepdaughter about the rising housing prices in Warrenton, a town in the northeastern Piedmont popular with refugees from eastern North Carolina and Virginia. With an antebellum population of 1,520, Warrenton doubled its inhabitants almost overnight, causing homeowners to dramatically increase rent and board. In 1861 Mary Lacy had moved to Warrenton with her husband, a Presbyterian minister and former president of Davidson College, their three young children, and two slaves. With housing at a premium in Warrenton, all seven members of the Lacy household crammed into one bedroom in a house that they shared with their landlord, Mr. Wilcox, and four refugee women, including one of Robert E. Lee's nieces. According to Mary Lacy, the "four ladies in the house [are] beautiful enough to make the reputation of a town, much less a house." Because of the demand for housing and food, their landlord had raised their board twice within the past year, leaving the family "in somewhat of a quandary what to do," as on her husband's modest ministerial salary they could not "afford to board at this rate." They felt inclined to move but could not find any less expensive housing or board in Warrenton and "where else to go we are perfectly at a loss." Like many refugees, Lacy believed that they could save money were they to procure housing that allowed them to feed themselves rather than boarding at another's table, noting that "I am very anxious to go to housekeeping, if we only knew where to go." She wondered if they could move to Raleigh, where they had lived prior to Reverend Lacy's tenure as Davidson College president, but her husband's ministry in Warrenton prevented that. Mary Lacy expressed to her stepdaughter that "I hope the way will be opened for us to go to some cheaper place."⁵⁴

Three months later, in October 1862, Mary and Drury Lacy were informed by their landlord that board would again be raised, this time by an additional thirty dollars per month. This third rate hike pushed them to leave Warrenton, as "it is now higher than we feel willing to pay & . . . it is higher than we are able to pay." Rev. Drury Lacy packed his books and prepared to find a new home. Mary Lacy wrote to her stepdaughter that although they had decided to leave, "we do not know where we shall go." Even though Warrenton had been her home for only slightly more than a year, Mary Lacy felt a sense of loss at the prospect of moving, noting that "Warrenton is one of the most charming little villages I know & I shall regret leaving it extremely."⁵⁵

The rising cost of food and housing, Reverend Lacy's work, and the threats of Union incursions into the eastern Piedmont left the couple wandering throughout the remainder of the war. After leaving Warrenton, Reverend Lacy took a position as a hospital chaplain in Wilson, sixty miles south of Warrenton and closer to Union forces stationed at New

Bern, Washington, and Plymouth. The location of their new home closer to the front lines initially concerned Mary Lacy, although she suppressed her fears, writing in July 1863 that "I used to be afraid of the Yankees coming to Warrenton (where there was not the slightest danger), but here where they can come at any time I scarcely feel a fear." While she claimed that she did not fear a Union invasion, she did worry about the rising cost of housing and food in Wilson, noting that although "we are living in the plainest sort of way," she feared that her landlord would "give us notice that he cannot keep us." Only a couple of evenings later, while Mary Lacy walked with her husband in Wilson, they heard that Union forces had arrived in nearby Rocky Mount. The couple immediately prepared to flee Wilson. In "a fuss and excitement," Mary Lacy packed a trunk with clothes, which she promptly sent to her stepdaughter in Charlotte. Reverend Lacy anxiously urged his wife to take their children to a safer location, although she decided to stay for the time being. Over the next few days, they received repeated warnings that Union soldiers could appear in Wilson at any time. Reverend Lacy eventually persuaded his wife to leave with the children for Warrenton. As their route passed close to areas Union soldiers were known to frequent, Drury Lacy waited anxiously to hear that his family had arrived in Warrenton.[56]

Mary Lacy returned to Wilson after the Union threat had passed, and the family continued to live in the shadow of the Federal army until November 1864, when they relocated to Raleigh. For more than two years, Mary Lacy had longed to move to Raleigh, where she believed that they would be safer. They managed to secure a house near the military hospital where Reverend Lacy had taken a position as a chaplain. After having lived as boarders with "two or three other families" in Warrenton and Wilson, Mary Lacy was glad to have a home of their own, though she observed that "it is very small & without any pantry, smoke house, or any place to store anything away. There are two rooms down stairs & two up, no passage & the stairs like a ladder." Mary Lacy wrote to her stepdaughter that "I am might glad to get back to Raleigh & yet I fear we shall have a hard time to live here."[57]

The experiences of Harriet Yellowley and Mary Lacy reveal the practical difficulties refugees faced securing housing. Many refugees discovered that providing enough food for themselves and their slaves was just as difficult as finding housing. The influx of white and black refugees into the region created unprecedented demands for food. Coupled with rampant Confederate inflation and shortages caused by Union blockade, even the wealthiest Confederate refugees had difficulties supplying their tables. One refugee concluded that the North Carolina interior had "too many servants & in consequence of such a high price of all edibles . . . [a] famine is approaching rapidly." After the outbreak of yellow fever in Wilmington, another refugee wrote that "the bible tells us that before the end of the World we will have War, pestilence & famine the two first is upon us—& the other is fast approaching." A refugee in Franklinton noted that "provisions [are] scarce and high." Fayetteville became "crowded with refugees from down the river," including many wealthy refugees who found "difficulty in procuring the bare necessities of life," such that "corn bread formed the sole bill of fare at meals in families accustomed to comfort and even luxury." A refugee in Hillsborough noted that "provisions [are] so hard to get & so enormously high. I give five dollars and a half for a bushel of meal, $1.30 for butter, & everything in proportion, & very scarce at these prices." Even planters who managed to secure farms discovered that they could not produce enough for their slaves to be self-supporting. Many refugee planters concluded that slave ownership had become more of a liability than an asset. One Confederate military official observed in 1862 that refugee "Negroes, who, from being producers, became consumers and add to our calamities."[58]

By the end of 1862 the North Carolina Piedmont had been transformed by the arrival of tens of thousands of refugees. Many refugees reconciled themselves to the fact that they could not return home until after the war ended. A homesick refugee from Virginia living near Raleigh recalled the last time she saw her home: "It never appeared more beautiful, never seemed more dear than when we left it, not knowing whether we would ever behold it again. We gazed through blinding tears, until the tops of the lofty oaks were lost in the distance, thinking of how the feet of the foe would desecrate every spot, and his hands delight to spoil whatever was dear to us." They had planned to return home as soon as the danger had passed, but "weeks have lengthened to months, and months into a year."[59] Unable to return home, they had become permanent refugees in Raleigh. Like the refugees on North Carolina's coast, Piedmont refugees greeted the end of 1862 with trepidation and fear, while at the same time laying the groundwork for refugee communities that would last for the duration of the war.

FOUR

Confederacy of Refugees

In the spring of 1864, William M. Boylan feared for the safety of his human property. The owner of three cotton plantations in Yazoo County, Mississippi, Boylan recognized that the presence of Union gunboats on the Mississippi River posed a threat to his property and a potential lure for his slaves. He had heard accounts of slaves running away to secure their freedom. He resolved to relocate approximately five hundred of his slaves to central North Carolina, where he believed they would be safely isolated from Union forces. Milly Henry, an eight-year-old girl in the spring of 1864, was one of the slaves Boylan selected for removal. Henry remembered that when Boylan gathered his slaves together to tell them of the relocation, he manifested a palpable anxiety about the situation. Boylan informed them that they would be removed to North Carolina in two days and that he "ain't gwine ter hyar no jaw 'bout hit." Henry was distressed to discover that she would be separated from her grandmother, her only family member, as many of the elderly and infirm slaves would stay in Mississippi.

A Raleigh native, Boylan had recently inherited land in both Mississippi and North Carolina, an inheritance that likely included both Milly Henry and her grandmother. Like many slaveholding families in the North Carolina Piedmont, the Boylans had established plantations in Mississippi during the 1830s and 1840s, moving thousands of slaves to the Black Belt, a migration that might have included Milly Henry's grandmother. With these plantations under threat, William Boylan concluded that his slaves would be safer in Raleigh. Milly Henry and Boylan's other slaves made the nearly nine-hundred-mile trek to North Carolina on foot and by covered wagon in about three weeks. She remembered that they camped along the side of the road and cooked over campfires. When they arrived in Raleigh, Boylan initially divided his slaves between two plantations he owned in Wake County. Within a few weeks, however, he decided, probably due to the high cost of provisions, to rent out many of his slaves, including Milly Henry. Over the next two years, she was rented to three different women. She worked for the first, a Miss Mary Lee, until "she got so pore she can't feed me." Her second renter, who neglected to provide her with shoes, beat her so severely that she ran away to her owner, pleading with Boylan to find another placement for her. She was with her third renter, a widow who ran a boardinghouse in Raleigh, when Yankee soldiers marched into the city in April 1865.[1]

By the time that William Boylan brought himself and his slaves to the North Carolina Piedmont in the spring of 1864, the region had already become overwhelmed by waves of refugees arriving from eastern North Carolina, Virginia, and across the Confederacy. In the final two years of the conflict, as Union armies advanced and the Confederacy contracted, white refugees increasingly congregated in the North Carolina Piedmont, where they believed the physical distance from the enemy would isolate them from the terrors of war and protect their human property. At times they could pretend that the war was not taking place. A disgruntled Greensboro resident complained in February 1863 that "our town is still full of Refugees, who give parties, dance and pass time as merrily as if our fair Country was not passing through a terrible Ordeal; as if all was peaceful & prosperous as in days gone by."[2] While some white refugees maintained the fiction in early 1863 that they could continue their lives unhindered by the war, they could not deceive themselves for long. In the final years of the Civil War, refugees in the North Carolina Piedmont experienced severe overcrowding, traumatic financial difficulties, food shortages, and epidemic disease. The tensions created by these forces served to undermine the social order and hierarchy that the refugees had sought to preserve. Most fundamentally, they undermined the strength of the South's peculiar institution, as refugeed slaves sought to expedite their freedom.

The arrival of thousands of black and white refugees in the North Carolina Piedmont radically transformed the racial, class, and labor profile of the region. Unfortunately, existing records make estimating the size of the Piedmont refugee population difficult. The Confederate government never conducted a census, and while local governments in other Confederate states conducted local enumerations, no county or municipality in North Carolina did so. The difficulties that white refugees had in securing housing throughout the war suggest that by early 1863 thousands of white refugees had descended on the Piedmont, particularly in urban areas, where schools, warehouses, and barns were converted into living spaces. Piedmont lawyer David Schenck estimated in January 1864 that "many thousands of exiles roam through the land, with tales of sorrow and affliction." According to Schenck, these "many thousands of exiles" included planters who had been "reduced to penury and want by the ravages and cruelty of the enemy" and "thousands of women and children, made widows and orphans constantly appeal for aid and sustenance."[3]

While the extent of the rise of the white refugee population can only be guessed at, firmer estimates can be made about the size of the refugeed slave population. Tax assessments from 1863 suggest that the slave population of many central North Carolina counties had increased significantly since the beginning of the war. Unfortunately, these tax assessments have survived for only six counties and most of these are incomplete.[4] In Orange County, where Hillsborough and Chapel Hill were popular destinations for eastern North Carolina planters, the slave population increased from 5,109 in 1860 to 6,103 in 1863 and probably exceeded 8,000 by the war's end.[5] The most complete records, those from Johnston and Cabarrus Counties, indicate that the slave population had increased by between 4 and 10 percent in the year since Burnside's invasion, and records from other central and western counties indicate a similar increase. Residents of Cabarrus County complained, however, that this figure undercounted the number of refugeed slaves living in their midst, as refugee slave owners refused to have their slaves enumerated, claiming that they had already paid taxes on them in their home county. In 1864, after receiving complaints from Cabarrus County residents, Richard C. Gatlin, the adjutant general of North Carolina, wrote to the local militia commander that he was to "place the slave owners who have lately taken their slaves from the Eastern Counties, to your County, on equality with the other slave owners of Cabarrus" and that their slaves should be taxed and impressed accordingly.[6] While these records make it impossible to accurately assess the number of refugeed slaves in the North Carolina Piedmont in 1863 or at any other point, they do suggest that the presence of refugeed slaves significantly altered the demographic profile of the region.

The presence of so many white and black refugees in the Piedmont, particularly in urban areas, contributed to an economic crisis that threatened to unravel the region's social order. Producing very little, refugees consumed vast quantities of food, medicine, cloth, and other goods in short supply. As economic parasites, refugees drove up the prices of housing, foodstuffs, and transportation. Compounded with inflationary pressures created by the overproduction of paper currency by the Confederate government, shortages created by the Union blockade, and unprecedented demands from the Confederate military for food and war materiel, consumption by refugees pushed prices for both staples and luxury items to unprecedented levels. Few areas of the Confederacy experienced as dramatic an increase in prices as central North Carolina, where prices for eggs, flour, and corn often exceeded thirty times their antebellum levels. When partnered with Confederate taxation, which grew increasingly onerous as the war progressed, inflationary pressures posed challenges to even the wealthiest refugees.[7] In March 1864 Macy Outten, a wealthy, childless widow from New Bern who had taken refuge in Hillsborough, complained that "I am growing quite despondent as it regards my pecuniary affairs, the heavy taxes which have been laid upon us is ruinous to persons in my situation." Required to pay taxes to the Confederate government for her property then under Union occupation, Outten later reflected that "the War has taught me to deny myself many things which I had once thought indispensable." Despite her difficulties, Outten recognized that her wealth insulated her from the worst effects of the Piedmont's economic crisis, noting that "I have got along remarkably well in spite of the taxes. Always had Meat which is more than many of my neighbors can say, and plenty of vegetables. . . . I cannot conceive how the poor manage to get along. They certainly must suffer for the necessities of life."[8]

Among the hardest hit by the Piedmont's economic crisis were nonslaveholding women. After the institution of the Confederate draft in 1862, they struggled to manage families and farms without their husbands' labor. Although their soldier husbands often sent home their wages, these never kept up with inflation, pushing female-headed yeoman families to the brink of starvation. In November 1864 Louisburg resident Anna Long Thomas Fuller observed that "the prospect for the winter is gloomy indeed. Prices are exorbitant. The poor must suffer, I'm sure. I hear there are a number of families in our community who have been without meat for months." Yeomen Piedmont women manifested their frustration in angry letters to Governor Zebulon Vance and Jefferson Davis, demanding that their husbands be returned to them or that the government provide some relief for their hunger. While most of these letters came from individuals, impoverished women frequently recognized that their situation was not unique and sent communal petitions, a nascent form of political organizing. For instance, in February 1863 soldiers' wives from Wayne County informed Governor Vance that "we hav seen the time when we could call our Littel chil31en and our Husbun to our tables and hav a plenty, and now wee have Becom Beggars and starvers an now way to help ourselves." They implored Governor Vance that "wee think it is hie time for us to get help in time our need." Dissatisfied with the government's response to their suffering, some yeomen Piedmont women encouraged their husbands to desert. Piedmont women's inability to secure affordable provisions for their families culminated in a series of bread riots beginning in 1863. The largest bread riot in North Carolina took place in Salisbury in March 1863, when "between 40 and 50 soldiers' wives, followed by a numerous train of curious female observers, made an attack on several of our businessmen . . . whom they regarded as speculators in the necessaries of life." Later in the war, women rioted for food in Greensboro, Bladenboro, and High Point and in smaller communities in Johnston, Granville, Orange, Alamance, and Montgomery Counties.[9]

Although they did not participate in bread riots, white refugees contributed to the exorbitant rise in prices that brought them about. By purchasing scarce food for themselves and their slaves, wealthy refugees drove up prices for poorer women. Despite their comparative wealth, white refugees were not immune to the economic crisis that permeated the North Carolina Piedmont. Possessing few transferable skills, most white refugees from the plantation districts of North Carolina, Virginia, and the Deep South had to rely on their accumulated wealth and human property to sustain themselves as refugees. For instance, Macy Outten, elderly and in poor health, had to live off of her inherited estate and the charity of her neighbors. Indeed, few white refugees found employment in the Piedmont. Since most refugees were women, children, and elderly men, employment options were limited. Outside of teaching and nursing, white refugee women had few options to earn an income, and even these were usually limited to women without children.[10] Some male refugees could find work as ministers and doctors, especially at military hospitals. Dr. James G. M. Ramsey, a refugee from Knoxville, tended to patients at the military hospital in Charlotte, while his wife tutored children in nearby Concord. Their income from these positions, however, was negligible, leading Ramsey to note that "my pecuniary resources were small and daily becoming smaller." Both he and his wife saw their work primarily as a form of Confederate patriotism rather than a source of income.[11]

Some refugee planters concluded that the best solution to this financial predicament was to sell some or all of their slaves. In January 1862 Rev. Henry Smith observed in his diary that Greensboro had become crowded with refugees and that "an immense number of people (black & white) are in town today. It is hiring day, & several negroes are to be sold." Prices for slaves, especially male slaves, increased dramatically during the war, such that the price for prime field hands exceeded $5,000 in 1865. However, while the absolute value of slaves increased during the war, when controlled for inflation, the prices for slaves actually declined significantly. This incongruous aspect of the wartime slave market was reflected in David Schenck's diary. In September 1862 Schenck claimed that prices for slaves had increased significantly. "Prices of negroes are enormous," Schenck noted, with "likely boys bringing $2000." However, Schenck noted in his diary in January 1865 that "Negroes are rapidly declining in price, in fact they can scarcely be sold at any price."[12] Dramatic fluctuations in slave prices scared away both buyers and sellers, as did the institution's uncertain future. Some slaveholders refrained from selling their slaves because they feared appearing unpatriotic, so tied was slaveholding to the Confederate identity. Others worried that selling slaves would expose them as debtors, which many white Southerners saw as dishonorable.[13] An advertisement for thirty slaves in Charlotte in March 1865 noted that "they are not offered for sale as a consequence of faults but simply because the owner lives where he cannot employ them to profit." Because of the uncertainty about the future of slavery, the slave market almost disappeared in the war's final years.[14]

While the market for selling slaves declined significantly after 1863, the market for renting slaves in the North Carolina Piedmont expanded tremendously throughout the war, as refugee slave owners sought to temporarily transfer the responsibility for feeding, housing, and clothing their slaves to someone else.[15] Renting out slaves, a well-established practice throughout the South, allowed slaveholding refugees to continue their commitment to the peculiar institution while absolving them of the responsibility to provide for their slaves far from home. For large planters, without land for their slaves to work, the rental market provided an easy way to relieve themselves of the considerable cost that housing and feeding their slaves entailed. As most rental contracts lasted a year, refugee slaveholders saw renting their slaves as a temporary panacea, allowing them time to evaluate their situation and postpone decisions about their own future and that of their slaves. For white refugees in central North Carolina whose husbands and sons were in the army, the absence of male family members to supervise slaves provided an additional motivation to rent out their slave property. Although plantation mistresses had long been accustomed to managing and disciplining slaves at home, as refugees they felt uncomfortable with the added burden of maintaining a slave system predicated on the threat and use of violence, as slaves increasingly used wartime conditions to test the limits of their enslavement.[16]

As early as March 1862, some Confederates were lamenting that the market for slave rentals had become so glutted that is was impossible to find someone to rent their slaves. Mary Boykin Chesnut observed in her diary that "labor [is] of no value at all. It commands no price whatever. People gladly hire out their negroes to have them fed and clothed. Which latter cannot be done." In the same month, Josiah Collins, a Washington County planter who had removed many of his slaves to Hillsborough, had to return ten of them to his plantation, despite the imminent threat posed by Union armies, because "he c[ou]ld get no work[,] all at a great cost." Collins confided to a friend that he "wished he had not attempted to bring them [to central North Carolina]—the expense is heavy, the profit very doubtful." While the rental market for young male slaves remained viable throughout the war, the market for women, children, and elderly men collapsed after 1863. With the devaluation of Confederate currency, some slave owners doubted the wisdom of renting their slaves. In an effort to dissuade his wife from renting their slaves, Kenelm Lewis informed her that even if she found someone interested in renting them, "the money you would get for the hire [of slaves] would not be of much use to you." Instead, he advocated that she "keep the mules & negroes at your father's."[17]

In the war's final years, when the cost of maintaining slaves exceeded their profitability, many slave owners were willing to rent their slaves without compensation. Eliza DeRosset proclaimed in January 1864 that she would rent one of her slaves for only "his victuals & clothes." By early 1865 some slave owners actually paid for others to care for their slaves. In January 1865 William Pettigrew received a letter from his overseer, who was attempting to find placements for his slaves for the year. He notified Pettigrew that he had to spend $2,000 to place one family and that he was having difficulty placing another slave. "I can't get any person to take Lucy at any price yet. I hav[e] offered $500 but that don't seem to be any thing to the people I hav[e] offered her to. I hav[e] tryed every person in 8 or 10 miles Round me."[18]

As the passage above indicates, planters like William Pettigrew found owning slaves more of a financial liability than an asset. While the financial difficulties from slave ownership were most pronounced at the end of the war, many planters began to see their slaves as toxic assets early in the conflict. In a letter asking for a loan in August 1862, Pettigrew framed his financial situation in the following terms: "as my lands are in the hands of the enemy, and as my negroes, most of whom are in the up country, have been hired, at a nominal sum, I begin to find my purse requires being replenished from without." Writing to an Alabama correspondent a few months later, Pettigrew described his current predicament. In March 1862, just after the fall of Roanoke Island, he had "removed my negroes to the Counties of Chatham & Moore [in the eastern Piedmont], regarding their location a safe one." In the intervening months, however, he had had difficulty securing employment and housing for his slaves and worried that Union soldiers could, within the next few months, occupy all of eastern North Carolina, such that "my negroes would be but fifty miles distant from the invader." As Pettigrew saw matters, he had three choices: "First, to leave my negroes where they are with the probability that, ere the 1st March next, all of them will have made their escape to the enemy; Secondly, to remove them to the western counties of N. Carolina, where food will be scarce & high & where large numbers of negroes are accumulating from the East. Or Thirdly, to remove them to the south, where the lands are more productive & grain more abundant."[19] After some deliberation, Pettigrew decided to keep his slaves in central North Carolina for the time being.

In January 1863 Pettigrew moved eighty of his slaves west to Davie County, a distance of approximately one hundred miles from their initial relocation in Chatham County. Prior to their forced migration, he had advertised to local farmers that his slaves were available for rent, noting that "the men and women are unusually good hands, and those hiring them I am sure will be pleased." Although he was able to find renters, prices had dropped significantly, such that he received only $125 for the men and $50 to $60 for the women. Pettigrew considered the price fair, as "the county is over supplied" with slaves, and in an effort to rationalize the low rental prices he was receiving for his slaves, he concluded that "safety is far more important than profit for one's negroes."[20]

While the expansion of slave hiring in the North Carolina interior may have been financially disastrous for slave owners, it was devastating to the emotional and social well-being of the slaves, as hiring out resulted in a further fragmentation of established slave communities and families. For instance, during the two years that Milly Henry spent in central North Carolina, she was rented out to three different masters, further separating her from the community in which she had grown up. Although William Pettigrew attempted to keep families together when he rented out his slaves, by leasing his eighty-seven slaves to fifteen different planters, he nonetheless fragmented a slave community and divided extended families.[21] In many cases, slave owners' motivations in keeping families together derived more from practicality than a disinclination to break apart families. Because it was generally much more difficult to find parties interested in renting women and children, slave owners preferred to rent out entire families in order to avoid the difficulty of placing women and children.

Many planters experienced difficulties in finding appropriate renters for their slaves. On several occasions William Pettigrew discovered that the individuals to whom he had rented his slaves were unable to provide them with adequate food and clothing. In January 1863 he wrote to Dr. Archibald Palmer, who had rented a family of slaves from Pettigrew, that one of the slaves had informed him that he "and his family have not, as yet, received all the clothing due them for the past year. My impression is that they are yet without their winter clothes, blankets, or quilts." Rented slaves often complained to their owners about their treatment. Osmyn, a DeRosset family slave, protested that his renters "have given him no clothes & he is much in need & begs to have his place changed."[22]

While most white refugees sought to sell or rent out their slaves, some more fortunate refugees saw the opportunity to expand their holdings. In June 1861 Michael Cronly, a prominent Wilmington merchant, decided to relocate his family and several domestic slaves to Laurinburg. Although Laurinburg was crowded with refugees, most of whom had come from Wilmington, such that "every available building was occupied, even school houses and stores," Cronly was able to purchase several properties in town. In 1864 Cronly "went South . . . and bought a great many negroes." Cronly was able to purchase the slaves at a discount because "the confusion and upsettings of war had thrown numbers of them on the market." In time, however, Cronly came to regret his decision, as it was impossible to find adequate food and clothing for his newly acquired slaves. "Most of them had nothing to do and consequentially got sick, and 'guffered.'" When Sherman's army marched through Laurinburg in March 1865 and their slaves departed in its wake, the Cronly family saw their leaving not as a misfortune but as "a blessing to us that the negroes had left, for they would have been only an additional care."[23]

When the rental market for slaves as agricultural workers became saturated, many slave owners decided that their best option would be to rent their slaves to one of several railroads being constructed in western and central North Carolina. Southern railroads had traditionally relied on slaves to perform the most taxing manual labor: wielding picks and shovels, cutting lumber, pushing wheelbarrows, and laying track. Since the 1830s, slave labor, much of it rented, had been instrumental in the construction of Southern railroads. According to the account of one anonymous fugitive slave published in 1838, slave owners sometimes used rental to a railroad as a form of punishment for recalcitrant slaves. Slaves rightly feared railroad work, as railroads developed reputations as brutal and dangerous workplaces. Building railroad beds, slaves pushed wheelbarrows loaded with dirt up wooden planks a foot and half wide; "if they lost their balance, they would fall from ten to twenty feet." During the two months that the anonymous fugitive slave worked on the railroad, "there was hardly a day that some of the slaves did not get crippled or killed." Not only were the physical demands of railroad construction taxing, but railroad overseers developed a reputation for brutality, pushing their temporary charges to perform. According to the anonymous fugitive slave, railroad overseers were quick to the lash, "cutting and slashing all the time. Every hour in the day we could hear the whip going." While slave owners customarily treated whipped slaves with brine, a painful but effective antiseptic, and allowed a brief period for recuperation, railroad overseers "did not use brine.... After we were whipped we had to go straight back to our work. They did not care whether we got well or not, because we were other people's niggers."[24]

During the Civil War, the Confederacy relied on railroads to provide transportation, food, and supplies to soldiers. The increase in traffic overtaxed the Southern railroad infrastructure, resulting in worn-out tracks, crumbling railroad beds, overburdened locomotives, and ultimately a significant increase in railroad accidents, many of them fatal. Unable to import new track to replace the worn-out track and without an adequate domestic supply, railroads cannibalized branch lines to repair the main trunk lines. All of these factors led to a significant increase in slave labor on railroads during the Civil War.[25] In May 1862, shortly after the Union invasion of New Bern and the exodus of slave owners from the region, the *Fayetteville Observer* recommended that refugee slave owners hire their slaves to the Piedmont Railroad, as "here will be a fine opportunity for those whose lands are in the hands of the enemy, or too much exposed to render their cultivation safe, to find employment for their negroes, in a locality that may be considered as safe from the ravages of the invader as any within the limits of the Confederacy."[26] Seen as a vital supply link between the interior and Confederate forces in and around Richmond, railroads in North Carolina received considerable support from both the state and national governments. Indeed, these ventures were so highly capitalized and the military need for the construction so urgent that they offered rental prices significantly above market rates (at least for male slaves), driving rental prices up.[27] The largest of these enterprises, the Piedmont Railroad, building the long-awaited connection between Danville and Greensboro, hired thousands of slaves, housing them in temporary tent cities along the tracks. At the height of construction in 1862–63, the Piedmont Railroad employed approximately twenty-five hundred slaves, and other railroads, including the North Carolina Railroad, the Western North Carolina Railroad, the Wilmington & Weldon Railroad, and the Raleigh & Gaston Railroad, employed thousands more.[28] Newspaper notices in Raleigh, Charleston, and Richmond advertised North Carolina railroads' seemingly insatiable appetite for slave rental labor. In February 1863 the Chatham Railroad placed an advertisement for three hundred slaves, noting that the "line runs through a healthy country, on a high ridge, and all hands employed on the road will be well fed and cared for." Hiring records from the North Carolina Railroad Company indicate that it relied heavily on refugeed slaves to maintain the railroad that ran from Goldsboro in the east through Raleigh, Greensboro, and Salisbury, ending at Charlotte. In 1862 the North Carolina Railroad hired 273 slaves, approximately one-third of whom came from refugee slave owners. Two years later it hired nearly three hundred slaves, with almost half of those from refugee slave owners.[29]

The rental of slave men to work on railroads in central North Carolina further divided slave families. While the railroads rented slave women as laundresses and occasionally to wield shovels and picks alongside the men, more than 95 percent of slaves rented by railroads were men, usually between the ages of fifteen and thirty.[30] Hired by a South Carolina planter to supervise his slaves working on a North Carolina railroad, an overseer noted that the men had a "great desire to hear from their families." The overseer requested that the planter inform him "so as to enable me to tell the fellows how their families are[;] it would have a good effect."³¹

Josiah Collins, a Washington County planter, was typical of the refugee slave owners who rented their slaves to the North Carolina Railroad. Census records for 1860 indicate that he was one of the wealthiest slave owners in North Carolina, with 328 slaves and hundreds of acres under cultivation at Somerset Plantation, not far from the Pettigrew brothers. Like many eastern planters, he relocated himself, his family, and their domestic servants to Hillsborough in April 1862. Collins left sixty-six slaves, primarily older men and women, at his Somerset Plantation, under the supervision of an overseer. He sent 171 slaves to a recently acquired plantation in Franklin County that he called "Hurry Scurry," a name that reflected the haste with which he removed his slaves there. Collins's decision to split his slaves between Washington, Orange, and Franklin Counties reflected a careful balance between his desire to protect his property in the Confederate interior with a practical consideration of the cost of removing and maintaining his slave property. Even after Union soldiers repeatedly visited Somerset Plantation during the spring and summer of 1863 and his overseer pleaded with him to remove his slaves, Collins refused to do so. Even news that his house had been vandalized and looted did not persuade him to relocate the remainder of his slaves to the Piedmont.³²

Unlike most refugees, Collins was able to acquire a new plantation for his refugeed slaves. Presumably, Collins expected that his slaves would, at minimum, produce enough to be self-sustaining. He planned for them not only to grow their own food but also to produce their own clothing and shoes. However, he quickly discovered that his ambitious scheme proved unwieldy, as he was unable to secure usable cotton cards and the farm never produced adequate foodstuffs. In May 1863 he received a letter from his friend Archibald Arrington, a Nash County planter and politician, who expressed his "doubts as to the purchase you made in Franklin [County]. I am apprehensive your people will not be able to raise a support on the farm & if so the deficiency will add to your already heavy expenses incurred for their maintenance & comfort. Your losses have been very great, but when you consider that others less prudent have been totally ruined you ought to feel thankful that you have saved so much from the hands of our ruthless invaders."³³ Shortly thereafter, Collins decided to rent thirty-seven of his slaves at Hurry Scurry, including his most valuable male slaves, to the railroad.

Despite the initial attraction, most slave owners soon discovered that working conditions on railroads imperiled the lives of their slaves. Poorly fed, housed, and clothed, slaves working on Confederate railroads suffered from disease, malnutrition, and exhaustion. Death and crippling injuries were common. Of the thirty-seven slaves rented out by Josiah Collins (and after his death in June 1863, by his widow) to the North Carolina Railroad, four died. In February 1862 Peter and Alexander, two slaves hired by the Wilmington and Manchester Railroad from a South Carolina refugee, were run over by a reversing train, killing Peter and significantly injuring Alexander. In November of that same year, a train accident on the Wilmington and Weldon Railroad killed a black brakeman who had been recently rented to the railroad.[34]

Under such working conditions, most slave owners rented their slaves to a railroad only if no other option was available. George Davidson, an Iredell County planter, stipulated in his rental contracts that his slaves "are not to [be] put to work on any Gold Mine, Rail Road, Iron Factories or any work connected therewith." In 1862 Catherine Edmondston's husband considered "the expediency of taking a Contract on the Coal Fields R R, so as to place our men hands at least in safety. O! the sword of Damocles hangs over our heads & it may fall at any moment."[35] The number of insurance claims filed for the deaths of rented slaves reflected the peril they faced working on Confederate railroads in central North Carolina. According to records of the North Carolina Mutual Insurance Company in Raleigh, the state's largest insurer of slaves, the rate of claims on slave policies nearly doubled during the Civil War.[36] One planter heard from a foreman overseeing his slaves rented to a railroad that "your negroes ar verry much Disatisfide tha cant satisfy those men on the Road with all tha can doo." His informant warned him that working conditions on the railroad, compounded with inadequate clothing and shoes, would likely result in high rates of mortality and desertion among the slaves. Furthermore, as the railroad charged planters for feeding and clothing the slaves against the rental price, the overseer thought it likely that "you will loose more than you will Make."[37]

Unable to find other renters to take his slaves, Charles Pettigrew rented them to work on the Piedmont Railroad in January 1863. Telling his wife that he did "not altogether like the treatment of the negroes, I conducted to go up the country to see if I could find a [new] place for the negroes." Failing in this endeavor, he went to visit the slaves, encamped some eighteen miles north of Greensboro. There he found them living on short rations (which the railroad charged at exorbitant rates against Pettigrew's account) and many of them "sick with something like measles." Their living conditions, he noted, were "dreadfully crowded and if summer finds them in this state I am sure there will be great death among them." Moreover, he observed that because of the military necessity for the railroad connection, his slaves were "not allowed one moment's leisure to rest, neither men nor women."[38]

For several months, Pettigrew attempted to find new employment for his slaves, without success. In April 1863 he visited them to find that their conditions had declined. They complained that they had been denied rations and were "never allowed to see the light of day at their quarters." Pettigrew also discovered through conversations with an acquaintance in Greensboro that slaves working on the railroad were often beaten severely and threatened with being shot. Although he contemplated buying a farm nearby and relocating his slaves there, Pettigrew kept most of his slaves working on the Piedmont Railroad despite the conditions. When he visited them a third time in August 1863, Pettigrew saw that his slaves "unquestionably work, very hard, and have asked me to take them from the road." Despite their pleas, Pettigrew rationalized keeping them on the railroad as they "would be much less satisfied with the scant amount of food I can supply them with on a farm."[39]

Pettigrew's admission that he could not properly provide for the material needs of his slaves undermined whatever paternalistic claims he had to mastery.[40] Despite their pleadings, Pettigrew appeared powerless to protect them from physical brutality. In short, Pettigrew forfeited the primary obligations that Southern slave owners claimed entitled them to own other people. Charles Pettigrew's dilemma was not uncommon, as many refugee slave owners found their claims to mastery slipping away. As historian Wayne Durrill has pointed out, slave removal created a "crisis in paternalism." Because slave owners could not adequately feed, clothe, house, or even protect their human property, slaves "protested loudly, slowed down their work, and, as a last resort, ran away or plotted their revenge in secret."[41]

While male slaves were frequently rented to railroads, refugee slave owners often rented both female and male slaves to hospitals, another wartime growth industry in central North Carolina. The first military hospital in North Carolina opened in Raleigh in May 1861 and others were soon established in Weldon, Wilson, Greensboro, Goldsboro, Tarboro, Salisbury, and Charlotte. By 1863 Raleigh was home to three general hospitals, making it a significant medical center within the Confederacy. By 1865 North Carolina was home to thirteen Confederate general hospitals and many smaller temporary and wayside medical facilities. The majority of the manual labor performed at these hospitals was conducted by rented slaves, many of whom had been brought to the North Carolina Piedmont by refugee slave owners. Josiah Collins's widow, for instance, rented out more than thirty of her slaves to four Confederate hospitals in 1864 and 1865. Like railroads, Confederate hospitals in central North Carolina advertised heavily to entice refugee slave owners to rent out their human property. Readers of the *Daily Confederate*, a Raleigh newspaper, would have found three different advertisements on December 17, 1864, to rent their slaves to nearby hospitals. Pettigrew Hospital in Raleigh looked to hire fifty or sixty slaves as "Nurses, Cooks, and Laundresses." The advertisement promised high rental prices, "good rations and comfortable quarters," though it noted that "the women must not be encumbered with children." Competing offers from hospitals in Kittrell's Springs and Wake Forest offered similar terms to "people wishing to hire their servants."[42]

While white doctors and nurses tended directly to wounded or ill soldiers, rented slaves performed the majority of the physical labor at Confederate hospitals. Slave men carried patients into the hospital, and when, as was often the case, the patients did not survive their stay, slaves carried their bodies out of the hospital and dug their graves. Rented slaves also cleaned privies, washed wounded soldiers, chopped wood, cleaned bedding, did laundry, and prepared and served meals. While some of these tasks would have been familiar to plantation slaves, the wartime hospital context often made them unfamiliar. Fearing that slaves made poor nurses, hospital officials attempted to closely supervise their labor, particularly when they had direct contact with patients. What little privacy or autonomy plantation slaves had within slave quarters or in the fields beyond an overseer's view disappeared under the close supervision of hospital administrators.[43]

The growing slave population and increased fears of slave rebellion led many communities in central and western North Carolina to expand slave patrols and in some communities to begin patrols for the first time. In 1861 Granville County doubled its slave patrols, and Davie County significantly increased pay for patrollers. Writing from Yanceyville, the seat of Caswell County in the northern Piedmont, James McKee informed his sister that "we have to keep a strict patrol over the negroes in this county as there is so many of them." The dramatic increase in its slave population led Yadkin

County to implement slave patrols for the first time. One farmer wrote to the county judge in 1864 that "I deem it necessary that some one should suggest to you the idea of having some patrols appointed for this district. If there ever was a time it was needed it is now." Removed slave William Sykes remembered that "de patteroller wus thick dem days."[44]

Fear of slave violence was not unwarranted, as violence by refugeed slaves appeared endemic in central North Carolina. In early 1863 two slave owners were murdered by their slaves in Orange County. In the aftermath of these murders, planter Paul Cameron wrote to Governor Vance, "As you might suppose the community is much excited and I am told a strong disposition prevails to take the matter in hand & execute the slaves without waiting the action of the court." Orange County sheriff Hugh Guthrie urged Vance to expedite the trial in order to pacify the panicked white populace. A young Wilmington refugee living in Laurinburg remembered that in early 1865 they uncovered "a dreadful plot . . . among the negroes to murder the white people and take possession of their property." Some white Piedmont residents sought to relocate themselves further west because of the threat posed by the increased slave population in central North Carolina. One Caswell County man wrote to a relative in Cherokee County that "if I go to the war, Fannie speaks of going up to the mountains and staying until I return as it is much safer up there than it is here as there is so many negroes here."[45]

These episodes of slave violence suggest that refugeed slaves were emboldened to forcefully resist their own enslavement. The case of Henrietta, one of Josiah Collins's slaves, is illustrative. With her six children, Henrietta was among the slaves that Collins removed from Washington County to his Hurry Scurry plantation in the Piedmont. Starting in early January 1863, Collins received several requests to hire house servants. Dr. F. M. Hubbard, a particularly persistent correspondent from Chapel Hill, wrote no fewer than five letters in January and February 1863, requesting to rent a capable cook, as his own "is an old woman—nearly seventy as I suppose—who is not infrequently disabled by her infirmities" and his only alternative was "putting my wife & daughters in the kitchen to roast & boil. I have no prospect of any cook but Henrietta, except as I have indicated: nor do I see how I can do well without one."[46] Somewhat reluctantly, Collins rented Henrietta to Hubbard in February 1863, separating her from her children.

Only three months later, however, Collins received a letter from Hubbard indicating that "I desire to return Henrietta to your keeping." Hubbard cited several reasons for no longer wishing to employ Henrietta. First, he noted that "I do not think she is happy or contented here, though she has little to do & I have tried to make her comfortable. She would do better, I think, among her old associates." Undoubtedly, Henrietta's separation from her children and other family members made her sullen. Second, Hubbard cited "the difficulty of providing food & clothing for my household. My salary has gone down, & prices have gone up so far beyond my expectation, & are like[ly] to go much higher, that I really fear I can not long continue to feed even all the mouths that I must now provide for." Like many residents of the central Piedmont, Hubbard was bearing the stress of rampant wartime inflation. He hoped that Collins was "ready to receive her again, as you were not desirous to part with her. If so I will return her to you whenever you may choose, & make such compensation for her services as you may think right." When Collins did not respond promptly to Hubbard's letter, Henrietta took matters into her own hands. In a tersely worded letter, Hubbard informed Collins that he was returning Henrietta immediately. "I return Henrietta to your keeping today," he wrote. "I should of course have waited till I had heard from you, but for the fact that my kitchen was set on fire yesterday morning, & I suspect by her agency. I am not willing to keep even for a day one of whom I have such apprehensions. I hope you will excuse . . . the lack of ceremony in my return of her to you."[47]

Refugeed slaves also appear to have run away in disproportionate numbers. Advertisements for fugitive slaves published in Piedmont newspapers between 1862 and 1865 suggest that slaves removed from eastern North Carolina often attempted to flee to Union lines, despite the considerable distance intended to mitigate such flight. An advertisement in the *Fayetteville Observer* announced in 1863 that a slave refugeed to Anson County had run away and that his owner believed he would "endeavor to get to the Yankees, having been raised, I think, somewhere in Eastern North Carolina." Similarly, the *Daily Confederate* in Raleigh speculated that a runaway slave in Graham would "endeavor to reach Newbern, where he was raised." While most refugeed slaves who ran away sought freedom by fleeing to Union-occupied eastern North Carolina, others attempted to reconnect with family members relocated elsewhere in central North Carolina. In June 1864 a refugee slave owner in Bladen County thought that a twenty-five-year-old slave who had recently run away "may be making his way up to Lincolnton, as his wife has been recently taken there [by her owner] . . . or he may be trying to get to the yankees." Similarly, a slave owner in Guilford County advertised in 1864 that a teenage male slave had run away. According to the advertisement, Orman had "formerly belonged to Col. Clark, of Newbern, but has been living in the counties of Alamance and Guilford since the commencement of the war. He has a wife living in Graham, and will probably be found lurking in that vicinity. He intimated to the balance of the negroes, some weeks ago, that he intended to go to the Yankees, and will perhaps, try to make his way to them."[48]

Rented refugeed slaves were particularly likely to run away, especially those rented to railroads, because of poor working conditions and inadequate supervision.[49] In late April 1864 the Raleigh and Gaston Railroad advertised a reward of fifty dollars for the return of a runaway rented slave; weeks later the High Shoals Iron Works in Gaston County offered seventy-five dollars for three runaways who had been rented from a Beaufort County refugee.[50] A month later, the Endor Iron Works in Chatham County advertised that two rented slaves had escaped, including "a desperate negro called Charles Hunter, who committed an assault on our Overseer and stole from him one of Colt's Navy Pistols, with which he is now armed."[51] In November 1864 the *Western Democrat* in Charlotte ran an advertisement for a runaway slave named Dick who had in the previous two years been rented to the North Carolina Railroad; the Wilmington, Charlotte, and Rutherford Railroad; and the Navy Yard in Charlotte.[52]

Refugee planters and slave renters complained that more passive forms of slave resistance also proliferated, especially work slowdowns. George Foushee complained to William Pettigrew that a slave he had rented, a cook named Mary Jane, was perpetually ill. During her first three weeks as Foushee's cook, she rendered "very little service." From his observations, Foushee concluded that "she don't seem to be very bad off, just sick enough to keep [her] from work," leading him to wonder if "a good deal of it is deception." Many rented slaves ran away to return to their owners and their families. Less than a week after he had rented out a slave boy to a neighbor, Rev. Henry Smith of Greensboro was surprised to find that he had returned. Reverend Smith recorded in his diary that Jim "complains of being sick ... [and] is very unwilling to go back." Over the next two months, Jim ran away from his renter at least three times, each time returning to Reverend Smith. Rufus Patterson reported "a general spirit of devilment" among slaves in Lenoir. "I deem it best to be constantly on the lookout. Our negroes need watching."[53]

Slave discipline seems to have relaxed somewhat in the war's final years, especially among slave renters, who often felt that they lacked the authority to discipline slaves and worried that forceful correction might encourage slaves to run away. While these concessions may have enabled slave renters to maintain some authority over an increasingly restless refugeed slave population, they undermined slave masters' claims to absolute authority over their slaves. As historian Stephen Ash has noted, "every concession granted to keep blacks at home, every appeal to argument instead of the whip, marked the further ebbing of the life force of the peculiar institution."[54]

White refugees had more to worry about than the erosion of mastery. The crowded conditions in the North Carolina Piedmont provided fertile ground for the spread of epidemic disease. The movement of millions of soldiers and civilians created vectors for contagious diseases, especially smallpox, while poor sanitation contributed to the spread of typhoid fever. The specter of disease loomed strongest in urban areas where thousands of refugees congregated. In January 1863 army chaplain A. W. Mangum reported that "the small pox is raging all about" Goldsboro. In September 1864 the *Fayetteville Observer* reported on a significant smallpox outbreak in Caswell County. A resident wrote that "the small pox is raging in our midst. . . . It has spread to a fearful extent, and I fear has become an epidemic." The newspaper noted that the epidemic seemed to be most virulent among slaves and that vaccination appeared to offer little immunity to the disease. A refugee living in Yanceyville, the largest town in Caswell County, observed that, "in addition to all the war troubles, we are surrounded with the smallpox." Throughout 1863 and 1864 Raleigh had repeated smallpox outbreaks. In March 1863 newspapers reported ten to fifteen cases and at least seven deaths from smallpox just north of Raleigh. In January 1864, because "the Small Pox has again appeared in the City of Raleigh," North Carolina surgeon general Dr. Edward Warren offered vaccinations "free of charge." By June 1864 newspapers were reporting that "there has been no time for eighteen months that we have not had small pox in Raleigh, and we believe the same may be said of Charlotte and other communities in the State. War always brings plague, pestilence and famine; in the small pox and other troubles that have afflicted us we have the plague and pestilence, while the famine is at the very threshold of thousands of families." The prevalence of disease in urban areas persuaded many white refugees to seek healthier environments. A refugee teacher from Virginia living in Concord, just north of Charlotte, wrote to a prospective employer in the eastern Piedmont that he sought a new home, as he had suffered "very much since I have been here from the typhoid and ague and fever." In his letter, the refugee teacher pressed his prospective employer about conditions near his new home: "Is your section subject to ague and fever? Have you good water?" Although disease proved less deadly among Piedmont refugees than it did among their counterparts in coastal North Carolina, its prevalence was partially a result of refugees' mobility and overcrowded living conditions.[55]

Many white refugee men discovered that leaving their homes not only challenged their livelihood, claims to mastery, and health but also undermined some of their rights of citizenship. By moving to the North Carolina Piedmont, many refugees became effectively disenfranchised. In July 1863 the North Carolina General Assembly passed a measure to clarify the voting rights of refugees. According to "An Act to Enable Refugees and Others to Vote for Members of Congress," refugees who could not vote in their home counties because of their occupation by the "public enemy" could vote "in the counties where they temporarily reside," but only so long as that county was within their congressional district. The measure did not create a mechanism for refugees temporarily living outside of their home congressional district to vote, effectively stripping most refugees of their suffrage. Of North Carolina's ten congressional districts at the time of the bill's passage, one was almost entirely under Union control and two others had a heavy Federal presence. For refugees from these counties to vote, they had to return home, where they would risk facing the dangers that had caused them to become refugees in the first place. Just prior to election day in November 1863, the *North Carolina Standard* reminded the many refugees in Raleigh that "refugees can vote for Congress in any County within the District in which they claim citizenship, but not out of it." The newspaper encouraged "refugees from the 2d and 3d Districts to be sure to return" as "the contest will be close, and a few votes" would likely decide the result of the elections. As predicted, voter turnout in the 1863 elections was very low, especially in the three coastal districts partially or wholly under Union occupation. The vast majority of votes cast in these races came not from refugees but from soldiers, who were allowed to vote in their camps. In the First Congressional District, representing the northeasternmost corner of the state, only 2,360 votes were cast, divided between four candidates. Refugees who came to North Carolina from outside the state had stronger legal protections for the ballot. In April 1863 the Confederate Congress passed a measure that allowed refugees from Virginia, Tennessee, and Louisiana, "driven from his home by the public enemy," to vote in military camps.[56] How many refugees availed themselves of this option, however, remains difficult to ascertain.

Although voting proved difficult, many refugees remained actively politically engaged. White refugees in the North Carolina Piedmont and their political representatives urged continuing the war long after many of their neighbors had soured on the conflict. By the summer of 1863, many native residents of the Piedmont had come to the conclusion that a Confederate military victory was unlikely and that the most viable resolution was a negotiated settlement with the North, a settlement that might preserve slavery even if it did not secure Confederate independence. Many Piedmont natives rallied around peace movement advocates such as Bryan Tyson, James Leach, and William Woods Holden, the last of whom emerged as the movement's leader and eventually its gubernatorial candidate. As the editor of Raleigh's *North Carolina Standard*, Holden had initially supported secession and served as an unofficial spokesman for Governor Zebulon Vance, only to break with Vance over the merits of continuing to fight after Confederate losses at Gettysburg and Vicksburg. The growing peace movement in the North Carolina Piedmont also provided a vehicle for opposing unpopular Confederate policies, especially conscription and burdensome taxation. The peace movement's opposition to conscription may have emboldened draft dodgers and deserters, who became a conspicuous presence in the Piedmont, especially in the western Piedmont counties of Guilford, Randolph, Forsyth, and Davidson, sometime known as the Quaker Belt. In the fall of 1863, peace movement candidates took six of North Carolina's ten seats in the Confederate Congress, including all of the Piedmont seats.[57]

In contrast to the enthusiasm with which Piedmont natives embraced the peace movement, white refugees in the Piedmont continued to support an aggressive prosecution of the war. With their homes under Union occupation and many of their slaves now living in Union refugee camps, refugees had little to gain from a negotiated settlement. Indeed, only a Confederate victory that included a reoccupation of territory taken by Union armies would allow refugees to return to their prewar prosperity. In the 1863 congressional elections, North Carolina's refugee districts (those under Union occupation) reelected pro-war candidates. While North Carolina's delegates in Richmond generally supported some form of negotiated peace after 1863, the representatives of the refugee districts, William N. H. Smith and Robert R. Bridgers, continued to push for independence through victory on the battlefield. Indeed, roll-call analysis of the Confederate Congress indicates that representatives from Union-occupied districts provided some of the strongest voices for an aggressive military policy and support for taxation and conscription. The political divide between refugees and native residents of the Piedmont culminated in the 1864 gubernatorial election between sitting governor Zebulon Vance and peace advocate William Woods Holden.[58] While the native population split fairly evenly between Vance and Holden, refugees overwhelming sided with Vance, whom many refugees believed provided the best available route to reclaiming their homes and property. In March 1864 the *Raleigh Weekly Progress* reported on "a meeting of the refugees from the counties East of the Chowan river" that endorsed Governor Vance in his reelection campaign, believing him alone capable of "guid[ing] the 'Old Ship of State' through the rough waves of a great revolution." In May 1864 the *Raleigh Daily Confederate* published "A Card to the Citizens, Soldiers, and Refugees of Pasquotank County, NC" from George Hinton, a candidate to be the county's representative in the state legislature. Unable to communicate directly with many of his constituents, who were scattered throughout the state or in military service, Hinton relied on newspapers to disseminate his message. Among other issues, Hinton expressed his opposition to a peace convention and his support for Governor Vance.[59] For George Hinton and the refugees he hoped to represent, nothing less than a continuation of the war effort, regardless of the costs, was acceptable.

While white refugee men found themselves shut out from the political process, white refugee women found themselves cut off from government relief aimed at helping soldiers' wives. Starting in December 1862, the North Carolina legislature passed a series of acts "for the Relief of the Wives and Families of Soldiers in the Army." Administered through county governments, the relief legislation allocated funds based on the white population in 1860. Underfunded and poorly managed, these relief efforts provided inadequate assistance to soldiers' families, many of whom never received aid.[60]

Refugee women and their children found themselves almost entirely excluded from these relief efforts. County governments routinely denied aid to refugee families if their soldier had enlisted in another county, giving preference to local soldiers' families. The Richmond County Relief Committee for Volunteers' Families, for instance, regularly refused to provide aid for any refugee woman whose "husband is not a volunteer of this County." In theory, the relief legislation provided that soldiers' families from Union-occupied counties could apply to a poor-relief commissioner from their home county, although there is little evidence that these commissioners were ever appointed. Nor could refugees seek aid if their home county was within Confederate lines, as many counties adopted policies limiting aid to those in residence. Adjacent Montgomery County refused to aid a family who had relocated to Richmond County, claiming that "it's not in accordance to their rules to assist families out of the County." The Richmond County Relief Committee lamented that many soldiers' families suffered because of these jurisdictional boundaries, noting that "it is desirable some uniform rule on this subject should be established." Responding to such concerns, the North Carolina legislature amended the relief legislation to clarify the eligibility of refugee families, such that "when any family of a soldier ... shall have removed from the county of his residence since the commencement of the war and shall have acquired a residence in another county, they shall be considered residents of the latter county and receive a share of such distribution." Despite this modification, however, many country relief committees, facing limited resources, continued to favor local families over refugees. By the end of the war, counties such as Wake, Orange, and Guilford that had sizable refugee populations became overwhelmed by indigent soldiers' families, some of whom went to the courts after being turned down for relief. In 1864 a soldier's wife from Rowan County successful argued in Wake County Court of Pleas and Quarter Sessions that she and her children should be eligible for "provisions ... as indigent soldiers family."[61]

Refugees continued to pour into the Piedmont during the war's final months. In January 1865 the mayor of Greensboro wrote to Governor Vance that his city had become "fill[ed] with strangers."[62] Union general William Tecumseh Sherman's invasion of South Carolina in February and March 1865 prompted thousands of South Carolinians to flee northward. Already overcrowded communities in the North Carolina Piedmont worried that the arrival of new refugees would overwhelm their scanty supply of housing and food. Anticipating that South Carolina refugees would inundate Charlotte, the *Western Democrat* urged potential refugees to remain at home. Only days before Columbia surrendered to Sherman, the newspaper declared, "We think it bad policy for families of women and children to leave their homes at the approach of the enemy." Instead, they should "remain at their own homes as long as they are permitted to do so. We know it is risky to stay, but it is also a serious risk to leave home with no certainty of finding shelter elsewhere. The interior towns are now crowded to overflowing, and vacant houses are not to be had. It is so in this place, and we learn the same is the case elsewhere."[63]

The siege and eventual burning of Columbia created a mass exodus northward, with the majority of refugees headed toward Charlotte. Among those who fled Columbia in advance of Sherman's army was Lydia Johnston, the wife of Confederate general Joseph E. Johnston. She remembered the chaos in the city, with "the poor people flying almost terror stricken to know what they could do—many leaving with only little bundles of clothes." Lydia Johnston left Columbia on the last train departing the city, hearing the "roar of the cannon in our ears" as the train left the depot. The journey north from Columbia to Charlotte took much longer than usual, as the overburdened locomotive managed to attain speeds only slightly faster than walking pace. When they arrived in Charlotte, Lydia Johnston and three hundred other refugee women aboard the train searched for shelter, but "none of us able to get rooms. . . . The sight of this town to-day is lamentable: women hunting in every direction for shelter—and the people themselves beginning to move off for a safer place." Cornelia Phillips Spencer noted that the "smoke of burning Columbia" sent into flight thousands of "panic-stricken refugees, homeless and penniless" who "brought every day fresh tales of havoc and ruin."[64]

Although most of the refugees fleeing Columbia were women and children, the refugee hegira included the editor of the *Daily South Carolinian*, who temporarily opened shop in the offices of the *Charlotte Bulletin*. In the final weeks of the war, the *Daily South Carolinian* published intermittent issues from Charlotte, some of which have survived. Less than a week after the burning of Columbia, the editor announced that "the publication of this journal having been resumed in Charlotte we shall continue, as heretofore, to give the latest and fullest intelligence of passing events." The editor claimed that he now ran the only daily newspaper representing the interests of South Carolinians. He hoped that the newspaper could serve as a social network for South Carolina refugees in Charlotte, noting, "If any of the citizens of Columbia or Charleston, now here as refugees, will send their address to this office, they will confer a favor on friends who may desire to find them. We propose to establish a directory for the use of all such, and shall endeavor to make our office headquarters for 'news from home.'"[65] As only two other issues of the *Daily South Carolinian* survive from their incarnation in Charlotte, it is impossible to say whether the proposed refugee directory ever came to fruition. It reflected, however, refugees' desire to maintain connections with their home and with each other.

A week after Sherman's assault on Columbia, with the city now in ashes, the *Western Democrat* noted that "Charlotte is now overrun with refugees. It is almost, if not quite, impossible to obtain shelter for those already here, and we hear that a large number of others are expected. Under the circumstances we think it nothing but right, that those abroad who may be fleeing the enemy, should be made acquainted with the state of affairs here, in order that they may seek refuge elsewhere." The newspaper claimed that Charlotte residents "have done and will do all that they can to assist the unfortunate, be they rich or poor, but they are now overtaxed, and we would therefore, in all kindness, advise those who may be leaving their homes, to go to the country, or some place other than Charlotte.... This town was crowded before the enemy advanced on Columbia, and consequentially it was impossible to accommodate many refugees from that direction." One Charlotte resident claimed that refugees arriving from Columbia occupied all available housing, noting that "my house is a perfect hotel." She complained that refugees consumed not only space but scarce provisions: "I have nearly exhausted all I have to eat—my eggs but few left—and very little flour—I feel worn out." Margaret Burwell, who ran Charlotte Female Institute with her husband, wrote in February 1865 that "there is the greatest crowd of refugees from South Carolina pouring into Charlotte, we are importuned every day to take Boarders, [that] I hate to hear the bell ring. I feel sorry for them but still I can't love my neighbors better than myself, & I really have as much as I can do now, & provisions are not to be had, price go up every day, eggs were five dollars a doz yesterday, today they are six."[66]

Many Charlotte residents and refugees feared that their city would be Sherman's next target. In late February 1865 Rev. A. W. Mangum wrote to his sister from Salisbury, not far from Charlotte, that "we are now in the mist of the worst features of the war. Day after day, it is thought that Sherman has been moving on Charlotte & this place since last Friday. First the refugees & plunder from Columbia scattered far and near along the road, crowding Charlotte particularly to its utmost capacity." Mangum had heard that the Confederate government had ordered all government property be removed from Charlotte and Salisbury, suggesting that it did not expect to hold the region. He noted that "night and day the citizens here are running off things or burying them." Fearing Union occupation, many retreated farther into the interior, leaving Charlotte for Greensboro. A Confederate soldier stationed near Greensboro noted that "the people of Charlotte is ... coming into Greensboro. This country is full of refugees. All of the valuable property that is easy to move is a coming and is in Greensboro."[67]

Sherman's army did not head north from Columbia to Charlotte but turned east toward Fayetteville, entering North Carolina during the first week of March 1865. On March 11, 1865, Sherman's forces occupied Fayetteville, with much of the town's civilian population fleeing. Their number included many refugees who had come to Fayetteville from coastal North Carolina. In a letter published in the *Raleigh Weekly Progress*, "A Refugee" described the "evacuation of Fayetteville," noting that after Confederate officials urged civilians to leave the town, "loved ones separated; fathers embracing their children; husbands and wives parted—but I must stop. The grief of such partings is too sacred for the public eye.... The confusion among citizens was, of course, intense."[68]

From Fayetteville, Sherman marched northwest toward Goldsboro, another community crowded with refugees. Among them were eighteen-year-old Elizabeth Collier's extended family (including her grandmother and her aunt), who had come to Everettsville, just south of Goldsboro, in August 1861 after the capture of Hatteras Island. According to her diary, Collier and her extended clan lived in her family's house until the occupation of Fayetteville. On March 11, 1865, she noted that "everybody is in the wildest state of excitement—Goldsboro is to be evacuated in less than 24 hours—Sherman has occupied Fayetteville." Delayed by the battles of Averasboro and Bentonville, on March 23, 1865, Sherman rendezvoused at Goldsboro with reinforcements who had marched from Wilmington, including nine regiments of U.S. Colored Troops. Rather than immediately march west on Raleigh, Sherman decided to rest and resupply his fatigued soldiers at Goldsboro. Foragers from Sherman's army visited the Collier residence shortly after their arrival in the area. Elizabeth Collier chronicled in her diary that foragers repeatedly confronted the women in the household (her father having taken to the woods when Union soldiers arrived), demanding food and threatening violence to body and property if not obeyed. Finding that their small town was "filled with Yankees & that they were plundering the houses," the Colliers secured a Union soldier to guard their house, although bummers looted "every thing out doors ... all provisions taken—fences knocked down—horses, cow, carriages & buggies stolen & every thing else the wretches could lay their hands on—even to the servants clothes." On March 27, when bummers eventually gained entrance to their home, Collier wrote, "Now they commenced their sacking of the house & did not cease until they had taken everything to eat the house contained." When told that the bummers would return later that night to burn the house down, Elizabeth Collier and her family fled to a neighbor's house and, when that residence came under threat, to Goldsboro. There Collier applied to Union general John M. Schofield for a pass to cross into Confederate lines. Although granted the pass, Collier and her mother were permitted to take only two trunks with them. Surprisingly, Elizabeth Collier, the formerly wealthy daughter of slaveholders, did not despair over having to abandon most of her worldly belongings but rejoiced when she saw Confederate soldiers again, noting in her diary that "I really do not think I was ever so happy in all my life, as I was when I first saw our men—rebel soldiers in the grey jackets." Like many refugees, Collier and her family went to Hillsborough, where they stayed until the end of the conflict.[69]

The final weeks of the war made even Piedmont natives into potential refugees. In early March 1865, Lucy Bryan, a Raleigh native, wrote to her friend and old classmate Sue Capehart, a refugee from Bertie County living in Granville County, less than forty miles to the north. She revealed that Raleigh residents worried about Sherman's inevitable march west from Fayetteville to the state capitol, as "everybody seems to be in a state of excitement about the Yankees." Bryan claimed that she tried not to obsess about their imminent arrival, though the tone of her letter suggests that she failed in this effort. She also distinguished between her own situation and that of her friend, who had experienced difficulty in securing housing in the Piedmont, noting that "I know you feel so good, having a home of your own, how disagreeable it must be to be a refugee. We have certainly been particularly blessed in that respect, for which I am more than thankful." Three weeks later Lucy Bryan faced the prospect of becoming a refugee herself. She wrote to Sue Capehart on March 23, 1863, that she had been "busy packing up my 'rags' (for they are not much more) to get away from the Yankees. I have not had time to do anything scarcely."[70]

Most Piedmont residents, both refugees and natives, knew that their options for eluding the approaching Union army were limited. By the end of March 1865, not only was Sherman's army, more than ninety thousand strong, preparing to march west from Goldsboro, but Union raids led by Gen. George Stoneman had entered North Carolina from the west. Frequently dividing his forces, numbering some six thousand soldiers, Stoneman attacked Boone on March 28 and by April 10 had forced the surrender of Salem and Winston in the western Piedmont. Bounded by

Sherman in the east and Stoneman in the west, refugees and natives in the central Piedmont had nowhere left to go.

Despite these limited options, some Piedmont refugees and natives engaged in a frantic scrabble to put as much distance between themselves and Union troops as possible. With the boundaries of the Confederacy contracting around them, these refugees faced increasingly narrow choices about where they could run. The plight of Tennessee refugee Dr. J. G. M. Ramsey reflected the futile efforts that many refugees took to avoid becoming ensnared by the Union noose. Like many Charlotte residents, Dr. Ramsey believed that Charlotte would be Sherman's next target after Columbia. He noted that "Sherman was advancing through and desolating South Carolina and my office was in such danger as to lead me to prepare for a further hegira." Ramsey wrote to his wife that he "was going to, I knew not where, but that Sherman should not get either me or my money if I could help it." Holding bank reserves that he had brought from Knoxville, Ramsey buried his "treasure" in the secluded banks of the Catawba River, then took a train north to Greensboro, where his train broke down. There, in early April, he heard "rumors of the approaching crisis at Richmond" and of Stoneman's raid near Salem. Although Greensboro had been considered one of the safest and most secure locations within the Confederacy, this news brought about "a general stampede from Greensboro." What location could be safer than Greensboro, however, was unclear, as "we could get no further north and very little further south." Ramsey decided that west remained the only viable option and made his way to Salisbury. There he found that "every public and private house was full of people.... At the mansion house I found a small space between the feet of a small table unoccupied. I crept into it. The entire floor of the room was covered over with men, some snoring, some drunk, some sober. I slept little and rested none." His wife, Margaret Ramsey, who remained in Concord, just north of Charlotte, reflected in her diary on how the war had dispersed her family. On April 16, 1865, less than a week after her husband desperately huddled under a table in Salisbury, she noted that "now the household [was] scattered, no two together." Her children were spread across the country and "their father I know not where."[71]

Longtime Piedmont refugees recognized that Sherman's march into North Carolina meant the war was nearing its end and that no place within the Confederacy would be safe. The Cronly family, which had left Wilmington for Laurinburg in 1862, heard "rumors of the burning of Columbia and the terrible sufferings" of its residents. The news "greatly alarmed us, for we now fully realized that there was no escape for us from the same fearful visitation." They also worried about the behavior of their slaves. Although the Cronlys' slaves "performed their daily duties as usual ... they often had meetings at each others houses and were no doubt better posted as to Sherman's movement than" their owners. Indeed, the Cronlys suspected that their slaves engaged in clandestine "communications with the enemy."[72]

Refugees prepared both physically and psychologically for the eventual arrival of Union soldiers. Many refugees hid their valuables either on their person or in clandestine caches, burying their jewelry and silverware late at night, often worrying that their slaves would reveal its location. Stationed with his unit in defense of Petersburg, William Blount Rodman instructed his wife about what to do were Union soldiers to take Greensboro, where she had lived with their children as refugees since 1862. Although he thought it unlikely that the Confederacy would allow Greensboro to fall, he urged her to "have on hand at all times corn enough to feed the family on for about a month." If Union soldiers visited, she should "remain at home in the house, be calm, dignified and civil. If you can see any officer ask him for protection. Give them what they ask for if you have it, because they can take it. Conceal your jewelry about your person." Rodman tried to assuage his wife's fears about what would happen were Union soldiers to visit, noting that "I do not think you would be in any personal danger. I have never heard in all their raids and robberies of any personal injury done to a lady. Calmness and a dignified lady like bearing will tell on the rudest men as well as on gentlemen."[73]

Anticipating that Sherman's forces would occupy Raleigh within a month, Rev. Drury Lacy wrote to reassure his daughter in March 1865 that he and his wife were safe, saying, "Raleigh is considerably stirred up about the Yankees, though I have seen nothing like a panic." Although some people had fled Raleigh and government supplies were being relocated to Greensboro, Lacy noted that "I don't think of being a refugee, unless they occupy the place & compel everyone to take the oath. I shall have then to take my leave." Three weeks later Lacy again wrote to his daughter, saying, "We are at the edge of the Crater and it is crumbling beneath our feet every moment. Sherman's army are expected here some time this week.... If the enemy should come this week this is probably the last letter you will receive from me unless they in their vindictiveness banish me from the City, which they may do unless I take &

subscribe the Oath which I think they will inflict upon all who remain in the City."[74]

The final influx of refugees into the North Carolina Piedmont came during the fall of Petersburg and the evacuation of Richmond. On March 29, 1865, Jefferson Davis put his wife, Varina, their children, and a small entourage on a train bound for Charlotte, while he stayed in Richmond for the inevitable final assault of Union forces on Lee's army at Petersburg. At her husband's direction, Varina Davis brought very little with her, although he did provide her with a small purse of gold coins and a pistol for self-protection, instructing her on how to load and fire the weapon. Just before she boarded the train, Jefferson Davis told her that since she "cannot remain undisturbed in our own country," once in Charlotte, she should "make for the Florida coast and from there board a ship to a foreign country." For Varina Davis, this journey would mark her second iteration as a refugee in the North Carolina Piedmont, having spent the summer of 1862 in Raleigh during the Peninsula Campaign. Because of the poor state of the rolling stock and rail lines between Richmond and Charlotte, her journey took four days. Indeed, her train broke down shortly after it left Richmond, forcing her to spend the night aboard. Her route south, a route used less than a week later by her husband and most of the Confederate cabinet, took her over the Danville connection, the recently constructed but already worn-out railroad link between Danville, Virginia, and Greensboro, built primarily by refugeed slaves from eastern North Carolina. On April 1, 1865, en route to Charlotte, Varina Davis wrote to her husband from Greensboro that "rumors numerous & not defined" of Union raids engulfed the city. She expected that her party would be able to make it to Charlotte unhindered. In Charlotte Varina Davis rented a modest house from Abram Weill, a Jewish merchant. She encountered many other prominent Confederate refugees in Charlotte, including Lydia Johnston, the wife of Gen. Joseph Johnston, Myra Semmes, the wife of Confederate senator Thomas J. Semmes, and Confederate senator Louis T. Wigfall, who had fled Richmond with his family in early March 1865. There Varina Davis awaited information about the situation in Richmond.

Only a few days after her arrival in Charlotte, Varina Davis received word that Richmond had fallen and that her husband had evacuated. "The news of Richmond," she wrote her husband, "came upon me like the 'abomination of desolation.'" Jefferson Davis himself left Richmond on April 2, 1865, accompanied by the Confederate cabinet, after receiving a telegram from Robert E. Lee that he was abandoning Petersburg, twenty-five miles south of Richmond. His overloaded train made slow progress out of Richmond to Danville, where Davis sent a telegram to his wife alerting her of his departure from Richmond. Davis stayed in Danville less than a week, until news reached him that General Lee had surrendered at Appomattox Courthouse. From Danville, Davis moved fifty miles south to Greensboro, close to General Johnston's headquarters. Like the thousands of refugees then living in Greensboro, Davis hoped that this Piedmont city would isolate him from the threat of Union armies. Davis also hoped that Greensboro could serve as a temporary capitol for the Confederacy, from which he and the rest of the cabinet could devise a plan to continue the war. The Greensboro railroad depot operated as a de facto Confederate office, with many cabinet members residing in the train coaches. Davis himself stayed with the family of John Taylor Wood, his nephew and aide, whose wife and children had come to Greensboro as refugees. Receiving a hostile welcome from locals, who worried about the consequences if the Confederate president were captured in their town, and after receiving repeated disillusioning reports on the military situation, Davis and the rest of mobile Confederate government moved on to Charlotte. In the intervening days since Varina Davis had traveled from Greensboro to Charlotte, Stoneman's cavalry had cut the railroad lines between the towns, forcing the presidential entourage to travel by horse and wagon.

Jefferson Davis and his party arrived in Charlotte on April 18. He discovered upon his arrival that Varina Davis and their children had already moved on to South Carolina, because, as she wrote her husband, "rumors of a raid on Charlotte induced me to decide to come this side of Charlotte." As in Greensboro, Davis received a cool welcome in Charlotte, unable to find shelter except in a modest house owned by a Northern-born merchant, because of "a threat made by Stoneman's troopers to burn every house giving refuge to Jefferson Davis." While waiting to meet with his host, Davis received a telegram informing him of Abraham Lincoln's assassination. As Davis pondered the telegram's implications, a gathering crowd of soldiers and civilians demanded that he make a speech, one that ended up being one of his final public addresses as president of the Confederacy. The crowd undoubtedly included refugees who sought shelter in one of the few locations still nominally under Confederate control. Davis warned them of a coming "very great disaster," presumably a reference to Johnston's impending surrender to Sherman, then being negotiated at the Bennett homestead, just east of Hillsborough. Thanking his audience for their enthusiasm and apologizing for not being able to deliver better news, Davis called himself "a refugee from the capital of the country." Davis's self-identification as a refugee indicates how persuasive the refugee experience was in the Confederacy. Indeed, for the president of the Confederacy to label himself a refugee suggests that by the end of the war, it had become a confederacy of refugees.[75]

FIVE

In Good Hands, in a Safe Place

When Greensboro Female College opened its doors for the fall term in July 1863, Rev. Turner Jones, the school's president, proudly proclaimed that "every room in the building was engaged, many applications for rooms by letter, had been declined, and quite a number, who applied in person for admission, were under the necessity of returning home. A large faculty had been secured." Over the previous two years, the school's enrollment had doubled, now exceeding 240 students, with many of them coming from war-torn parts of the Confederacy. A local newspaper observed that the school flourished "mid the ravages of war, not only holds its course, but outstrips itself even in the days of prosperous peace." Looking forward to another academic year, Reverend Jones reflected that "apart from the uncertainties hanging over the future, in consequence of the fact that the storm of war was raging around us in the distance, the outlook was very encouraging."[1]

Less than a month after the start of the new school year, students were awoken at midnight by fire bells. The fire had started in the kitchens and quickly spread to the adjacent main school building, where the students and teachers lived. One student remembered being awakened by the screams of her classmates: "All was now confusion where but a few hours ago all had been so calm. Never, never shall I forget with what feelings of horror I sprang from my bed, for those cries.... The College was on fire and full of sleeping girls." Some of them fled outside in their nightclothes; others struggled to carry their trunks, ones they "could not have lifted at another time. Others were hurling them down the stairs, others throwing them from the windows." Miraculously, none of the students or teachers were hurt in the fire. Before sunrise, however, the structure itself was consumed in the flames, leaving "the whole building ... in a heap of ruins." The students, ranging in age from twelve to nineteen, huddled outside in their nightgowns and watched as their school was reduced to rubble. One student noted that her horror was mixed with awe, as the school became a "huge burning mass, when the flames had fully spread o'er it, clasping the tall pillars with their fiery arms, hissing and roaring like wild demons in their fury."

News of the fire spread quickly, and girls' parents and relatives rushed to Greensboro to retrieve them, though some girls had to stay with local families for several weeks because of delays in mail and transportation. Reverend Jones attempted to secure alternative locations to reopen the school, either in Greensboro or at one of the three dozen other female academies in the North Carolina Piedmont, quickly discovering that a building adequate for more than 240 students could not be acquired for any price. Most of the students managed to secure positions at other female academies, many of them transferring to Warrenton Female College. One newspaper worried that "the burning of Greensboro College will increase the crowd at other schools." The school's administration made concerted efforts after the fire to rebuild. By 1865 an intensive fundraising effort had amassed enough money to begin construction on a new building. "A large quantity of lumber" and more than half a million bricks had been secured with the intention of reopening the school in the fall. However, lamented Reverend Jones, "the change in the condition of the country, caused by the close of the war, arrested the progress of the work. Our money lost its value. Bond and accounts became, for the most part, worthless. The building materials were taken by the Federal army, and, of necessity, the enterprise was temporarily abandoned." The school would not reopen until 1873.[2]

The Civil War had a devastating effect on higher education in the South. As young men joined the Confederate ranks, the enrollment of men's institutions dropped precipitously, leading many schools and colleges to close, with those remaining open serving only a fraction of their antebellum enrollment. Most women's schools fared little better, with female academies across the South closing their doors for the duration of the conflict, due to low enrollment, financial insolvency, or appropriation by Confederate forces to be used as hospitals. Many Southerners worried that the war could create an entire generation of uneducated men and women.[3] A widely reprinted editorial from May 1861 lamented, "It is deeply to be regretted that the present disturbed state of affairs is having such a disastrous effect upon the schools of the country. Several of our most flourishing institutions of learning, both male and female, either have already suspended or are expecting shortly to suspend. It is of the utmost importance that our schools should be maintained, and that our children should be educated."[4]

North Carolina's female academies proved the exception to this rule. Not only did the female academies in North Carolina remain open and financially viable during the Civil War, but their enrollment increased significantly during this period, often to double their antebellum levels. North Carolina's female academies flourished during the Civil War because they became seen as places of refuge, sites where parents could send their teenage daughters away from the front lines. Located primarily in the Piedmont, more than three dozen female academies in North Carolina survived and even prospered when so many educational institutions in the Confederacy closed their doors. Despite efforts by teachers and principals to maintain a sense of normality for their refugee students and operate their schools as if their nascent country were not fighting for its independence, the war had a significant effect on the students who attended these female academies. While at school, these young women were physically and psychologically separated from both their homes and the front lines. They sought to make sense of a world that was changing rapidly around them, yet from which they were comparatively isolated within the confines of female academies.

Although the more than five thousand young women who studied, lived, and came of age at female academies in North Carolina saw themselves as refugees, their experiences differed significantly from those of most other refugees. Most notably, they did not suffer from the severe shortages of food and housing that plagued other refugees. Despite the material differences that separated them from most other refugees in the Piedmont, the students, their parents, and their teachers maintained that they were refugees. Many students, such as Lucie Malone, a Salem Female Academy student from Alabama, described themselves and many of their classmates as "refugees." Malone was proud to call herself a refugee, later writing that her friends at school included many "other refugees & among them two from Newberne, NC, nieces of a sea Captain, Capt. Wallace, who ran the blockade to Bermuda & England." The head teachers at North Carolina's female academies were regularly praised for sheltering refugee students. Richard Henry Battle lauded St. Mary's principal, Rev.

Aldert Smedes, for his leadership, noting that "during the war its rooms and dormitories were crowded as never before," including "a number of refugees." Margaret Burwell of Charlotte Female Institute received similar commendation: "In addition to her large household of pupils Mrs. Burwell extended her limits to their utmost capacity to receive the girl refugees who sought safety from an invading army." So too did Salem Female Academy's Rev. Robert de Schweinitz, who was praised for his ability to keep the school open and running, as it was "no light task to feed and clothe and protect 250 or 300 pupils in this establishment, many of them refugees from different parts of the country." Therefore, although female academy students did not resemble refugees in the traditional sense, both they and their broader communities saw them as refugees. These young refugees' experiences within the protected enclaves of female academies complicate any effort to reduce the Civil War refugee crisis to a single narrative.[5]

The female academy movement in North Carolina began in the early nineteenth century, as Southern slaveholding families sought to create educational opportunities for their daughters that would prepare them for the particular social and cultural demands that came with becoming a plantation mistress. Many historians have recognized that female academies served an important role in coming of age for young women in the antebellum South. For most upper-class white women, their years at school proved to be the only time in their lives in which they lived away from home and family, offering what historian Anya Jabour has described as "an alternative definition of southern womanhood, one that revolved around self-improvement and female community rather than around self-sacrifice and male dominance."[6] Entering the schools as girls, they left as women.

By 1860 the development of higher education for women had advanced to a point where there were more educational options for elite young women than for young men in North Carolina. On the eve of the Civil War, Governor John W. Ellis remarked that North Carolina had thirteen female and six male colleges, with fifteen hundred female and nine hundred male college students. To be sure, the distinction between colleges and other institutions of secondary or higher education was ill defined, and the difference between those schools that described themselves as colleges, seminaries, or academies was negligible. Regardless of the nomenclature, the students at female colleges or academies considered themselves to be social and intellectual peers of their counterparts at male institutions. Although they tended to be three or four years younger than their brothers and cousins at Wake Forest, Davidson, or the University of North Carolina, the students at North Carolina's female academies came from the same cultural background and social demographic as those who populated male institutions.[7]

The election of Abraham Lincoln and the subsequent secession of seven Southern states placed North Carolina's female academies in a precarious position. Like Virginia, North Carolina remained within the Union throughout the secession winter, joining the Confederacy only after the firing on Fort Sumter and Abraham Lincoln's call for troops in April 1861. For students attending school during this period, the threat and possibility of war created anxiety and excitement. Rosa Biddle, a student at Chowan Female Baptist Institute in Murfreesboro wrote in a letter home to New Bern after Abraham Lincoln's election in November 1860, "The papers say that Lincoln is elected by 150 majority & that S. Carolina is ready & Virginia is nearly ready & N. Carolina will soon begin to get ready. I don't think it can be so but I trouble myself so little about it that I don't take time to read the papers enough to find out whether it is so or not! I think Pa will come if there was any danger at hand & besides I don't have time to trouble myself about such things." Three months later she wrote again, pleading with her father to "tell me all the news about war & every thing of the kind whether you think we will have war or not, or whether those states that have threatened to secede & if Old No Carolina is likely to or not." A student at St. Mary's School in Raleigh expressed a similar anxiety about the consequences of Lincoln's election. "This week is elections," she wrote home. "Such excitement! I never did see among people before. The girls talk as if they were the greatest politicians, but ask them the difference between the whig and democrat they say they do not know; neither do I. I have tried to find out, but in vain.... Today at intermission the schoolroom was the sound of the tower of babel... for there was such a noise about the politics.... They say that Lincoln is elected.... All of us are like tigers about Lincoln's election."[8]

In April 1861 Rosa Biddle received a letter from a childhood friend who attended Louisburg Female College: "If the people there talk as much about wars & secession as they do here I am certain you are quite tired of it; for it seems to me I hear nothing else." On April 17, less than a week after Fort Sumter, Rosa wrote to her father,

> So war is declared! I am sorry this continent is shaken with civil war, one which has stood for so many years & on such a firm basis. I begin to think

dear Pa that the end of all things is not far hence, predictions are so fast being fulfilled. How important that we all should be preparing to meet it.... Write me something about the state of this most favored of all countries what you think will be the termination of these commotions. I hope it is only a cloud, & that the sun will soon burst forth in all its magnificent glory.

Pauline Hill, a student at Louisburg Female College, wrote in her journal that "ever since the school opened this winter we have heard nothing talked about but war. Fort Sumter has fallen, and all over the South and in our State they are forming companies."[9]

The uncertain state of North Carolina within the Confederacy temporarily reduced enrollment in female academies, as parents hesitated before placing their daughters in a potentially precarious position. St. Mary's student Kate Curtis wrote shortly before North Carolina's secession from the Union that "there has been such a panic in school about the times, that many of the girls have written home, entirely misrepresenting the state of affairs here and have been sent for. Some left yesterday, and some this morning."[10]

After the firing on Fort Sumter and North Carolina's secession from the Union, wealthy Southern parents began to send their daughters away from areas in the Confederacy where the threats of war loomed largest. Although North Carolina's female academies had always attracted some out-of-state students, their numbers swelled starting in 1861 and increased every year thereafter. They also attracted an increasing number of students from North Carolina's coastal counties, the one area of the state threatened and (after 1862) occupied by Union forces. Rev. A. G. Stacy, president of Lenoir's Davenport Female College, boasted in 1863 that "the success of the institution has exceeded the most sanguine expectations of its friends[;] a larger number of pupils have been in attendance than at any former period. Six states in the Confederacy have been represented and in North Carolina, 10 counties." In 1863 Salem Female Academy reported that of its 310 students, nearly half came from outside of North Carolina, including from "Tennessee 32, Georgia 24, Virginia 21, Alabama 19, Mississippi 18, South Carolina 15, Florida 9, Texas 4, Louisiana 2, [and] Arkansas 2." A St. Mary's student observed in 1862 that "there are a good many Wilmington girls here.... The school is larger than it has been some years at the commencement of the session." Another St. Mary's student remembered that "quite a number of them [students] then at St. Mary's were there for protection, since their homes were in Federal lines early in the War."[11]

These refugee students included the daughters of many prominent Confederate politicians and military leaders, leading Lou Sullivan, a St. Mary's student, to observe in February 1863 that "the school is pretty full. There are over a hundred boarders who have already come in.... There are a good many girls here who are daughters, or near relations of distinguished characters." The most famous of these was Robert E. Lee's daughter Mildred, who attended St. Mary's from 1862 to 1863. Fearing that his daughter would be captured by Union forces, Lee arranged for her to be transferred from a school in Winchester, Virginia, to St. Mary's School in Raleigh. Some of her classmates were daughters of prominent Confederates, including Lucia Polk, daughter of Gen. Leonidas Polk, and Laura Pearson, daughter of the North Carolina Supreme Court's chief justice. Prior to Mildred Lee's arrival at St. Mary's, Varina Davis had made the school her home between early July and late August 1862. In May 1862 Jefferson Davis had sent his young wife with their children to Raleigh, fearing for her safety during the Peninsula Campaign. Varina Davis originally stayed at the Yarborough House, which she found "terribly crowded, and very rough." Moving to St. Mary's, located just outside of downtown Raleigh, Davis remarked in a letter to her husband that the accommodations "are very plain, but the ladies are sensible & kind, the girls polite & gentle ... the whole grounds are free to the children." She remained at St. Mary's until after Second Manassas, when it was deemed safe for her and the children to return to Richmond.[12]

Some parents worried about sending their daughters so far from home during wartime. Edmund Pendleton of Virginia wrote to his daughter Elizabeth that "as at present advised, I am inclined to think that the Moravian School [Salem Female Academy] at Salem NC will be the best for you. The objection to it is its distance from where your mother & myself will probably be." Despite his misgivings, Pendleton sent his daughter to Salem Female Academy, where she stayed for the duration of the war. Living in Union-occupied coastal North Carolina, Richard Creecy also expressed concerns about the distance between himself and his daughter Bettie, a student at St. Mary's in Raleigh. Despite these concerns, Creecy wrote to his daughter that he felt that she should stay at St. Mary's, where "you are in good hands, in a safe place."[13]

The influx of refugee students led to a dramatic increase in enrollment in almost all of North Carolina's female academies. St. Mary's School, for instance, had 78 boarding students on the eve of the Civil War. By the war's end, the school's enrollment had increased to 125 boarders.

Salem Female Academy witnessed an even more dramatic increase in enrollment, from 152 to more than 320 students. At many schools, enrollment continued to increase throughout the war, with many schools hosting a record number of students in the spring of 1865. Even in the war's final months, when almost all educational institutions in the Confederacy had closed, North Carolina's female academies continued to attract new students. In February 1865, even though the Confederate economy had utterly collapsed and military defeat was imminent, Carolina Female College in Ansonville was able to report that "the second term of this institute begins ... under very favorable auspices. It is already nearly filled up to its ability to accommodate boarders."[14]

Both students and teachers began to see the female academies as places of refuge. In a sermon in the fall of 1861, the principal of St. Mary's School in Raleigh told his students that they should be thankful for "our comparative immunity from the consequences of war." Students became convinced early in the war that they were safer at school than they would be at home. St. Mary's student Kate Curtis wrote home in late April 1861 that "I should think we were quite as safe and well protected here as we could be at home." A student at Salem Female Academy remembered, "Those long years in the sheltered nest, while the storm rage around and beyond, ... not for a single day was the regular routine interrupted, but life moved on in its accustomed grooves with its little every day ups and downs."[15]

Indeed, many schools began to employ this idea of schools as places of refuge in their advertising. In May 1861 the principal of Greensboro Female College urged parents in an advertisement that, despite the onset of war, "their daughters will be perfectly safe at Greensboro." An 1863 advertisement for Louisburg Female College noted that the school was "remote from the lines of the public enemy." Similarly, an 1864 advertisement for Davenport Female College noted that the school was in a "locality remote from Yankee invasion." Concord Female College recommended itself "to those in the South desiring a safe and pleasant retreat for pupils during the war.... This college has suffered less from the war than any other of a like kind of which we have heard."[16]

Despite their physical isolation, students at female academies often found their connections to home strengthened. Letters to and from parents at home took on an increased importance, especially when that home was threatened by invasion. Letters between parents and children commonly began with entreaties to write more often. In these letters, both parents and children exhibited an anxiety about their separation in the time of national crisis. They also reveal significant gendered differences in how mothers and fathers communicated with their daughters (and how daughters communicated with their mothers and fathers). While fathers often wrote to their daughters at school to reassure them that their home and family were safe, embodying the traditionally male role of the protector of the household, mothers were more likely to console their daughters on emotional issues, such as homesickness.

For students whose homes were in territory occupied by the Union army, direct correspondence was often impossible, and families developed elaborate procedures to communicate through intermediaries. For instance, the correspondence between Bettie Crecy at St. Mary's and her parents on Nag's Head was often interrupted or delayed by the presence of Union forces on the Outer Banks. Richard Creecy wrote his daughter that "I cannot account for you not receiving our letters regularly. We write quite often. We have written twice since we got home from Nags Head. Your ma proposes that you number your letters & we will number ours." Unable to communicate directly through the mail, the family devised plans to communicate through relatives in nearby Norfolk where mail delivery was more regular, plans that frequently went awry. After several months of pleading for shoes and clothing, Bettie's parents sent her a parcel delivered by a family friend to the rail yard. Several days after she was to receive her long-awaited package, Bettie received a letter that informed her that "the box of clothing which was in E. [Elizabeth] City to be sent to the Express office in Norfolk for you was burnt with the Hotel on Monday morning [by Union soldiers]. Don't be distressed. We don't apprehend any danger. But we are without any mail."[17]

As the war progressed, many students found corresponding with home almost impossible. By 1863 the Confederate Postal Service had begun to collapse, resulting in highly irregular mail delivery. Writing to her daughter at St. Mary's, one mother lamented that "the letters now take ten days to come" from Raleigh to their home in Asheville. Bettie Dobson, a student at Gilmer's Female Academy in Mt. Airy, complained in a letter to her sister that "I have not received a letter from you in nine weeks, and I must by that think you all have forgotten me."[18]

Many students manifested their anxiety and psychological isolation through severe homesickness. While such longings for home were typical among antebellum schoolgirls, within the context of the Civil War, when many of the girls' homes and families were under physical threat, these natural feelings became exacerbated.[19] A student at Edgeworth Female Seminary wrote to her mother, "[I] wish I had never heard of Greensboro. I am terribly homesick.... O Mama I must come home. I don't think I can stand it for ten long months. Won't you take us South with you when you go through here?" Two weeks later, her anxiety had not abated, and she wrote, "I am just as homesick as I can be, you have no idea my precious Ma how much I would give to see and kiss you. I feel as if I did not care about learning anything more." Min Curtis wrote to her mother that her St. Mary's classmate "Mary Easton cries the whole time to go home. She is so dreadfully homesick, the first thing I hear in the morning is Mary E. sobbing and crying fit to kill herself."[20]

Almost all of the students had a close family member who was fighting in the war, and therefore news from the front became a matter not only of political and military interest but of significant personal importance. When students received letters from brothers, fathers, uncles, and cousins in the Confederate army, news and rumors spread among the students, who speculated about the consequences for their loved ones and for their new country. More often than not, however, schoolgirls complained that they did not know enough about the welfare of those in the military. A student at Davenport Female College in Lenoir wrote to her uncle that he must "when you write give me the war news." A student at Edgeworth Female Seminary wrote, "We have not heard any news since we have been here so we have nothing to distract our attention but I feel very anxious to here [hear] from our army, so please write and tell us if their [there] is any."[21]

At Louisburg Female Institute, Pauline Hill recorded the movements of the Union and Confederate armies carefully (although not always accurately) in her journal and noted when battles imperiled her family members or those of her classmates. On August 20, 1861, she noted that "a terrible battle has been fought at Manassas.... I have four cousins in the army. Charlie, my brother, says he wishes he was old enough to go, too." A year later, during the Peninsula Campaign, she wrote that "there are sad hearts in Louisburg, for we don't know how many of our dear boys were killed or wounded." Lou Sullivan, a St. Mary's student, wrote home in 1864 that "we are still in suspense about the recent battles. But very little news has been received. Lizzie has heard nothing from her brother." Lucy Walke, a student at St. Mary's, remembered that after significant battles, both students and teachers anxiously awaited news about their loved ones' welfare. One "lovely Sunday in the summer of '64" proved to be particularly memorable. "We knew," she recalled, "on Saturday that a fierce battle was raging many of the girls had near and dear relatives in the army." A telegram arrived during the Sunday morning chapel service, informing the principal that he had lost a third son in the Confederate war effort.[22]

The information that students did receive from home or from relatives on the front lines tended to downplay any risks to person or property. In his correspondence with his daughter at St. Mary's, Richard Creecy repeatedly attempted to reassure her that he and her mother were safe. Although "Fort Hattress has been taken," he wrote her in August 1861, "we do not think there is any danger here, so you need not be uneasy about us." Two weeks later he informed her that there were "1500 Southern troops on Roanoke Island. No danger here." In letter after letter, the Creecy parents attempted to temper any fears that their daughter may have had for their safety. After repeatedly assuring his daughter that Union forces would never attack Roanoke, when the attack did happen in February 1862, Richard Creecy told his daughter that "you must not distress yourself about it," as he assured her that the attack would undoubtedly fail. When Union forces proceeded to take and occupy Roanoke, Richard Creecy continued to maintain that the presence of enemy soldiers a few miles from their home should not elicit concern, as "we do not think we are in any danger in the country and don't wish you to be alarmed about it." Despite her parents' repeated claims that family and property were safe, Bettie Creecy evidently found the Union occupation of North Carolina's coastal counties worthy of alarm. Reading panic in his daughter's letters, Richard Creecy continued to maintain their safety: "We are all safe & well and do not anticipate any harm. . . . You must not be distressed. You magnify dangers because you are not near them."[23]

Despite what Richard and Mary Creecy told their daughter, they were more forthcoming with their other correspondents, revealing that they were deeply fearful about the presence of Union forces near their home.[24] By sending their daughter to St. Mary's, they hoped to shelter her not only from potential violence but also from the anxiety that the threat of violence would evoke. In a letter to St. Mary's principal Aldert Smedes shortly after his daughter's arrival at the school in the fall of 1861, Richard Creecy wrote, "We are in the midst of excitement, confusion, & with some consternation, caused by the attack of Fort Hatteras and the complete defeat of our troops. . . . Sustain Betty as well as you can, under the alarm that she will suffer as the report reaches her. Under the unfortunate disaster which has befallen us, Mrs. Creecy thought it would be better for Betty to return, but I regard your situation as much less perilous than ours, and I have full confidence in your parental care, kindness & watchfulness."[25] This letter and others like it indicate that parents wanted school administrators not only to keep their daughters safe from physical harm but to engage in willful deception to protect their emotional and psychological well-being.

The absence of adequate and reliable information about loved ones in combat created the ideal conditions for rampant rumoring and conjecturing on the part of female academy students. Taking whatever fragmentary evidence they could accumulate about their relatives and the movements of the armies, they imagined scenarios to fill in the gaps in their knowledge. In these speculative ventures, they posited battlefield experiences for their loved ones that were based in part on the sanitized accounts they received in the mail, their readings of romantic literature, and their fertile adolescent imaginations.[26] Often their imagined war differed significantly from the actual events on the battlefield. For instance, Pauline Hill of Louisburg Female College evidently believed that Robert E. Lee had launched a third invasion of the North in the summer of 1864, occupying portions of Maryland.[27]

This anxiety about the fate of loved ones led some students to embrace spiritualism.[28] By conducting séances, they hoped to learn about relatives and friends on the front lines. Lizzie Montgomery remembered that the students at St. Mary's

> would hang a shawl before the window, light the gas and for hours, on Saturdays, cluster around the table. We soon found out a medium, and through the moving of the table, in reply to our calling over the alphabet, we asked many questions and thought we gained satisfactory replies. I recall that the sweetheart of one of the girls had just been killed on the battlefield in Virginia. It was known he was wild and dissipated and utterly fearless. The table spelled out that he wished to communicate with her, and the message that followed—"Remorse," caused a panic and we left off table turning for some time.

Spiritualism was also popular among students at Greensboro Female College. Sophie Richardson recalled that "our favorite pastime on Friday nights, on Saturdays when there were no study hours, was Spirit rapping. It was quite a fad in those days, and there were some wonderful things told us in some mysterious way."[29]

Like others on the Confederate home front, students at female academies in North Carolina experienced a significant shift in material conditions caused by the war. The Union blockade of Confederate ports dramatically limited the availability of imported food, clothing, medicine, and other consumer goods. When available at all, many goods sold at prohibitively high prices, forcing Confederates of all classes to do without or to use inventive substitutes.[30]

Wartime shortages visibly manifested themselves in the physical appearance of female academy students. Because of a severe textile shortage, almost all schools abandoned their strict antebellum dress codes. St. Mary's students had for decades been distinguished by a dress code of light blue or white dresses with pale blue ribbons. According to the mother of two St. Mary's students, shortages made finding appropriate school clothes impossible, such that "it is quite useless to speak of calico and shirting which Min [her daughter] needs, but must do without, even if she goes to St. Mary's." A similar situation existed at Louisburg Female College. By March 1862, Pauline Hill took pride in "our first homespun dresses," noting that hers was "blue, grey, and black check" with a "Garibalidi waist."[31] For her, this change in apparel was one way in which she could manifest her Confederate patriotism.[32] Two years later, however, she was less enthusiastic about the clothing shortage's effects, claiming that "it is getting to be a serious thing how we are to get clothes to wear. We have cut up our linen sheets for underclothes and handkerchiefs." Schoolgirls from privileged backgrounds were reduced to ransacking their trunks "to get the trimmings." Despite her misgivings, Hill maintained that she and her classmates were "willing to do without many of these things if we could only have peace."[33] However, repeated requests for clothing were a regular theme in correspondence between schoolgirls and their parents, requests that more often than not went unfulfilled.

Shortages also transformed their diets. With the Confederate military receiving priority for foodstuffs, a decline in agricultural production in the South, and imported foods like coffee and sugar unavailable, female academies provided their students with a cuisine derived from local produce. Kate Curtis wrote home in early 1861 about the steps St. Mary's principal, Aldert Smedes, had taken to ensure that the school would be adequately provisioned. "We might, perhaps," Smedes told his students, "be obliged to forego some of luxuries, but we wouldn't be pinched for want of food." According to Curtis, Smedes's statement "just 'brought down the house.' The girls have been anxiously enquiring what the luxuries are, so that they may enjoy them before they are taken away." Lou Sullivan wrote to her parents in 1864 that Reverend Smedes had "introduced a new dish for breakfast—fried okra. You have no idea how nice it is when fried brown. Try it." Although she thought that the new cuisine was innovative, she recognized that her classmates did not always agree with her. "Though our fare is coarse," she wrote to her parents, "it agrees with me. Our supplies are a little better, we have molasses 2 times a week & Sunday night we had cakes, 3 a piece. The girls complain considerably of the fare, I never have left the table without being satisfied & common is it is I always enjoy it. I believe Dr. Smedes furnishes the tables as nicely as he can, everything is so very scarce & dear around here." Smedes himself was impressed with his students' willingness to accommodate the new menu, arguing that "such is the patriotism of our girls that they not only are content, but even grow fat upon the plainest fare."[34]

Despite their occasional complaints, students at female academies fared far better materially than almost anyone else on the Confederate home front. Although school administrators had difficulties at times securing provisions to support their robust student populations, at no point during the war did students at female academies experience real material hardship.[35] A student at Salem Female Academy remembered being reminded by the school's principal of how fortunate they were. After being caught stealing sugar from the dining room, the students were called into the chapel, where they were admonished for their infraction and reminded

> how much better they lived there than at their own homes, because coffee and sugar were not found in every man's house during the war. We had well furnished tables three times a day, and a luncheon at four o'clock. On the Principal's birthday we had big dinners, and the girls had big pockets made for the occasion, and the spoils we carried off lasted several days! But it was no easy task to provide for two hundred and fifty girls entrusted to their care, in addition to the other members of the large family, and Principal and Steward had their hands full.[36]

For the slaves who worked at North Carolina's female academies, the schools functioned more as prisons than as places of refugee. Slaves provided almost all of the manual labor at these schools, including cooking, cleaning, and laundry service. At St. Mary's, slave boys brought lunches and carried the schoolbooks for day students. At least one student brought her own slave to do her laundry and attend to her personal needs. Lou Sullivan remembered that every Saturday the students found "the freshly laundered clothes deposited on the foot of each bed by the long procession of smiling Negro washerwomen." At the Nash and Kollack school in Hillsborough, it was customary for younger students to bring their "Negro mammy" with them. When David Bell brought his three daughters to the school from Washington, North Carolina, as refugees in 1863, he was sure to leave a female slave to care for his daughters. Similarly, Hannah Emerson Williard, a thirteen-year-old refugee also from Washington, brought an elderly slave named Caroline (whom she called "Nussie") with her in order to care for her "clothes and look after her in such other ways as might be necessary." Although most slaves at the school slept in quarters separate from the main school building, Caroline slept next to Hannah, ready to attend to her at any hour.[37]

For these slaves, the schools' increased enrollments brought additional labor and burdens, as schools rarely purchased or hired additional slaves in proportion to the growth in enrollment. Margaret Burwell, wife of the Charlotte Female Institute headmaster Rev. Robert Burwell, wrote to her son in February 1865 that the school was "dirty beyond endurance" because her slaves "Mary Ann & Hannah have taken their usual spells. Hannah has not cooked for three weeks & Mary Ann has not been in the house more than two days since you left. . . . Our school is much larger than we anticipated."[38] Whether Mary Ann's and Hannah's illnesses were real or feinted, they were probably brought about by continued labor in an overcrowded school.

Although slave management was never part of the formal curriculum of female academies, the proper treatment of slaves naturally and regularly appeared in the context of religious instruction. In a sermon he regularly delivered to his female charges, St. Mary's headmaster Aldert Smedes implored them to treat their slaves with humanity. "In a community like ours, where we are surrounded in such numbers by servants born in our own house," Smedes argued, "surely the pious daughter need not go far, perhaps not beyond the precincts of her own abode, to find suitable objects of her benevolence." The object of such benevolence, Smedes claimed, was that slaves would become "more faithful servants of their masters upon earth [and] might also invest them with the freedom of the skies." Bettie Creecy, from a slave-owning Pasquotank County family, wrote to her father that Smedes had assigned her to write an essay on the "Catechetical Instruction of Servants."[39]

The dramatic increase in enrollment in North Carolina's female academies necessitated the hiring of additional teachers, and many of these positions were filled with refugees from war-torn areas of the Confederacy. By the end of the war, at least half of the teaching staff at St. Mary's were refugees.[40] At Concord Female Academy in Statesville, all but one member of the faculty were refugees, including the school's president, who had fled from Georgia in 1863, where he had been president of Rome Female College until that school was closed after Yankee raids.[41] Indeed, almost all of the schools in this study had at least one refugee teacher.

These refugee teachers filled vacancies created by male teachers departing for military service and Northern-born teachers who felt uncomfortable teaching in the South after secession.[42] A recent graduate of Lima Academy in New York, Maria Flint was hired by Warrenton Female Academy in 1860 to teach music, French, German, and English. Although she was impressed by the grounds of the school and the wealth of her students, whom she described in her diary as "mostly planter's daughters from the country around," Flint expressed anxiety about the prevalence of slavery at the school and in the town. After Lincoln's election, she and another Northern teacher left for Union lines. Although the war encouraged Southern women to enter the teaching profession, female academies in North Carolina often experienced a shortage of teachers. "Teachers were scarce," claimed one Confederate memoirist, "but many of our women filled the places vacated by soldiers. The boarding schools of St. Mary's, Raleigh, Greensboro, and Salem were kept open, as was the Charlotte Female Institute." With some relief, Margaret Burwell proudly reported in 1864 that her school had "a very full corps of Teachers."[43]

From the very beginning of the conflict, students at North Carolina's female academies expressed their devotion to the Confederate cause. A month before North Carolina officially seceded from the Union, Kate Curtis wrote home from St. Mary's that "we have now three flags of the 'Southern Confederacy' waving from our windows. Saturday morning some people from town rode by here with their flags, and their cries of 'secession'. That first made us think of displaying our zeal, and all hands were immediately at work upon 'red, white, & blue.'" In an August 1861 letter home, Emma Kimberly, a student at St. Mary's, wrote, "The South is certainly right in everything. . . . Providence is certainly on our side." In April 1861 students at St. Mary's devoted themselves during a two-day holiday to producing war supplies. According to one student, "During that time we made 167 mattresses, and hemmed 118 towels," a feat that she proudly noted exceed those produced by military academy cadets in nearby Hillsborough. Kate McKimmon remembered that "the first five years if the Sixties found me as I still am, an un[re]constructed rebel! As a school girl at St. Mary's, I enjoyed marching with our 'crowd,' when with paper caps, Confederate flag, and a drum we paraded around the grove."[44]

The Civil War had only a subtle effect on the educational experience at North Carolina's female academies. Comparing school bulletins from the Civil War to those from both before and after the war indicate that the subjects and texts studied remained largely unchanged.[45] For instance, students at Chowan Female Baptist Institute continued to study the same subjects throughout the middle decades of the nineteenth century: arithmetic, poetry, Latin (Caesar, Ovid, Virgil), French, Paley's *Natural Theology*, and "Trigonometry and Mensuration."[46] While many primary schools in the Confederacy adopted new textbooks printed in the South and intended to promote Confederate nationalism, female academy students read the same texts that they had prior to the Civil War.[47] Although they were not directly exposed to a nationalist curriculum, female academy students would have been aware of Confederate textbooks, as many of them were written by teachers at female academies.[48]

While the official curriculum remained relatively static, students and teachers used the classroom assignments to reflect on war-related issues. On April 20, 1861—shortly after the firing on Fort Sumter—students at Louisburg Female College were assigned the debate topic "Has the South the Right to Secede?" In the fall of 1862 the older students at St. Mary's School were assigned to write an essay on "Our Opinions of the Present War," while younger pupils were assigned the topic "On Leaving Home."[49] Unfortunately, the products of these assignments have not survived, although one may presume the result, given the students' ardent Confederate nationalism.

While the curriculum did not change dramatically, the purpose of female education did undergo a subtle but significant shift during the Civil War. With many of the state's male teachers in the Confederate army, graduates of female academies were increasing called on to teach. An editorial in the *North Carolina Journal of Education* opined, "We again call upon the ladies to come to the rescue; to occupy our vacant school houses, and train up the children to take the places of those who are now pouring out their blood to defend our homes." The leaders of the state educational association publically appealed to young women's patriotism to entice them to teach. In notices published in newspapers across the state, they asked educated young women, "Will you not as patriots, come forward in this hour of your country's trial, when every strong arm is needed to defend you and your homes from a merciless foe? . . . Teach, not for the pay, and, it may be, not for the love of the work, but teach for the sake of the children of the State, who must grow up in ignorance, if you do not instruct them."[50]

Students and faculty at female academies responded to this demand for teachers. Nowhere was this transformation more evident that at Concord Female College in Statesville. In 1864 the college's new president, Rev. J. M. M. Caldwell, instituted a "teachers department" to help train the school's graduates to become educators. Caldwell, the scion of a famous Presbyterian family, had come to Concord after fleeing from Georgia, where he had been head of Rome Female College, which had closed after Yankee raids in the area. In an address to the students at Concord shortly after Caldwell's installation, Dr. James Ramsay argued that the war had fundamentally changed the purpose of female higher education in the South. "Your fathers and brothers are, perhaps, far away upon fields of strife and blood," Ramsay told the students, "and your mothers and sisters toiling and economizing at home while you are placed here. You are not here that you may idle your time away in listless folly, and indulge your fancy and pride in dress and pleasure. . . . No! No!! . . . It is to prepare for the journey of life that you are placed here. Learn to labor, and labor to learn." Dr. Ramsay urged the students to use their education productively rather than ornamentally and to consider teaching as a possible vocation.[51]

For more than three years, because of their location in the Confederate interior, female academies in North Carolina protected their students from the horrors of war and the threat of Yankee invasion. In the war's final months, however, as the Confederacy collapsed and Union soldiers marched into central North Carolina, students at female academies came face-to-face with a war that they, their parents, and their teachers hoped they never would experience. Indeed, female academies, which had served as places of refuge for most of the conflict, became, in the war's final months, venues for intense interactions between their students and both Confederate and Union soldiers. Because their campuses were almost all located in urban areas, near railroad junctions, and had large, open groves, North Carolina's female academies became the preferred campground for both retreating Confederate and advancing Union forces. These brief but intense interactions between schoolgirls and soldiers provided a unique venue for young women who had spent the duration of war physically separated from the conflict itself to express their thoughts and feelings on the Confederacy and its imminent defeat. Even when most Southerners, soldiers and civilians alike, had become convinced that the Confederacy would fail in its quest for independence, schoolgirls in central North Carolina remained committed Confederate nationalists and resistant to Union occupation.

A handful of parents removed their daughters from female academies in anticipation of Union occupation of central North Carolina. In January 1865 Bessie Cain's father wrote to a friend that "we regret very much to learn that our dear Bessie will not be able to continue her education at St. Mary's at this time, but perhaps it is all for the best, as we are fearful that if Wilmington is taken, Raleigh will fall into the hands of the Yankees & you would be miserable to have your dear children within the Yankee lines & separated so far from us all."[52] One month later, however, Bessie returned to St. Mary's, where she stayed until the war's conclusion. Although the surviving correspondence does not indicate why her parents changed their mind about removing Bessie from school, the threat of Union occupation of Asheville may have persuaded them to keep their daughter in the more protected location in Raleigh. Expressing a similar anxiety about the safety of their daughter, Catherine Hanes's parents decided to move her from Salem Female Academy to Statesville Female Academy in the fall of 1864 so that she would be closer to their home in Davie County.[53] However, in the war's final months, most parents did not have the option of removing their daughters from school. Most families felt that their daughters were safer at school in central North Carolina than they would be at home.

For many schoolgirls, the sight of retreating Confederate soldiers in the spring of 1865 marked the first time that they had seen so many gray uniforms since the soldiers had departed nearly four years earlier. A student from St. Mary's recorded in her scrapbook that "the confederate soldiers came marching in each one with a blooming sprig of lilac tucked in his hat, like plumes, though almost barefoot, wearing ragged and worn uniforms. Unshaved and gaunt they were but unconquered still. The girls gladly took their dinner from the table to the soldiers in the grove." Susan Collier, a student at St. Mary's, expressed surprise and concern that the army before them did not conform to her imagined ideal of Confederate manhood, noting in her diary that "I was really surprised to see our men so desponding but they were the least class of men and did not feel like the men that are in the Army of their free wills fighting for their all."[54]

Despite their misgivings at the soldiers' appearance, the schoolgirls at St. Mary's reveled at the opportunity to see and talk with retreating Confederate soldiers. After persuading their reluctant principal, the students lined themselves along the fence separating the school's grove from Hillsborough Road. Susan Collier recalled their enthusiasm in her journal: "Just to think to see our dear soldiers.... How we all rushed when we knew we could go. We had a charming time feeding the soldiers. We girls gave them our dinners. They were so grateful for it. We gave them water also. I was quite exhausted carrying great tubs of water, but we were all willing to do any and every thing for our dear soldiers." Students at Louisburg Female College responded similarly to the "crowds of weary, hungry soldiers ... thronging our streets." Pauline Hill recorded in her diary that "they are so worn out they fall down on the sidewalks and sleep. We all do everything for them we can, feeding them and caring for the sick ones."[55]

The passing of the Confederate army brought about feelings of elation and regret. Susan Collier recalled that "all the girls seem wild with joy, though we know tomorrow at this time we will be left desolate. Perfectly so. But we are determined to have a nice, nice time." After a day of talking, dining, and flirting with Confederate soldiers, the students at St. Mary's watched uneasily as General Wheeler's cavalry rode by, protecting the Confederate rear. "We girls watched the last one," wrote Susan Collier. "Oh what a night we all spent. Expecting the Yankees every moment."[56]

Students at female academies expressed deep fear and anxiety for their safety as Union forces approached. Maggie Ramsay wrote from Concord Female Academy in Statesville to her father in Richmond that "we heard if they burnt the College the Yankees would not let you take anything out. Some of the girls put on nearly all the clothing they had. If the Yankees had come they would have seen some fleshy looking girls."[57] Their fears that Union forces would ransack the school and even impose themselves sexually on students were not without justification. As Sherman's forces marched through Georgia and the Carolinas, they regularly invaded private female spaces within the home, leading one North Carolina woman to complain that "there was no place, no chamber, trunk, drawer, desk, garret, closet, or cellar that was private to their unholy eyes."[58] While the rape of white Confederate women by Union soldiers was comparatively rare (at least by the standards of nineteenth-century warfare), the belief that Union soldiers preyed on vulnerable women was widespread.[59]

These fears proved to be largely unfounded, as Union soldiers demonstrated a remarkable degree of civility. Even Bessie Cain, a committed Confederate nationalist, had to admit in her diary that Union soldiers "thus far ... have treated us with the greatest possible kindness & respect." Her fear of sexual and physical violence returned, however, after news of

Lincoln's assassination reached the troops encamped in St. Mary's grove. "We knew that on the least provocation the Yankees would do anything they wanted to us," she wrote in her diary. "How uneasy we were! Last night we were frightened to death. They [sic] officers thought they could restrain their soldiers, but they thought if the news about Lincoln spread among the soldiers, they would set fire to houses & how a tremendous uproar; the noise would be heard up here & then St. Mary's would be set on fire. We all slept in our clothes having filled the pocket of our dresses with anything we wanted particularly to save."[60]

The principals of female academies often played a decisive role in protecting their institutions from the potential threat posed by Union forces. When General Stoneman's forces threatened Salem in 1865, the principal of Salem Female Academy joined a delegation led by "the Mayor of the town, and several prominent citizens" to confront the brigade before it entered the community. They successfully negotiated a surrender of the town and arranged for Union soldiers to protect the academy from looters.[61]

While the principals attempted to negotiate a careful détente with Union forces, the students took every opportunity to insult and antagonize Union soldiers and officers. Emboldened by the protected status granted to them by their race, gender, and age, schoolgirls openly expressed their continued loyalty to the Confederacy and their hatred and revulsion at the thought of reunion with the North. At Louisburg Female College, Pauline Hill, who had rejoiced upon seeing retreating Confederate soldiers, fumed when Union soldiers arrived a few days later. "I shall never forget my feelings [of anger] when I saw the first Yankees," she wrote in her diary.[62]

Female academy students took particular umbrage at the sight of the Union flag. With several thousand Union soldiers encamped in the grove adjacent to the school, St. Mary's students were confronted with tangible evidence of Confederate defeat. Bessie Cain noted in her diary, "This morning O horrors the United States flag was hoisted in the grove." In a sign of defiance, "every morning, when the United States flag was raised, [the St. Mary's students] rushed to the windows and drew the curtain, that they might not look upon it." Correctly interpreting this behavior as hostile, Union "Gen. Howard gladdened their hearts by making them martyrs to their cause. He sent in word to the principal that unless all such expressions of dislike to the United States flag were stopped he would close the school." Students at Louisburg Female College expressed the same outrage at the presence of Union soldiers on their school grounds. One resident described the horror of occupation: "The town is full of Yankee soldiers riding and walking up and down every street and coming in our yards and kitchens. . . . Their tents are pitched in the college. . . . The reality is upon us that we are a subjugated people. Two very large US flags are unfurled and waving in the breeze." Anna Maria Clewell, a student at Salem Female Academy, repeatedly crossed the street rather than walk underneath the Union flag hanging from the requisitioned Union headquarters near the school. When confronted by Union soldiers, who threatened to arrest her for insulting the flag, Anna maintained her Confederate nationalism, shouting at the soldiers that "I will not live under it. I am going to South America or Mexico, or somewhere out of the United States. *I am not going to live under it.*"[63]

Female academy students also expressed their anger and nationalism when confronting Union officers. When Gen. William T. Sherman visited St. Mary's in April 1865, the students initially treated him respectfully, presumably at the request of their principal, who was eager to maintain cordial relations with the soldiers who occupied the grounds around the school. When Sherman turned to leave, however, their tone changed dramatically. When Sherman turned to give the building a final look, he found the students "all making such mouths as only angry school girls can make, while some more daring ones were absolutely shaking their pretty little fists at him." A student at Chowan Female Baptist Institute displayed a similar antipathy to Union officers. When a captain asked if she would play for him on the school's piano, she replied, "I don't play anything but Southern songs" and proceeded to regale him and his men with "Dixie" and "Bonnie Blue Flag." Even after Union occupation, female academy students continued to express their disbelief that their beloved Confederacy had been defeated. Bessie Cain wrote in her diary that "after fighting four years in a noble cause, and after gaining so many brilliant victories, how could we have been defeated?"[64]

The Civil War experience of female academy students shaped their later development in two significant ways. First, they increasingly saw education not only as a symbol of social status but as a means of financial advancement. Whereas antebellum schoolgirls usually returned home to marry, have children, and run a plantation, the Civil War generation and those who followed them went into teaching in record numbers. The Civil War marked a watershed in the gender demographics of teaching in North Carolina. What had been a male-dominated profession before the Civil War gradually transitioned into a female field. On the eve of the Civil War, less than 8 percent of public school teachers in North Carolina were women.⁶⁵ The gendered transformation of teaching began during the war itself, as female academy graduates replaced male teachers who had entered the Confederate Army. Surviving county records indicate that the number of female primary school teachers in North Carolina doubled between 1861 and 1865, while the number of male teachers declined by an equal measure, though men continued to hold more than half of available teaching posts.⁶⁶ In 1899 Mont Amoena Female Seminary in Mount Pleasant proudly reported that 69 percent of its graduates since 1859 had become teachers and that the school had graduated few "parlor boarders" interested only in ornamental education. By 1900 teaching had become a female-dominated occupation in North Carolina.⁶⁷

Their particular vantage point from within female academies also shaped how schoolgirls would later remember and memorialize the Civil War. Spared from the horrors of the front lines and from many of the deprivations that most Confederates experienced on the home front, the students at female academies saw the war in largely celebratory terms. According to Kate McKimmon, who attended St. Mary's from 1861 to 1866, "Tho' much interested in 'The War' my class-mates and I were too young to realize any of the horrors of it."⁶⁸ They maintained their unflagging passion for the Confederate cause long after most Southerners had recognized the futility of the war efforts and reconciled themselves to defeat.

As adults, the students at North Carolina's female academies became the architects of the Lost Cause.⁶⁹ In North Carolina and across the former Confederacy, students who had attended school in North Carolina during the Civil War helped to establish chapters of the United Daughters of the Confederacy, ladies' memorial associations, and other organizations committed to preserving a particular memory of the Confederate past. Kate McKimmon, who later taught at St. Mary's and became the founding secretary of the North Carolina Division of the United Daughters of the Confederacy, was described by a classmate as "possessed of two supreme loyalties—the Confederacy and the Church. One wonders if this early experience [seeing Yankee soldiers] did not serve to deepen that inborn devotion to the Confederate cause." McKimmon herself believed that her schoolgirl patriotism informed her later work with the United Daughters of the Confederacy, claiming that "the first five years of the Sixties found me as I still am, an un[re]constructed rebel!" Similarly, Sallie Southall Cotten, who attended Wesleyan Female College and Greensboro Female College during the Civil War, held leadership positions within the United Daughters of the Confederacy and helped to establish the North

Carolina Federation of Women's Clubs, an organization that helped to orchestrate Lost Cause commemoration.[70] Women such as McKimmon and Cotten used the United Daughters of the Confederacy and other Lost Cause organizations to promote a version of the Confederate experience that drew heavily from their atypical vantage point in the relatively safe and well-provisioned sanctuaries provided by female academies.[71]

The refugee students at North Carolina's female academies shared few experiences with other Piedmont refugees. Although they complained about the unavailability of luxury items, they never suffered the kind of genuine hardship that most white refugees lived with. Physically isolated and sheltered from news about the war's progress that might disturb them, refugee students at female academies maintained their loyalty to the Confederate cause long after many other white refugees in the Piedmont had abandoned it. Their exceptional experiences demonstrate the diversity within the North Carolina refugee crisis. Not only did the refugee experience in the Piedmont differ significantly from that on the coast and the white refugee experience in the Piedmont differ significantly from that of the black slaves they brought with them, but within the white refugee population in the Piedmont no single narrative typifies a wide range of experiences. Female academy students' self-identification as refugees reveals how North Carolina's refugee crisis took on many different faces.

SIX

A Home for the Rest of the War

When Katherine Polk Gale arrived in Asheville in the summer of 1863 via stagecoach, she breathed a sigh of relief, hoping that her long refugee odyssey might finally be at an end. She proclaimed that "the drive up the lovely French Broad river was charming the scenery was beautiful; peace & plenty ruled everywhere; the country was shut in from the world, it seemed almost impossible for the desolations of the war to reach the happy homes along the route." With three children in tow, all under the age of three, Katherine Polk Gale was exhausted from nearly two years of forced relocations preceding her arrival in Asheville, where she would settle for the remainder of the war. When the stagecoach pulled in front of the rented house, she was greeted by her mother, Frances Polk, and her four younger sisters and one sister-in-law, all of whom had relocated to the site the previous December, hoping that it would serve "as a home for the rest of the war; as that was consider a safe retired place."

Married in 1858 and with a young daughter born in 1860 and a son in 1861, Katherine Polk Gale knew that the beginning of hostilities would greatly disrupt her new family in Yazoo, Mississippi. Her father, Leonidas Polk, a prosperous sugar planter and Episcopal bishop for Louisiana, was commissioned a general in the Confederate army in June 1861. Her brother and uncles also joined the Confederate ranks, although her husband was one of the few men in the family who did not enlist. While the men planned for war, the women looked out for the security and safety of themselves and their children. Among the first decisions made during the summer of 1861 was to relocate Mary Gale, Katherine Polk Gale's teenage stepdaughter, from a school in Nashville to St. Mary's School in Raleigh, "that being a good school & a safe place."

Katherine Polk Gale spent the winter of 1861 with her husband and children at their Holly Bend plantation on the Yazoo River, just north of Vicksburg. Their peace was upset, however, in February 1862 when the Union capture of Fort Donelson on the Cumberland River and Fort Henry on the Tennessee River necessitated the evacuation of Nashville, where her mother and sisters were spending the winter. She later recalled that "my Mother, with her large family, had to leave at an hour's notice; for she did not wish to be caught in the enemy's lines & be cut off from her husband & sons. They were to take the last train leaving the city, took time to save nothing but their valuables & clothes & left the house unoccupied.... The only idea with them was to get away, out of the reach of the Federals." Her mother headed to New Orleans, which then still remained in Confederate hands, a trip described as taking "many weary hours" as "they could get nothing along the way to eat." They only had a few months of peace before the Union occupation of New Orleans under Gen. Benjamin Butler began on the first of May 1862. Although concerned about Butler's infamous General Order No. 28, which said that a woman who expressed hostility to Union soldiers would be treated as a woman of the town "plying her avocation," Frances Polk and her daughters were, according to Katherine Polk Gale, "not annoyed in that way; for my sisters never went on the streets & my Mother rarely."

While her mother and sisters were afraid to leave the house in New Orleans, Katherine Polk Gale worried that her home would be flooded. Gen. Ulysses S. Grant's efforts to siege Vicksburg included breaching a levee on the Yazoo River, inundating the surrounding countryside, such that "we were soon surrounded by water; snakes and frogs were seen swimming in all directions." Fearing that the children might drown, the family relocated to Jackson, some forty miles away. Over the next year, the Polk and Gale families wandered the Confederacy in search of a place of safety, spending brief periods in Mobile, Richmond, and Raleigh. During this period, two events transformed Katherine Polk Gale's family. First, her husband enlisted in the Confederate army, serving as an aide-de-camp to his father-in-law, Gen. Leonidas Polk. Second, she gave birth to her third child, a daughter. With the exception of Gen. Leonidas Polk and William Gale, the entire family reunited outside of Asheville in May 1863 for what they hoped would be a peaceful and uneventful existence for the duration of the war. With more than fifty slaves brought from Mississippi, the extended family assumed that the remoteness of their new home would provide some semblance of normality.

Hundreds of other refugees joined the Gale-Polk clan in the North Carolina mountains, particularly in Buncombe and Henderson Counties. Katherine Polk Gale recalled that "we met some extremely agreeable people in Asheville, great hospitality was shown us by people in the town & the surrounding country, many charming friendships were formed; for Asheville & 'Flat Rock' about twenty-five miles away, was the summer resort for many charming, cultivated people, especially from the Carolinas."[1] As a refugee destination, western North Carolina lacked many of the amenities present in the Piedmont. The towns in the mountain counties were smaller than those in the Piedmont; Asheville, by far the largest town in the region, had fewer than one thousand residents in 1860. Most mountain towns consisted of little more than a church, a smattering of dwellings, and (in county seats) a courthouse. Travel to and within the mountains proved challenging. Chartered in 1855, the Western North Carolina Railroad was only partially completed by 1861 and ran only a few miles past Morganton, leaving the western fifth of the state cut off from direct rail traffic. Travel into the region was conducted primarily via two turnpike roads. Built in 1828, the Buncombe Turnpike ran from the Saluda Gap on the South Carolina border, along the French Broad River to Asheville, and through Warm Springs to the Tennessee line. In 1851 it was joined by the Asheville and Greenville Plank Road.[2] Although daily stages ran from Greenville, South Carolina, to Asheville, many travelers found the route tiring and expensive. West of Asheville, mountain travel proved difficult and slow, and in inclement weather, nearly impossible.

While most of the refugees in the Piedmont came from Virginia and eastern North Carolina, the orientation of the mountain turnpikes meant that most of the refugees entering western North Carolina came from South Carolina and, to a lesser extent, from east Tennessee. The South Carolina refugees who ended up in western North Carolina were part of a mass exodus from the Low Country to Columbia, Greenville, and Spartanburg. Those who ended up in North Carolina tended to be among the wealthiest of South Carolina refugees, including many of the Low Country planter elite. The most important destinations for refugees lay along the turnpike roads, especially the remote hamlet of Flat Rock.

Nestled in the Blue Ridge Mountains, the small town of Flat Rock became an enclave for a number of refugee South Carolina planters. Starting in the 1820s, Low Country planters had established summer retreats

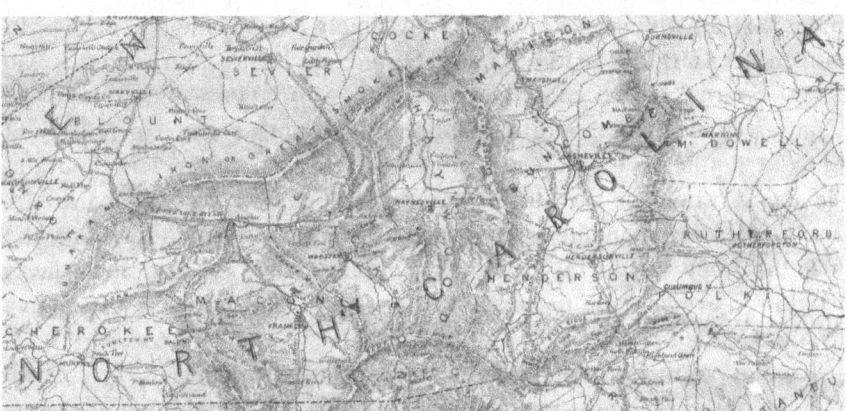

Figure 7. The North Carolina mountains. John R. Niernsee and John McRae, "Map of the Reconnaissance of the South Carolina Passes in Connection with those of Western North Carolina and Tennessee." Jeremy Francis Gilmer Papers, Southern Historical Collection, Wilson Library, University of North Carolina, Chapel Hill.

in Flat Rock, escaping the heat, humidity, and malaria that made living in or around Charleston unbearable and dangerous. By the 1850s, this summer retreat of the planter class had grown to several hundred people, including representatives from some of the most wealthy and politically connected families from South Carolina. The register for St. John in the Wilderness Episcopal Church, established by South Carolina planters in 1836, reveals that the remote hamlet attracted Low County aristocracy, including the Pinckneys, Middlestons, Memmingers, Hugers, and Lowdnes, leading the town to be nicknamed "Little Charleston."[3]

The Civil War transformed Flat Rock in two significant respects. First, South Carolina planter families decided to make Flat Rock a permanent retreat rather than a temporary respite from the Low Country miasma. Traditionally, they had arrived in Flat Rock in June and left by fall. After the Union incursions to the Sea Islands and coastal rice plantations in late 1861 and 1862, however, many South Carolina planters sought a permanent refuge in the remote mountain hamlet, sheltering friends and family members seeking a secure locale for the war. Many of the refugee planters who arrived in 1861 or 1862 did not leave Flat Rock until 1865.

Second, refugee planters brought hundreds of slaves with them. While they had always brought some of their domestic slaves with them on their summer retreat, the threat posed to their plantations by Union forces caused them to remove hundreds of field hands to Flat Rock, an environment radically different from their Low Country rice plantation homes. In November 1861 Union forces under Samuel du Pont captured Port Royal on the South Carolina coast, placing the entire Atlantic seaboard between Charleston and Savannah under threat. Du Pont's seizure included not only a significant Confederate port but also more than ten thousand slaves, who became the nucleus for the famous Port Royal Experiment. For Low Country planters just outside of Union-occupied territory, the fear that they would be visited by Union soldiers or that their slaves would run away to join those at Port Royal provided a powerful incentive to remove them.[4]

Coastal South Carolina planters faced a similar calculus as their North Carolina brethren in deciding whether, when, where, and how to remove their slaves from the threat posed by Union forces. In September 1861 William Elliott, an elderly South Carolina cotton and rice planter, warned his son, then serving in the Confederate army, that he should remove his slaves to the interior. "Your plantation at Hilton Head will be in imminent danger [from Union occupation]," he wrote. "I advise you to move off most your hands, carrying what provisions you can collect and what cotton you can take away without exposing your hands." At seventy-three years of age, Elliott had, through inheritance and marriage, acquired thousands of acres of prime Low Country farmland and more than two hundred slaves. He had established a home in Flat Rock in 1848, with the family spending most of their summers there, escaping the Low Country heat and humidity. His daughter Mary, wife of his fellow South Carolina planter Andrew Johnstone, had already decided not to return to Charleston for the winter, and her husband had begun the process of removing their slaves to Flat Rock. Presumably she expected to return to their plantation shortly, as "such a move could only be temporary I imagine—for in the pine region they were going to, there would be no provision or work to occupy them."[5]

Low Country rice planters faced one significant complication that their tobacco- and cotton-planting neighbors to the north did not. Unlike tobacco or cotton fields, which benefited from a period of laying fallow, rice cultivation required carefully managed irrigation, run through a complex and delicate system of canals and dikes. Without constant supervision and maintenance, these irrigation systems would collapse, resulting in the need for expensive and timely repairs when the planter and his slaves returned. In a series of letters, the cousins Susan and Harriott Middleton explained the rationale behind their families' (and many other planters') decision to remove their slaves to Flat Rock and other sites in western North Carolina. On January 31, 1862, Susan observed that "the [Low Country] planters are in anxiety about their negroes," with many of them planning on removing them to the interior. By May 1862, Harriott's father, Henry A. Middleton, had decided to remove most of their slaves to their home in Flat Rock. In Greenville, South Carolina, after disembarking from the train from Charleston and prior to boarding the stage for Flat Rock, Harriott wrote to Susan that "the agitation amongst the servants in town [Charleston] was becoming very unpleasant and we did not care to subject ours to it any longer." In response, Susan, who remained in Charleston, envied her cousin, noting, "How lucky you all are in having a comfortable home in a fine climate ready for you!" Her family had attempted to find a refugee home in Columbia but had found that "there is so much difficulty here [Columbia], in this mean little town, in finding a place of refuge, even at an exorbitant price, the extortions which are practiced upon the low-country refugees, by the so-called 'best people in Columbia,' are enough to disgrace the place forever."[6]

The flight of Low Country planters, their families, and their slaves in late 1861 and 1862 clogged the roads to western North Carolina. One refugee noted his discomfort in September 1862 as he waited for the "Stage to leave Greenville [South Carolina] for Flat Rock at 1 A.M." During the fourteen-hour trip, the passengers sat in lamplit darkness on the overcrowded stagecoach until sunrise. "Precious close packing it was, ten inside," noted the refugee in his diary. "One of the ten was an immense fat negro woman, the washerwoman for no less a person than the Secretary of the Treasury at Richmond, Mr. Memminger, whose family were at Flat Rock." When Mary Boykin Chesnut's niece Mary Williams traveled from Greenville to Flat Rock, she complained about being crowded with "four or five other persons in a most dilapidated old rattle-trap of a stage," traveling through "sleet and snow and slush ... over the great corkscrew roads across the mountains." When one of the overworked horses died, the party marched to the next house along the road, a distance of twelve to fifteen miles, until "our feet became stiff and cold and our hair frozen to our faces."[7]

The arrival in Flat Rock of refugee planters and their slaves exposed class tensions within the Blue Ridge that had been festering for decades. One observer noted that throughout the antebellum period, South Carolina planters "contributed but little to the general improvement of the country. Their slaves furnished them labor, and store goods were furnished from abroad. The natives were kept at a great distance, and if they were employed at all, only for menial occupations at inadequate remuneration. A feeling of great bitterness sprung up between both classes."[8] Although South Carolina planters had been visiting the area for more than two decades, there remained a significant social distance between the locals and the summer residents of Flat Rock. For their part, the planters rarely interacted directly with locals, preferring to socialize with their Low Country compatriots. Planters in Flat Rock, for instance, built and attended their own Episcopal church, St. John in the Wilderness, rather than attend services at any of the several Methodist or Baptist churches in the area where locals worshipped. Prior to 1861, St. John's remained open only during the summer, when Low Country planters were in residence. Nestled among pine trees, St. John in the Wilderness had been remodeled in 1852 by the famed Charleston architect Charles C. Jones, who modeled the structure on a Tuscan hill church, including a square bell tower and round-arched windows. A gallery at the lower end of the church provided pews for slaves, while wealthy summer residents, such as Charleston judge Mitchell King, routinely paid fifty dollars to rent a pew at St. John's, considerably more than mountain yeoman farmers could afford.[9] Compared to the humble, rough-hewn churches of the surrounding communities, the ornate brick edifice of St. John in the Wilderness must have seemed like a cathedral.

This social distance, built and maintained during the 1840s and 1850s, allowed planters to mythologize their mountain neighbors. At times they admired the mountain yeoman's apparent individualism and ruggedness. For instance, a child of Civil War refugees noted that

> to many of the South Carolina rice planters the Mountain White was an interest and much admired revelation. We might say that in more ways than one he lived in high places: he was lofty in his habitat and in his opinion of himself. Having wrested his living from the mountain steeps, he very properly had a high estimate of his own abilities and was able to look with undaunted eyes upon these "flat-landers". Though he might be as poor as a pike staff, the mountaineer was independence itself, and his honesty was such that it was said you could leave an ax (an ax being a most highly prized tool) and come back the next day and find it where you left it on the road.

Other outsiders developed negative stereotypes, emphasizing the financial, intellectual, and moral poverty of the region. One described the mountain residents as "poor tenants of small farms, or parts of farms or still ruder mountaineers, dwelling in squalid log huts, and living by fishing, by occasional day's work in the gold mines, by illicit distilling, roguery of all sorts and other invisible means of support."[10]

The house of C. G. Memminger, a South Carolina lawyer, politician, and Confederate secretary of the treasury, was representative of the social divide between the South Carolina aristocracy in Flat Rock and the neighboring yeoman farmers. While modest compared to their Low Country plantations and Charleston residences, the summer residences in Flat Rock dwarfed in both scale and grandeur the modest homes of neighboring locals. Memminger decided that his summer cottage, built in 1838 atop a steep hill overlooking the valley below, was worthy of a name. He dubbed it Rock Hill and used that name rather than Flat Rock when addressing his correspondence. Other Charlestonians in Flat Rock adopted a similar pretense, with neighboring houses designated Beaumont, Argyle, and Tranquility. With approximately nine thousand square feet of living space, not including the numerous outbuildings, Memminger's house featured fifteen-foot ceilings and ornate molding. He decorated the house with five crates of furniture imported from Germany, including twenty-four dining chairs, a dressing bureau, and a tea table. Most of the property's more than two hundred acres were wooded and rocky, inappropriate for commercial agriculture (Memminger called it "miserably barren"), but very picturesque. The view from his front porch consisted of a small lake, nearby Glassy Mountain, and on clear days, the Blue Ridge Mountains in the distance.[11]

As historians John Inscoe and Gordon McKinney have demonstrated, the mountains of North Carolina contained a greater socioeconomic diversity than many contemporaries and historians have supposed. Although the region had few slaves or slave owners, especially in the counties bordering Tennessee, the practice was not entirely foreign. According to figures calculated by Inscoe and McKinney, slaves composed approximately 10 percent of the regional population and slave owners maintained a significant position within the local political and economic hierarchy.[12] Yet South Carolina planters, whether they were summer visitors prior to the Civil War or refugees during it, appeared largely ignorant of the social complexity within the local populace. They rarely, if ever, mentioned locals by name in their diaries and correspondence and preferred to socialize only with other Low Country South Carolinians.

In their economic relationships, South Carolina planters also preferred to keep local residents at arm's length. While small truck gardens on their property provided fruits and vegetables, planters purchased flour, corn, and animal fodder produced by local yeoman farmers. Rather than buy these items directly from the farmers, however, planters usually purchased them from a local merchant, who served as an economic conduit between the planters and locals. In Flat Rock this role was filled by Henry T. Farmer, a merchant, miller, and innkeeper.

Due to its low slave population, western North Carolina developed a reputation as a hotbed for Unionism. However, recent scholarship has suggested that Unionism in western North Carolina was neither as robust nor as universal as had been supposed. Like people in the rest of North Carolina, mountain residents were hesitant about secession until after Fort Sumter. Indeed, support for secession was probably stronger in the mountains than it was in the Piedmont. During the first two years of the conflict, western North Carolina supported the Confederate war effort with the same fervor as the rest of state, with more than four thousand volunteers from mountain counties enlisting by October 1861 and more than eight thousand by the year's end. Not all mountain residents, however, responded favorably to the call for arms. A Baptist minister wrote to Governor Clark in August 1861 that most mountain farmers "have no negroes to defend and will not take up arms for the South."[13]

As the war progressed, many mountain residents soured on the Confederate cause. The turning point for many of them was the implementation of the Confederate draft. The passage of the conscription act in April 1862 marked the first significant turning point in the relationship between Low Country refugee planters and their mountain neighbors. During the winter of 1861–62, the *rage militaire* had diminished, and dropping enlistment prompted the Confederate Congress to enact the first conscription act in American history. The act made all able-bodied white men between the ages of eighteen and thirty-five liable for military service for three years. It also extended the service of men who had one-year enlistments for an additional two years. This blanket enlistment had several significant loopholes. First, those with the means to do so could purchase substitutes from among the "persons not liable for duty." Since most men of fighting age were subject to the draft, the price of substitutes (most of whom were foreign nationals or above draft age) rose to $6,000 by late 1863, well out of the price range of all but the most wealthy Southerners. Second, certain occupational categories were except from the draft, including government officials, clergymen, and teachers. Widely unpopular throughout the South, the new conscription law drew the particular ire of mountain yeomen, who saw clear class bias in the legislation. Although many of the men of draft age had already enlisted, the draft threatened the already depleted labor force to the extent that many mountain residents worried about starvation. One Stokes County farmer noted that "if all the conscripts from my county are taken off, it will be impossible for those left behind to make support for another year."[14]

Some mountain residents vowed to resist conscription. Although most mountain men begrudgingly joined the Confederate army, a few fled into the mountains rather than submit to conscription, forming the nucleus of draft resisters' bands that would grow and proliferate over the next three years. According to one Yadkin County resident, "When the time came for them to go, perhaps 100 in this county took to the woods, lying out day and night to avoid arrest." Although it is difficult to assess the size and number of these bands during the summer of 1862, rampant rumors suggest that they were not insignificant. By 1863 Governor Vance estimated that at least twelve hundred armed deserters, many of them in deserter bands, roamed "the mountains and inaccessible wilds of the west."[15] Furthermore, many mountain soldiers who had enlisted in 1861 for twelve months felt that the two-year extension of their service infringed on their liberty. Matthew Love, a lieutenant in the Twenty-Fifth North Carolina Regiment, wrote to his father in Henderson County, not far from the refugee enclave of Flat Rock, that "there is a great deal of dissatisfaction in camp concerning the press law[.] some say they are going home when their times is out regardless of consequences."[16]

Flat Rock refugees largely dismissed the mountain residents' complaints about conscription. Mary Johnstone wrote to her mother that "we have had a conscript commotion in this county and several others, the ignorant natives, asserting that there was no law to compel me to enlist, and many of them threaten to take to the Balsam [Mountains] and there resist to the death. When it came to the test, however, most of those liable formed into Volunteer companies." Mary Johnstone presumed that their reluctance to enlist resulted from their hostility to a war they saw as benefiting the planter class rather than hardscrabble farmers. This hostility manifested itself not only in resistance to the Confederate draft but also in animosity directed at the South Carolina refugee planters. Mary Johnstone wrote that "a great deal of animosity is felt against the low country gentlemen it seems, ('this being a rich man's war')," resulting in one of her relatives being "assaulted by one of these outlaws, who sneaked behind him, and gave him a violent blow on his head with a rock, stunning him for the time, . . . and Mr. Lowndes has had a gentle hint that 'he is to be hung.' They are too cowardly a race to give me any anxiety tho' I should much regret the necessity of shooting any of them."[17] The palpable disdain in Mary Johnstone's letter reflected the low opinion that most refugee planters held of their mountain neighbors.

Approximately 130 Henderson County men submitted to the Confederate conscription in July 1862, forming Company B of the Sixty-Fourth North Carolina Regiment. Instead of fighting against Union forces, the Sixty-Fourth Regiment was detailed primarily with patrolling the North Carolina and Tennessee mountains for deserters, duty that disheartened and discouraged the soldiers. Although they rarely caught deserters, when they did, the deserters received brutal treatment. In the case of the notorious Shelton Laurel Massacre in January 1863, thirteen captured Madison County Unionists, ranging in age from thirteen to sixty-four, were executed.[18]

Ironically for a unit tasked with hunting deserters, many soldiers in Company B abandoned their assignment. Within a year after its formation, nearly half of the company had deserted, one of the highest rates of desertion in the entire Confederacy.[19] Almost none of the deserters from Company B returned to Confederate service, preferring to remain outlaws. At least two dozen of the deserters eventually joined the Second North Carolina Mounted Infantry, one of two Union regiments formed in Tennessee from Unionists and Confederate deserters. Led by Capt. George Kirk, the Second North Carolina Mounted Infantry conducted raids into western North Carolina during the latter half of the conflict. In September 1863 the remainder of Company B was captured by Union forces near the Cumberland Gap in Tennessee. Sent to a Union prison camp in Illinois, many of the soldiers died of disease, while others decided that enlistment in the Union military was superior to languishing in confinement.[20]

Henderson County locals directed much of their hostility toward Mary Johnstone's husband, Andrew Johnstone, a South Carolina rice planter. Johnstone's plantations near Georgetown were home to more than two hundred slaves. Johnstone had purchased more than eight hundred acres in Flat Rock in the 1830s, erecting his summer house (Beaumont) there in 1839. Built of granite, Beaumont featured eighteen rooms spread over two stories. In 1861 Johnstone relocated himself, his wife, his children, and most of his slaves to Flat Rock year-round, fearing for their safety in coastal South Carolina. Johnstone surmised that his family and human property would be secure within the confines of his Flat Rock estate, as far from Union armies as one could be within the Confederacy.[21]

Two weeks after the initial confrontation over conscription, Mary Johnstone wrote to her mother that her husband had received "a written warning from 'the citizens of Crab Creek, Mud Creek, Willow Little River, and other parts of the country' to remove from the state within a week all of his negroes until the war is over, or failing to do so they will come and remove Mr. J with his negroes, not choosing to leave their wives and children among so many negroes." Rumors of the threats against Johnstone spread quickly in the Flat Rock refugee community. Mary Boykin Chesnut, visiting her sister in Flat Rock during the summer, wrote to her husband that "we had a fright here. The North Carolina people threatened to burn down Mr. Andrew Johnstone's place because he brought his negroes here." Harriott Middleton wrote to her cousin that "the country people here objected to Mr. Johnston's bringing up his negroes from the plantation saying it would raise the price of provisions. A hundred men swore to put him and his people beyond the state line."[22]

It is unclear why Andrew Johnstone became the subject of the particular ire of mountain farmers. Harriott Middleton's supposition that their anger resulted from fear that the presence of the refugeed slave population would lead to an increase in food prices appears justified. Johnstone himself knew that his property in Flat Rock could not sustain the nearly fifty people now living there. He had already decided, like many large planters, to divide his slaveholdings, placing the "old people and children" in Santee, South Carolina, while bringing up his house slaves and prime field hands to Flat Rock. Andrew Johnstone believed it was imperative to keep the "prime darkies" nearby, "thinking the risks immense in keeping them in such accessible positions" near possible Union invasions. Even with their slaves divided, the Johnstones found it challenging to acquire adequate sustenance for themselves and their slaves in Flat Rock. Mary Johnstone lamented that "the difficulties this year are so numerous that many have determined to do without." However, with financial resources far exceeding the average mountain resident, Mary Johnstone was able to procure four hundred pounds of flour for fifty dollars, as well as "plenty of bread, beef, and fine mutton." Despite her temporary ability to purchase foodstuffs in Flat Rock, Mary Johnstone worried that the local supply would soon evaporate. She wrote to her mother, then contemplating joining them, that she "had better save as much of your bacon, lard, rice, salt, peas, and everything eatable to bring with you as you possibly can. Times will I fear be even more hard than they are now." Finding adequate provisions for livestock also proved problematic. During the summer of 1862, Mary Johnstone lamented, "Provisions are so high that teams are not to be had." Later that year Mitchell King agreed that "provisions here [in Flat Rock] for both man & beast are expected to be quite exorbitant."[23]

Flat Rock refugees quickly organized to protect Johnstone. After hearing of the threat, Mitchell King rode out to Andrew Johnstone's house and encountered Johnstone en route. Nearly eighty years old, King was a plantation owner and judge in South Carolina who had been among the first to purchase land in Flat Rock. In poor health and mourning the recent death of his son at the battle of Secessionville, King nevertheless felt that he had to take action in response to the threat against Johnstone. According to King's diary, the men conversed at length about the "Conspiracy agt. Souther[n] men." Together they went to see Rev. Charles Pinckney, who concurred that "action [was] essential," especially against Unionists rumored to be in the area. They agreed to have a "defensive gathering at Johnstons Friday." Around Johnstone's dinner table, the refugee planters discussed their options. They agreed to have a rotating watch at Johnstone's house each evening. Capt. George Cuthbert, on leave from Lee's army after being wounded in battle, volunteered to take the first shift. The men also agreed to send for additional ammunition to defend themselves.[24]

The defensive measures taken on Johnstone's behalf temporarily prevented direct physical confrontation between refugee planters and their Henderson County neighbors. A month after the threats against Andrew Johnstone began, however, five refugee planters were arrested and taken to the Henderson County jail in Hendersonville, accused of "having beaten an old country woman nearly to death." Found "tied to her bed, and dreadfully bruised and cut up," Mrs. Corn accused the refugee planters of assaulting her. The five accused, however, were unlikely assailants, as they consisted of an elderly Episcopal clergyman, a doctor, their wives, and an unmarried young woman. When the refugee planter community, which had gathered that morning at St. John in the Wilderness Church for a Thanksgiving service, heard of the arrest, "the whole church convulsed." Timely intervention with the sheriff by Andrew Johnstone and Henry Farmer and a brief trial secured their release. To Harriott Middleton, this incident illustrated the "bitter feeling entertained here to the low country people." Mary Johnstone was more pointed in her analysis, asking, "Did you ever hear of such impertinence?"[25]

The apparent attack on Mrs. Corn in September 1862 coincided with two significant changes in the Confederate conscription law. First, it was amended to raise the upper age limit to forty-five. For many mountain families, this enlargement of the draft engulfed many male heads of household on the eve of the harvest, when their labor was most needed. Second, the Confederate Congress simultaneously exempted from the draft one white man on every plantation with more than twenty slaves. The ostensible purpose of the infamous "Twenty-Negro Law" was to ensure that slaves would be supervised, preventing them from running to Union lines, which by late 1862 was becoming endemic in many parts of the Confederacy.[26]

The approaching harvest and the reversal of Lee's army at Antietam in September 1862 pushed refugee planters to reconsider their situation. Many of those who had come to Flat Rock the previous summer envisioned their stay in the mountains as merely an extended version of their usual summer retreat. By the fall of 1862, however, it became clear that the war's end was nowhere in sight. The conflicts between refugee planters and their mountain neighbors had deteriorated significantly, and many refugee planters worried that they would be unable to secure sufficient provisions to feed themselves and their slaves in the future.

Newly elected governor Zebulon Vance complained to President Jefferson Davis in October 1862 that "thousands are flying from our Eastern Counties with their slaves to the centre & West to devour the very short crops and increase the prospect of starvation."[27] Born in Buncombe County, Vance knew instinctively how the introduction of thousands of refugeed slaves into the North Carolina mountains would compromise the ability of the region's subsistence farmers to feed themselves, especially with the yeoman workforce conscripted into the Confederate army.

Many mountain residents worried about the danger presented by so many Low Country slaves. In February 1863 a group from Yadkin County calling themselves "Confederate Friends" urged Governor Vance to remove refugeed slaves from the region because they threatened public safety. If Vance did not act soon, they warned, "we will Bee Ablige to put Some of them to deth for this." Later that year Vance received a letter from a Buncombe County slaveholder who informed him that many whites in the region feared that the importation of so many slaves would result in "negro Ravages."[28] Two days before Christmas, 1863, Henry Farmer "summ[on]ed all the Gentlemen to a meeting at Flat Rock" because "it was reported that the negroes in Transylvania (French Broad) were to demolish the white." They organized a patrol, with Andrew Johnstone and Dr. Thomas Means taking responsibility for Flat Rock. According to Mary Johnstone, the measures were unnecessary: "Of course it was all a farce. The darkies all expected the patrol and receiving them politely the next day." Johnstone surmised that the rumors about a slave "insurrectionary attempt" had been started by "some of the Militia men who were sent off from here, and wished to be recalled for home protection.... I do not imagine the negroes had the remotest intention of mischief, but the accidental absence of some of the proprietors may have alarmed the natives."[29]

While Mary Johnstone dismissed the threat posed by refugeed slaves, Katherine Polk Gale's family near Asheville had their house burned to the ground by a disgruntled slave. After being awoken by screams in the middle of the night, Katherine Gale initially believed that they were the victims of a Yankee raid, only to discover that their house was on fire. Gale rushed her children out of the house and joined the line passing buckets of water from the cistern to the house. After interrogating the other slaves, "we were all compelled to come to the conclusion it was the work of 'Josh' the cook, who had a very bad temper." The property of Katherine Gale's mother, Josh had been brought to Asheville from New Orleans and had supposedly threatened arson in the past. When Josh's role in the fire was uncovered, the family arranged for him to be sent to Atlanta, which General Polk, Katherine Gale's father, was defending. En route, Josh escaped.[30]

As in other parts of the Confederacy, refugees in the mountains struggled to secure sufficient food. In February 1863 Henry Middleton worried that he was "quite at a loss to imagine how it will be possible for me to make my limited income, even under the most economic management, pay the expenses of the war." He bemoaned the exorbitant prices he had to pay for meager foodstuffs and the expenses necessary to maintain not only his family but the slaves he had brought with him, noting that he recently paid seven dollars to mend a pair of slave shoes. "Unless something is done, and done soon to change the course which things are going," he wrote, "I can not see anything ahead but utter bankruptcy and ruin." Henry's daughter Harriott concurred in a letter to her cousin that same month, noting that "people here are taken up with the difficulty of getting any thing to eat and to wear. No beef to be killed, and not bacon or poultry to be bought!" As the adult daughter of a planter and unaccustomed to manual labor, Harriott remarked to her cousin that while they had insufficient food, "we have indeed a spinning wheel, and weaving machine, and intend to manufacture cloth!" Several months later, Harriott elaborated on their dietary difficulties, noting that "we are not starving but living on bacon, rice and hominy. Those who can, eat bacon. The unfortunates who can't go without meat. I am in the latter class, which has so distressed Mamma, that she has sacrificed two chickens." Harriott worried that the immediate gratification of eating chicken came at the cost of future eggs, noting that "I felt quite overwhelmed.... how shall I be able to eat this chicken when I think of the dozens of eggs and broods of chickens I am devouring."[31]

Andrew Johnstone decided that he could make better use of his slaves in the mountains were he to acquire additional land. In September 1862 Mary Johnstone wrote to her mother that "Mr. J. is thinking of getting some lands on the river to plant if the war continues. Our prospects for the winter are gloomy enough, as the absolute scarcity of food is becoming alarming." Two months later Andrew Johnstone left Flat Rock in search of additional places to house his slaves, some of whom were still at his Low Country plantations, although his wife lamented that "it seems impossible to get food, shelter, and lands to cultivate provision." Johnstone planned to keep many of the women and children at an encampment at Santee, roughly halfway between Charleston and Columbia, and entertained the idea of "sending the men ... to work upon a N.C. Railroad." When his expedition took longer than Mary Johnstone anticipated, she noted, "I hope he will be back soon or the darkies here will die from idleness."[32]

By the spring of 1864 Johnstone had put nearly one hundred acres of his Flat Rock estate into cultivation, as well as an additional sixty acres along the French Broad River. Unlike most refugee planters, the Johnstones had a wagon and team, facilitating the transition of their Flat Rock estate to agricultural production. At Mary Johnstone's father's estate in Flat Rock, refugeed slaves had to work without the benefit of a plow because he could not afford to feed the draft animals.[33] According to Mary Johnstone, most refugee planters had to pay "4 dollars a bushel for corn" to be delivered to them by locals. Even with the additional land under cultivation, the Johnstones struggled to procure sufficient food for themselves and their slaves at Flat Rock. Mary Johnstone lamented that they had difficulty purchasing additional foodstuffs from locals, since "the country people having taken to eat their own poultry, butter, & eggs." Mountain farmers, who had traditionally sold their surpluses to Flat Rock summer residents, found that the Confederate tax-in-kind and the conscription of male labor into the Confederate army necessitated conserving whatever temporary surpluses they produced. To refugee planters, this conservation by mountain farmers amounted to hoarding. Mary Johnstone spoke approvingly of efforts by government officials to "put a stop to the hoarding of corn by the farmers and obliging them to take in payment Confederate money which they have refused heretofore."[34]

By March 1864 the situation for the Middleton family and other refugees in Flat Rock had grown worse. Harriott Middleton grieved, "We are in a present state of disagreeable corn uncertainty." The local merchant from whom they had been purchasing corn for themselves and their slaves informed them that "he cannot send us another ear! And what are we to do! ... I have never heard of genteel people starving." In March 1864 the food shortage was compounded when soldiers under Gen. James Longstreet's command marched through western North Carolina on a foraging expedition, stripping the region of food. Impressing horses and mules, Longstreet's soldiers seized much of the previous year's grain harvest, leaving already destitute mountain farmers even more imperiled. Harriott Middleton wrote to her cousin that "as we were looking at the soldiers[,] an old man passed us on his way from the mill and said ... 'It's a sad sight for us. They will leave us nothing to eat.'" Mary Johnstone lamented to her mother that "three thousand of Longstreet's men passed thro' here a few since going to Johnston and stripped the all [foodstuffs] that was left." One mountain resident wrote to Governor Vance, complaining that Longstreet's men had "come down through McDowell, Burke & Caldwell [Counties] & have nearly consumed all the grain they could pick up on their tracks. What are poor day laborers to do for bread when every crib in the land is depleted to the lowest possible standard. ... I see a dark day ahead for the poor sons of toil and in fact for us all unless some unforeseen good luck should happen."[35]

Accustomed to luxurious dining at their South Carolina plantations, the Middleton family and other refugees were compelled to eat whatever was available. In March 1864 Harriett Middleton noted that the family had been regularly eating potato soup, which she described as "but disguised hot water." In sharing the recipe with her cousin, she noted its "demoralizing effects," but as they had been "so long debarred from luxuries," they "could not enjoy them!" Mary Johnstone observed that "the prices of everything and scarcity are excessive. If you meet a neighbor they can only talk of the impossibility of getting anything to eat. Many of them have no meat for days."[36]

If wealthy white refugees worried about the state of their diet, their slaves fared far worse. Rations, especially meat rations, were cut back significantly. In March 1864 Laura Norwood noted that "our negroes have been doing with less.... We have had a very inadequate supply of bacon for this year, and no prospect of being able to get any more I have of late allowed the men 1/3 of a pound of bacon a day." Refugee planters in Flat Rock also struggled to find adequate housing for their slaves. Unlike their Low Country plantations, their summer residences in Flat Rock had few slave cabins and were completely inadequate for the number of slaves refugeed during the Civil War. Furthermore, many of the slave cabins and converted barns that planters used to house their slaves were never intended to be occupied during winter months, exposing the poorly clad slaves to bitterly cold drafts. In October 1862 the Johnstone's gardener, a local farmer named Cartwright, informed his employer and landlord that he would no longer live in the small house on the Johnstone estate, as "he could not stand the negroes—their dancing and fighting at night was too much for him." Rather than regret losing the man who had cared for their property for many years, Mary Johnstone observed that she wished the Cartwright family "would vacate now instead of in a month that we might have their house for the negroes."[37]

Many of the slaves refugeed to Flat Rock and other mountain communities suffered from ill health, undoubtedly enhanced by the inadequate food, shelter, and clothing. In November 1861 Mary Johnstone complained that "in spite of the fine weather, we have had the servants all ailing with pains & aches." Like many of their refugee planter neighbors, the Johnstones sought out Dr. Mitchell King to tend to their ailing slaves. According to his medical ledger, Dr. King, the son of the elderly judge Mitchell King and the only practicing physician in Flat Rock, treated dozens of cases of diphtheria, scarlet fever, and typhoid. Writing to her mother, Mary Johnstone noted that under Dr. King's care, their slaves' heath had improved, such that "the negroes with diphtheria are also well, so is the man with the dropsy.... [I] have been very busy lately (or rather Nonie Gran and Eleanore have) in making comforts for the negroes having obtained some cotton, and using all the quilts and curtains to be found." Despite Dr. King's efforts, the ravages of disease took a significant toll on refugeed slaves in Flat Rock, including Johnstone's slave Nonie Gran, an elderly nurse who had cared for the Johnstone children and most recently for other sick slaves. Having died after "three weeks of unceasing pain and restlessness," Nonie Gran appeared unrecognizable with her emaciated body in a black burial gown and muslin cap. Andrew Johnstone arranged to have her buried in the family's enclosure at St. John in the Wilderness but had the funeral service performed at his house, as "it would be impossible for family and servants all to get to the church." Nonie Gran's name does not appear in the church's register of deaths; however, the ledger does indicate that Nonie Gran was not the only refugeed slave in Flat Rock to succumb to disease during the Civil War. According to the incomplete records kept by the church at least a dozen slaves shared her fate, including five who died during a one-month period at the height of summer in 1864.[38]

Like slave-owning refugees in the Piedmont, many Low Country refugees attempted to rent out their slaves in order to reduce the burden of feeding and housing them. Unlike the Piedmont, however, the mountains had no major employer of refugeed slave labor to rival the railroads or hospitals that rented much of the surplus slave labor in central North Carolina. The closest analogue in the mountains was the Asheville Armory, a wartime factory that rented a handful of refugeed slaves in 1862 and 1863. As in Flat Rock, locals in Asheville resented the economic and social competition posed by refugeed slaves, severely whipping a South Carolina slave named Allen, who was discovered without a pass from the armory. In some parts of the North Carolina mountains, slave trading remained robust throughout the Civil War, and slave renting appeared to have increased, with mountain masters such as Nicholas Woodfin, Calvin Cowles, and Walter Lenoir taking advantage of wartime dislocations.[39]

Some mountain residents saw the widespread availability of slaves on the market as an opportunity to enter the slaveholding ranks for the first time. In March 1864 Mary Bell purchased her first three slaves, a family that had been removed from Charleston, South Carolina. Shortly after their purchase, she wrote to her husband, a dentist then serving in the Confederate army in Alabama, "I told you that you need not be surprised if [I] made a nigger trade. Well I have done it." Because of some shrewd investments, Mary Bell had some disposable income, which her husband urged her to invest. "I don't think it a good policy to keep money on hand," he wrote her from the army. "I want you to invest what you have in something; either for a negro or land." In weighing these alternatives, Mary Bell must have been struck by the effect that the recent arrival of hundreds of white and black refugees had on the respective prices of slaves and land. While the price of land in Macon County, a western county with a miniscule antebellum slave population, had increased significantly since the beginning of the war, due to the increased demand created by white refugees, the price of slaves, if controlled for inflation, had decreased significantly. Given the alternative, Mary Bell's purchase seemed to make good financial sense. During her year as a member of the slaveholding class, she expressed mixed feelings about the wisdom of her purchase. On the one hand, she regretted that the slaves did not work as hard as she had hoped, writing to her husband that "these low country negroes are not like ours in their work or anything else." In a moment of desperation, Mary complained that Patsy "is like all other south niggers—don't know much about the work as we do" and contemplated selling the slaves if "they do not make my crib full of corn." On the other hand, she considered purchasing additional slaves, a venture that her husband encouraged.[40]

In and around Flat Rock, however, few opportunities existed for refugee slave owners to rent their slaves. Several Flat Rock refugees attempted to rent their slaves to the railroads in the Piedmont. In October 1862 Susan Middleton noted that some eighty of her family's slaves were sent to Greensboro to work on the Piedmont Railroad. She observed that "they seemed quite willing to go, and in good spirits, declar[ing] that they had no idea of going to the Yankees," while at the same time she urged her cousin to "get an up-country place, and move their families, where they would be safe." Recognizing the weakness of Confederate currency, some refugee slaveholders rented their slaves for food. The Polk family rented "some twenty excellent negro men & their families" to neighboring farmers in exchange for "supplies of Bacon, wheat, flour, potatoes, etc.; in that way provisions for the family were secured so long as hostilities lasted."[41]

Like other refugees, Low Country refugees in Flat Rock anxiously anticipated news from home and from the front lines. With the nearest telegraph station nearly eighty miles away in Morganton, Flat Rock refugees depended on the sporadic mail delivery via the Buncombe Turnpike. In the aftermath of the battle of Port Royal in November 1861, refugee planters in Flat Rock worried about the fate of their Low Country plantations. Unable to wait for news to reach them, they sent an express coach to Greenville, South Carolina, the nearest railroad terminus, for the most recent updates, but, observed Mary Johnstone, "as yet we have no news, and the suspense is harassing." A month later, Mary Johnstone noted that "the mail continues to be the chief object of interest." News of war developments came too slowly and late for most refugee planters in Flat Rock.

When Union forces occupied New Orleans in May 1862, it took nearly a month for the news to reach Flat Rock, and then details were sparse. In September 1862, more than four months later, Mary Johnstone complained, "How slowly we get news. Our New Orleans neighbors must feel pretty blue about their property." Although she never named them explicitly, the New Orleans neighbors Johnstone referred to were probably the Urquhart and Fisk families. These refugee families had arrived in Flat Rock after leaving Union-occupied New Orleans in June 1862, having received permission from Gen. Benjamin Butler to leave the city. During their absence from New Orleans, they knew that their adjacent homes were used by Union officers, although the exact state of their homes remained a mystery until their return to the city in the fall of 1865.[42]

When inclement weather washed out the roads, mail delivery often ceased for days at a time, leading Mary Johnstone to observe, "In consequence of bad weather and horrible roads we have been without mails since Monday, a privation severely felt in these anxious times." Katherine Polk Gale regretted that "letters took a long time to come; they gave but meager news; but in our mountain home how we watch for the coming mail; only three time a week; but some one in our large circle, always got news from the absent ones, of only a few lines on the march." When news did reach Flat Rock, it was rarely good. Low Country refugees received accounts, often second- and thirdhand, that their plantations had been burned or occupied by Union soldiers. Many refugee planters also regularly received news that their slaves in South Carolina had fled to Union lines. In May 1862 Mitchell King noted in his diary that he had heard about a "steamer stolen from our wharves last night by negroes & carried to the Lincolnites." Two months later, the Johnstones learned that two dozen slaves they had left at Santee had attempted to run to the Union-occupied enclaves on the coast. While some had been captured by Confederate patrols, most of them had managed to make it to the Sea Islands. When Union raids on the Combahee River district in June 1863 imperiled several refugees' plantations, Mary Johnstone wrote to her mother that "after the raid upon the Combahee neighborhood where we hear the negroes were packed up ready to leave, I feel extremely uneasy. I do not think Jacob's faithfulness will prevent a stampede from Social Hall, and the success at Combahee will only renew the wish of the Oak Lawn darkies to test freedom for themselves." While the Johnstones' plantations survived that raid, several of their refugee neighbors' homes fell to the torch. When Flat Rock residents received the June 4, 1863, issue of the *Charleston Mercury*, they discovered that the Middleton, Manigault, and Lowdnes plantations had gone up in flames during the raid, Union soldiers "pillaging the premises of these gentlemen, the enemy set fire to the residences, outbuildings and whatever grain, etc., they could find ... taking with them between 600 and 700 negroes." In the months to come, Mary Johnstone wrote to her mother that Flat Rock refugees "dread to hear of some new trouble [in South Carolina] in the shape of negro raids."[43]

The forced separation from home brought about severe homesickness in some refugee planters. On Christmas Day 1863, after more than a year in Flat Rock, Harriott Middleton expressed her longing for home in a letter to her cousin, noting, "I wonder if you feel the same intense love which I do for that low country, weather, atmosphere.... The very thought of that low lying, dimly colored landscape, sometimes flooded with sunshine, sometimes veiled in haze, stirs my heart and thoughts in a way that only one or two others ideas in the world can produce." When Ann Stuart, a Flat Rock refugee from Beaufort, South Carolina, died in May 1862, her family inscribed her tombstone in the St. John in the Wilderness graveyard with the epitaph that she had died "driven in her last years from her beloved home by the casualties of war." Less than a year after Stuart's death, her daughter grieved that as "an Exile from Home & Motherless, this has been the darkest & saddest season of my life.... It often makes my heart ache to think of my beautiful Home in ruins & of my dear old Beaufort in the hands of the Enemy. I sometimes think I will never feel at Home."[44]

During the summer of 1863, tensions between Flat Rock refugee planters and their neighbors intensified. The increasing size and strength of deserter gangs, formed the previous summer, terrorized the civilian population. In an 1863 letter to the Confederate secretary of war, Rev. Thomas Atkin of Asheville "and other citizens of Western North Carolina" argued that "the safety and security of [their] homes and property ... [were] seriously menaced and openly assaulted by herds of disloyal citizens and gangs of deserters from the Confederate army.... In the event, the conscripts ... are taken into the Confederate service, we shall doubtless fall an easy prey to the malicious hands of marauders, which now openly parade themselves in the different counties, west of the Blue Ridge." In a letter to her husband, then serving in the Confederate army, Sarepta Revis of Henderson County wrote that "the war has commenced hear [sic] at last.... There is more deserters than there is malishey [Home Guard] hear."[45]

Although many mountain residents worried about the looming presence of bushwhacker gangs, these deserter bands posed a particular threat to refugee planters in Flat Rock, who felt that they had become the preferred target. Not only were they significantly wealthier than their Henderson County neighbors, but as Low Country South Carolinians, they represented the secessionist impulse, a physical manifestation of a war and a government that many mountain residents had soured on. In a worried letter to her cousin, Harriott Middleton noted that "a hundred deserters are lurking around, and in consequence the militia of the County has been ordered out." Constantly outnumbered, members of the Henderson County Home Guard were both apprehensive and ineffective against deserters. With deeper social and familial connections to the deserters than to refugee planters in Flat Rock, the Home Guard was reluctant to intervene when refugee planters were targeted. Harriott Middleton complained in October 1863 that "there was another horse theft in the neighborhood last night.... It is said that the magistrates are afraid of taking any measures to prevent the robberies, for fear that their own will be taken, and hitherto only the horses of the Low country people have been taken." Some refugee planters concluded that while they had successfully escaped war on the South Carolina coast, they had found another one in the North Carolina mountains. Mary Johnstone lamented in April 1863 that a state of war had broken out in Flat Rock, as "the tories threatened to burn out the Lowlanders."[46]

Refugee planters' growing paranoia about deserters caused them to be on edge. In a letter to her cousin in December 1863, Harriott Middleton revealed that the rumors of outlaw and deserter bands had gotten the better of her: "I quite alarmed the house hold last night. There was a series of most mysterious noises in the house—wood falling down, steps walking about, the doors visibly shaken.... I stood it for a long time, but when I heard the doors being tried alternately, and the falling of the umbrella which stood in the corner, I rushed into Mama's room and declared some person must be there. She rang the bell violently, and soon Isabella and a servant came rushing to our assistance. They searched every where and could find nothing." After a lengthy hunt, they surmised that the noises had been made by a large cat.[47] Although Harriott Middleton intended the episode to assuage and amuse her cousin, it indicates the extent to which their fears of attack permeated refugee planters' thoughts and dreams.

The looming threats against Andrew Johnstone came to fruition one evening in early June 1864. As the family completed their dinner, a band of six men rode up to Johnstone's Beaumont estate. Johnstone excused himself from the table to greet the men, who presented themselves as a detachment from the Confederate army searching for deserters. After asking for forage for their horses, the men came into the house for dinner, with Johnstone's slave Annie scrabbling to prepare a second dinner from their meager pantry. Johnstone's daughters followed their father's lead in extending hospitality to the visitors, playing for them on the piano and "German music box." Johnstone's fifteen-year-old son, Elliott, noticed that some of the men had paused by the hat rack in the hall, trying on the hats. When the visitors "became too free in their manners," Johnstone sent his daughters upstairs, whispering to them as they retired to watch for signs of pilfering. Recent robberies in the area, especially committed against wealthy refugees, had put Johnstone and other refugee planters on guard against theft. Andrew Johnstone silently handed his son the key to the upstairs wardrobe, where he kept a loaded English fowling piece.

Although disturbed by their guests' behavior, Andrew, Mary, and Elliott Johnstone continued to entertain the men. Alarmed by the threats against her husband and rumors of deserter bands roaming the mountains, Mary Johnstone tried to make conversation with their guests, nervously brushing flies away from the food, while Elliott slipped out and seized the gun from the upstairs wardrobe. After a tense meal and coffee made with rye, the leader of the gang, described in some sources as the "Sergeant," demanded that Andrew Johnstone fill their satchels with food, a request to which Johnstone acquiesced. Calling to his men, some of whom had retired to the passageway outside the dining room, the Sergeant pulled his pistol on Johnstone, declaring, "You are my prisoner, Sir." When Johnstone reached for his small pocket revolver, a constant companion since the first threats against him in Flat Rock, the Sergeant fired. The bullet passed through Johnstone's body and into the wall behind. Hearing the shot as he returned downstairs, Elliott Johnstone exchanged fire with one of the other men in the hallway, receiving a grazing wound in his shoulder. In the confusion that followed, the mortally wounded Andrew Johnstone fired wildly at his assailants as they bolted from the house, collapsing shortly thereafter.

While Mary Johnstone cradled her dying husband, Elliott pursued the attackers. On the porch, he found one man lying on his back, whom he initially presumed dead, until the man raised his pistol to fire at Elliott. Before he could fire, Elliott wrestled the pistol from the fallen intruder and "shot him where he lay," before pursuing the other bushwackers. In an exchange of fire between Elliott Johnstone on the porch and his father's assailants in the nearby woods, the teenage refugee managed to mortally wound two of them; in "his just anger," the wounds left "lasting marks for repentance." When neighbors, alarmed by the gunfire, came to Elliott's aid, the remaining men fled into the woods. By the time Elliott returned to his father's side, Andrew Johnstone had less than an hour to live.[48]

Immediately after Andrew Johnstone's murder, a posse drawn from Flat Rock's refugee community and Home Guard soldiers searched the nearby woods and fields in pursuit of his attackers. Not far from the house, they found a wounded man and "gave him no quarter, [but] killed and buried him on the spot." They later captured another wounded man in the woods and "if both barrels of I'On Lowndes' gun had not snapped, he would have killed him also." After a brief stint in the Hendersonville jail, the wounded man was court-martialed in Asheville as a deserter and sentenced to hang in Morganton. The soldiers escorting him "pretended to give him a chance to escape and shot him."[49]

The identities and motivations of the men who attacked Johnstone remain unclear. Oral tradition within Flat Rock suggests that they had come via "a trail through the Dark Swamp from the general direction of Brevard."[50] Several sources, including a letter written more than forty years later by Elliott Johnstone, point to the Kuykendall gang, a band of deserters led by three brothers from Henderson County who had deserted from the Confederate army. The gang's leader and the most likely suspect in Andrew Johnstone's murder, Jahu Kuykendall, enlisted in the Sixteenth North Carolina Regiment in March 1862 and was wounded at the battle of Gaines Mill but deserted in July 1863. He enlisted in the Second North Carolina Mounted Infantry Regiment, a Union regiment raised in Tennessee, in October 1863, only to desert a few months later. Throughout 1864 and 1865, "Kuykendoll and his gang of deserters" had terrorized the residents of Flat Rock, "restricting their operations generally to the breaking into and pillaging the houses of the South Carolinians." In addition to Andrew Johnstone's murder, the Kuykendall gang reportedly attacked the home of Beatrix and Eliza De Choiseul, daughters of the French consul to Charleston, beating Beatrix "with the butt of a pistol to insensibility," leaving her unconscious with "a terrible sabre cut on her head," while they "pillaged the house at their leisure." The gang also attacked Mary Boykin Williams's home. Awakened at two in the morning by a loud knock at the door, Mary's mother yelled from an upstairs window that there was nothing left in the house to steal. The gang first threatened to burn the house down, then broke open the door, attacking Mary's mother and attempting to rape Mary's sister. When the women fought back, the men looted the house and fled.[51]

After her husband's murder, Mary Johnstone debated moving her family to Greenville, South Carolina, fearing that her son would be targeted for killing his father's murderer. As refugee families rallied around her in the aftermath of her husband's murder, Mary Johnstone felt that she "could not unless in absolute danger to my children leave this place, although at first I felt inclined to rush from it forever." Her brother urged her to relocate, as Elliott's "life will be forfeited if he is not brought away." Two weeks after his father's murder, Elliott moved to Greenville on the counsel of friends. Mary Johnstone remained steadfast in her determination to stay in Flat Rock, although she asked her brother to remain with her, ostensibly to "assist in the council of war." With the family's Low Country plantations under Union control, Mary Johnstone deliberated with her brother, weighing the "discomfort, expense, and ruination of the only home which this family possesses, which a removal will cause . . . against the possible danger which may ensue from their remaining here." Their decision was complicated by the absence of her husband's will, which they believed was in South Carolina. Without it, it would be difficult to sell Beaumont or find alternative housing in Greenville.[52]

While Mary Johnstone resisted leaving Flat Rock, many other refugees quickly concluded that the situation in the North Carolina mountains was more hazardous than they had anticipated. After Andrew Johnstone's murder and the attack on their home, Mary Boykin Williams and her family fled Flat Rock to Greenville, South Carolina, where they were joined "by many of those who had fled like ourselves from the terror of the deserters." Their number included Elliott Johnstone, "with his partly healed arm," and Beatrix De Choiseul, "with a part of her raven black hair cut off and a plastered with black court-plaster." Crammed into a small house in Greenville, the Flat Rock refugees, driven for a second time from their homes, "sat and talked over our experiences," wondering if they would ever return to Flat Rock or to the Low Country.[53]

A month after her husband's murder, Mary Johnstone left Flat Rock for Greenville, joining her son, who had managed to secure temporary housing for them there. On the eve of her departure, she wrote to her sister that "I am to leave tomorrow this home, made so beautiful and comfortable for us by my darling husband, and I may not have courage to write again soon. It is a great trial to desert this home. I feel as if I were still near him here, tho' I listen in vain for his steps, his voice, and miss oh so much those little hourly attentions—a flower, a beautiful cherry."[54] With the status of her husband's estate in limbo, the family struggled to survive the war's final year in Greenville, a struggle than continued well after the war's conclusion as Mary Johnstone fought to assert her claim to her husband's property. In 1868 the former plantation mistress was reduced to teaching school in order to support herself and her children.

Most South Carolina refugee planters remained in Flat Rock after Andrew Johnstone's murder, albeit with significantly increased concerns for their own security. C. G. Memminger, who had recently joined his family in Flat Rock after resigning as the Confederate secretary of the treasury, fortified his house against possible attacks. Because of the threat posed by "a gang of deserters from the Confederate Army," Memminger removed the steps from the front of the house, barricaded the ground floor windows with sandbags and wooden spikes, and cut gun ports in doors and walls in case the house were sieged. From within his fortified domicile, Memminger wrote to Jefferson Davis that a "state of anarchy" prevailed in Flat Rock. "The condition of this corner of North Carolina is exceptional. Its loyal population is all in the army. The mountains here afford strongholds to the deserters and outlaws from North Carolina, South Carolina, Georgia, and Tennessee. They have already organized two bands and have driven away some of the inhabitants, and they seem to proceed only against the low country people and the families of soldiers who are absent in the army." Memminger implored Davis to step up the military presence in the area and to take draconian measures against deserters. Given how thinly spread the Confederate forces were at the end of 1864, Davis's response was unsurprising. While "the outrages and depredations enumerated call for means of repression," additional resources were unavailable.[55]

Unbeknownst to Memminger, at least one of these bands spent the night in an outbuilding on his estate. At approximately the same time that Memminger wrote his letter to Jefferson Davis, four Union soldiers who had escaped from a POW camp in South Carolina followed the same route that refugee planters had taken to Flat Rock, hoping to reach Union lines in Tennessee. They entered Flat Rock at night, slipping past a sleeping watchman guarding the bridge into the hamlet. In the heart of the refugee planter enclave, however, the four Union soldiers were discovered by an armed patrol of four men, the leader of which burnished a sword. After a failed attempt to persuade the patrol that they were Confederate soldiers on leave, the fugitives fled into the woods and took shelter at the summit of Glassy Mountain, less than a mile from Memminger's home.[56]

Fearing that they would be tracked during daylight by dogs, the fugitive Union soldiers plotted to leave Flat Rock as soon as they could. They knew, however, that traveling during the daytime would be suicidal. Hungry, tired, and scared, their misery was compounded when the morning rains turned to sleet, and by noon into snow. It grew much colder as the day progressed, and heavy winds froze the poorly dressed soldiers, who hid under rocky outcroppings as they tried to preserve their body heat. From this vantage point, they noticed a small patch of cultivated land at the base of the mountain. Overcome by hunger, they descended from their rocky shelter, only to discover that the cabbages were frozen solid to the ground and could not be removed without great effort. While bent over prying the frozen cabbages from the frozen ground, they were discovered by four grown women. When they attempted their usual ruse of pretending to be Confederate soldiers, they discovered that the women were Unionists, "boldly asserting their full sympathy with the Federal arms." After a thorough interrogation by the women, they revealed their identity as Union soldiers and their intention to escape to Union lines at Knoxville. Feasting on corn bread and apples, the men rejoiced at meeting the rumored "'good Union people' of North Carolina" in the mountains.[57]

After feeding the hungry soldiers, the women offered them shelter in the garret of their house. The sisters revealed that they "lived in a rebel neighborhood and were tenants to a rebel landlord." George Hadley, one of the four Union soldiers, who later chronicled their adventure, did not name the "rebel landlord" the women rented from, except to say that he was a former Confederate cabinet officer, undoubtedly a reference to Memminger.[58] The sisters sheltered the men in a small hidden chamber in the upper story of their home that they had constructed to conceal their brother from Confederate conscription gangs. They also arranged for the fugitive Union soldiers to rendezvous with an outlaw gang headquartered near Flat Rock who would guide them to Knoxville. The sisters warned them that this gang "are bad men, at least they are so regarded by both rebels and Unionists; they have the reputation of killing many people and robbing many more; they have been declared outlaws by the proper authorities, and one thousand dollars reward offered for their arrest."[59]

After several days in hiding, the men were led by the gang leader's sister to their hideout in the Blue Ridge Mountains. According to John Hadley, the outlaws were dressed in coarse, threadbare clothes and armed with Springfield rifles. The leader, Jerry Vance, possessed long, dark hair that grew to his eyes, a dark beard, and a "wool hat so full of holes." Vance's gang looked "so much like rebel soldiers" that Hadley feared for their safety. After some tense negotiations, Jerry and his younger brother Jack agreed to lead Hadley and his men over the mountains to Knoxville in exchange for $400, "payable in gold and silver." As they prepared for their journey to Knoxville, Hadley learned that Jerry and Jack Vance had both deserted from the Confederate army and Jack had also deserted from the Union army. They had lived as outlaws for the previous two years, living in rudimentary cabins, barns, and caves. Their band consisted of eight men in similar circumstances, who "expressed the most inveterate hate for rebels" and "regarded every man a rebel who had valuables." The gang "now lived on spoils . . . sacking every 'fine house.'" Their cave was furnished with silverware, jewelry, and other items plundered from nearby homes, including one of their more recent acquisitions, a life-sized portrait of George Washington, liberated from the "parlor of a rebel."[60]

Given that John Hadley routinely employed pseudonyms in his narrative, the Vance brothers were probably the Kuykendall brothers, leaders of the Henderson County gang who were likely responsible for Andrew Johnstone's murder. Although only one of several such bands in the region, the Vance-Kuykendall gang undoubtedly perpetrated much of the violence and robbery committed against Low Country refugee planters in Flat Rock. According to Hadley, their "depredations were so notorious that the rebel authorities had published a solemn proclamation of outlawry against them." In the month prior to Hadley's arrival in Flat Rock, the homes of several refugee planters in Flat Rock had been burglarized, including "five men [who] robbed Mrs. Singleton's house in broad daylight," and "Burrell's and Mr. Pringle's houses being both robbed twice."[61] Even more shocking was the attack on the home of Col. Joseph Bryson, not far from Flat Rock. Colonel Bryson had gone to bed early, when eight men arrived at his house, asking to see him. When his wife, two daughters, and a slave stepped out on the porch to greet the visitors, "the men at the gate fired on them, killing Mrs. Bryson instantly, and inflicting painful and dangerous wounds upon the young ladies." The *Asheville News* attributed the murder to Colonel Bryson's identification as "an active Southern man." Bryson had been active during the previous two years in attempting to reduce the presence of outlaws and deserters in Henderson County. In June 1863 he had led a failed expedition to round up deserters. Bryson claimed that the "outlaws are a terror to the citizens, and especially to the soldiers wives who are alone" and that they had threated his life and the life of any Confederate officer who would attempt to conscript them. The death of Bryson's wife, surmised one Flat Rock refugee, was no accident but "deliberate, intentional murder."[62]

Prior to escorting Hadley and his men to Knoxville, the Vance-Kuykendall brothers insisted on one final robbery, of a refugee doctor in Flat Rock. Initially the Vance-Kuykendall brothers demanded that the fugitive Union soldiers join them; however, after pleading that they "felt no desire for the romance of robbing, and probably, murdering," and that they "could not wish to punish and rob a man who has done us no harm," the Vance-Kuykendall brothers relented, allowing Hadley and his men to stay at their hideout under guard. Although he did not witness the attack in person, Hadley gathered from subsequent conversations that when the Vance-Kuykendall gang arrived at the house, they found the doctor and his family sitting around the fireplace.[63] They fired a volley at them and then rushed into the house. The doctor fled immediately out the back door into the woods, leaving his wife and three children in the hands of the Vance-Kuykendall gang. The gang ransacked the house in search of valuables, tying a noose around the doctor's wife's neck, threatening to hang her. Under beds in the house, they found three black men hiding, who were made to dance for their amusement. The Vance-Kuykendall gang left the house largely empty-handed after three hours and promptly left with Hadley and his men for Knoxville, fearing that they would be pursued.

Hadley does not give the name of the doctor, although circumstantial evidence suggests that it may have been Dr. Thomas Means, a refugee planter from South Carolina. According to records from the 1860 census, Dr. Means owned more than sixty slaves on his St. Helena plantation. He had come with his family to Flat Rock in early 1862, bringing several slaves with him. In September 1862 he had his wife had been arrested and detained for the assault of Mrs. Corn, until they were liberated through Andrew Johnstone and Henry Farmer's intervention. Just prior to the Vance-Kuykendall gang's attack, Dr. Means had been warned via message left with a slave on a neighboring estate that were he not to leave the area, "he would be put in his coffin."[64]

During the final year of the war, Flat Rock remained almost entirely cut off from the rest of the Confederacy. Mail delivery essentially stopped and travel in and out of the mountains became more difficult. Mary Johnstone claimed that "the annoyances of travelling now a days are enough to deter all voluntary locomotion." With deserter gangs a ubiquitous threat, planter refugees spent the final months of the war bunkered in their mountain estates. Nine years old in 1865, Edward Memminger, son of C. G. Memminger, later remembered that the Confederate surrender did not bring about an end to hostilities in the mountains, as "after the surrender at Appomattox, the Union troops came through Flat Rock and ... pillaged some of the houses and took whatever they wanted. In the day the men of the family 'took to the woods' to escape the soldiers and had to come back at night to defend the house from a gang of deserters from the Confederate Army, who had turned bandits and terrorized the community with their burglaries and other offences."[65]

Many Low Country planters who took refuge in the North Carolina mountains emerged from the war bankrupt. While their Low Country estates were sacked by Union armies, refugee planters "found no better treatment in the interior; the mountaineers hated them as cordially as did the Yankees, and visited their places with like vengeance. Many of their residences were burned down, the flocks and cattle destroyed, they themselves driven away by threats, violence and assassination. It was a wheel within a wheel, and none pitied them, for they were mainly instrumental in putting the first in motion. Unaccustomed to labor, and raised in luxury and affluence, they were reduced to great wretchedness and poverty."[66]

The slaves taken to the North Carolina mountains were among the last of those east of the Mississippi to be liberated. George Robertson, a refugee in Asheville, remembered a "great negro hegira immediately after their realization of the fact they were free." Numbering in the "hundreds and hundreds," newly emancipated freedmen and freedwomen celebrated by leaving their former owners. Robertson was struck by the fact that, rather than march southeast, where most of the refugeed slaves had lived prior to the Civil War, "they moved almost en masse towards Tennessee," following the Union army. For refugeed slaves, emancipation gave them the opportunity to relocate on their own terms. Among the crowd of "negroes, freedmen of all sorts and sizes," one figure stood out to Robertson: "A rather boney horse on whose back were piled sundry and divers bundles, sacks packed with clothing. On top of this pile sat an elderly negro woman of generous proportions, her bonnet hanging over her back, held there by ribbons. She was astride the sacks, holding the reins in hands that were swinging with the motions of riding, and she was shouting at the top of her voice. 'Glory, glory! We's free, we's free. Glory, Halleluia!'"[67]

Compared to other North Carolina refugees, the refugee planters of the North Carolina mountains did not suffer the same threats of disease, overcrowding, and famine that menaced refugees on the coast and in the Piedmont. Although they complained about shortages, their material wealth allowed them to live in conditions not too dissimilar to their accustomed antebellum luxury. Their greatest fear turned out to be not the Union army or starvation but the hostility of the local populace, who had come to view their presence as a threat to their economic well-being and as an embodiment of the class divisions within the Confederacy. Committed secessionists and slave owners, the refugee planters sought sanctuary in a corner of the Confederacy with comparatively little investment in either secession or slavery. For some, like the murdered Andrew Johnstone, this sanctuary proved to be anything but.

Epilogue

When Clara Dargan heard that Confederate general Robert E. Lee had surrendered to Union general Ulysses S. Grant at Appomattox Courthouse in April 1865, her first thought was "I must go home." Like most white refugees, Dargan, a sixteen-year-old from Columbia, South Carolina, living in Chatham County, North Carolina, longed to return home as soon as the war ended. Shortly after Christmas 1864, Dargan had been sent to "the interior of North Carolina, . . . when it was considered unsafe to remain in the possible line of march of Sherman's merciless myrmidons." Without mail for weeks, Dargan had no news from home or from family members, which the war had scattered. Despite her fervent desire to return home, Dargan found that "transportation was impossible. Railroads were destroyed; horses and mules of any worth had been seized by friends or foes; vehicles of all sorts were apprehended or in a state of utter dilapidation." With her refugee home more than forty miles from the nearest railroad stations in Raleigh and Greensboro, Dargan had to stay in Chatham County for several months after the Confederate surrender, until she could take a "spavined mule and dilapidated buggy" to Greensboro. There she boarded a train home, horrified that the other passengers were "a motley crowd, consisting chiefly of 'citizens of African descent' and Yankee soldiers." Except for a confrontation with Union soldiers in Salisbury, her trip south from Greensboro through Charlotte was uneventful. Once she entered South Carolina, however, she saw the "'desolation of desolation.' Not a fence or house or living animal where once I had remembered such happy homesteads." When she finally arrived at home, she found "a chimney here, a blackened ruin there, the silence as of death, attested the pathway of the destroyer. One wondered where all the former dwellers in these homes had gone. Where were their cows and chickens, and hogs, and cattle?"[1]

Confederate surrenders at Appomattox, Bennett Place, and elsewhere did not bring an end to the North Carolina refugee crisis. Reconstruction changed the terms but did not fundamentally alter the debates over land, resources, and mobility that the refugee crisis had created. As in earlier phases of the crisis, a refugee's geographical and social position shaped the options available to him or her. Many white Confederate refugees, like Clara Dargan, had longed to return home, only to experience profound disappointment, despair, and alienation upon their return. Financial uncertainty and a decimated transportation infrastructure imperiled their return home. For many black North Carolinians, the Confederacy's demise did little to transform their immediate humanitarian catastrophe, as the refugee camps continued to grow. Newly emancipated African Americans continued to seek protection in the small shadow of safety created by the occupying Union army. With only a small footprint in North Carolina, the army and the newly chartered Freedmen's Bureau proved largely impotent in efforts to protect black and white Unionist refugees from violence and discrimination at the hands of former Confederates and slave owners. Officials with the thinly staffed Freedmen's Bureau often demonstrated more interest in returning black refugees to agricultural labor than in meeting their immediate humanitarian needs. In their efforts to prevent black refugees from becoming dependent upon the government, Freedmen's Bureau officials were unwittingly aided by recalcitrant white North Carolinians who sought to forcibly return African Americans to the plantation and reclaim land granted to black refugees, using the twin tools of law and violence to do so. Unwilling to surrender the gains made during the war, African Americans resisted efforts to break up refugee communities and curtail their mobility, maintaining that freedom of movement was a hallmark of their freedom. As in earlier phases of the refugee crisis, black political mobilization was fundamentally intertwined with their physical mobility.[2]

For Clara Dargan, the journey home marked the end of her experience as a refugee. In her absence, her home had been radically transformed, rendering it almost unrecognizable. Many white refugees shared Dargan's longing for home and disappointment when they eventually returned. When Lavinia Roberts, a refugee from New Bern, returned home in April 1865, she discovered that her house had burned to the ground. "Not even the ashes of my old home remained," she noted years later, as "the provident Yankees had gathered them up with the bricks from chimneys, basement, wine cellar, and even from the pavement in the street. The very earth had been carried, so that where flowers and shrubs once grew, was a stagnant pond." The daughter of a wealthy planter and wife of an equally wealthy lawyer, Roberts had been accustomed to a life of "ease and luxury." Forced to flee in 1862 during the Burnside invasion, she had lived for three years on a modest farm in Warren County, where she with her children were "generally hungry, our clothes had been thread-bare, and we had many trial and tribulations." Despite her difficulties as a refugee, returning home proved even more challenging. Arriving nearly penniless, she "began life over again."

With only sixty cents in her pocket, she rented two rooms for herself and her eight family members, "one to sleep in, one to live in." Included among that number was her husband, Frederick Roberts, who had been discharged with tuberculosis from his service in the Fifth North Carolina Cavalry in 1863. Lavinia described her husband as "a war wreck, broken down in health and spirits." Their five children, three of whom had been born while their mother was a refugee, were all ill; her oldest son died less than a week after the family's return to New Bern. Lavinia Roberts blamed her son's death on the twenty thousand black refugees expelled from Sherman's army a few months earlier, many of whom took up residence in James City, just across the river from her home. When smallpox broke out among them, they "were allowed to walk the streets of New Bern with the disease in all its stages [and] took great pleasure in rubbing against the white people." Of her family's own slaves, now free, only one remained, whom Roberts described as a "young, incompetent, and indifferent servant." The Robertses had left their other former slaves in Warren County, as they had "no money to pay the traveling expenses of the servants."

Like many white refugees in the North Carolina Piedmont, Lavinia Roberts had yearned since leaving New Bern in 1862 for the opportunity to return home and reestablish the life she had led prior to the war. As someone who "loved the old South," she longed for "the ease, the comfort, the refinement, the culture we once enjoyed." What she found instead was a set of challenges just as difficult as any she faced when she was a refugee. "With bowed heads and aching hearts," Roberts wrote of her return to New Bern, "we began the battle of life again."[3] For almost all refugees, regardless of race, class, or gender, the cessation of hostilities rarely resulted in an uncomplicated return to their antebellum lives.

Instead, it created a new chapter of the refugee experience. Many refugees, like Lavinia Roberts, attempted to return home, only to find that the home they had dreamt of for years no longer existed. Other refugees saw the end of the war as an opportunity to create a new life for themselves, sometimes making their refugee homes permanent. The variety of postwar experiences suggests that the Civil War refugee crisis did not end with the Confederate surrender but commenced a new phase in which refugees had to make difficult decisions about where and how to rebuild their lives.

Like Lavinia Roberts and Clara Dargan, most white refugees returned to their homes at the end of the war, although many found their homes transformed. Even those whose houses remained intact found that the homes they returned to bore only passing resemblance to the homes they had left. Only ten years old when she became a refugee, Ellen Bellamy was still becoming accustomed to her family's new home when she was forced to leave it. When the war began, her family had recently moved into an enormous Greek revival mansion in downtown Wilmington. Completed only weeks before the attack on Fort Sumter, the mansion featured twenty-two rooms, replete with modern amenities, including running hot and cold water and gas chandeliers. Her father, Dr. John Bellamy, a wealthy physician and landowner, had advocated secession and had chaired the welcoming committee when Jefferson Davis visited Wilmington in May 1861. Ellen Bellamy had left Wilmington with her family in September 1862, moving to Floral College in Robeson County, where they lived with other Wilmington refugees. Her parents believed that they would be safer there from both the threat of Union invasion and yellow fever. Unlike most refugees, the Bellamys periodically returned to their Wilmington mansion. After the occupation of Wilmington in February 1865, her parents' vacant home had been commandeered as Union headquarters. When the Bellamys attempted to return to Wilmington in September 1865, they found that their house remained occupied by Federal soldiers, including Gen. Joseph Hawley, an abolitionist and one of the founders of the Republican Party in Connecticut. Neighbors who had stayed in Wilmington told the Bellamys that their home had been defiled by raucous interracial parties held in the mansion. "My parents . . . repeatedly tried to get possession of their home," Bellamy later wrote, "to no avail." On one visit, the Bellamys felt humiliated to be stopped at the front door by a "nigger soldier" and then "entertained by Mrs. Hawley, in [their] own parlor." When, months later, after Dr. Bellamy received a presidential pardon, they eventually reclaimed their house, the Bellamys found it in a deplorable state, with tobacco stains caking the floors and mantel. Even in her old age, Ellen Bellamy believed that their home retained some corrupting pollution from its temporary occupation. Although the physical structure remained intact, for Ellen Bellamy, it would never again be the same house.[4]

The return of white refugees such as Lavinia Roberts and Ellen Bellamy coincided with the return of Confederate soldiers. James Rumley, a Confederate sympathizer who stayed in Beaufort during its Union occupation, noted in his diary in May 1865 that both Confederate soldiers and refugees "whom we have not seen for three year past, appear daily in the streets . . . as they did in better days." In New Bern, Wilmington, Beaufort, and other sites on the North Carolina coast, white refugees and former Confederate soldiers came home to communities occupied (and largely dominated) by Union soldiers and black refugees. When the Northern journalist Whitelaw Reid visited coastal North Carolina in early May 1865 as part of a government delegation to assess conditions in the postwar South, he observed the tensions created by the interaction of black and white refugees, returning soldiers, and Union soldiers. In Wilmington, Reid noted that the streets were filled with white "refugees from the late theatre of military operations." One family walked alongside a "crazy cart, with wheels on the eve of a general secession," pulled by an ill-nourished horse and carrying "tables, chairs, a bedstead, a stove, and some frying pans." White refugees, Reid believed, "seemed hopeless, and in some cases, scarcely knew where they wanted to go." He also observed that many black refugees had congregated in Wilmington, most of them arriving within the previous few months, as Union occupation provided protections unavailable on the coastal plantations outside the city. Their plight was complicated by the "constant return of old proprietors, and the general confusion and uncertainty as to the ownership of real estate." Many black refugees told Reid that they lived in fear of white violence and of reenslavement once Federal soldiers left.[5]

Most of the black refugees Reid encountered in Wilmington had only recently arrived in the city, entering after its Union capture in February 1865. When Reid visited New Bern, he encountered black refugees who had lived in refugee communities for more than three years. He described the Trent River settlement (now James City) as a "remarkable city of log cabins, outside the city limits, which now really form the most interesting part of the ancient town of Newbern." He noted that while New Bern had an antebellum population of between five and six thousand people, "these newly-built cabins on the outskirts, alone, contain over ten thousand souls." When Reid visited during the first week of May 1865, he noted that very few of the city's antebellum white residents remained, claiming that New Bern had been "deserted by its former inhabitants, and filled by Union refugees from all parts of the State." Reid observed, however, that these wartime conditions were rapidly changing with the cessation of hostilities. During the same week that Reid visited, "men, whose faces have not been seen in Newbern for nearly four years, are beginning to appear again, with many an anxious inquiry about property." According to Reid, these returning soldiers and white refugees expected to find their property "to have been carefully preserved for them during their hostile absence." As in Wilmington, Reid observed that more often than not, New Bern's returning white residents found their homes occupied by Union soldiers and black and white refugees.[6]

Many out-of-state refugees stayed in North Carolina because they could not return home or knew that there was little left for them there. By the end of the war, Tennessee refugees James and Margaret Ramsey had lived near Charlotte since 1864. Cut off from their home in Knoxville, Dr. Ramsey complained that "we knew nothing of the large property we had left in Tennessee." Nearly penniless and desperate for any information about his home, Ramsey had throughout the war sought out any scrap that could offer insight. From rumors gathered from "the banished members of my household, from other exiles and refugees," and from the occasional Union newspaper that slipped through the lines, he learned that "the property was either burnt or destroyed or lawlessly sold, alienated or confiscated." Even if he wanted to return to his Tennessee home, it is unclear whether he had the means to do so. The formerly wealthy planter and physician and his wife had been reduced to "our joint fortune of forty-two dollars ... on which to start the world again." At sixty-eight years of age, Ramsey worried not only about how he and his wife would support themselves but also about his children, who had also been impoverished by the war: "Our daughters were not better provided for. Our four surviving sons were equally penniless." Although many formerly wealthy Southerners found themselves relatively impoverished at the end of the war, for refugees like Ramsey, their distance and isolation from home made their pecuniary dilemmas that much more vexing. "We were in North Carolina among strangers and many of them as much impoverished as ourselves," Ramsey later noted. "What was best to do? This was the question now to be solved."

Margaret Ramsey shared her husband's despair and anxiety about their situation at the end of the war. Two weeks after Johnston's surrender at Bennett Place, Margaret Ramsey compared their plight to that of the Babylonian exile: "Like the Jews when they were in captivity how we have yearned for our homes—'By the rivers of Babylon there we sat down, yea, we went when we remembered Zion.'" Like her husband's, Margaret Ramsey's sadness was mingled with confusion about where and how to live. "Everything in confusion," she wrote in her diary, "don't know what we are to do." Accustomed to a life of luxury, she had been reduced to "teaching for my board." She mourned for her distant Knoxville home that existed now only in memory. Once, while walking near her refugee home near Charlotte, she found herself in a place that reminded her of home. Overcome by emotion, she "sat down on a stump and gave vent to my feelings." In her mind, she could see her "beautiful home" with its "large and stately trees," along with images of fields, rivers, and majestic bluffs. "All of these I was once mistress of," she wrote, barely able to contain her tears. "Now the old mansion," she lamented, "is in ashes."

As much as they missed their home in Knoxville, the Ramseys decided to remain near Charlotte. Although Knoxville rested only across the Smoky Mountains from where they now found themselves, the Ramseys believed that they could not afford the journey. Shortly after the Confederate surrender, they decided "that as we have not the means to get away from North Carolina we would stay where the waves of revolution and disaster had floated us. We were as badly wrecked as mariners can be if they are not drowned." They were not the only refugees stranded in the North Carolina Piedmont at the end of the war; their neighbors included "refugees and exiles from New Orleans." Like the Ramseys, these neighbors were "perfectly destitute." With their property in Knoxville in limbo, tied up in convoluted court proceedings that dragged on for years, the Ramsey family remained in the Charlotte area, renting small residences that they numbered Exile's Retreat No. 1 through No. 3. Although Dr. Ramsey returned to Knoxville periodically, primarily to participate in legal hearings to reclaim his property, he no longer felt at home there, the city having been transformed in their absence. Joined by their daughters after the war, the Ramseys lived modestly, rarely interacting with the local populace. Margaret Ramsey complained that "there is but little generosity here—the people have no sympathy for refugees and those who have lost all . . . no sociality—no friendship—no attention to strangers." Despite their unhappiness in North Carolina, the Ramseys remained there until 1872, when they finally returned to Knoxville.[7]

While many wealthy white refugees chose to remain in North Carolina, especially in the Piedmont, so too did many African Americans who had been forcibly brought to the state by their owners. Freedom came to Milly Henry when she saw Union cavalry riding up Fayetteville Street in Raleigh. Henry had arrived in Raleigh a year earlier, having been brought from Mississippi by her owner, and rented out to a series of employers, the last of whom ran a boardinghouse. Years later Henry remembered that "de Yankees wus good ter me" but that in the immediate aftermath of the war, it "shore wus hard ter git a job." In a 1937 interview conducted as a part of the New Deal WPA Federal Writers' Program, Henry did not indicate why she stayed in Raleigh after the war. Her only known relative, her grandmother, had died in 1864 or 1865 in Mississippi, cutting her only meaningful tie to her native state. The interview transcript suggests that Milly Henry lived her entire life after emancipation in Raleigh, her home less than a mile from the site where she first saw Union soldiers.[8]

Although Milly Henry decided to remain in Raleigh, many African Americans in the North Carolina Piedmont, both natives and refugees alike, celebrated the Union victory and emancipation by exercising their ability to relocate, leaving their former masters and plantations. Controlling black mobility had been one of the defining features of slavery. For many freedmen and freedwomen, leaving their former owner's gaze without a pass proved the first tentative test of their freedom. By heading out on the road, former slaves placed physical and symbolic distance between themselves and their lives in bondage. A Freedmen's Bureau official in North Carolina observed that "to be sure of their freedom, many [freedmen] thought they must leave the old scenes of oppression and seek new homes." For many black refugees, returning home was less of a priority than finding lost family members. In May 1865 the journalist Whitelaw Reid observed that dozens of black refugees in Wilmington were "hunting up children and wives, from whom they had been separated." A few months later in Concord, John Dennett, another Northern journalist chronicling the South after the war, "met a middle-aged negro plodding along, staff in hand, and apparently very footsore and tired." He had been sold away from his family just as the war was beginning, and "as soon as he learned he was free determined to return to North Carolina to try to find his wife and children." By the time he met Dennett, he had journeyed for nearly two months and walked more than six hundred miles. In the quest to reunite with lost family members, many African Americans relied on newspaper advertisements. In March 1866 Augustus and Lutitia Bryant of Augusta, Georgia, placed an advertisement requesting information about the whereabouts of their five children, whom they had not seen since 1862. When last they had heard, their children had been taken to Charlotte, North Carolina.[9]

When Eliphalet Whittlesey, Freedmen's Bureau assistant commissioner for North Carolina, arrived in Raleigh in June 1865 to assume control of "all subjects relating to 'refugees, freedmen, and abandoned lands'" within the state, he found "hundreds of whites refugees and thousand blacks . . . occupying every hovel and shanty, living upon government rations, without employment and with comfort, many dying for want of proper food and medical supplies." From his Raleigh headquarters, Whittlesey observed that these were not static populations but that refugees, "both white and black, were crowding into the towns, and literally swarming around every depot," in desperate need of government aid. Whittlesey observed that the distribution of rations by the Freedmen's Bureau caused them to be "besieged from morning till night by freedmen, some coming many miles on foot."

Whittlesey claimed that his primary aim was "to aid the destitute, yet in such a way as not to encourage dependence." He ordered bureau agents to distinguish between those "really deserving" rations from the "throng of beggars" in search of a handout, instructing them to deny rations to those able to work. Under Whittlesey's supervision, "the homeless and helpless [black refugees] were gathered in camps, where shelter and food could be furnished." New refugee camps were established in Raleigh, Greensboro, Salisbury, and Charlotte. Freedmen's Bureau agents clearly intended these camps to exist only as temporary measures. At the "Freedmen's camp" in Salisbury, "the negroes are quartered in comfortable shanties," but were denied rations unless physically unable to work. Although "quite a large number [of black refugees] are received every day," they were allowed to stay only until "proper employ is obtained for them," such that "none may go there with expectation of remaining in idleness."[10]

Freedmen's Bureau agents in the North Carolina Piedmont struggled to implement Whittlesey's contradictory instructions to provide aid but avoid dependence. For Capt. John C. Barrett, a Union soldier from Indiana and a Freedmen's Bureau agent in Charlotte, African Americans' postwar migrations initially suggested chaos. Barrett noted in a letter to Whittlesey that "the whole population of Blacks were completely wild . . .

straggling over the country in search of freedom." He soon realized, however, that many African Americans in or near Charlotte were not native to the area but had been brought there during the war by their refugee owners. Although empowered to provide transportation for black refugees within North Carolina, Barrett did not have the authority under Freedmen's Bureau regulations to provide for those traveling to other states. By midsummer 1865 Barrett observed that fifteen to twenty black refugees arrived in Charlotte daily en route to South Carolina and Georgia, few of whom had the means to make it home. Indeed, Barrett estimated that Charlotte had more than five hundred homeless black refugees from eastern North Carolina, Virginia, Georgia, Tennessee, and across the former Confederacy. Barrett established a refugee camp on the outskirts of Charlotte to house these indigent refugees. Like many other Freedmen's Bureau agents, Barrett worked diligently to limit black refugees' dependence on government assistance, especially those able to find work and housing elsewhere. However, despite his concerted efforts, the refugee camp remained open until at least May 1866.[11]

At the same time that Barrett supervised the opening of new black refugee camps in the Piedmont, other Freedmen's Bureau officials pressed for the closing of the established refugee settlements in coastal North Carolina. In September 1865 Dr. M. K. Hogan, the Freedmen's Bureau's surgeon in chief for North Carolina toured the black refugee camps in eastern North Carolina. Like many Freedmen's Bureau officials, Hogan feared that black refugees would become dependent on the government and believed that refugee camps should either become permanent, self-sufficient settlements or be disbanded. At the Trent River settlement he found five thousand refugees living "as a town, with streets, &c. . . . in good comfortable log houses," only one thousand of whom were receiving government rations. Although James City, as many of its residents now called the Trent River settlement, remained one of the most populous communities in the state, almost half of its wartime population had left. When Hogan visited other mainland camps, he also found that they had become largely depopulated. The colony on Roanoke Island remained robust, though smaller than its wartime apex, with approximately thirty-five hundred refugees, mostly composed of soldiers' families. Hogan noted that twenty-two hundred refugees on Roanoke received government rations but that the majority of these were children under the age of fourteen. Although Hogan approved of the progress that black refugees had made in becoming independent of the government dole, he worried about the alarming number of black refugees who suffered from "intermittent and remittent fevers," noting that they had little access to proper medical treatment.[12]

Despite the Freedmen's Bureau's efforts to close refugee camps in coastal North Carolina, black refugees and Northern aid workers struggled to maintain civic institutions established during the war. Schools remained the backbone of the black refugee communities in eastern North Carolina. In October 1865 Eliphalet Whittlesey reported that North Carolina had sixty-three black schools serving 5,624 students. Of these sixty-three schools, at least half were located in refugee communities. One Roanoke Island teacher observed the zeal with which her students learned geography, "their favorite study." The subject undoubtedly had special meaning for a class made up of refugees who were now considering where to live in the postwar world. While maintaining schools remained a priority for black political leaders, so too did working for political and economic equality. Held in Raleigh's African Methodist Church in September 1865, the North Carolina Freedmen's Convention brought more than one hundred delegates from thirty-four counties. Although the delegates advocated for suffrage, the right to testify in court and serve on juries, and other political rights, they proclaimed that "our first and engrossing concern in our new relation, is how we may provide shelter and an honorable subsistence for ourselves and [our] families."[13] With North Carolina's black population in a state of flux, the delegates to the Freedmen's Convention recognized the importance of securing homes in establishing and maintaining freedom.

As in other parts of the former Confederacy, Freedmen's Bureau officials in North Carolina attempted to restrict postwar black mobility, urging African Americans to establish agricultural labor contracts, often with their former owners. They were particularly keen to push African Americans out of urban areas and back onto plantations. White North Carolinians also sought to place significant restrictions on black mobility. The black code established by North Carolina's first postwar legislature included several provisions limiting African Americans' freedom of movement, including a vagrancy provision that provided for fines, imprisonment, and hard labor at a workhouse.[14] The persistence of black mobility in the face of these twin threats suggests the extent to which freedmen and freedwomen saw the freedom of movement as a hallmark of emancipation.

Returning white refugees in eastern North Carolina asserted their claims to the land on which black refugee camps were built. Many black refugees assumed that they owned their homes and the plots on which they were built. This belief was particularly present in James City and Roanoke Island. In both locations, black refugees had constructed communities based on the promises made by Horace James and other Union officials that the settlements were permanent. Indeed, from the beginning of the Union occupation of eastern North Carolina, questions about legal title to land and property remained ambiguous, especially with respect to the parcels on which the refugee communities were built. Horace James himself had repeatedly used language throughout the war that suggested that black refugees owned the land on which they lived, noting in an annual report that they were "absolute owners of the soil."[15] Despite his public statements, James also made concerted efforts to purchase the land on which the refugee camps were built from its prewar owners. At the end of the war, the Freedmen's Bureau inherited this legal ambiguity. Under President Andrew Johnson's generous and largely indiscriminate amnesty policy, landowners in eastern North Carolina asserted their ownership, claiming that black refugees were squatting on their land and demanding that the Freedmen's Bureau aid them in collecting rents.

On Roanoke Island, Freedmen's Bureau officials discovered that the refugee camp, now stretching over more than one thousand acres, was built on land owned by twenty-five different parties. Starting in July 1865, these antebellum owners began asserting to Freedmen's Bureau officials that they rightfully owned the land. Foremost among them was Isaac Meekins, whose homestead formed the heart of the refugee community, housing not only black refugees but a delegation of missionary teachers from the National Freedmen's Relief Association, who had built a school on the property. Meekins demanded that the property be turned over to him, refusing offers by both the Freedmen's Bureau and the National Freedmen's Relief Association to purchase the land. In October 1866, more than a year after Isaac Meekins began lobbying, the Freedmen's Bureau officially recognized his legal title. Buoyed by Meekins's successful efforts, other white property owners on Roanoke Island began pressing for return of their property. The long occupation by refugees had transformed a section of Roanoke Island from thinly populated farmsteads to a densely populated and developed town. This transformation was documented by one white property owner who noted, "My land was taken for the benefit of freedmen when they sought Roanoke Island as a place of refuge; was laid off into acre lots, streets opened, and cutting the timber, they built several houses, which they continue to occupy."

Facing pressures from white landowners who wanted to reclaim their land and from Freedmen's Bureau officials in Washington who wanted to limit black refugees' dependence on government, local Freedmen's Bureau agents struggled to reduce the refugee population on Roanoke Island. Increasingly, bureau agents limited access to rations, hoping to induce able-bodied refugees to leave the island in search of employment on the mainland. By May 1866 rations were distributed to only two hundred of the fifteen hundred black refugees on the island. Although Roanoke's refugee population had declined significantly since the end of the war, many bureau officials complained that their dispersal had not progressed rapidly enough. In June 1866 Whittlesey ordered that bureau agents "clear the island at once." Despite these pressures, the remaining black refugees on Roanoke steadfastly refused to leave the island. Many believed that they owned the land on which they had been living since 1863. In the same month that Whittlesey ordered the refugee camp vacated, a Union official reported that "most of the freedmen believe the lands upon which they live are their own, or that the government will yet give them land." Others feared "the oppression & injustice of their old masters" on the mainland. Rumors of violence perpetrated against former slaves were rampant on Roanoke. Indeed, one refugee who had recently left the island had been "shot down in cold blood," his family returning to Roanoke after his murder. "Is there any wonder," noted one Northern teacher who remained on the island, that "they hesitate about leaving a place of safety?" By January 1867 the population of the refugee colony had declined to 950, 17 of whom received government rations. In May 1867 Gen. Nelson A. Miles, Whittlesey's successor as the Freedmen's Bureau's assistant commissioner for North Carolina, ordered the Roanoke Island settlement broken up, putting a final end to the refugee community that had begun there more than five years earlier.[16]

At James City, black refugees also engaged in a lengthy fight to keep land and homes they had concluded to be rightfully and legally their own. As in Roanoke and other black refugee sites, Freedmen's Bureau agents tried to encourage James City residents to leave by cutting off rations. Many local whites favored breaking up the settlement. In April 1866 the *New Berne Daily Times* argued that "in the Trent River Settlement ... there are about two thousand darkies, nearly all of whom are dependent on the government. ... All such should be driven out of the camp and made to support themselves." By February 1867 the population of James City had been reduced to 1,760. In October 1867 a North Carolina Freedmen's Bureau official noted that "since the last annual report all the colonies have been broken up and the properties upon which they are settled restored to the owners. This has been accomplished by gradual, systematic measures resulting in no disadvantage or suffering to the former occupants." This statement was not entirely true, as the James City settlement remained. The Freedmen's Bureau ended all aid to the residents of James City by the end of 1868, effectively ending the federal support for black refugees that had begun in 1862.[17]

The legal fight over the property on which James City was built dragged on for decades. The Evans family claimed ownership of the land on which James City was built. Freedmen's Bureau officials pleaded with the Evans family to sell the property to the black residents of James City, only to be rebuffed. Many of James City's residents refused to accept that they did not own the land on which many of them had been living since 1863, insisting that they had been given clear title to the properties that they had worked and improved. Until 1880 the legal status of the James City property remained in limbo. Although the Evans family and the black residents claimed ownership, neither pressed their case in court. In 1880 the Evans family sold the James City property to the Bryan family of New Bern, who began to demand rents from its residents. James City residents offered the Bryan family $2,000 to purchase six hundred acres of land, which they refused. When efforts to collect rents proved difficult, the Bryan family attempted to evict the black families that had been living in James City for nearly two decades. The residents of James City vigorously defended their claim to the land in court, delaying final judgment until 1891, when the state supreme court ruled in favor of the Bryans. Threatened with eviction, the residents of James City signed leases with the Bryans.[18]

As the case of James City suggests, the Civil War refugee crisis did not end with Confederate surrender. Many refugees struggled for years to reestablish lives and homes. Recognizing the size and severity of the refugee crisis during the American Civil War should force historians to reconsider how they conceptualize the Confederate home front. In North Carolina and across the Confederacy, the Civil War drove civilians to leave their homes, with some running away from and others toward the front lines. It shattered the traditional Southern attachment to place, one that emphasized the connection between family and community. Acknowledging the Civil War refugee crisis should push scholars to reevaluate what Confederate soldiers meant when they wrote in their diaries that they were fighting for their homes and families, when so many of their families were far from home. For many Confederate soldiers and refugees, home had become an abstraction rather than a physical place. For black refugees who fled to Union lines, the war also redefined the meaning of home. Abandoning their plantation homes, places of bondage and domination under slavery, black refugees created new homes as bastions of freedom.[19]

The refugee crisis took on many different faces: the experiences of fugitive slaves on the North Carolina coast, refugee students at female academies in the Piedmont, and refugee planters in the North Carolina mountains diverged on more points than they shared. The diversity of refugee experiences within the Civil War South—black and white, enslaved and free, Confederate and Unionist—reveals a whole that is more than the sum of its parts. Taken together, the picture that emerges exposes a humanitarian crisis driven by mobility, shaped by unprecedented economic pressures and disease vectors, and exacerbated by Confederate and Union governments unwilling or unable to provide meaningful relief. The complexity of the refugee crisis in North Carolina and across the Confederacy suggests that the traditional distinctions between the home front and the military front were illusions. Just as Union and Confederate armies traversed the Southern landscape, so too did refugees. Their dynamic mobility destroyed the human geography of the Old South and proved instrumental in both emancipation and Confederate defeat. Even those refugees who sought to isolate themselves from the Civil War could not detach themselves from its reach.

NOTES

Abbreviations

DU	Special Collections, Perkins Library, Duke University, Durham, N.C.
ECU	Special Collections, Joyner Library, East Carolina University, Greenville, N.C.
HL	Huntington Library, San Marino, Calif.
NCDAH	North Carolina Department of Archives and History, Raleigh
OR	*The War of the Rebellion: A Compilation of the Official Records of the Union and Confederate Armies.* 70 vols. Washington, D.C.: GPO, 1880–1901
SCL	South Caroliniana Library, University of South Carolina, Columbia
SHC	Southern Historical Collection, Wilson Library, University of North Carolina, Chapel Hill

Introduction

1. Herrington, "The Refugee's Niece"; Herrington, *The Captain's Bride*. The name of the town of New Bern was in the nineteenth century variously spelled New Bern, Newbern, and Newberne. Quotations retain the original spelling, while I have elected to use the modern spelling elsewhere.

2. Massey, *Refugee Life*, xii. The biographical description of Massey is drawn from George Rable's excellent introduction to the new paperback edition of *Refugee Life*; C. Myers, "Mary Elizabeth Massey"; Heath, "Mary Elizabeth Massey."

3. On the Freedmen and Southern Society Project, see Berlin et al., *Freedom*; Glymph, *Out of the House of Bondage*; Glymph, "This Species of Property"; Schwalm, *A Hard Fight for We*; J. Downs, *Sick from Freedom*; Hahn, *The Political Worlds of Slavery and Freedom*; Sternhell, *Routes of War*. Also see Click, *Time Full of Trial*; Litwack, *Been in the Storm So Long*; Mobley, *James City*; Camp, *Closer to Freedom*, 117–38. On the biracial aspects of the Confederate refugee crisis, see Mohr, *On the Threshold of Freedom*; Inscoe, "Mountain Masters as Confederate Opportunists."

4. For a recent review of the historiography of the Confederate home front, see Mobley, *Weary of War*, 165–68; and DeCredico, "The Confederate Homefront." Also see Cashin, "Into the Trackless Wilderness."

5. Sternhell, *Routes of War*, 7.

6. Two exceptions to this were the American Freedmen's Inquiry Commission, which used "Negroes as Refugees" as a subhead in a report, and the American Missionary Association, which insisted that "colored refugees" was a better term than "freedman" or "contraband" to describe African Americans who had fled to Union lines. "Colored Refugees," *American Missionary* 6 (February 1862): 29; American Freedmen's Inquiry Commission, *Preliminary Report*, 3–14; Click, *Time Full of Trial*, 77–78, 145; Meekins, "Unionism and the Arcane Origin of 'Buffalo.'"

7. Taylor, *The Internal Enemy;* Jasanoff, *Liberty's Exiles;* Pybus, *Epic Journeys of Freedom;* Schama, *Rough Crossings;* Gatrell, *The Making of the Modern Refugee*, 21.

8. Manning, "Working for Citizenship," 190.

9. Rable, *Civil Wars*, 183; J. Downs, *Sick from Freedom*, 21; Hahn, *The Political Worlds of Slavery and Freedom*, 61; Sternhell, *Routes of War*, 5; Blight, *A Slave No More*, 160.

10. I have drawn on recent scholarship on refugees and internally displaced peoples, especially Lischer, *Dangerous Sanctuaries;* R. Cohen and Deng, *Masses in Flight;* Helton, *The Price of Indifference.* My work has also been shaped by accounts of contemporary refugee experiences, notably, Moorehead, *Human Cargo;* Dau and Sweeney, *God Grew Tired of Us;* Bashir and Lewis, *Tears of the Desert.* I also benefited tremendously from attending and participating in the Conference on Critical Refugee Studies held at the University of Wisconsin-Milwaukee in November 2011. Recent studies suggest that refugees experienced significant psychological consequences. See Fazel, Wheeler, and Danesh, "Prevalence of Serious Mental Disorder"; Geltman et al., "Lost Boys of Sudan"; Sundquist et al., "Posttraumatic Stress Disorder."

Chapter 1. Gwine to Liberty

1. Colyer, *Report of the Services Rendered*, 1.
2. J. Downs, *Sick from Freedom*, 46–48.
3. Watson, *A History of New Bern;* Sandbeck, *The Historic Architecture of New Bern.*
4. Judkin Browning, *Shifting Loyalties*, 55.
5. Diary entry, January 26, 1862, Clarrisa Phelps Hanks Papers, Special Collections, Joyner Library, East Carolina University, Greenville, N.C. (hereafter ECU); Judkin Browning, *Shifting Loyalties*, 52; Bryan, *A Grandmother's Recollection*, 25; Curtis, "A Journal of Reminiscences," 288.
6. Denny, *Wearing the Blue*, 104; Curtis, "A Journal of Reminiscences," 289.
7. Barrett, *The Civil War in North Carolina*, 123; *Official Records of the Union and Confederate Navies*, ser. 1, vol. 7, p. 372.
8. On the white evacuation of towns in eastern North Carolina such as New Bern, see R. B. MacRae to his brother, September 1, 1861; W. G. McRae to Don [?], August 21, 1862, MacRae Family Papers, Special Collections, Perkins Library, Duke University (hereafter DU).
9. Horace James, letter, *Congregationalist*, March 22, 1862; Day, *My Diary of Rambles*, 46; Burnside to Stanton, March 21, 1862, in *The War of the Rebellion: A Compilation of the Official Records of the Union and Confederate Armies* (Washington, D.C.: Government Printing Office, 1880–1901) ser. 2, vol. 1, p. 812 (hereafter OR); Emmerton, *A Record of the Twenty-Third Regiment*, 95; Judkin Browning, "Visions of Freedom and Civilization," 79; Rawick, *The American Slave*, 15:227–28; Greenwood, *First Fruits of Freedom*, 33.
10. Colyer, *Report of the Services Rendered*, 22; *New York Times*, June 10, 1862.
11. Franklin and Schweninger, *Runaway Slaves;* W. Robinson, *From Log Cabin to Pulpit*, 29–32; Parker, *Recollection of Slavery Times*, 30, 58, 76, 82, 85–90.
12. Cecelski, *Waterman's Song*, 205; Denny, *Wearing the Blue*, 91–92; Drake, *The History of the Ninth New Jersey*, 85–86. Also see Gould, *Diary of a Contraband*, 104–5; Judkin Browning, *The Southern Mind under Union Rule*, 86.

13. Barrett, *The Civil War in North Carolina*, 156–62; Hess, *Lee's Tar Heels*, 93–96; W. Brown, *The Negro in the American Rebellion*, 212.

14. Leaming, *Hidden Americans*, 222–86; Sayers, Burke, and Henry, "The Political Economy of Exile"; OR, ser. 2, vol. 1, p. 812; Colyer, *Report of the Services Rendered*, 19–20.

15. Graham, *Ninth Regiment New York Volunteers*, 216.

16. Colyer, *Report of the Services Rendered*, 23; Walls, *Joseph Charles Price*, 24–30.

17. Martinez, *Confederate Slave Impressment*, 21; Evans, *To Die Game*, 6; Hauptman, *Between Two Fires*, 66, 77–84; "Our War Experience," Cronly Family Papers, DU; Rawick, *The American Slave*, 14:81.

18. Franklin and Schweninger, *Runaway Slaves*, 210–12; Berlin et al., *Slaves No More*, 16; Camp, *Closer to Freedom*, 123–27.

19. J. Abbott, "Heroic Deeds of Heroic Men," 8; Day, *My Diary of Rambles*, 51; Esther Williams, "Roanoke Island," *National Freedman* 1 (April 1, 1865): 93–94; Clapp, *Letters to the Home Circle*, 150; Judkin Browning, *The Southern Mind under Union Rule*, 48; Mann, *History of the Forty-Fifth Regiment*, 83–84.

20. Day, *My Diary of Rambles*, 64, 74, 76; Roe, *Fifth Regiment Massachusetts Volunteer Infantry*, 185–86; Putnam, *The Story of Company A*, 136, 184–85; Mann, *History of the Forty-Fifth Regiment*, 84, 323.

21. Mann, *History of the Forty-Fifth Regiment*, 208; Day, *My Diary of Rambles*, 76.

22. Greenwood, *First Fruits of Freedom*, 33–35; Putnam, *The Story of Company A*, 114.

23. Hadden, *Slave Patrols*, 172–73; Berlin et al., *Freedom*, ser. 1, 1:94.

24. Ash, *When the Yankees Came*, 163; Kirwan, *Memorial History*, 393–94; Henry Jones to J. Donnell, September 14, 1862, Bryan Family Papers, DU, quoted in Ash, *When the Yankees Came*, 166.

25. James, *Annual Report*, 4.

26. Mann, *History of the Forty-Fifth Regiment*, 107–8.

27. Graham, *Ninth Regiment New York Volunteers*, 228–29; diary entry, April 17, 1862, William J. Creasey Papers, Southern Historical Collection, Wilson Library University of North Carolina at Chapel Hill (hereafter SHC). For a similar incident, see "Incidents of Three Years Trip at Soldiering," Charles Henry Tubbs Letters, North Carolina Department of Archives and History (hereafter NCDAH).

28. Rowland Hall to his father, May 26 1863, Julia Ward Stickley Papers, NCDAH.

29. Oakes, *Freedom National*, 118–40, 186–89, 209–11; Berlin, *Slaves No More*, 6–32; Gerteis, *From Contraband to Freedman*, 11–32; Siddali, *From Property to Person*. On the use of the word "contraband," see Masur, "A Rare Phenomenon of Philological Vegetation."

30. OR, ser. 1, vol. 9, pp. 352–53, 359–60, 363–64.

31. Berlin et al., *Freedom*, ser. 1, 1:81.

32. Click, *Time Full of Trial*, 33, 38; Oakes, *Freedom National*, 210–11; OR, ser. 1, vol. 9, pp. 369–70.

33. William H. Doherty to Abraham Lincoln, May 13, 1862, Abraham Lincoln Papers, Library of Congress.

34. OR, ser. 2, vol. 1, p. 813.

35. Colyer, *Report of the Christian Mission*, 2–10; Bishop, *Memorial Record of the New York Branch*, 9–12; Henry, "The United States Christian Commission," 374–76; Raney, "In the Lord's Army"; Silkenat, "A Typical Negro."

36. Howard, "The Freedmen during the War," 381–82; Colyer, *Report of the Services Rendered*, 1; Click, *Time Full of Trial*, 38.

37. Colyer, *Report of the Services Rendered*, 6.

38. Ibid., 9; Judkin Browning, "Visions of Freedom and Civilization," 81.

39. Colyer, *Report of the Services Rendered*, 14–15; *Liberator*, July 11, 1862; *Philadelphia Inquirer*, July 17, 1862.

40. Colyer, *Report of the Services Rendered*, 22.

41. Singleton, *Recollections of My Slavery Days*, 8.

42. William Loftin to his mother, March 18, 1862, William F. Loftin Papers, DU; Judkin Browning, *The Southern Mind under Union Rule*, 36–37; OR, ser. 1, vol. 9, p. 477; H. Jones to J. R. Donnell, December 1863, Bryan Family Papers, DU, quoted in Cecelski, *Waterman's Song*, 159.

43. Berlin et al., *Slaves No More*, 18; *Worcester Daily Spy*, April 26, 1862, quoted in Greenwood, *First Fruits of Freedom*, 35.

44. "New England Anti-Slavery Convention," *Liberator*, June 6, 1862; Clapp, *Letters to the Home Circle*, 126.

45. Emmerton, *A Record of the Twenty-Third Regiment*, 96; Rowland Hall to his sister, February 13, 1863, Julia Ward Stickley Papers, NCDAH.

46. Hubbard, *Campaign of the Forty-Fifth Regiment*, 18; Putnam, *The Story of Company A*, 130–31.

47. Putnam, *The Story of Company A*, 140–41; B. Myers, *Rebels against the Confederacy*; Denny, *Wearing the Blue*, 90–91; Putnam, *The Story of Company A*, 171.

48. OR, ser. 1, vol. 18, pp. 745–47; Durrill, *War of Another Kind*, 91.

49. Ash, *When the Yankees Came*, 177; Mann, *History of the Forty-Fifth Regiment*, 109; OR, ser. 1, vol. 4, p. 619.

50. Ash, *When the Yankees Came*, 179–80.

51. *North Carolina Times* (New Bern), March 23, 1864. On Quakers in Civil War North Carolina, see Bynum, "Occupied at Home"; Zuber, "Conscientious Objectors in the Confederacy."

52. Derby, *Bearing Arms*, 96; Sternhell, *Routes of War*, 129–32. For an example of a passport issued to a white refugee, see pass dated May 10, 1862, Foscue Family Papers, SHC.

53. Clapp, *Letters to the Home Circle*, 15; Haines, *Letters from the Forty-Fourth*, 37; Budington, *A Memorial of Giles F. Ward*, 61; "Incidents of Three Years Trip at Soldiering," Charles Henry Tubbs Letters, NCDAH.

54. Mildred Wallace, "The Sacrifice or Daring of a Southern Woman during the War between the States," diary fragment, December 7, [1865], Benjamin Franklin Royal Papers, SHC; *Old North State*, February 18, 1865.

55. "Heroines of the Confederacy, New Bern and Vicinity, 1861–1865," Elizabeth Moore Collection, ECU; Anderson, *North Carolina Women of the Confederacy*, 16–20; Carbone, *Civil War in Coastal North Carolina*, 128; Lowry, *Swamp Doctor*, 104, 108.

56. Clapp, *Letters to the Home Circle*, 22; Derby, *Bearing Arms*, 162; James E. Glazier to Annie Monroe, September 23, 1862, James E. Glazier Papers, Huntington Library (hereafter HL); Stephen Tippett Andrews to Maggie, May 6, 1863, Stephen Tippet Andrews Papers, SHC; Rowland Hall to mother, February 13, 1863, Julia Ward Stickley Papers, NCDAH; Marcotte, *Private Osborne*, 94–95; Roe, *Fifth Regiment Massachusetts Volunteer Infantry*, 240.

57. Colyer, *Report of the Services Rendered*, 34.
58. Foner, *Free Soil, Free Labor, Free Men*; G. Downs, *Declarations of Dependence*, 46–47.
59. Colyer, *Report of the Services Rendered*, 6.
60. Ibid., 34.
61. Walcott, *History of the Twenty-First*, 106.
62. Colyer, *Report of the Services Rendered*, 33; Schwalm, "Between Slavery and Freedom," 140–41; Judkin Browning, "Visions of Freedom and Civilization," 81; Clapp, *Letters to the Home Circle*, 16, 30, 41; Roe, *Fifth Regiment Massachusetts Volunteer Infantry*, 135–36; Hubbard, *Campaign of the Forty-Fifth Regiment*, 23.
63. Rowland Hall to his sister, June 13, 1862, Julia Ward Stickley Papers, NCDAH; Putnam, *The Story of Company A*, 172.
64. Denny, *Wearing the Blue*, 226–27; Judkin Browning, "Visions of Freedom and Civilization," 81.
65. Colyer, *Report of the Christian Mission*, 14.
66. Colyer, *Report of the Services Rendered*, 14, 31.
67. Emmerton, *A Record of the Twenty-Third Regiment*, 95; Denny, *Wearing the Blue*, 104; George F. Weston to "Dear Sir," February 15, 1863, New Bern Occupation Papers, SHC; Click, *Time Full of Trial*, 26–28.
68. Clapp, *Letters to the Home Circle*, 15; Day, *My Diary of Rambles*, 47.
69. Colyer, *Report of the Services Rendered*, 6.
70. Denny, *Wearing the Blue*, 104; Ash, *When the Yankees Came*, 19.
71. Barrett, *The Civil War in North Carolina*, 127; Colyer, *Report of the Christian Mission*, 16; Colyer, *Report of the Services Rendered*, 40–42.
72. Haines, *Letters from the Forty-Fourth*, 91; Colyer, *Report of the Services Rendered*, 36; Click, *Time Full of Trial*, 35.
73. Roe, *Fifth Regiment Massachusetts Volunteer Infantry*, 155; Mann, *History of the Forty-Fifth Regiment*, 218. Also see Hubbard, *Campaign of the Forty-Fifth Regiment*, 80–82.
74. James Glazier to his parents, March 19, 1862; James Glazier to Annie Monroe, June 24, 1862, James E. Glazier Papers, HL.
75. Haines, *Letters from the Forty-Fourth*, 114.
76. Fenn, "A Perfect Equality Seemed to Reign." For a description of Jonkonnu in eastern North Carolina just prior to the Civil War, see Jacobs, *Incidents in the Life*, 179–80.
77. H. Williams, *Self Taught*, 15; Click, *Time Full of Trial*, 35, 85; Colyer, *Report of the Services Rendered*, 43–44.
78. OR, ser. 1, vol. 9, pp. 396–97; N. Brown, *Edward Stanly*; Barrett, *The Civil War in North Carolina*, 127.
79. Carbone, *Civil War in Coastal North Carolina*, 80–81; Recruitment poster, May 1, 1862, Henry Toole Clarke Papers, NCDAH.
80. Judkin Browning and Smith, *Letters from a North Carolina Unionist*, 17; Wyeth, *Leaves from a Diary*, 36.
81. *Letter from Hon. Edward Stanly*, 6; N. Brown, *Edward Stanly*, 204.
82. OR, ser. 1, vol. 9, p. 400; Colyer, *Report of the Services Rendered*, 44. Also see *New York Times*, June 10, 1862.
83. Coyler, *Report of the Services Rendered*, 44–47; *New York Times*, June 4, 1862.
84. Colyer, *Report of the Services Rendered*, 47–51; *New York Times*, June 4, 1862; N. Brown, *Edward Stanly*, 208; *Christian Recorder*, June 21, 1862.

85. *New York Times,* June 4, 10, 1862; Greenwood, *First Fruits of Freedom,* 44.
86. Rowland Hall to his sister, June 13, 1862, Julia Ward Stickley Papers, NCDAH; *New York Times,* June 4, 1862; Daniel Reed Larned to his sister, May 28, 1862, Larned Papers, cited in N. Brown, *Edward Stanly,* 209; Judkin Browning and Smith, *Letters from a North Carolina Unionist,* 15.
87. Graham, *Ninth Regiment New York Volunteers,* 220–21.
88. Colyer, *Report of the Services Rendered,* 52; N. Brown, *Edward Stanly,* 210–212.
89. Colyer, *Report of the Services Rendered,* 52–55; N. Brown, *Edward Stanly,* 228–32; Harris, "Lincoln and Wartime Reconstruction," 165–66; Greenwood, *First Fruits of Freedom,* 56.
90. Barrett, *The Civil War in North Carolina,* 128; Colyer, *Report of the Christian Mission,* 17; Colyer, *Report of the Services Rendered,* 59–60.

Chapter 2. Crowded with Refugees

1. Cecelski, *Fire of Freedom,* 111.
2. *Old North State,* January 7, 1865; Cecelski, *Fire of Freedom,* 160–64. Also see *Freedman's Journal* 1:3 (March 1865).
3. *Congregationalist,* January 30, 1863.
4. Ash, *When the Yankees Came,* 151; Oakes, *Freedom National,* 362–67. On the Emancipation Proclamation, see Franklin, *The Emancipation Proclamation;* Guelzo, *The Emancipation Proclamation;* Holzer, Medford, and Williams, *The Emancipation Proclamation;* Foner, *The Fiery Trial,* 240–50.
5. George F. Weston to "Dear Sir," February 15, 1863, New Bern Occupation Papers, SHC; Judkin Browning, "Visions of Freedom and Civilization," 78; Clapp, *Letters to the Home Circle,* 129; Roe, *Fifth Regiment Massachusetts Volunteer Infantry,* 191.
6. Roe, *Fifth Regiment Massachusetts Volunteer Infantry,* 192; Clapp, *Letters to the Home Circle,* 129; Gustavus Jocknick to John Wilkin, March 11, 1863, Gustavus Jocknick Papers, HL; Silber and Sievens, *Yankee Correspondence,* 97–98.
7. *New York Times,* December 5, 1862.
8. Clapp, *Letters to the Home Circle,* 173; *Friend,* 37:17 (1863): 135.
9. N. Brown, *Edward Stanly,* 249–53; OR, ser. 1, vol. 19, p. 525.
10. Mann, *History of the Forty-Fifth Regiment,* 230; Mary L. Peabody to Edward Kinsley, March 22, 1863, Edward W. Kinsley Papers, DU.
11. Mann, *History of the Forty-Fifth Regiment,* 211.
12. Colyer, *Report of the Services Rendered,* 35; Clapp, *Letters to the Home Circle,* 139, 149–50. On black literacy in slavery, see H. Williams, *Self Taught.*
13. Clapp, *Letters to the Home Circle,* 158; James, *Annual Report,* 7; Haines, *Letters from the Forty-Fourth,* 88.
14. Clapp, *Letters to the Home Circle,* 172–73, 219; R. Reid, *Freedom for Themselves,* 13.
15. Ash, *When the Yankees Came,* 44–45. On the importance of oaths in the South, see Wyatt-Brown, *Southern Honor,* 55–57.
16. James E. Glazier to Annie Monroe, October 24, 1862; James E. Glazier to his parents, November 6, 1862, James E. Glazier Papers, HL.
17. Meekins, *Elizabeth City,* 62–65, 79; OR, ser. 1, vol. 18, pp. 1050–51.

18. Donaghy, *Army Experience of Capt. John Donaghy*, 111. Also see *New York Herald*, May 11, 1863.

19. Josiah Wood to Laurania, June 28, 1863, Josiah Wood Papers, DU.

20. Singleton, *Recollections of My Slavery Days*, 8–9.

21. OR, ser. 1, vol. 16, p. 525. Also see Meekins, *Elizabeth City*, 61–64; William Loftin to his mother, January 22, 1863, William F. Loftin Papers, DU.

22. Clapp, *Letters to the Home Circle*, 176.

23. Click, *Time Full of Trial*, 40–41; Reilly, "Reconstruction through Regeneration"; James, *The Two Great Wars of America*, 27; Day, *My Diary of Rambles*, 87.

24. Although Wild was authorized to raise four regiments in North Carolina, he raised only three. Originally named the First, Second, and Third Regiments North Carolina Colored Volunteers, they were later rechristened the Thirty-Fifth, Thirty-Sixth, and Thirty-Seventh Regiments U.S. Colored Troops. Kingman, *Memoir of Gen. Edward Augustus Wild*, 5–7.

25. Cecelski, *Fire of Freedom*, 1–62.

26. Mann, *History of the Forty-Fifth Regiment*, 301–2, 446–49; unpublished memoirs, Edward W. Kinsley Papers, W. E. B. DuBois Library, University of Massachusetts, Amherst; Cecelski, *Fire of Freedom*, xiii–xvi, 73–74, 78–80. On the Confederacy's policy on black POWs, see Manning, *What This Cruel War Was Over*, 160–61; McPherson, *Marching toward Freedom*, 81–82; McCurry, *Confederate Reckoning*, 301–8.

27. Haines, *Letters from the Forty-Fourth*, 93–95, 109; Rowland Hall to father, June 10, 1863, Julia Ward Stickley Papers, NCDAH.

28. Roe, *Fifth Regiment Massachusetts Volunteer Infantry*, 244; *Weekly Anglo-African*, August 22, 1863, quoted in Trudeau, *Voices of the 55th*, 37; Mann, *History of the Forty-Fifth Regiment*, 324.

29. Roe, *Fifth Regiment Massachusetts Volunteer Infantry*, 244–45; Trudeau, *Voices of the 55th*, 15; Helen James letter, December 12, 1863, *Friend* 37:17 (1863), 135.

30. James, *Annual Report*, 4.

31. Haines, *Letters from the Forty-Fourth*, 109. Also see Mobley, *James City*, 5.

32. Helen James letter, December 12, 1863, *Friend* 37:17 (1863), 135.

33. Click, *Time Full of Trial*, 57–71; Horace James to the Public, June 27, 1863, Letters Received, Department of North Carolina, Record Group 393, pt. 1, series 3238, box 2, National Archives, Washington, D.C. Also see G. Downs, *Declarations of Dependence*, 63.

34. Click, *Time Full of Trial*, 47–49.

35. *Christian Recorder*, July 4, 1863, quoted in Redkey, *A Grand Army of Black Men*, 91.

36. Click, *Time Full of Trial*, 27–28, 51, 82–83, 85–86; "Letter from Miss E. James," *American Missionary* 8 (February 1864): 39–40; Sarah Freeman, "A Letter to Be Read and Circulated, in Public and Private Meeting, in Aid of the Freedmen," *Freedmen's Advocate* 1 (November 1864): 38.

37. Barrett, *The Civil War in North Carolina*, 202–7; Olnhausen, *Adventures of an Army Nurse*, 133; "Letter from Miss E. James," *American Missionary* 8 (February 1864): 39–40; James, *Annual Report*, 7; Reilly, "Reconstruction through Regeneration," 39.

38. Goss, *Soldier's Story of His Captivity*, 55–57; Olnhausen, *Adventures of an Army Nurse*, 141–42; Jordan and Thomas, "Massacre at Plymouth," 156–58.

39. Jordan and Thomas, "Massacre at Plymouth," 125–93; Carbone, *Civil War in Coastal North Carolina*, 112–20; *Daily Confederate*, April 30, May 3, 1864; Goss, *Soldier's Story of His Captivity*, 61.

40. OR, ser. 2, vol. 7, pp. 459–60.

41. Barrett, *The Civil War in North Carolina*, 220–21; Reilly, "Reconstruction through Regeneration," 40; Jesse Harrison to his mother, April 28, 1864, Jesse Harrison Papers, DU; *North Carolina Times* (New Bern), May 7, 14, 1864; Putnam, *The Story of Company A*, 319; Judkin Browning and Smith, *Letters from a North Carolina Unionist*, 206; James, *Annual Report*, 8–9.

42. *North Carolina Times*, April 13, 1864; James, *Annual Report*, 10.

43. L. Abbott, *The James City Project*; Wheaton and Reed, *James City, North Carolina*; Mobley, *James City*; James, *Annual Report*, 8–9.

44. James, *Annual Report*, 39–42.

45. Stanley, "Beggars Can't Be Choosers"; J. Downs, *Sick from Freedom*, 55–57; G. Downs, *Declarations of Dependence*, 64–65; James, *Annual Report*, 7, 12–13.

46. James, *Annual Report*, 10–12.

47. Ibid., 15; Click, *Time Full of Trial*, 133–35.

48. James, *Annual Report*, 30; Reilly, "Reconstruction through Regeneration," 55.

49. *New York Times*, August 5, 1863; Cecelski, *Fire of Freedom*, 86–89.

50. Cecelski, *Fire of Freedom*, 108–9, 114–17.

51. Hood, *Sketch of the Early History*, 89–91. Also see S. Martin, *For God and Race*, 51–54; Hildebrand, *The Times were Strange and Stirring*, 46.

52. Cecelski, *Fire of Freedom*, 129–33.

53. Ibid., 133, 137, 245, 256, 277; Foner, *Freedom's Lawmakers*, 88–89; Beckel, *Radical Reform*, 44; *Minutes of the Freedmen's Convention*, 21; Bernstein, "Participation of Negro Delegates," 391.

54. W. Black, "Civil War Letters of E. N. Boots," 219; *North Carolina Times*, September 9, 1864; Judkin Browning, *The Southern Mind under Union Rule*, 155.

55. OR, ser. 1, vol. 33, pp. 870–71; *Murder of Union Soldiers*, 23; Gordon, "In Time of War"; Collins, "War Crimes or Justice?"

56. Judkin Browning and Smith, *Letters from a North Carolina Unionist*, 191, 221.

57. "Horrors of the Rebellion," *New York Times*, March 18, 1864.

58. Judkin Browning and Smith, *Letters from a North Carolina Unionist*, 206.

59. *North Carolina Times*, May 14, 1864. The quotation is from Proverbs 11:25.

60. *North Carolina Times*, May 14, June 18, December 24, 1864; Judkin Browning and Smith, *Letters from a North Carolina Unionist*, 213; Clapp, *Letters to the Home Circle*, 112.

61. R. Reid, *Freedom for Themselves*, 221; J. Downs, *Sick from Freedom*, 24; Long, *Doctoring Freedom*, 51–60.

62. Stanley, "Beggars Can't Be Choosers," 1276–88; Judkin Browning and Smith, *Letters of a North Carolina Unionist*, 208; *North Carolina Times*, January 23, July 16, 1864.

63. Click, *Time Full of Trial*, 94–95.

64. James, *Annual Report*, 9; *Anti-Slavery Reporter*, May 1, 1865.

65. *Report of the Joint Committee on Reconstruction*, 2:204. Also see Homer A. Cooke Military Records, SHC.

66. Mrs. F. Roberts, "Historical Incidents," 5.

67. On prostitution during the Civil War, see Clinton, *Public Women and the Confederacy*; Barber, "Depraved and Abandoned Women"; D. Williams, *Bitterly Divided*, 80; J. Jones, "A Tale of Two Cities"; Cole, "Upon the Stage of Disorder"; Massey, *Bonnet Brigades*, 262–64; Rable, *Civil Wars*, 194–95; Wiley, *The Life of Johnny Reb*, 51–55.

68. Lowry, *Swamp Doctor*, 169, 179, 181–83.

69. Sparrow, "Recollections of the Civil War," 58; Edmund J. Cleveland diary, April 6, 1865, SHC.

70. William J. Creasey diary, June 5, 24, 1862, SHC. Also see James Glazier to Annie G. Monroe, June 24, 1862, James Edward Glazier Papers, HL; Haines, *Letters from the Forty-Fourth*, 112.

71. Edwards, *Scarlett Doesn't Live Here Anymore*, 109; Schwalm, *A Hard Fight for We*, 102; Fellman, *Inside War*, 211; Frankel, *Freedom's Women*, 39–40; Humphreys, *The Marrow of Tragedy*, 73.

72. Schwartz, *A Woman Doctor's Civil War*, 34; Barber and Ritter, "Physical Abuse . . . and Rough Handling," 54.

73. James, *Annual Report*, 6; *Liberator*, October 21, 1864; Roe, *Fifth Regiment Massachusetts Volunteer Infantry*, 152; Clapp, *Letters to the Home Circle*, 211; Haines, *Letters from the Forty-Fourth*, 111; Olnhausen, *Adventures of an Army Nurse*, 151; Butler, *Autobiography and Personal Reminiscences*, 411–12.

74. J. Downs, *Sick from Freedom*, 42–64; Meier, *Nature's Civil War*; Long, *Doctoring Freedom*, 44–60; Humphreys, *Intensely Human*, 6–8; Humphreys, *The Marrow of Tragedy*, 76–102.

75. Judkin Browning and Smith, *Letters from a North Carolina Unionist*, 172. Also see J. Downs, "The Other Side of Freedom."

76. Judkin Browning and Smith, *Letters from a North Carolina Unionist*, 226–33; Rawick, *The American Slave*, 14:373; "Letter from Miss E. James," *American Missionary* 8 (February 1864): 39–40; Helen James letter, December 12, 1863, *Friend* 37:17 (1863): 135.

77. T. Farnham and King, "The March of the Destroyer." Estimates vary as to the number of soldiers and civilians killed during the yellow fever epidemic. Horace James estimated that fifteen hundred whites and one thousand blacks died in the epidemic. See James, *Annual Report*, 17. Also see Benjamin, *Great Epidemic*.

78. William H. Jackson to George A. Root, October 28, 1864, George A. Root Letters, DU; Day, *My Diary of Rambles*, 149; Thorpe, *History of the Fifteenth Connecticut Volunteers*, 76–77; Putnam, *The Story of Company A*, 318–19; Olnhausen, *Adventures of an Army Nurse*, 152; Diary of Chas. A. Torunier, October 21, 1864, New Bern Historical Society Collection, ECU; Reilly, "Reconstruction through Regeneration," 82–83.

79. Thorpe, *History of the Fifteenth Connecticut Volunteers*, 76–77, 235. African Americans may have had increased immunity to yellow fever. See Humphreys, *Intensely Human*, 49.

80. Olnhausen, *Adventures of an Army Nurse*, 151–52.

81. Kirwan, *Memorial History*, 250.

82. J. Downs, *Sick from Freedom*, 35; Lowry, *Swamp Doctor*, 185. Also see Foster, "Limitations of Federal Health Care," 353–54. On black folk medicine, see Gorn, "Black Magic"; Fett, *Working Cures*.

83. Judkin Browning, *The Southern Mind under Union Rule*, 132, 136–37, 150–52.
84. Cecelski, *Fire of Freedom*, 158–60.
85. Diary of Chas. A. Torunier, January 17, 1865, New Bern Historical Society Collection, ECU; Silber and Sievens, *Yankee Correspondence*, 108.
86. *North Carolina Times*, February 7, 1865; Diary of Chas. A. Torunier, February 5, 1865, New Bern Historical Society Collection, ECU; "Roanoke Island," *National Freedman* 1 (April 1, 1865): 93–94.
87. *North Carolina Times*, January 21, 1865; Olnhausen, *Adventures of an Army Nurse*, 146.
88. Barrett, *Sherman's March through the Carolinas*, 137; Reilly, "Reconstruction through Regeneration," 86.
89. Nicholas, *Story of the Great March*, 252. Also see Campbell, *When Sherman Marched North*, 86.
90. Reilly, "Reconstruction through Regeneration," 86; James, *Annual Report*, 57–58; *North Carolina Times*, March 25, 1865; OR, ser. 1, vol. 47, pt. 1, pp. 164–65; Evans, *Ballots and Fence Rails*, 37–38; *Wilmington Herald*, March 21, 1865.
91. *Wilmington Herald*, March 17, 24, April 4, 1865; Fonvielle, *The Wilmington Campaign*, 451; Evans, *Ballots and Fence Rails*, 39.
92. Reilly, "Reconstruction through Regeneration," 84; Hamilton, *Reconstruction in North Carolina*, 148; Fonvielle, *The Wilmington Campaign*, 452; *Congregationalist*, April 28, 1865; J. Downs, *Sick from Freedom*, 69.
93. *Freedmen's Record*, May 1865, quoted in Greenwood, *First Fruits of Freedom*, 78; Gage, *From Vicksburg to Raleigh*, 292–93; James, *Annual Report*, 57.
94. *North Carolina Times*, April 4, 1865.
95. Mary Ann Starkey to Edward Kinsley, April 20, 1865, Edward W. Kinsley Papers, DU.
96. On the Freedmen's Bureau, see Cimbala and Miller, *The Freedmen's Bureau and Reconstruction*; Foner, *Reconstruction*, 142–70.
97. McFeely, *Yankee Stepfather*; Howard, *Autobiography*, 164; *Statutes at Large*, 13:507–9.
98. James, *Annual Report*, 64; *Congregationalist*, August 18, 1865; Mobley, *James City*, 32; *Report of the Joint Committee on Reconstruction*, 2:182, 187, 192.
99. *Report of the Joint Committee on Reconstruction*, 2:182–89; Stanley, "Beggars Can't Be Choosers," 1283.
100. Mobley, *James City*, 44–45; Reilly, "Reconstruction through Regeneration," 103–104; *Report of the Joint Committee on Reconstruction*, 2:190.
101. Berlin et al., *Freedom*, ser. 2, 729–30.

Chapter 3. Driven into Exile

1. Bryan, *A Grandmother's Recollection*, 25; Bryan, *Echoes from the Past*, 17–20; scrapbooks, Mary Norcott Bryan Papers, SHC; Mrs. F. Roberts, "Historical Incidents," 4; Barrett, *The Civil War in North Carolina*, 105.
2. The poem can be found in the Mary Bryan's scrapbooks, Mary Norcott Bryan Papers, SHC. It is unclear in which newspaper the poem was originally published. The clipping indicates that the author of the poem was an "M.E.S." in Snow Hill,

Greene County. Mary Bryan added a note to her scrapbook that the author was Eliza Scott, a friend of hers from New Bern and a fellow refugee. Mary Bryan later quoted from the poem in *A Grandmother's Recollection of Dixie*, in which she describes the author as "a very old lady refugeed from here [New Bern] during the war" to "a little village at the head waters of the Neuse" (33).

3. Giles Underhill to his children, December 8, 1862, Ransom Lee Papers, DU.

4. Berlin et al., *Freedom*, ser. 1, vol. 1, pp. 676–77.

5. Auman, "Neighbor against Neighbor"; Crofts, *Reluctant Confederates*; Bynum, *Long Shadow*; Domby, "Loyal to the Core"; Dodge, "Cave-Dwellers of the Confederacy."

6. Susie Mallett to Peter Mallett, September 7, 1861, Peter Mallett Papers, SHC; diary, September 1, 1861, David Schenck Papers, SHC. On Schenck, see Stewart, *David Schenck*.

7. Barrett, *The Civil War in North Carolina*, 66–130.

8. Massey, *Refugee Life*, 237; William S. Pettigrew to Charles L. Pettigrew, October 14, 1862, Pettigrew Family Papers, SHC; Wiley, *Southern Negroes*, 5; diary, October 9, 1862, Cushing Biggs Hassell Papers, SHC; *Milton Chronicle*, November 14, 1862.

9. Blair, *Virginia's Private War*, 77; Cashin, *First Lady of the Confederacy*, 125; Rable, *Civil Wars*, 197; Murray, *Wake*, 1:197; McGee, "On the Edge of the Crater," 175.

10. Bell, *Mosquito Soldiers*, 51; Sprunt, *Chronicles of the Cape Fear River*, 283–88. For other examples of Wilmington residents fleeing to the interior in 1862 because of the yellow fever outbreak, see Bellamy, *Back with the Tide*, 4; Joseph Blount Cheshire, "Some Account of My Life for My Children," NCDAH; J. E. Metts to James Isaac Metts, October 13, 1862, James Isaac Metts Papers, SHC.

11. *Wilmington Journal*, November 27, 1862; Nicholas Schenck diary, 28–29, ECU; D. W. K. Dix to Don MacRae, September 24, 1862, MacRae Family Papers, DU; William Calder to Phila Calder, April 23, September 15, 1862, Calder Family Papers, SHC.

12. The role of the *Aedes aegypti* mosquito as a carrier for yellow fever was not discovered until the twentieth century. See Carrigan, "Yellow Fever."

13. Nicholas Schenck diary, 28–29, ECU; *Fayetteville Observer*, September 29, 1862; Zebulon Vance to Harriet Vance, October 2, 1862, Zebulon Vance and Harriet Espy Vance Papers, NCDAH.

14. "Some Incidents of the War as Personally Experienced," Cronly Family Papers, DU; Eliza Oswald Hill diary, October 12, 25, 1862, Papers of Eliza Oswald Hill, Albert and Shirley Small Special Collections Library, University of Virginia; Marie Louise Du Brutz Reston Memoirs, SHC.

15. William Henry to Eliza DeRosset, October 3, 1862; Bella DeRosset to Eliza DeRosset, October 3, 1862; Cattie Kennedy to Eliza DeRosset, October 8, 1862, DeRosset Family Papers, SHC.

16. Alice DeRosset to Mary DeRosset Curtis, December 23, 1861, Moses A. Curtis Papers, SHC; John Benbury to Harriet Benbury, January 22, 1862, Benbury and Haywood Family Papers, SHC; Massey, *Refugee Life*, 15. Census records indicate that Benbury owned twenty-four slaves in 1860.

17. Harriet A. Yellowley to Edward C. Yellowley, September 20, October 28, 1862, Edward C. Yellowley Correspondence, Henry T. King Collection, ECU.

18. *North Carolina Standard*, May 7, August 6, 1862.

19. William Holland Thomas to Zebulon Baird Vance, November 22, 1862, in F. Johnston, *Papers of Zebulon Baird Vance*, 1:385–86; Inscoe and McKinney, *The Heart of Confederate Appalachia*, 212.

20. Diary, July 8, 1863, February 28, 1865, Cushing Biggs Hassell Papers, SHC.

21. Crabtree and Patton, *Journal of a Secesh Lady*, 273; William S. Pettigrew to James C. Johnston, November 26, 1862; William S. Pettigrew to Wesley Johnson, December 18, 1862, Pettigrew Family Papers, SHC. Pettigrew eventually did move many of his slaves to Davie County.

22. Crabtree and Patton, *Journal of a Secesh Lady*, 287.

23. Rawick, *The American Slave*, 15:329–30.

24. *Greensboro Daily News*, December 22, 1940; Tristim Skinner to Eliza Skinner, April 6, 1862, Skinner Family Papers, SHC.

25. OR, ser. 1, vol. 29, pt. 1, pp. 911–14; Creecy, *Grandfather's Tales*, 155–56; Sarah Espy diary, December 17–18, 1863, Alabama Department of Archives and History, Montgomery; Clampitt, *Confederate Heartland*, 51; Levine, *Fall of the House of Dixie*, 195.

26. Caroline Pettigrew to her mother, March 22, 1862, Pettigrew Family Papers, SHC. Also see Durrill, *War of Another Kind*, 68–90; contract, May 6, 1862, B. C. Beckwith Papers, NCDAH.

27. William Henry Thurber to Eliza DeRosset, October 28, 1862, DeRosset Family Papers, SHC; Bardaglio, "African American Childhood in Wartime," 221–24. Also see Ripley, "The Black Family in Transition," 371–74; Litwack, *Been in the Storm So Long*, 30–36; Mohr, *On the Threshold of Freedom*, 104. On the fragility of cross-plantation marriages, see Gutman, *Black Family*, 131–39; Fraser, *Courtship and Love*; West, *Chains of Love*; R. Griffin, "Goin' Back Over There"; West, "Surviving Separation."

28. "An Interesting and Romantic Narrative," *Anglo-African*, June 11, 1864, quoted in Wood, *When the Roll Is Called Up Yonder*, 14–15.

29. Caroline Pettigrew to Charles Pettigrew, February 26, 1862, Pettigrew Family Papers, SHC; Berlin, *Freedom*, ser. 1, vol. 1, p. 676; Crabtree and Patton, *Journal of a Secesh Lady*, 118; diary, February 22, 1862, David Schenck Papers, SHC.

30. Spencer, *Last Ninety Days*, 264; Crabtree and Patton, *Journal of a Secesh Lady*, 117.

31. Martinez, *Confederate Slave Impressment*; Ash, *When the Yankees Came*, 164; M. Bowen to Charles Pettigrew, March 1, 1863, Pettigrew Family Papers, SHC; Mobley, *Weary of War*, 73–74.

32. A. W. Mangum to his sister, January 19, 29, 1863, Mangum Family Papers, SHC; "A Voyage of a Refugee Sailor-Soldier, from the Interior of North Carolina to the Interior of South Carolina, Ending at Kingsville, January, 1864," HL.

33. MacBryde, *Ellie's Book*, 33; Massey, *Refugee Life*, 56–57.

34. Cashin, "Into the Trackless Wilderness," 42; Crabtree and Patton, *Journal of a Secesh Lady*, 119; *Norfolk Christian Sun*, February 14, 1862.

35. Massey, *Refugee Life*, 51; McDonald, *A Woman's Civil War*, 166.

36. Cashin, "Into the Trackless Wilderness," 29–33. On sexual purity, see Scott, *The Southern Lady*; Friedman, *The Enclosed Garden*. On the role of antebellum plantation mistresses and slave management, see Clinton, *The Plantation Mistress*; Fox-Genovese, *Within the Plantation Household*.

37. Bynum, *Unruly Women*; Bolton, *Poor Whites of the Antebellum South*; Cecil-Fronsman, *Common Whites*.
38. Ash, *When the Yankees Came*, 18–20.
39. Massey, *Refugee Life*, 71–81; McGee, "On the Edge of the Crater," 195.
40. Spencer, *Last Ninety Days*, 264; *Raleigh Register*, May 21, 1862; *Papers of Jefferson Davis*, 8:187, 199.
41. Stoops, *The Heritage*, 62. For more on refugees at female academies in central North Carolina, see chapter 5.
42. Jane Meares to Kate Meares, October 28, 1862, John W. and Augustus Williams Papers, SHC; *Western Democrat*, May 20, 1862.
43. Eliza A. DeRosset to her sister, December 10, 1862, DeRosset Family Papers, SHC; Paul Cameron to George Mordecai, November 25, 1862, George W. Mordecai Papers, SHC.
44. Crow and Barden, *Live Your Own Life*, 152.
45. *North Carolina Standard*, June 25, 1862. For other property ads targeting refugees, see *North Carolina Standard*, August 9, December 9, 1863; *Daily Confederate*, September 1, October 29, 1864; *Greensboro Patriot*, January 26, 1865; *Christian Advocate*, November 11, 1863.
46. *Daily Confederate*, October 26, 1864.
47. *Biblical Recorder*, reprinted in *North Carolina Standard*, April 9, 1862; *Salisbury Watchman*, quoted in *North Carolina Standard*, May 14, 1862; *Christian Advocate*, May 13, 1863.
48. Sharpe, "Diary of a Confederate Refugee," 10; McCallum, *Martin County during the Civil War*, 18–20, 107–8; *Daily Confederate*, June 6, 1864.
49. Hamilton, *Papers of William A. Graham*, 5:417–18.
50. Lloyd Beall to David Swain, August 29, 1864, David Swain Papers, NCDAH.
51. Harriet Yellowley to Edward C. Yellowley, September 13, 1862, Edward C. Yellowley Correspondence, Henry T. King Collection, ECU. On Edward C. Yellowley, see entry in Powell, *Dictionary of North Carolina Biography*, 6:291.
52. Harriet Yellowley to Edward C. Yellowley, November 16, 1862, Edward C. Yellowley Correspondence, Henry T. King Collection, ECU.
53. Harriet Yellowley to Edward C. Yellowley, November 27, December 6, 1862, Edward C. Yellowley Correspondence, Henry T. King Collection, ECU.
54. Mary Lacy to Bessie Dewey, July 3, 1862, Drury Lacy Papers, SHC.
55. Mary Lacy to Bessie Dewey, October 2, 1862, Drury Lacy Papers, SHC.
56. Mary Lacy to Bessie Dewey, July 17, 21, 24, 1863; Drury Lacy to Bessie Dewey, August 3, 1863, Drury Lacy Papers, SHC.
57. Mary Lacy to Bessie Dewey, November 8, 1864, Drury Lacy Papers, SHC.
58. Lou to Kate DeRosset, April 1863, DeRosset Family Papers, SHC; Eliza Oswald Hill diary, September 28, 1862, Papers of Eliza Oswald Hill, Albert and Shirley Small Special Collections Library, University of Virginia; R. Barrus to Caroline Foscue, November 19, 1862, Foscue Family Papers, SHC; *War Days in Fayetteville*, 21; Aunt Julia to Mary Scott, May 15, 1863, Mary French Scott Papers, DU; W. J. Clarke to Z. B. Vance, November 27, 1863, Z. B. Vance Papers, DU, quoted in Barrett, *The Civil War in North Carolina*, 181.
59. *Spirit of the Age*, June 15, 1863.

Chapter 4. Confederacy of Refugees

1. Rawick, *The American Slave*, 14:400–402; Censer, "Southwestern Migration." Boylan was born in Raleigh in 1803 and moved to Mississippi as a young man. His father was William Boylan, a prosperous planter and politician; see Powell, *Dictionary of North Carolina Biography*, 1:205.

2. Carrie to her aunt, February 3, 1863, Samuel Finley Patterson Papers, DU.

3. Diary, January 19, 1864, David Schenck Papers, SHC.

4. In February 1863 North Carolina enacted a tax on slaves and property. See *Revue Law*; 1863 Tax Assessors List, Ashe County, NCDAH; Warren County Assessment, 1863, Steed and Phipps Family Papers, SHC; 1863 Tax List, Johnston County, NCDAH; 1863 Tax List, Cabarrus County, NCDAH; 1863 Tax List, Wayne County, NCDAH; Wynne, "Confederate Tax Assessments."

5. Kenzer, *Kinship and Neighborhood*, 86.

6. Richard C. Gatlin to Col. J. C. Barnhardt, January 11, 1864, Militia Letterbook, N.C. Adjutant General's Department, General Records, 1807–1950, NCDAH, quoted in Martinez, "For the Defense of the State," 130.

7. Silkenat, *Moments of Despair*, 159–63; Mobley, *Weary of War*, 40–42; Dodge, "Domestic Economy in the Confederacy."

8. Macy Outten to John Isaac Brown, March 31, August 15, 1864, January 27, 1865, John Isaac Brown Papers, NCDAH.

9. King, *Anna Long Thomas Fullers' Journal*, 32; Margaret M. Smith et al. to Gov. Vance, February 4, 1863, Zebulon B. Vance Governor's Papers, NCDAH. Also see McCurry, *Confederate Reckoning*, 133–68, 174–99; Bynum, *Unruly Women*, 111–29, 145–46; Escott, *Many Excellent People*, 52–58, 65–67; Bynum, "War within a War"; Simkins and Patton, *The Women of the Confederacy*, 127; D. Williams, *Bitterly Divided*, 91; Mobley, *Weary of War*, 42–43.

10. On refugees working as teachers, see chapter 5. On refugees working as nurses, see Dawson, *Our Women in the War*, 146–48. Also see Massey, *Refugee Life*, 160–64.

11. Hesseltine, *Dr. J. G. M. Ramsey*, 218.

12. Rev. J. Henry Smith diary, January 1, 1862, Henry Smith Richardson Papers, SHC; B. Nelson, "Some Aspects of Negro Life," 164; Martinez, "Slave Market in Civil War Virginia"; Wiley, *Southern Negroes*, 86–90; diary, September 1, 1862, January [?], 1865, David Schenck Papers, SHC.

13. On the relationship between debt and honor, see Silkenat, *Moments of Despair*, 141–58; Greenberg, *Honor and Slavery*, 51–86; Wyatt-Brown, *Southern Honor*, 23, 73, 345.

14. *Charlotte Daily Bulletin*, March 3, 1865, quoted in B. Nelson, "Some Aspects of Negro Life," 164. For the uncertainty of slavery's future in central North Carolina, see R. B. Johnston to Thomas D. Johnston, December 7, 1863, Thomas D. Johnston Papers, SHC; diary entry, September 1, 1861, January 1865, David Schenck Papers, SHC. For western North Carolinians who sought to capitalize on the depressed market for slaves, see Inscoe and McKinney, *The Heart of Confederate Appalachia*, 212; Inscoe, "Mountain Masters as Confederate Opportunists."

15. On slave renting, see J. Martin, *Divided Mastery*; Perry, "A Profitable, but Risky Business," 141–45. Also see B. Nelson, "Some Aspects of Negro Life," 161–64.

On the increasing in renting during the war, see *Fayetteville Observer*, January 9, 1862; Wiley, *Southern Negroes*, 94.

16. Faust, *Mothers of Invention*, 62–79; Weiner, *Mistresses and Slaves*, 155–84; Glymph, *Out of the House of Bondage*, 97–136.

17. Woodward, *Mary Chesnut's Civil War*, 304; Caroline Pettigrew to her mother, March 4, 22, 1862, Pettigrew Family Papers, SHC; Kenelm H. Lewis to Elizabeth Lewis, July 27, 1863, Kenelm H. Lewis Papers, NCDAH.

18. Eliza DeRosset to her sister, January 14, 1864, DeRosset Family Papers, SHC; John A. Campbell to William S. Pettigrew, January 24, 1865, Pettigrew Family Papers, SHC.

19. William S. Pettigrew to Joshua Swift, August 12, 1862; William S. Pettigrew to Oliver H. Prince, October 22, 1862, Pettigrew Family Papers, SHC.

20. Durrill, *War of Another Kind*, 146–47.

21. Rawick, *The American Slave*, 14:400–402; Durrill, *War of Another Kind*, 74.

22. William S. Pettigrew to Dr. Archibald Palmer, January 16, 1863, Pettigrew Family Papers, SHC; Eliza DeRosset to her sister, December 15, 1863, DeRosset Family Papers, SHC.

23. "Our War Experience," Cronly Family Papers, DU.

24. "Recollections of Slavery by a Runaway Slave," *Emancipator*, August 23, September 13, 20, October 11, 18, 1838.

25. K. Battle, *Memories of an Old Time Tar Heel*, 177.

26. *Fayetteville Observer*, May 19, 1862.

27. Inscoe and McKinney, *The Heart of Confederate Appalachia*, 212–13; B. Nelson "Some Aspects of Negro Life," 158–61.

28. C. Brown, "A History of the Piedmont Railroad Company"; Trelease, "A Southern Railroad at War"; R. Black, *The Railroads of the Confederacy*, 148–53, 227–29; S. Nelson, *Iron Confederacies*, 28–40.

29. *Charleston Mercury*, October 21, 1862; B. Nelson, "Some Aspects of Negro Life," 161; *Fayetteville Observer*, February 16, 1863; *North Carolina Standard*, February 11, 1863; Trelease, "A Southern Railroad at War," 5, 15; Turner, "Slaves Hired."

30. On the division of labor among slaves on a railroad, see Thomas, *The Iron Way*, 21.

31. Allan Maifarlam [?] to Elias VanderHorst, March 18, 1863, VanderHorst Family Papers, South Carolina Historical Society, Charlotte, quoted in Schwalm, *A Hard Fight for We*, 88.

32. Hardy Hardison to Collins, March 27, 1863; Lloyd Bateman to Collins, June 1, 1863; Girard Phelps to Collins, March 14, 1863, Josiah Collins Papers, NCDAH. Also see Tarlton, *Somerset Place and Its Restoration*, 40–43; Redford, *Somerset Homecoming*, 118–20.

33. Durrill, *War of Another Kind*, 163; A. H. Arrington to Collins, May 13, 1863, Josiah Collins Papers, NCDAH.

34. "Private List–Negroes where hired 1863"; "Negroes where hired for 1864," Josiah Collins Papers, NCDAH; Ash, *Black Experience*, 37; *Fayetteville Observer*, November 3, 1862.

35. Rental contract, September 20, 1864, Davidson Family Papers, DU; Crabtree and Patton, *Journal of a Secesh Lady*, 285.

36. Savitt, "Slave Life Insurance," 594. The North Carolina Mutual Insurance Company of Raleigh should not be confused with the North Carolina Mutual Insurance Company of Durham, an African American owned company established in 1898.

37. J. M. Zohler to Williams Middleton, November 9, 1862, Middleton Family Papers, South Carolina Historical Society, Charleston, quoted in Schwalm, *A Hard Fight for We*, 88.

38. Charles Pettigrew to Jane Pettigrew, January 8, 12, 23, 1863, Pettigrew Family Papers, SHC.

39. Charles Pettigrew to Jane Pettigrew, April 3, August 6, 1863, Pettigrew Family Papers, SHC.

40. The role of paternalism in American slavery remains a contentious topic. The traditional exposition of the idea can be found in Genovese, *Roll, Jordan, Roll*. For recent assessment of Genovese's concept of paternalism, see Sinha, "Eugene D. Genovese"; Johnson, "A Nettlesome Classic Turns Twenty-Five."

41. Durrill, *War of Another Kind*, 164–65.

42. Schwalm, *A Hard Fight for We*, 87; Cunningham, "Edmund Burke Haywood," 153; H. Johnston, *Records of the Wilson Confederate Hospital*; Cunningham, "Confederate General Hospitals," 386; "Negroes where hired for 1864"; "Negroes where hired for 1865," Josiah Collins Papers, NCDAH; *Daily Confederate*, December 17, 1864.

43. Shurr, "Inside the Confederate Hospital," 144–57; Schultz, *Women at the Front*, 17, 38.

44. James L. McKee to Nancy Avaline Jarrett, May 5, 1861, Nancy Avaline Jarrett Papers, SHC; Hadden, *Slave Patrols*, 172, 174, 187; Rawick, *The American Slave*, 15:330.

45. Kenzer, *Kinship and Neighborhood*, 86; Bynum, *Unruly Women*, 116–17; "Our War Experience," Cronly Family Papers, DU; James L. McKee to Nancy Avaline Jarrett, August 17, 1861, Nancy Avaline Jarrett Papers, SHC.

46. F. M. Hubbard to Josiah Collins, January 17, February 7, 1863, Josiah Collins Papers, NCDAH.

47. F. M. Hubbard to Josiah Collins, June 8, 17, 1863, Josiah Collins Papers, NCDAH.

48. *Asheville News*, November 3, 1864; *Fayetteville Observer*, August 25, 1862, March 16, November 23, 1863, June 2, 1864; *Daily Confederate*, February 13, 23, March 9, April 7, 8, June 5, 13, 20, 25, 30, August 18, 1864.

49. *Richmond Daily Dispatch*, September 2, 23, 1862, February 1, 1864.

50. *Daily Confederate*, April 28, May 3, 1864.

51. *Fayetteville Observer*, June 9, 1864. Also see Endor Iron Works Ledger, SHC.

52. *Western Democrat*, November 8, 1864.

53. Schneider, "Institution of Slavery," 179; William C. Campbell to William S. Pettigrew, May 9, 22, 1862, Pettigrew Family Papers, SHC; Durrill, *War of Another Kind*, 76; Rev. J. Henry Smith diary, January 1, 9, 21, 25, February 11, March 1, 1862, Henry Smith Richardson Papers, SHC; Rufus L. Patterson to his father, December 8, 1864, Jones and Patterson Family Papers, SHC, quoted in Inscoe, "Mountain Masters as Confederate Opportunists," 97.

54. Morgan, *Emancipation in Virginia's Tobacco Belt*, 97–98; Ash, *When the Yankees Came*, 167.

55. Cashin, "Into the Trackless Wilderness," 43–45; A. W. Mangum to his sister, January 19, 1863, Mangum Family Papers, SHC; *Fayetteville Observer,* September 12, 29, 1864; James McKee to Nancy Avaline Jarrett, March 1, 1863, Nancy Avaline Jarrett Papers, SHC; *Spirit of the Age,* March 23, 1863; *Daily Confederate,* February 6, 1864; *Raleigh Weekly Progress,* June 14, 1864; William H. Owen to Alexander Elliot, December 16, 1864, Alexander Elliot Papers, SHC.

56. *Public Laws, Called Session,* 4; *North Carolina Standard,* November 4, 1863; Martis, *Historical Atlas,* 57, 70, 136; Yearns, *The Confederate Congress,* 42–43; *A Bill to Be Enacted; Journal of the Congress,* 6:298–301.

57. Kruman, *Parties and Politics in North Carolina,* 249–65; Auman, "Neighbor against Neighbor," 114–411; Raper, "William W. Holden"; Yates, "Governor Vance"; Harris, *William Woods Holden,* 127–55; McCurry, *Confederate Reckoning,* 124–32; Escott, *Many Excellent People,* 45–49.

58. T. Alexander and Beringer, *Anatomy of the Confederate Congress,* 133, 228–29; Mobley, "Zebulon B. Vance," 434–54; Manning, "Order of Nature."

59. *Raleigh Daily Confederate,* May 10, 1864; *Raleigh Weekly Progress,* March 13, July 12, 19, 1864.

60. Escott, "Poverty and Government Aid," 469; McCurry, *Confederate Reckoning,* 199–201.

61. Relief Committee for Volunteers' Families–Richmond County, 1861–1863, Leak and Wall Family Papers, SHC; *Public Laws, Called Session,* 16; *Public Laws, Adjourned Session,* 26; Wake County Pleas and Quarter Sessions Minutes, 1859–65, 596, NCDAH.

62. Mayor of Greensboro to Z. B. Vance, January 19, 1865, Zebulon B. Vance Governor's Papers, NCDAH.

63. *Western Democrat,* February 14, 1865.

64. Wright, *A Southern Girl in '61,* 228–29; Spencer, *Last Ninety Days,* 46.

65. *Daily Confederate,* March 8, 1865; *Daily South Carolinian,* March 9, 1865.

66. *Western Democrat,* February 21, 1865; Greenwood, *On the Home Front,* 14; Van Noppen, "The Significance of Stoneman's Last Raid," 350; Margaret Burwell to Robert Burwell, February 16, 1865, Edmund S. Burwell Papers, SHC.

67. Bradley, *This Astounding Close,* 6; A. W. Mangum to his sister, February 24, 1865, Mangum Family Papers, SHC; Aaron Thompson to [?], February 21, 1865, Thomas Nixon Papers, DU.

68. Bradley, *This Astounding Close,* 14–15; *Raleigh Weekly Progress,* March 28, 1865.

69. Hollowell, *War-Time Reminiscences,* 29; Elizabeth Collier Diary, August 30, 1861, March 11, April 20, 1865, SHC; Bradley, *This Astounding Close,* 26–40. For another refugee experience in the Goldsboro area, see Harriet Cobb Lane, "Some War Reminiscences," Lillie Vause Archbell Papers, SHC; Lane, *For My Children.* On the looting of homes by Sherman's soldiers, see Campbell, *When Sherman Marched North,* 75–92.

70. Lucy H. Bryan to Sue Capehart, March 3, 23, 1865, Capehart Family Papers, SHC.

71. Hesseltine, *Dr. J. G. M. Ramsey,* 220–21; Diary of Margaret B. Crozier Ramsey, April 16, 1865, J. G. M. Ramsey Papers, SHC.

72. "Some Incidents of the War as Personally Experienced," Cronly Family Papers, DU.

73. William Blount Rodman to Camilla Holliday Rodman, February 19, 1865, William Blount Rodman Papers, ECU.
74. Drury Lacy to Bessie Dewey, March 20, April 10, 1865, Drury Lacy Papers, SHC.
75. The primary source record contains contradictory accounts of Varina and Jefferson Davis's flights from Richmond, including the date that Jefferson Davis arrived in Charlotte and the circumstances under which he heard of Lincoln's assassination. J. Davis, *Rise and Fall*, 2:661–85; V. Davis, *Jefferson Davis*, 2:575–78, 582–88, 610–30; *Papers of Jefferson Davis*, 11:491, 513–14, 540, 549–50; Thomson, "How Jefferson Davis Received the News"; Harrison, *Recollections Grave and Gay*, 205–25; Stephen R. Mallory Diary and Reminiscences, SHC; diary, April 8–11, 1865, John Taylor Wood Papers, SHC; Cooper, *Jefferson Davis, American*, 522–30; C. Johnson, *Pursuit*, 1–149; Cashin, *First Lady of the Confederacy*, 152–63.

Chapter 5. In Good Hands, in a Safe Place

1. An earlier version of this chapter appeared as Silkenat, "'In Good Hands, in a Safe Place': Female Academies in Confederate North Carolina," *North Carolina Historical Review* 83 (January 2011): 40–71. It is used with the generous permission of the *North Carolina Historical Review*.
2. T. Jones, "Historical Sketch of Greensboro Female College," 168–73; *Christian Advocate*, April 16, May 27, August 19, September 2, 1863, January 17, 1865; *Greensboro Patriot*, August 13, 1863; *People's Press*, August 13, 1863; Powell, *Higher Education in North Carolina*, 76.
3. Stillman, "Education in the Confederate States of America"; Eaton, *Waning of the Old South Civilization*, 103–9; Downey, "Light of Learning"; Cook, "Mt. Lebanon University"; Akers, *First Hundred Years of Wesleyan College*; Coulter, *College Life in the Old South*; Gray, "Corona Female College"; Duncan, "Impact of the Civil War"; Pusey, "Lexington Female Academy"; Hollow, "Development of the Brownsville Baptist Female College."
4. *Greensboro Patriot*, May 31, 1861.
5. Because the enrollment records for many schools are incomplete or nonexistent, the figure of five thousand students who attended female academies in North Carolina during the Civil War is a rough estimate based on existing enrollment records. Autobiographical Sketch of Lucie Blackwell Malone Thompson, Thompson Family Papers, SHC; R. Battle, *Historical Sketch of St. Mary's School*, 7–8; "Death of Rev. Robert de Schweinitz," *Academy*, October 1901, Salem College Archives; Anderson, *North Carolina Women of the Confederacy*, 38–39. Also see Brooks, "Extracts from a School Girl's Journal," 61.
6. Jabour, *Scarlett's Sisters*, 47–82; Pope, "Preparation for Pedestals"; C. Farnham, *Education of the Southern Belle*; Stowe, "The Not-So-Cloistered Academy"; Ott, *Confederate Daughters*; Censer, *North Carolina Planters and Their Children*, 23, 43–46; Clinton, *The Plantation Mistress*, 124–37; Roberts, *The Confederate Belle*; Marten, *The Children's Civil War*.
7. Powell, *Higher Education in North Carolina*, 7; Pope, "Preparation for Pedestals," 29. On the culture of antebellum Southern men's colleges, see T. Williams, *Intellectual Manhood*; Pace, *Halls of Honor*; Coulter, *College Life in the Old South*. On

military academies, see Green, *Military Education*; Andrew, *Long Gray Lines*. Also see Tolley, "Science for Ladies, Classics for Gentlemen"; Walbert, "Endeavor to Improve Yourself."

8. Rosa Biddle to her mother, November 14, 1860; Rosa Biddle to her father, January 20, 1861, Samuel Biddle Papers, DU; Emma Kimberly to John Kimberly, November 6, 1860, Kimberly Family Papers, SHC.

9. Annie E. Brodie to Rosa Biddle, April 14, 1861; Rosa Biddle to her father, April 15, 1861, Samuel Biddle Papers, DU; Brooks, "Extracts from a School Girl's Journal," 59.

10. Kate Curtis to her brother, April 27, 1861, Moses Ashley Curtis Papers, SHC.

11. Rev. A. G. Stacy, quoted in Ruth Jane Trivette, "Davenport College: The Early Years," *Lenoir News-Topic*, May 23, 1957, Davenport College Collection, Greensboro College Archives, Greensboro, N.C.; *People's Press*, May 22, 1863; Fannie Patton to Charlotte Kerr, January 24, 1862, James W. Patton Papers, SHC; Montgomery, *St. Mary's of Olden Days*, 25.

12. Lou Sullivan to her parents, February 17, 1863, Lou Sullivan Papers, St. Mary's School Archives, Raleigh, N.C.; Montgomery, *St. Mary's of Olden Days*, 16; Salley, *Life at St. Mary's*, 35–36; Stoops, *The Heritage*, 62–65; Coulling, *The Lee Girls*, 106–8, 112, 120–21, 128, 130; *Papers of Jefferson Davis*, 8:199, 271.

13. Edmund Pendleton to Elizabeth Pendleton, February 6, 1863, Elizabeth Pendleton Coles Papers, SHC; Richard Creecy to Bettie Creecy, March 3, 1862, Creecy Family Papers, SHC.

14. Stoops, *The Heritage*, 37, 72; R. Battle, *Historical Sketch of St. Mary's School*, 7–8; Fries, *Historical Sketch of Salem Female Academy*, 20–21; *People's Press*, June 9, 1864; *Christian Advocate*, February 14, 1865.

15. Stoops, *The Heritage*, 61; Kate Curtis to brother, April 27, 1861, Moses Ashley Curtis Papers, SHC; Fries, *Historical Sketch of Salem Female Academy*, 21.

16. *Greensboro Patriot*, May 28, 1861, August 1, 1864; *Christian Advocate*, April 23, November 26, 1863; Willard, *Louisburg College Echoes*, 54; Moose, *History of Mitchell Community College*, 32.

17. Richard Creecy to Bettie Creecy, October 17, 1861, February 18, 1862, Creecy Family Papers, SHC.

18. Dietz, *Postal Service*; Sarah Cain to Elizabeth Cain, March 12, 1864, John Bailey Lancaster Papers, SHC; Bettie Dobson to Mary Dobson, March 11, 1865, Dobson Family Papers, SHC.

19. On homesickness at antebellum schools, see Miles, "Forgotten Scholars," 238; Jabour, *Scarlett's Sisters*, 47. On homesickness among Confederate refugees, see Mobley, *Weary of War*, 6–7.

20. Fannie Wirt to her mother, August 4, 16, 1863, Edward McCrady L'Engle Papers, SHC; Min Curtis to Mary Curtis, August 11, 1864, Moses Ashley Curtis Papers, SHC.

21. Fanny Moody to M. D. L. Moody, August 10, 1863, Sims Family Papers, SHC; Fannie Wirt to her mother, August 16, 1863, Edward McCrady L'Engle Papers, SHC.

22. Brooks, "Extracts from a School Girl's Journal," 60–61; Lou Sullivan to her parents, May 17, 1864, Lou Sullivan Papers, St. Mary's School Archives; Walke, "A Few Recollections," 14.

23. Richard Creecy to Bettie Creecy, August 31, September 12, 1861, February 8, 13, March 3, 1862, Creecy Family Papers, SHC.

24. Creecy later described the situation in eastern North Carolina as "a time of horrors, . . . brotherhood and civilization were rudely sundered." Creecy, *Grandfather's Tales*, 235–36.

25. Richard Creecy to Aldert Smedes, August 31, 1861, Creecy Family Papers, SHC. Richard and Mary Creecy used both "Betty" and "Bettie" in correspondence with their daughter.

26. On the role of rumor in the Confederacy, see Phillips, "The Grave Vine Telegraph," 753–88. Also see Cashin, "Into the Trackless Wilderness," 48.

27. Brooks, "Extracts from a School Girl's Journal," 63.

28. On spiritualism during the Civil War era, see Faust, *This Republic of Suffering*, 180–85; Schantz, *Awaiting the Heavenly Country*, 46–47.

29. Montgomery, *St. Mary's of Olden Days*, 20; Sophie Richardson Patrick letter, 1937, Greensboro College Archives.

30. Massey, *Ersatz in the Confederacy*; Mobley, *Weary of War*, 33–48.

31. Stoops, *The Heritage*, 51; Mary Curtis to her sister, May 12, 1863, Moses Ashley Curtis Papers, SHC; Brooks, "Extracts from a School Girl's Journal," 60.

32. On the Confederate textile shortage and the use of homespun as a symbol of Confederate patriotism, see Faust, *Mothers of Invention*, 220–26, 269–70; Ott, *Confederate Daughters*, 52–54; Massey, *Ersatz in the Confederacy*, 79–98; G. Roberts, *The Confederate Belle*, 79–84.

33. Brooks, "Extracts from a School Girl's Journal," 64.

34. Kate Curtis to her brother, April 27, 1861, Moses Ashley Curtis Papers, SHC; Lou Sullivan to her parents, April 13, August [?], 1864, Lou Sullivan Letters, St. Mary's School Archives; Aldert Smedes, untitled circular, March 14, 1864, St. Mary's School Archives.

35. For accounts of the lengths to which school administrators went to secure provisions and other supplies, see Fries, *Historical Sketch of Salem Female Academy*, 21; Memoir of Augustus Fogel, Moravian Church Archives, Salem, N.C.; F. Griffin, *Less Time for Meddling*, 264–65; Robert Burwell to Edmund Burwell, March 14, 1863; Margaret Burwell to Edmund Burwell, September 30, 1863; Robert Burwell to Edmund Burwell, September 10, 1864; and Margaret Burwell to Edmund Burwell, September 21, 1864, Edmund Strudwick Burwell Papers, SHC. In 1864–65 many schools accepted foodstuffs for tuition in lieu of highly inflated Confederate currency. Account books provide insight into how schools managed to feed and supply so many students. See Aldert Smedes, account book, St. Mary's School Archives; account book of Augustus Fogel, Salem College Archive; Edgeworth Female Academy Account Book, Greensboro Historical Museum Archives, Greensboro, N.C.

36. Fries, *Historical Sketch of Salem Female Academy*, 21.

37. Stoops, *The Heritage*, 44, 52; McKimmon, "Some Notes of Happenings," 11; Lou Sullivan to her parents, undated, Lou Sullivan Papers, St. Mary's School Archives; Nash, *Ladies in Making*, 19, 26–27.

38. Margaret Burwell to Edmund Burwell, February 16, 1865, Edmund Strudwick Burwell Papers, SHC.

39. Smedes, *She Hath Done What She Could*, 7; Richard Creecy to Bettie Creecy, December 21, 1861, Creecy Family Papers, SHC.

40. The school had refugee teachers from Maryland, Virginia, and Fayetteville, North Carolina. Montgomery, *St. Mary's of Olden Days*, 23–25.

41. Moose, *History of Mitchell Community College*, 39–40.

42. Although male teachers were exempt from the Confederate draft, many enlisted. According to Calvin Wiley, "Our schools contributed their full share to the ranks of the brave and patriotic army which volunteered its services in defense of our rights and freedoms." Southern schools had traditionally employed a significant number of Northern-born teachers. Stillman, "Education in the Confederate States of America," 61–71, 83, 153, 265–68; *North Carolina Journal of Education* 4 (1861): 193–207.

43. Autobiography, Maria Florilla Flint Hamblen Papers, SHC; Anderson, *North Carolina Women of the Confederacy*, 105; Margaret Burwell to Edmund Burwell, September 21, 1864, Edmund Strudwick Burwell Papers, SHC.

44. Kate Curtis to her brother, April 22, 27, 1861, Moses Ashley Curtis Papers, SHC; Emma Kimberly to John Kimberly, August 3, 1861, Kimberly Papers, SHC; Anderson, *North Carolina Women of the Confederacy*, 127.

45. On the curriculum of antebellum female academies, see Jabour, *Scarlett's Sisters*, 55–61; Clinton, *The Plantation Mistress*, 31–33.

46. Catalogue of Chowan Female Baptist Institute, 1853–54, 1856–57, 1867–70, Chowan University Archives, Murfreesboro, N.C. Also see Hixson, "Academic Requirement of Salem College."

47. There has been considerable scholarly attention to the issue of Confederate textbooks: Stillman, "Education in the Confederate States of America," 196–254; Bernath, *Confederate Minds*, 125–33, 199–205; Weeks, *Confederate Textbooks*; Rable, *The Confederate Republic*, 179–83; Marten, *The Children's Civil War*, 33, 52–61.

48. Edgeworth Female Academy principal Richard Sterling published (with Edgeworth teacher J. D. Campbell) several primary textbooks during the Civil War, including *Our Own First Reader, Our Own Second Reader, Our Own Third Reader, Our Own Fourth Reader, Our Own Fifth Reader, Our Own Primer*, and *Our Own Spelling Book*. He also opened his own printing business to produce textbooks. See Carroll, "Sterling, Campbell, and Albright." Samuel Lander, principal of High Point Female Seminary and later Lincolnton Female Seminary, published *Our Own Primary Arithmetic* in 1863 and the *Verbal Primer* in 1865. Female academy graduates also produced Confederate textbooks. Greensboro Female College graduate Marinda Branson Moore produced *The Geographical Reader for Dixie Children* in 1863. See O. Davis and Parks, "Confederate School Geographies."

49. Brooks, "Extracts from a School Girl's Journal," 59; Bettie Creecy to Kate Curtis, February 5, 1862, Moses Ashley Curtis Papers, SHC.

50. Noble, *History of the Public Schools*, 239; Stillman, "Education in the Confederate States of America," 265–68; *North Carolina Journal of Education* 5 (1862): 62; *People's Press*, January 12, 1865.

51. Ott, *Confederate Daughters*, 97; Moose, *History of Mitchell Community College*, 39–42; James G. Ramsay, "An Address Delivered by Hon. James G. Ramsay, M.D., before the Young Ladies of Concord Female College at Statesville, May

29th, 1863," 17–18, North Carolina Collection, Wilson Library, University of North Carolina at Chapel Hill.

52. John Bailey to Sarah Cain, January 22, 1865, John Bailey Lancaster Papers, SHC.

53. John Hanes to Catherine Hanes, undated, Catherine E. Hanes Papers, SHC.

54. Undated scrapbook, St. Mary's School Archives; Susan Collier diary, April 11, 1865, St. Mary's School Archives.

55. Susan Collier diary, April 11, 1865, St. Mary's School Archives; Brooks, "Extracts from a School Girl's Journal," 68.

56. Susan Collier diary, April 11, 1865, St. Mary's School Archives.

57. Maggie Ramsay to Margaret Ramsay, April 4, 1865, John Graham Ramsay Papers, SHC.

58. Quoted in Frank, "Bedrooms as Battlefields," 33.

59. Frank, "Bedrooms as Battlefields," 40–41; Barber and Ritter, "Physical Abuse . . . and Rough Handling"; Faust, *Mothers of Invention*, 200; Feimster, "General Benjamin Butler"; Cashin, "Into the Trackless Wilderness," 47–48.

60. Bessie Cain diary, April 16, 18, 1865, John Bailey Lancaster Papers, SHC.

61. Fries, *Historical Sketch of Salem Female Academy*, 21.

62. Brooks, "Extracts from a School Girl's Journal," 68.

63. Bessie Cain diary, April 16, 1865, John Bailey Lancaster Papers, SHC; Clarke, "General Sherman in Raleigh," 226; King, *Anna Long Thomas Fullers' Journal*, 46; "Endurin' the War," typed manuscript compiled by Gertrude Jenkins containing the narrative of Margaret Elizabeth Clewell, 1908, Gertrude Jenkins Papers, DU.

64. Clarke, "General Sherman in Raleigh," 226; Knight and Creech, *A History of Chowan College*, 164; Bessie Cain diary, April 29, 1865, John Bailey Lancaster Papers, SHC.

65. Censer, *The Reconstruction of Southern Womanhood*, 166–83; Noble, *History of Public Schools*, 245.

66. Stillman, "Education in the Confederate States of America," 268–69. Male teachers with more than twenty students were exempt from the Confederate draft.

67. *Mont Amoenian* 2:2 (February 1899): 7–8, Kirkman Family Papers, SHC; Lelouids, *Schooling in the New South*, 73–78.

68. McKimmon, "Some Notes of Happenings," 10.

69. Janney, *Burying the Dead*; Mills and Simpson, *Monuments to the Lost Cause*; Foster, *Ghosts of the Confederacy*; Wilson, *Baptized in Blood*; Cox, *Dixie's Daughters*; Sims, *Power of Femininity*, 129–51.

70. Salley, *Life at St. Mary's*, 48; Anderson, *North Carolina Women of the Confederacy*, 127; Smith and Wilson, *North Carolina Women Making History*, 201–4.

71. Although slightly younger than the generation examined by Pete Carmichael, female academy students experienced the Civil War as a similarly transformative event. See Carmichael, *The Last Generation*.

Chapter 6. A Home for the Rest of the War

1. Katherine Polk Gale, "Recollections of the Southern Confederacy," Gale and Polk Family Papers, SHC.

2. Sondley, *Asheville and Buncombe County*, 117; Inscoe and McKinney, *The Heart of Confederate Appalachia*, 27.

3. Brewster, *Summer Migrations and Resorts*, 7, 63–66; Memminger, *Historical Sketch of Flat Rock*, 8–12; Allston, *Early Sketch*; McCandless, *Slavery, Disease and Suffering*, 259.

4. McPherson, *Battle Cry of Freedom*, 370–72; Rose, *Rehearsal for Reconstruction*.

5. Schwalm, *A Hard Fight for We*, 108–15; William Elliott to William Elliott, September 24, 1861; Mary Johnstone to her mother, n.d., Elliott and Gonzales Family Papers, SHC.

6. Schwalm, *A Hard Fight for We*, 108; Leland, "Middleton Correspondence," 39, 65.

7. Diary of Reverend Malet, quoted in Allston, *Early Sketch*, 31; Mary Boykin Williams Harrison Ames, "Childhood Recollections," Williams-Chesnut-Manning Family Papers, South Caroliniana Library, University of South Carolina (hereafter SCL).

8. O'Connell, *Catholicity in the Carolinas and Georgia*, 443.

9. Bishir, Southern, and Martin, *Guide to the Historic Architecture*, 318; Pinckney, "Register of St. John-in-the-Wilderness" (April 1962): 106; 1861 receipt, Mitchell King Papers, SHC.

10. Allston, *Early Sketch*, 22; Hamilton and Cameron, *Papers of Randolph Abbott Shotwell*, 2:280.

11. Patton, *Flat Rock*, 11. C. G. Memminger's house was later owned by the poet and historian Carl Sandburg and is now a National Historic Site. See *Carl Sandburg Home National Historic Site, Connemara Main House*, 8–19. On Memminger, see Jordan, "Schemes of Usefulness"; Capers, *Life and Times of C. G. Memminger*.

12. Inscoe and McKinney, *The Heart of Confederate Appalachia*, 18.

13. Crofts, *Reluctant Confederates*, 145; Inscoe and McKinney, *The Heart of Confederate Appalachia*, 83–111; Trotter, *Bushwhackers*, 37; Alex J. Cansler to [Henry T.] Clark, August 20, 1861, Clark Governor's Papers, NCDAH; Poteat, *Henry Toole Clark*, 109.

14. McPherson, *Battle Cry of Freedom*, 430–32; Inscoe and McKinney, *The Heart of Confederate Appalachia*, 111–15; Trotter, *Bushwhackers*, 39–40; Barrett, *The Civil War in North Carolina*, 183–84.

15. Barrett, *The Civil War in North Carolina*, 185; OR, ser. 4, vol. 2, p. 674; Trotter, *Bushwhackers*, 137–44.

16. Quoted in Inscoe and McKinney, *The Heart of Confederate Appalachia*, 113.

17. Mary Johnstone to her mother, July 13, [1862?], Elliott and Gonzales Family Papers, SHC.

18. *North Carolina Troops*, 15:183–92; Paludan, *Victims*, 56–98.

19. On desertion in western North Carolina, see King-Owen, "Conditional Confederates"; Bardolph, "Confederate Dilemma"; Guiffre, "Desertion as Politics," 246–63; R. Reid, "Test Case of 'Crying Evil'"; Inscoe and McKinney, *The Heart of Confederate Appalachia*, 113–17.

20. Inscoe and McKinney, *The Heart of Confederate Appalachia*, 134–36; Bumgarner, *Kirk's Raiders*; Barrett, *The Civil War in North Carolina*, 233–37; Trotter, *Bushwhackers*, 113–19; *North Carolina Troops*, 15:183–92.

21. Bishir, Southern, and Martin, *Guide to the Historic Architecture*, 320–21; Trotter, *Bushwhackers*, 176.

22. Mary Johnstone to her mother, August 3, [1862?], Elliott and Gonzales Family Papers, SHC; Woodward, *Mary Chesnut's Civil War*, 455; Leland, "Middleton Correspondence," 169.

23. Mary Johnstone to her mother, February 2, [1862?], [summer 1862], September 21, 1862, [June?] 21 [1863?], n.d., Elliott and Gonzales Family Papers, SHC; "List of Negroes at Beaumont," Johnstone Family Papers, SCL; Mitchell King to MacMillan King, October 15, 1862, Mitchell King Papers, SHC.

24. Helsley, "Mitchell King Builds His Dream Home"; Mitchell King diary, August 2, 1862, Mitchell King Papers, SHC; Leland, "Middleton Correspondence," 168; Woodward, *Mary Chesnut's Civil War*, 422–23.

25. Leland, "Middleton Correspondence," 172; Mary Johnstone to her mother, September 21, [1862], Elliott and Gonzales Family Papers, SHC.

26. McPherson, *Battle Cry of Freedom*, 611–12; A. Robinson, *Bitter Fruits of Bondage*, 129–30, 278–79.

27. Inscoe and McKinney, *The Heart of Confederate Appalachia*, 211.

28. Confederate Friends to Vance, February 17, 1863; William Pickens to Vance, March 2, 1863, Zebulon B. Vance Papers, NCDAH, quoted in Schneider, "Institution of Slavery," 242–43.

29. Mary Johnstone to Emmie, December 27, [1863], Elliott and Gonzales Family Papers, SHC.

30. Katherine Polk Gale, "Recollections of the Southern Confederacy," Gale and Polk Family Papers, SHC.

31. Hunt, "High with Courage and Hope," 109; Leland, "Middleton Correspondence," 99, 100.

32. Mary Johnstone to her mother, [September 1862], November 9, 1862; Mary Johnstone to sister Emma, [October 26, 1862], Elliott and Gonzales Family Papers, SHC.

33. A. H. Elliott to [?], n.d., Elliott and Gonzales Family Papers, SHC; Schwalm, *A Hard Fight for We*, 112.

34. Mary Johnstone to her mother, March 15, [1863? 1864?], Elliott and Gonzales Family Papers, SHC.

35. Barrett, *The Civil War in North Carolina*, 240–41; Trotter, *Bushwhackers*, 143; Leland, "Middleton Correspondence," 40; Mary Johnstone to her mother, March 15, [1864?], Elliott and Gonzales Family Papers, SHC; Calvin Cowles to Gov. Zebulon Vance, April 4, 1864, Calvin Cowles Papers, NCDAH.

36. Leland, "Middleton Correspondence," 41–42; Mary Johnstone to her mother, March 15, [1864?], Elliott and Gonzales Family Papers, SHC.

37. Laura Norwood to Walter Lenoir, March 15, 1864, Lenoir Family Papers, SHC; Mary Johnstone to her sister Emma, [October 26, 1862], Elliott and Gonzales Family Papers, SHC.

38. Mary Johnstone to her mother, [November 1861], November 9, 1862, [April 25, 1863?], Elliott and Gonzales Family Papers, SHC; medical ledger, Mitchell King Papers, SHC; Pinckney, "Register of St. John-in-the-Wilderness" (October 1962): 233–34.

39. Inscoe and McKinney, *The Heart of Confederate Appalachia*, 176–81; Inscoe, "Mountain Masters as Confederate Opportunists," 85–100.

40. Inscoe, "Civil War's Empowerment of an Appalachian Woman"; Inscoe, "Mountain Masters as Confederate Opportunists," 94–95; Inscoe and McKinney, *The Heart of Confederate Appalachia*, 218–22.

41. Leland, "Middleton Correspondence," 205; Katherine Polk Gale, "Recollections of the Southern Confederacy," Gale and Polk Family Papers, SHC.

42. Trotter, *Bushwhackers*, 142; Mary Johnstone to her mother, December 1, 1861, [September 1862?], n.d., Elliott and Gonzales Family Papers; *New Orleans Architecture*, 5:38.

43. Mary Johnstone to her mother, July 13, 1862, [June 1863?], August 15, [1863], n.d., Elliott and Gonzales Family Papers, SHC; Katherine Polk Gale, "Recollections of the Southern Confederacy," Gale and Polk Family Papers, SHC; Leland, "Middleton Correspondence," 217; Mitchell King diary, May 13, 1862, Mitchell King Papers, SHC; *Charleston Mercury*, June 4, 1863.

44. Leland, "Middleton Correspondence," 218; Webber, "St. John's in the Wilderness," 56; Annie Stuart to Emmie, January 29, [1863?], Elliott and Gonzales Family Papers, SHC.

45. T. W. Atkin to J. A. Seddon, July 29, 1863, Z. B. Vance Papers, NCDAH, quoted in Barrett, *The Civil War in North Carolina*, 184; Sarepta Revis to Daniel W. Revis, June 7, 1863, Daniel Revis Letters, NCDAH.

46. Leland, "Middleton Correspondence," 99, 212; Mary Johnstone to her mother, April 10, [1863?], Elliott and Gonzales Family Papers, SHC.

47. Leland, "Middleton Correspondence," 217–18.

48. "Murder of Mr. Andrew Johnstone," SCL; *Charleston Daily Courier*, June 10, 1864; *Daily Confederate*, June 20, 1864; Memminger, *Historical Sketch of Flat Rock*, 15–16; Patton, *Flat Rock*, 42–43; "Murder of Andrew Johnstone, Esq.," Special Collections, University of Tennessee, Knoxville; Ralph Elliott to his mother, June 15, 1864, Elliott and Gonzales Family Papers, SHC; Inscoe and McKinney, *The Heart of Confederate Appalachia*, 128–29; Trotter, *Bushwhackers*, 176–78.

49. "Murder of Mr. Andrew Johnstone," SCL.

50. Patton, *Flat Rock*, 43.

51. "Murder of Mr. Andrew Johnstone," SCL; "Murder of Andrew Johnstone, Esq.," Special Collections, University of Tennessee, Knoxville; Mary Boykin William Harrison Ames, "Childhood Recollections," Williams-Chesnut Manning Family Papers, SCL; Allston, *Early Sketch*, 35; Ralph Elliott to his mother, June 15, 1864, Elliott and Gonzales Family Papers, SHC; *Asheville News* quoted in *Daily Confederate*, June 20, 1864.

52. Ralph Elliott to his mother, June 15, 1864, Elliott and Gonzales Family Papers, SHC; Mary Johnstone to her mother, June 24, 1864; Ralph Elliott to his mother, June 20, 25, 1864; Mary Johnstone to her sister, [July 1864?], Elliott and Gonzales Family Papers, SHC.

53. Mary Boykin Williams Harrison Ames, "Childhood Recollections," SCL.

54. Mary Johnstone to her sister, [July 1864?], Elliott and Gonzales Family Papers, SHC.

55. Memminger, *Historical Sketch of Flat Rock*, 14; *Carl Sandburg Home National Historic Site, Connemara Main House*, 61–62; *Papers of Jefferson Davis*, 11:199–202; OR, ser. 1, vol. 46, pt. 2, p. 1013.

56. Hadley, *Seven Months a Prisoner*, 120–25.
57. Ibid., 125–33.
58. The sisters have been identified as Martha, Elizabeth, and Alice Hollingsworth. See Helsley and Jones, *Guide to Historic Henderson County*, 48; Patton, *Flat Rock*, 44–45; *Carl Sandburg Home National Historic Site, The Swedish House*, 21.
59. Hadley, *Seven Months a Prisoner*, 133–40.
60. Ibid., 145–46. The painting in question may be a Rembrandt Peale portrait of George Washington, now housed in the Detroit Museum of Art. The painting was once owned by Mrs. Lewis S. Jervey, a South Carolina refugee in Flat Rock, who was a descendant of the painting's original owner, Gen. Christopher Gadsden.
61. Letter fragment, [November 1864], Elliott and Gonzales Family Papers, SHC. On Martha Singleton, see Crawford, "Martha Rutledge Kinloch Singleton."
62. *Asheville News*, quoted in *Western Democrat*, November 8, 1864; OR, ser. 4, vol. 2, p. 732; Inscoe and McKinney, *The Heart of Confederate Appalachia*, 129; letter fragment, [November 1864], Elliott and Gonzales Family Papers, SHC.
63. Letter fragment, [November 1864], Elliott and Gonzales Family Papers, SHC.
64. Ibid.
65. Mary Johnstone to her mother, [1864?], Elliott and Gonzales Family Papers, SHC; Memminger, *Historical Sketch of Flat Rock*, 14.
66. O'Connell, *Catholicity in the Carolinas and Georgia*, 443.
67. Robertson, *A Small Boy's Recollections*, 102–4.

Epilogue

1. MacLean, "Return of a Refugee."
2. Egerton, *The Wars of Reconstruction*, 70–107; G. Downs, *After Appomattox*.
3. Mrs. F. Roberts, "The Aftermath"; Mrs. F. Roberts, "Historical Incidents"; Ashe, *Cyclopedia of Eminent and Representative Men*, 2:127–28.
4. Bellamy, *Back with the Tide*, 3–8; Bishir, *The Bellamy Mansion*. Mrs. Hawley's version of entertaining the Bellamys came be found in W. Reid, *After the War*, 47.
5. Judkin Browning, *The Southern Mind under Union Rule*, 176; W. Reid, *After the War*, 49.
6. W. Reid, *After the War*, 29.
7. Hesseltine, *Dr. J. G. M. Ramsey*, 220–77; Diary of Margaret Ramsey, 7–12, James Gettys McGready Ramsey Papers, SHC.
8. Rawick, *The American Slave*, 14:400–404.
9. Litwack, *Been in the Storm So Long*, 229–32, 292–301; W. Cohen, *At Freedom's Edge*, 3; *Report of the Joint Committee on Reconstruction*, 187; W. Reid, *After the War*, 49; Dennett, *The South As It Is*, 130; H. Williams, *Help Me Find My People*, 157.
10. *Report of the Joint Committee on Reconstruction*, 182–87; *Union Banner*, June 30, 1865.
11. Price, "John C. Barnett."
12. *Raleigh Daily Standard*, September 29, 1865; R. Alexander, *North Carolina Faces the Freedman*, 7; J. Downs, *Sick from Freedom*, 65–145.
13. "From Miss Ella Roper," *American Missionary* 9 (July 1865): 157–58; Hahn, *A Nation under Our Feet*, 123–24; Cecelski, *Fire of Freedom*, 186.

14. Escott, *Many Excellent People*, 119–22, 130–31; R. Alexander, *North Carolina Faces the Freedman*, 1–14, 40–49; Sternhell, *Routes of War*, 176; Litwack, *Been in the Storm So Long*, 367–68, 379–86; James Browning, "The North Carolina Black Code," 467.

15. James, *Annual Report*, 24; Click, *Time Full of Trial*, 154–55.

16. Click, *Time Full of Trial*, 153–90.

17. Mobley, *James City*, 55, 61, 64–65.

18. Ibid., 76–88.

19. Southern ideas of home are explored in Levine, *Fall of the House of Dixie*; Glymph, *Out of the House of Bondage*; Sternhell, *Routes of War*.

BIBLIOGRAPHY

Manuscripts

Alabama Department of Archives and History, Montgomery
  Sarah Espy diary

Albert and Shirley Small Special Collections Library, University of Virginia, Charlottesville
  Papers of Eliza Oswald Hill

Chowan University Archives, Murfreesboro, N.C.
  Catalogue of Chowan Female Baptist Institute (1853–54, 1856–57, 1867–70)

Greensboro College Archives, Greensboro, N.C.
  Davenport College Collection
  Sophie Richardson Patrick letter (1937)

Greensboro Historical Museum Archives, Greensboro, N.C.
  Edgeworth Female Academy Account Book

Huntington Library, San Marino, Calif.
  James E. Glazier Papers
  Gustavus Jocknick Papers
  "A Voyage of a Refugee Sailor-Soldier, from the Interior of North Carolina to the Interior of South Carolina, Ending at Kingsville, January, 1864"

Library of Congress, Washington, D.C.
  Abraham Lincoln Papers

Moravian Church Archives, Winston-Salem, N.C.
  Memoir of Augustus Fogel

National Archives, Washington, D.C.
  Record Group 393

North Carolina Collection, University of North Carolina, Chapel Hill
  James G. Ramsay, "An Address Delivered by Hon. James G. Ramsay, M.D., before the Young Ladies of Concord Female College at Statesville, May 29th, 1863"

North Carolina Department of Archives and History, Raleigh
  Ashe County Tax Assessors List, 1863
  B. C. Beckwith Papers
  Isaac Brown Papers
  Cabarrus County Tax List, 1863
  Joseph Blount Cheshire, "Some Account of My Life for My Children"
  Henry Toole Clarke Papers

262 Bibliography

    Josiah Collins Papers
    Calvin Cowles Papers
    Johnston County Tax List, 1863
    Kenelm H. Lewis Papers
    Daniel Revis Letters
    Julia Ward Stickley Papers
    David Swain Papers
    Charles Henry Tubbs Letters
    Zebulon Vance and Harriet Espy Vance Papers
    Zebulon B. Vance Governor's Papers
    Wake County Pleas and Quarter Sessions Minutes, 1859–1865
    Wayne County Tax List, 1863

Salem College Archives, Winston-Salem, N.C.
    Account book of Augustus Fogel
    "Death of Rev. Robert de Schweinitz." *Academy* (October 1901)

South Carolina Historical Society, Charleston
    Middleton Family Papers
    VanderHorst Family Papers

South Caroliniana Library, University of South Carolina, Columbia
    Johnstone Family Papers
    "Murder of Mr. Andrew Johnstone"
    Williams-Chesnut-Manning Family Papers

Southern Historical Collection, Wilson Library, University of North Carolina, Chapel Hill
    Stephen Tippet Andrews Papers
    Lillie Vause Archbell Papers
    Benbury and Haywood Family Papers
    Mary Norcott Bryan Papers
    Edmund Strudwick Burwell Papers
    Calder Family Papers
    Capehart Family Papers
    Edmund J. Cleveland Diary
    Elizabeth Pendleton Coles Papers
    Elizabeth Collier Diary
    Homer A. Cooke Military Records
    William J. Creasey Papers
    Creecy Family Papers
    Moses Ashley Curtis Papers
    DeRosset Family Papers
    Dobson Family Papers
    Alexander Elliot Papers
    Elliott and Gonzales Family Papers
    Endor Iron Works Ledger
    Foscue Family Papers

Gale and Polk Family Papers
Jeremy Francis Gilmer Papers
Maria Florilla Flint Hamblen Papers
Catherine E. Hanes Papers
Cushing Biggs Hassell Papers
Nancy Avaline Jarrett Papers
Thomas D. Johnston Papers
Kimberly Family Papers
Mitchell King Papers
Kirkman Family Papers
Drury Lacy Papers
John Bailey Lancaster Papers
Leak and Wall Family Papers
Edward McCrady L'Engle Papers
Lenoir Family Papers
Peter Mallett Papers
Stephen R. Mallory Diary and Reminiscences
Mangum Family Papers
James Isaac Metts Papers
George W. Mordecai Papers
New Bern Occupation Papers
James W. Patton Papers
Pettigrew Family Papers
James Gettys McGready Ramsey Papers
John Graham Ramsay Papers
Marie Louise Du Brutz Reston Memoirs
Henry Smith Richardson Papers
Benjamin Franklin Royal Papers
David Schenck Papers
Sims Family Papers
Skinner Family Papers
Steed and Phipps Family Papers
Thompson Family Papers
John W. and Augustus Williams Papers
John Taylor Wood Papers

Special Collections, Joyner Library, East Carolina University, Greenville, N.C.
  Clarrisa Phelps Hanks Papers
  Elizabeth Moore Collection
  New Bern Historical Society Collection
  William Blount Rodman Papers
  Nicholas Schenck diary
  Edward C. Yellowley Correspondence, Henry T. King Collection

Special Collections, Perkins Library, Duke University,
Durham, N.C.

Samuel Biddle Papers
Cronly Family Papers
Davidson Family Papers
Jesse Harrison Papers
Gertrude Jenkins Papers
Edward W. Kinsley Papers
Ransom Lee Papers
William F. Loftin Papers
MacRae Family Papers
Thomas Nixon Papers
Samuel Finley Patterson Papers
George A. Root Letters
Mary French Scott Papers
Josiah Wood Papers

Special Collections, University of Tennessee Library, Knoxville
"Murder of Andrew Johnstone, Esq."

St. Mary's School Archives, Raleigh, N.C.
Susan Collier diary
Aldert Smedes, untitled circular, March 14, 1864
Aldert Smedes account book
Lou Sullivan Papers
Undated scrapbook

W. E. B. DuBois Library, University of Massachusetts, Amherst
Edward W. Kinsley Papers

Newspapers
American Missionary (New York)
Anti-Slavery Reporter (London)
Asheville News
Charleston Daily Courier
Charleston Mercury
Christian Advocate (Raleigh)
Christian Recorder (Philadelphia)
Congregationalist (Boston)
Daily Confederate (Raleigh)
Daily South Carolinian (Columbia)
Fayetteville Observer
Freedmen's Advocate (New York)
Freedman's Journal (Boston)
Friend (Philadelphia)
Greensboro Daily News
Greensboro Patriot
Liberator (Boston)
Milton Chronicle

National Freedman (New York)
New York Herald
New York Times
North Carolina Journal of Education (Greensboro)
North Carolina Standard (Raleigh)
North Carolina Times (New Bern)
Norfolk Christian Sun
Old North State (Beaufort)
People's Press (Salem)
Philadelphia Inquirer
Raleigh Register
Richmond Daily Dispatch
Spirit of the Age (Raleigh)
Union Banner (Salisbury)
Weekly Progress (Raleigh)
Western Democrat (Charlotte)
Wilmington Herald

Published Primary Sources

Abbott, John S. C. "Heroic Deeds of Heroic Men." *Harper's New Monthly Magazine* 30 (December 1864): 3–20.
American Freedmen's Inquiry Commission. *Preliminary Report Touching the Condition and Management of Emancipated Refugees*. New York: John F. Trow, 1863.
Anderson, Lucy London. *North Carolina Women of the Confederacy*. Fayetteville, N.C.: Cumberland Printing, 1926.
Battle, Kemp Plumber. *Memories of an Old Time Tar Heel*. Chapel Hill: University of North Carolina Press, 1945.
Battle, Richard H. *An Historical Sketch of St. Mary's School*. Charlotte: Observer Printing, 1902.
Bellamy, Ellen D. *Back with the Tide*. Wilmington, N.C.: Bellamy Mansion Museum, 2002.
Benjamin, W. S. *The Great Epidemic in New Berne and Vicinity*. New Berne, N.C.: Geo. Mills Joy, 1865.
Berlin, Ira, et al. *Freedom: A Documentary History of Emancipation, 1861–1867*. 5 vols. New York: Cambridge University Press; Chapel Hill: University of North Carolina Press, 1995–2008.
A Bill To Be Enacted To Provide for Holding Elections for Representatives in the Congress of the Confederate States, in States Occupied by the Forces of the Enemy. Richmond, Va.: The House, 1863.
Bishop, Nathan. *A Memorial Record of the New York Branch of the United States Christian Commission*. New York: Gray & Green, 1866.
Black, Wilfred W. "Civil War Letters of E. N. Boots from New Bern and Plymouth." *North Carolina Historical Review* 36 (1959): 205–23.
Blight, David. *A Slave No More*. New York: Harcourt, 2007.
Brooks, Pauline Hill. "Extracts from a School Girl's Journal during the Sixties." *Collegian*, July 1903.

Brown, William Wells. *The Negro in the American Rebellion.* Boston: Lee & Shepard, 1867.

Browning, Judkin. *The Southern Mind under Union Rule: The Diary of James Rumley, Beaufort, North Carolina, 1862–1865.* Gainesville: University Press of Florida, 2009.

Browning, Judkin, and Michael Thomas Smith, eds. *Letters from a North Carolina Unionist.* Raleigh, N.C.: Division of Archives and History, 2001.

Bryan, Mary Norcott. *Echoes from the Past.* New Bern, N.C., 1921.

———. *A Grandmother's Recollection of Dixie.* New Bern, N.C.: Owen G. Dunn, 1912.

Budington, William Ives. *A Memorial of Giles F. Ward, Jr.* New York: Anson D. F. Randolph, 1866.

Butler, Benjamin. *Autobiography and Personal Reminiscences of Major-General Benj. F. Butler.* Boston: A. M. Thayer, 1892.

Clapp, Henry Austin. *Letters to the Home Circle.* Edited by John R. Barden. Raleigh, N.C.: Division of Archives and History, 1998.

Clarke, Mary Bayard. "General Sherman in Raleigh." *Old Guard* 4 (April 1866): 226–32.

Colyer, Vincent. *Report of Christian Mission to the United States Army.* New York: Whitehorne, 1862.

———. *Report of the Services Rendered by the Freed People to the United States Army, in North Carolina, in the Spring 1862, After the Battle of Newbern.* New York: V. Colyer, 1864.

Crabtree, Beth G., and James W. Patton, eds. *Journal of a Secesh Lady: The Diary of Catherine Ann Devereux Edmondston, 1860–1866.* Raleigh, N.C.: Division of Archives and History, 1979.

Creecy, Richard B. *Grandfather's Tales.* Raleigh, N.C.: Edwards & Broughton, 1901.

Crow, Terrell Armistead, and Mary Moulton Barden, eds. *Live Your Own Life: The Family Papers of Mary Bayard Clarke, 1854–1886.* Columbia: University of South Carolina Press, 2003.

Curtis, William A. "A Journal of Reminiscences of the War." *Our Living and Our Dead* 2:3 (May 1875): 281–90.

Davis, Jefferson. *The Rise and Fall of the Confederate Government.* New York: Appleton, 1881.

Davis, Varina. *Jefferson Davis: Ex-president of the Confederate States of America.* New York: Belford, 1890.

Dawson, Francis W. *Our Women in the War.* Charleston, S.C.: News & Courier, 1885.

Day, David L. *My Diary of Rambles.* Milford, Mass.: King & Billings, 1884.

Dennett, John Richard. *The South As It Is.* Baton Rouge: Louisiana State University Press, 1995.

Denny, Joseph Waldo. *Wearing the Blue in the 25th Mass. Volunteer Infantry.* Worchester, Mass.: Putnam & Davis, 1879.

Derby, William P. *Bearing Arms in the Twenty-Seventh Massachusetts Regiment of Volunteer Infantry.* Boston: Wright & Potter, 1883.

Dodge, David. "Cave-Dwellers of the Confederacy." *Atlantic Monthly* 68 (1891): 514–21.

———. "Domestic Economy in the Confederacy." *Atlantic Monthly* 58 (August 1886): 229–43.
Donaghy, John. *Army Experience of Capt. John Donaghy.* Deland, Fla.: E. O. Painter, 1926.
Drake, J. Madison. *The History of the Ninth New Jersey Veteran Vols.* Elizabeth, N.J.: Journal Printing House, 1889.
Emmerton, James Arthur. *A Record of the Twenty-Third Regiment Mass. Vol. Infantry in the War of Rebellion.* Boston: William Ware, 1886.
Fries, Adelaide L. *Historical Sketch of Salem Female Academy.* Salem, N.C.: Crist & Keehln, 1902.
Gage, Moses D. *From Vicksburg to Raleigh.* Chicago: Clarke, 1865.
Goss, Warren Lee. *The Soldier's Story of His Captivity at Andersonville, Belle Isle, and Other Rebel Prisons.* Boston: Lee and Shepard, 1867.
Gould, William B., IV. *Diary of a Contraband: The Civil War Passage of a Black Sailor.* Stanford, Calif.: Stanford University Press, 2002.
Graham, Matthew J. *Ninth Regiment New York Volunteers.* New York: E. P. Coby, 1900.
Hadley, J. V. *Seven Months a Prisoner.* Indianapolis: Meikel, 1868.
Haines, Zenas T. *Letters from the Forty-Fourth Regiment M.V.M.* Boston: Herald Job Office, 1863.
Hamilton, J. G. de Roulhac, ed. *Papers of William A. Graham.* Raleigh, N.C.: State Department of Archives and History, 1973.
Hamilton, J. G. de Roulhac, and Rebecca Cameron, eds. *Papers of Randolph Abbott Shotwell.* Raleigh: North Carolina Historical Commission, 1931.
Harrison, Mrs. Burton. *Recollections Grave and Gay.* New York, 1911.
Herrington, William D. *The Captain's Bride: A Tale of the War; and, The Deserter's Daughter.* Edited by W. Keats Sparrow. Raleigh: Division of Archives and History, North Carolina Department of Cultural Resources, 1990.
———. "The Refugee's Niece." *Mercury*, May 7, 1864.
Hesseltine, William B., ed. *Dr. J. G. M. Ramsey: Autobiography and Letters.* Knoxville: University of Tennessee Press, 2002.
Hollowell, James Monroe. *War-Time Reminiscences and Other Selections.* Goldsboro, N.C.: Goldsboro Herald, 1939.
Hood, James Walker. *Sketch of the Early History of the African Methodist Episcopal Zion Church.* Charlotte, N.C.: A. M. E. Zion Publishing House, 1914.
Howard, O. O. *Autobiography.* New York: Baker & Taylor, 1907.
———. "The Freedmen during the War." *New Princeton Review* 1 (1886): 373–85.
Hubbard, Charles E. *Campaign of the Forty-Fifth Regiment, Massachusetts Volunteer Militia.* Boston: J. S. Adams, 1882.
Jacobs, Harriet. *Incidents in the Life of a Slave Girl.* Boston, 1861.
James, Horace. *Annual Report of the Superintendent of Negro Affairs in North Carolina, 1864.* Boston: W. F. Brown, 1865.
———. *The Two Great Wars of America.* Boston: W. F. Brown, 1862.
Johnston, Frontis, ed. *The Papers of Zebulon Baird Vance.* Raleigh: North Carolina Department of Archives and History, 1963.
Johnston, Hugh Buckner. *Records of the Wilson Confederate Hospital.* Wilson, N.C., 1954.

Jones, Turner M. "Historical Sketch of Greensboro Female College." In *Centennial of Methodism in North Carolina*, edited by L. S. Burkhead, 159–78. Raleigh, N.C.: John Nichols, 1876.

Journal of the Congress of the Confederate States of America. Washington, D.C.: GPO, 1905.

King, Myrtle C., ed. *Anna Long Thomas Fullers' Journal, 1856–1890: A Civil War Diary.* Alpharetta, Ga.: Priority Publishing, 1999.

Kingman, Bradford. *Memoir of Gen. Edward Augustus Wild.* Boston, 1895.

Kirwan, Thomas. *Memorial History of Seventeenth Regiment Massachusetts Volunteer Infantry.* Salem, Mass.: Salem Press, 1911.

Lane, Harriet Cobb. *For My Children.* N.p., n.d.

Leland, Isabella Middleton. "Middleton Correspondence, 1861–1865." *South Carolina Historical Magazine* 63 (1962): 33–41, 61–70, 164–74, 204–10.

Letter from Hon. Edward Stanly, Military Governor of North Carolina, to Col. Henry A. Gilliam. New Bern, N.C., 1862.

Lowry, Thomas P., ed. *Swamp Doctor: The Diary of a Union Surgeon in the Virginia and North Carolina Marshes.* Mechanicsburg, Pa.: Stackpole Books, 2001.

MacBryde, Ann Campbell, ed. *Ellie's Book: The Journal Kept by Ellie M. Andrews.* Davidson, N.C.: Briarpatch Press, 1984.

MacLean, Clara Dargan. "Return of a Refugee." *Southern Historical Society Papers* 13 (1885): 502–15.

Mann, Albert W. *History of the Forty-Fifth Regiment, Massachusetts Volunteer Militia.* Boston: W. Spooner, 1908.

Marcotte, Frank B., ed. *Private Osborne, Massachusetts 23rd Volunteers.* Jefferson, N.C.: McFarland, 1999.

McDonald, Cornelia Peake. *A Woman's Civil War.* Madison: University of Wisconsin Press, 1992.

McKimmon, Kate. "Some Notes of Happenings at St. Mary's during Her School Days, by the Oldest Inhabitant." *St. Mary's Muse* 10 (April 1906): 10–11.

Minutes of the Freedmen's Convention, Held in the City of Raleigh, on the 2nd, 3rd, 4th and 5th of October, 1866. Raleigh, N.C.: Standard Book and Job Office, 1866.

Montgomery, Lizzie Wilson. *The St. Mary's of Olden Days.* Raleigh, N.C.: Bynam Printing, 1932.

Murder of Union Soldiers in North Carolina. Washington, D.C.: U.S. War Department, 1866.

Nicholas, George Ward. *The Story of the Great March.* New York: Harper, 1865.

O'Connell, J. J. *Catholicity in the Carolinas and Georgia.* New York: D. & J. Sadlier, 1879.

Official Records of the Union and Confederate Navies in the War of the Rebellion. 30 vols. Washington, D.C.: GPO, 1894–1922.

Olnhausen, Mary Phinney von. *Adventures of an Army Nurse in Two Wars.* Boston: Little, Brown, 1903.

Papers of Jefferson Davis. 13 vols. Baton Rouge: Louisiana State University Press, 1971–2012.

Parker, Allen. *Recollection of Slavery Times.* Worchester, Mass.: Chas. W. Burbank, 1895.

Pinckney, Elise. "Register of St. John-in-the-Wilderness, Flat Rock." Pts. 1-3. *South Carolina Historical Magazine* 63 (April 1962): 105-11; (July 1962): 175-81; (October 1962): 232-37.
Public Laws of the State of North Carolina: Passed by the General Assembly, at Its Adjourned Session of 1863. Raleigh, N.C.: W. W. Holden, 1863.
Public Laws of the State of North Carolina: Passed by the General Assembly, at Its Called Session of 1863. Raleigh, N.C.: W. W. Holden, 1863.
Putnam, Samuel H. *The Story of Company A, Twenty-Fifth Regiment Mass. Vols. in the War of the Rebellion*. Worchester, Mass.: Putnam, Davis, 1886.
Rawick, George P., ed. *The American Slave: A Composite Autobiography*. Westport, Conn.: Greenwood Press, 1972-79.
"Recollections of Slavery by a Runaway Slave." *Emancipator*, August 23, September 13, 20, October 11, 18, 1838.
Redkey, Edwin S. *A Grand Army of Black Men: Letters from African-American Soldiers in the Union Army, 1861-1865*. Cambridge: Cambridge University Press, 1992.
Reid, Whitelaw. *After the War*. London: Moore, Wilstach & Baldwin, 1866.
Report of the Joint Committee on Reconstruction. Washington, D.C.: GPO, 1866.
Revue Law Passed by the General Assembly of State of North Carolina. Raleigh, N.C.: W. W. Holden, 1863.
Roberts, Mrs. Frederick C. "The Aftermath." *Carolina and the Southern Cross* (February 1914): 4-7.
———. "Historical Incidents—What 'Our Women in the War' Did and Suffered—Within the Lines." *Carolina and the Southern Cross* 2 (April 1914): 4-7.
Robertson, George F. *A Small Boy's Recollections of the Civil War*. Clover, S.C.: George F. Robertson, 1932.
Robinson, William H. *From Log Cabin to Pulpit*. Eau Claire, Wis.: James H. Tifft, 1913.
Roe, Alfred S. *The Fifth Regiment Massachusetts Volunteer Infantry in Its Three Tours of Duty, 1861, 1862-63, 1864*. Boston: Fifth Regiment Veterans Association, 1911.
Salley, Katherine Batts. *Life at St. Mary's*. Chapel Hill: University of North Carolina Press, 1942.
Schwartz, Gerald, ed., *A Woman Doctor's Civil War: Esther Hill Hawks' Diary*. Columbia: University of South Carolina Press, 1989.
Sharpe, J. A. "Diary of a Confederate Refugee." *Historical Papers, Historical Society of Trinity College*, series 3 (1899): 8-16.
Silber, Nina, and Mary Beth Sievens. *Yankee Correspondence: Civil War Letters between New England Soldiers and the Home Front*. Charlottesville: University of Virginia Press, 1996.
Singleton, William Henry. *Recollections of My Slavery Days*. Peekskill, N.Y.: Highland Democrat, 1922.
Smedes, Aldert. *She Hath Done What She Could*. Raleigh, N.C.: Seaton Gales, 1851.
Sparrow, Annie. "Recollections of the Civil War." In *Washington and the Pamlico*, edited by Ursula F. Loy and Pauline M. Worthy, 51-64. Raleigh, N.C.: Edwards & Broughton, 1976.

Spencer, Cornelia Phillips. *The Last Ninety Days of the War in North Carolina.* New York: Watchman, 1866.
Statutes at Large, Treaties, and Proclamations of the United States of America. Vol. 13. Boston: Little, Brown, 1866.
Thomson, A. W. "How Jefferson Davis Received the News of Lincoln's Death." *Independent* 52 (1900): 436.
Thorpe, Sheldon B. *History of the Fifteenth Connecticut Volunteers.* New Haven, Conn.: Price, Lee & Adkins, 1893.
Trudeau, Noah Andre. *Voices of the 55th.* Dayton, Ohio: Morningside House, 1996.
Turner, Grace. "Slaves Hired by the North Carolina Rail Road in 1862 and 1864." *North Carolina Genealogical Society Journal* 25 (1999): 22–33.
Walcott, Charles Folsom. *History of the Twenty-First Regiment Massachusetts Volunteers.* Boston: Houghton Mifflin, 1882.
Walke, Lucy. "A Few Recollections, 1863–1864." *St. Mary's Muse* 10 (April 1906): 12–14.
War Days in Fayetteville. Fayetteville, Ark.: Judge, 1910.
The War of the Rebellion: A Compilation of the Official Records of the Union and Confederate Armies. 70 vols. Washington, D.C.: GPO, 1880–1901.
Woodward, C. Vann. *Mary Chesnut's Civil War.* New Haven, Conn.: Yale University Press, 1981.
Wright, Louise Wigfall. *A Southern Girl in '61.* New York: Doubleday Page, 1905.
Wyeth, John J. *Leaves from a Diary.* Boston: L. F. Lawrence, 1878.
Wynne, Frances Holloway. "Confederate Tax Assessments for Rowan County, North Carolina, 1863." *Journal of the Afro-American Historical and Genealogical Society* 7 (1980): 51–59.

Secondary Sources

Abbott, Lawrence E., Jr., *The James City Project: Test Excavations at a 19th Century Freedman Community.* Winston-Salem, N.C.: Wake Forest University Archeology Laboratories, 1988.
Akers, Samuel Luttrel. *The First Hundred Years of Wesleyan College: 1836–1936.* Savannah, Ga.: Beehive, 1976.
Alexander, Roberta Sue. *North Carolina Faces the Freedman.* Durham, N.C.: Duke University Press, 1985.
Alexander, Thomas B., and Richard E. Beringer. *The Anatomy of the Confederate Congress.* Nashville, Tenn.: Vanderbilt University Press, 1972.
Allston, Susan Lowndes. *Early Sketch of St. John in the Wilderness and Flat Rock, North Carolina.* N.p., 1964.
Andrew, Rod, Jr. *Long Gray Lines: The Southern Military School Tradition, 1839–1915.* Chapel Hill: University of North Carolina Press, 2001.
Ash, Steven V. *The Black Experience in the Civil War South.* Santa Barbara, Calif.: Praeger, 2010.
———. *When the Yankees Came.* Chapel Hill: University of North Carolina Press, 1995.
Ashe, Samuel A. *Cyclopedia of Eminent and Representative Men of the Carolinas.* Madison, Wis.: Brant & Fuller, 1892.

Auman, William T. "Neighbor against Neighbor: The Inner Civil War in the Central Counties of Confederate North Carolina." PhD diss., University of North Carolina at Chapel Hill, 1988.

Barber, E. Susan. "'Depraved and Abandoned Women': Prostitution in Richmond, Virginia, across the Civil War." In *Neither Lady Nor Slave: Working Women of the Old South*, edited by Susanna Delfino and Michele Gillespie, 155–73. Chapel Hill: University of North Carolina Press, 2002.

Barber, E. Susan, and Charles F. Ritter. "'Physical Abuse . . . and Rough Handling': Race, Gender, and Sexual Justice in the Occupied South." In *Occupied Women: Gender, Military Occupation, and the American Civil War*, edited by LeeAnn Whites and Alecia P. Long, 49–64. Baton Rouge: Louisiana State University Press, 2009.

Bardaglio, Peter. "African American Childhood in Wartime." In *Divided Houses: Gender and the Civil War*, edited by Catherine Clinton and Nina Silber, 213–29. New York: Oxford University Press, 1992.

Bardolph, Richard. "Confederate Dilemma: North Carolina Troops and the Deserter Problem." *North Carolina Historical Review* 66 (1989): 61–86, 179–210.

Barrett, John G. *The Civil War in North Carolina*. Chapel Hill: University of North Carolina Press, 1963.

———. *Sherman's March through the Carolinas*. Chapel Hill: University of North Carolina Press, 1996.

Bashir, Hamilia, and Damien Lewis. *Tears of the Desert: A Memoir of Survival in Darfur*. New York: Ballantine, 2008.

Beckel, Deborah. *Radical Reform: Interracial Politics in Post-Emancipation North Carolina*. Charlottesville: University of Virginia Press, 2010.

Bell, Andrew. *Mosquito Soldiers: Malaria, Yellow Fever, and the Course of the American Civil War*. Baton Rouge: Louisiana State University Press, 2010.

Berlin, Ira, Barbara J. Fields, Steven F. Miller, Joseph P. Reidy, and Leslie Rowland. *Slaves No More*. New York: Cambridge University Press, 1992.

Bernath, Michael T. *Confederate Minds: The Struggle for Intellectual Independence in the Civil War South*. Chapel Hill: University of North Carolina Press, 2010.

Bernstein, Leonard. "The Participation of Negro Delegates in the Constitutional Convention of 1868 in North Carolina." *Journal of Negro History* 34 (1949): 391–409.

Bishir, Catherine W. *The Bellamy Mansion*. Wilmington, N.C.: Bellamy Mansion Museum, 2004.

Bishir, Catherine, Michael T. Southern, and Jennifer F. Martin. *A Guide to the Historic Architecture of Western North Carolina*. Chapel Hill: University of North Carolina Press, 1999.

Black, Robert C. *The Railroads of the Confederacy*. Chapel Hill: University of North Carolina Press, 1952.

Blair, William A. *Virginia's Private War*. New York: Oxford University Press, 1998.

Bolton, Charles C. *Poor Whites of the Antebellum South*. Durham, N.C.: Duke University Press, 1994.

Bradley, Mark L. *This Astounding Close*. Chapel Hill: University of North Carolina Press, 2000.

Brewster, Lawrence Fay. *Summer Migrations and Resorts of South Carolina Low-County Planters.* Durham, N.C.: Duke University Press, 1947.

Brown, C. K. "A History of the Piedmont Railroad Company." *North Carolina Historical Review* 3 (1926): 198–212.

Brown, Norman D. *Edward Stanly: Whiggery's Tarheel "Conqueror".* Tuscaloosa: University of Alabama Press, 1974.

Browning, James B. "The North Carolina Black Code." *Journal of Negro History* 15 (1930): 461–73.

Browning, Judkin. *Shifting Loyalties: The Union Occupation of Eastern North Carolina.* Chapel Hill: University of North Carolina Press, 2011.

——. "'Visions of Freedom and Civilization Opening before Them': African Americans Search for Autonomy during the Military Occupation in North Carolina." In *North Carolinians in the Era of the Civil War and Reconstruction*, edited by Paul D. Escott, 69–100. Chapel Hill: University of North Carolina Press, 2008.

Bumgarner, Matthew. *Kirk's Raiders.* Hickory, N.C.: Piedmont Press, 2000.

Bynum, Victoria E. *The Long Shadow of the Civil War: Southern Dissent and Its Legacies.* Chapel Hill: University of North Carolina Press, 2010.

——. "Occupied at Home: Women Confront Confederate Forces in North Carolina's Quaker Belt." In *Occupied Women: Gender, Military Occupation, and the American Civil War*, edited by Alecia P. Long and LeeAnn Whites, 155–70. Baton Rouge: Louisiana State University Press, 2009.

——. *Unruly Women.* Chapel Hill: University of North Carolina Press, 1992.

——. "'War within a War': Women's Participation in the Revolt of the North Carolina Piedmont, 1863–1865." *Frontiers* 9 (1987): 43–49.

Camp, Stephanie. *Closer to Freedom.* Chapel Hill: University of North Carolina Press, 2004.

Campbell, Jacqueline Glass. *When Sherman Marched North from the Sea.* Chapel Hill: University of North Carolina Press, 2003.

Capers, Henry D. *The Life and Times of C. G. Memminger.* Richmond, Va.: Everett Waddey, 1893.

Carbone, John S. *The Civil War in Coastal North Carolina.* Raleigh: North Carolina Division of Archives and History, 2001.

Carl Sandburg Home National Historic Site, Connemara Main House, Historic Structure Report. Atlanta: National Parks Service, 2005.

Carl Sandburg Home National Historic Site, The Swedish House, Historic Structure Report. Atlanta: National Parks Service, 2005.

Carmichael, Peter S. *The Last Generation: Young Virginians in Peace, War, and Reunion.* Chapel Hill: University of North Carolina Press, 2005.

Carrigan, Jo Ann. "Yellow Fever: Scourge of the South." In *Disease and Distinctiveness in the American South*, edited by Todd L. Savitt and James Harvey Young, 55–78. Knoxville: University of Tennessee Press, 1988.

Carroll, Karen C. "Sterling, Campbell, and Albright: Textbook Publishers, 1861–1865." *North Carolina Historical Review* 63 (1986): 169–98.

Cashin, Joan E. *First Lady of the Confederacy: Varina Davis's Civil War.* Cambridge, Mass.: Harvard University Press, 2006.

———. "Into the Trackless Wilderness: The Refugee Experience in the Civil War." In *A Woman's War: Southern Women, Civil War, and the Confederate Legacy*, edited by Edward D. C. Campbell Jr. and Kym S. Rice, 29–53. Richmond: Museum of the Confederacy and University of Virginia Press, 1996.

Cecelski, David S. *The Fire of Freedom: Abraham Galloway and the Slaves' Civil War*. Chapel Hill: University of North Carolina Press, 2012.

———. *The Waterman's Song: Slavery and Freedom in Maritime North Carolina*. Chapel Hill: University of North Carolina Press, 2001.

Cecil-Fronsman, Bill. *Common Whites*. Lexington: University Press of Kentucky, 1992.

Censer, Jane Turner. *North Carolina Planters and Their Children, 1800–1860*. Baton Rouge: Louisiana State University Press, 1984.

———. *The Reconstruction of Southern Womanhood, 1865–1895*. Baton Rouge: Louisiana State University Press, 2003.

———. "Southwestern Migration among North Carolina Planter Families." *Journal of Southern History* 57 (1991): 407–26.

Cimbala, Paul A., and Randall M. Miller. *The Freedmen's Bureau and Reconstruction: Reconsiderations*. New York: Fordham University Press, 1999.

Clampitt, Bradley. *Confederate Heartland*. Baton Rouge: Louisiana State University Press, 2011.

Click, Patrick C. *Time Full of Trial: The Roanoke Island Freedmen's Colony, 1862–1867*. Chapel Hill: University of North Carolina Press, 2001.

Clinton, Catherine. *The Plantation Mistress*. New York: Pantheon, 1982.

———. *Public Women and the Confederacy*. Milwaukee: Marquette University Press, 1999.

Cohen, Roberta, and Francis M. Deng. *Masses in Flight: The Global Crisis of Internal Displacement*. Washington, D.C.: Brookings Institute, 1998.

Cohen, William. *At Freedom's Edge: Black Mobility and the Southern White Quest for Racial Control, 1861–1915*. Baton Rouge: Louisiana State University Press, 1991.

Cole, Jeannine. "'Upon the Stage of Disorder': Legalized Prostitution in Memphis and Nashville, 1863–1865." *Tennessee Historical Quarterly* 68 (2009): 40–65.

Collins, Donald E. "War Crimes or Justice? Gen. George Pickett and the Mass Execution of Deserters in Civil War Kinston, North Carolina." In *The Art of Command in the Civil War*, edited by Steven E. Woodworth, 50–83. Lincoln: University of Nebraska Press, 1998.

Cook, Philip C. "Mt. Lebanon University in Peace and War." *North Louisiana History* 9 (1978): 55–63.

Cooper, William J. *Jefferson Davis, American*. New York: Knopf, 2000.

Coulling, Mary P. *The Lee Girls*. Winston-Salem, N.C.: John F. Blair, 1987.

Coulter, Merton E. *College Life in the Old South*. New York: Macmillan, 1928.

Cox, Karen L. *Dixie's Daughters: The United Daughters of the Confederacy and the Preservation of Confederate Culture*. Gainesville: University Press of Florida, 2003.

Crawford, Lindsay. "Martha Rutledge Kinloch Singleton: A Slaveholding Widow in Late Antebellum South Carolina." *Proceedings of the South Carolina Historical Association* (2009): 15–26.

Crofts, Daniel W. *Reluctant Confederates: Upper South Unionists in the Secession Crisis*. Chapel Hill: University of North Carolina Press, 1993.

Cunningham, H. H. "Confederate General Hospitals: Establishment and Organization." *Journal of Southern History* 20 (1954) 376–94.
———. "Edmund Burke Haywood and Raleigh's Confederate Hospitals." *North Carolina Historical Review* 35 (1958): 153–66.
Dau, John Bul, and Michael S. Sweeney. *God Grew Tired of Us*. Washington, D.C.: National Geographic, 2007.
Davis, O. L., Jr. and Serena Rankin Parks. "Confederate School Geographies, I: Marinda Branson Moore's Dixie Geography." *Peabody Journal of Education* 40 (1963): 265–74.
DeCredico, Mary. "The Confederate Homefront." In *A Companion to the Civil War and Reconstruction*, edited by Lacy K. Ford, 258–76. Malden, Mass.: Blackwell, 2005.
Dietz, August. *The Postal Service of Confederate States of America*. Richmond, Va.: Dietz, 1929.
Domby, Adam H. "'Loyal to the Core from the First to the Last': Remembering the Inner Civil War of Forsyth County, North Carolina, 1862–1876." M.A. thesis, University of North Carolina at Chapel Hill, 2011.
Downey, Tom. "'The Light of Learning Extinguished within Our Borders': The College Hospitals, Columbia, South Carolina, 1862–1865." *Proceedings of the South Carolina Historical Association* (1994): 117–22.
Downs, Gregory P. *After Appomattox: Military Occupation and the Ends of War*. Cambridge, Mass.: Harvard University Press, 2015.
———. *Declarations of Dependence*. Chapel Hill: University of North Carolina Press, 2011.
Downs, Jim. "The Other Side of Freedom: Destitution, Disease, and Dependency among Freedwomen and Their Children during and after the Civil War." In *Battle Scars: Gender and Sexuality in the American Civil War*, edited by Catherine Clinton and Nina Silber, 78–103. New York: Oxford University Press, 2006.
———. *Sick from Freedom*. New York: Oxford University Press, 2012.
Duncan, Richard R. "The Impact of the Civil War on Education in Maryland." *Maryland Historical Magazine* 61 (1966): 37–52.
Durrill, Wayne K. *War of Another Kind: A Southern Community in the Great Rebellion*. New York: Oxford University Press, 1990.
Eaton, Clement. *The Waning of the Old South Civilization, 1860–1880s*. Athens: University of Georgia Press, 1968.
Edwards, Laura F. *Scarlett Doesn't Live Here Anymore*. Urbana: University of Illinois Press, 2000.
Egerton, Douglas R. *The Wars of Reconstruction*. New York: Bloomsbury Press, 2014.
Escott, Paul D. *Many Excellent People: Power and Privilege in North Carolina, 1850–1900*. Chapel Hill: University of North Carolina Press, 1985.
———. "Poverty and Government Aid for the Poor in Confederate North Carolina." *North Carolina Historical Review* 61 (1984): 462–80.
Evans, William McKee. *Ballots and Fence Rails*. Chapel Hill: University of North Carolina Press, 1967.
———. *To Die Game: The Story of the Lowry Band, Indian Guerrillas of Reconstruction*. Baton Rouge: Louisiana State University Press, 1971.
Farnham, Christie Anne. *The Education of the Southern Belle*. New York: New York University Press, 1994.

Farnham, Thomas J., and Francis P. King. "'The March of the Destroyer': The New Bern Yellow Fever Epidemic of 1864." *North Carolina Historical Review* 73 (1996): 435–83.
Faust, Drew Gilpin. *Mothers of Invention.* Chapel Hill: University of North Carolina Press, 1996.
———. *This Republic of Suffering: Death and the American Civil War.* New York: Knopf, 2008.
Fazel, M., J. Wheeler, and J. Danesh. "Prevalence of Serious Mental Disorder in 7000 Refugees Resettled in Western Countries: A Systematic Review." *Lancet,* April 9–15, 2005, 1309–14.
Feimster, Crystal. "General Benjamin Butler and the Threat of Sexual Violence during the American Civil War." *Daedalus* (Spring 2009): 126–34.
Fellman, Michael. *Inside War.* New York: Oxford University Press, 1989.
Fenn, Elizabeth. "'A Perfect Equality Seemed to Reign': Slave Society and Jonkonnu." *North Carolina Historical Review* 65 (1988): 127–53.
Fett, Sharla M. *Working Cures: Healing, Heath, and Power on Southern Slave Plantations.* Chapel Hill: University of North Carolina Press, 2002.
Foner, Eric. *The Fiery Trial.* New York: Norton, 2010.
———. *Freedom's Lawmakers: A Directory of Black Lawmakers during Reconstruction.* Baton Rouge: Louisiana State University Press, 1996.
———. *Free Soil, Free Labor, Free Men.* New York: Oxford University Press, 1970.
———. *Reconstruction.* New York: Harper & Row, 1988.
Fonvielle, Chris E. *The Wilmington Campaign.* Mechanicsburg, Pa.: Stackpole Books, 2001.
Foster, Gaines M. *Ghosts of the Confederacy: Defeat, the Lost Cause, and the Emergence of the New South, 1865 to 1913.* New York: Oxford University Press, 1987.
———. "The Limitations of Federal Health Care for Freedmen, 1862–1868." *Journal of Southern History* 48 (1982): 349–72.
Fox-Genovese, Elizabeth. *Within the Plantation Household.* Chapel Hill: University of North Carolina Press, 1999.
Frank, Lisa Tendrich. "Bedrooms as Battlefields: The Role of Gender Politics in Sherman's March." In *Occupied Women: Gender, Military Occupation, and the American Civil War,* edited by LeeAnn Whites and Alecia P. Long, 33–48. Baton Rouge: Louisiana State University Press, 2009.
Frankel, Noralee. *Freedom's Women.* Bloomington: Indiana University Press, 1999.
Franklin, John Hope. *The Emancipation Proclamation.* Garden City, N.Y.: Doubleday, 1963.
Franklin, John Hope, and Loren Schweninger. *Runaway Slaves: Rebels on the Plantation.* New York: Oxford University Press, 1999.
Fraser, Rebecca J. *Courtship and Love among the Enslaved in North Carolina.* Jackson: University of Mississippi Press, 2007.
Friedman, Jean E. *The Enclosed Garden: Women and Community in the Evangelical South, 1830–1900.* Chapel Hill: University of North Carolina Press, 1985.
Gatrell, Peter. *The Making of the Modern Refugee.* Oxford: Oxford University Press, 2013.

Geltman, P. L., W. Grant-Knight, S. D. Mehta, C. Lloyd-Travaglini, S. Lustig, J. M. Landgraf, and P. H. Wise. "The 'Lost Boys of Sudan': Functional and Behavioral Health of Unaccompanied Refugee Minors Re-settled in the United States." *Archives of Pediatric and Adolescent Medicine* 159:6 (June 2005): 585-91.

Genovese, Eugene D. *Roll, Jordan, Roll: The World the Slaves Made.* New York: Random House, 1976.

Gerteis, Louis S. *From Contraband to Freedman.* Westport, Conn.: Greenwood Press, 1973.

Glymph, Thavolia. *Out of the House of Bondage.* New York: Cambridge University Press, 2008.

———. "'This Species of Property': Female Slave Contrabands in the Civil War." In *A Woman's War: Southern Women, Civil War, and the Confederate Legacy,* edited by Edward D. C. Campbell and Kym S. Rice, 55-71. Richmond: Museum of the Confederacy and University of Virginia Press, 1996.

Gordon, Lesley J. "'In Time of War': Unionists Hanged in Kinston, North Carolina, February 1864." In *Guerillas, Unionists and Violence on the Confederate Home Front,* edited by Daniel E. Sutherland, 45-58. Fayetteville: University of Arkansas Press, 1999.

Gorn, Elliott J. "Black Magic: Folk Beliefs of the Slave Community." In *Science and Medicine in the Old South,* edited by Ronald L. Numbers and Todd L. Savitt, 295-326. Baton Rouge: Louisiana State University Press, 1989.

Gray, Ricky Harold. "Corona Female College, 1857-1864." *Journal of Mississippi History* 42 (1980): 129-34.

Green, Jennifer R. *Military Education and the Emerging Middle Class in the Old South.* Cambridge: Cambridge University Press, 2008.

Greenberg, Kenneth S. *Honor and Slavery.* Princeton, N.J.: Princeton University Press, 1996.

Greenwood, Janette Thomas. *First Fruits of Freedom: The Migration of Former Slaves and Their Quest for Equality in Worchester, Massachusetts.* Chapel Hill: University of North Carolina Press, 2010.

———. *On the Home Front: Charlotte during the Civil War.* Charlotte, N.C.: Mint Museum, 1982.

Griffin, Francis. *Less Time for Meddling: A History of Salem Academy and College, 1772-1866.* Winston-Salem, N.C.: John F. Blair, 1979.

Griffin, Rebecca J. "'Goin' Back Over There to See That Girl': Competing Social Spaces in the Lives of the Enslaved in Antebellum North Carolina." *Slavery and Abolition* 25 (2004): 94-113.

Guelzo, Allen C. *The Emancipation Proclamation.* New York: Simon & Schuster, 2004.

Guiffre, Katherine. "Desertion as Politics in the North Carolina Confederate Army." *Social Science History* 21 (1997): 246-63.

Gutman, Herbert. *The Black Family in Slavery and Freedom, 1750-1925.* New York: Vintage, 1976.

Hadden, Sally. *Slave Patrols.* Cambridge, Mass.: Harvard University Press, 2001.

Hahn, Steven. *A Nation under Our Feet.* Cambridge, Mass.: Harvard University Press, 2003.

———. *The Political Worlds of Slavery and Freedom.* Cambridge, Mass.: Harvard University Press, 2009.

Hamilton, J. G. de Roulhac. *Reconstruction in North Carolina.* New York: Columbia University, 1914.
Harris, William C. "Lincoln and Wartime Reconstruction in North Carolina, 1861–1863." *North Carolina Historical Review* 63 (1986): 149–68.
———. *William Woods Holden: Firebrand of North Carolina Politics.* Baton Rouge: Louisiana State University Press, 1987.
Hauptman, Laurence M. *Between Two Fires: American Indians in the Civil War.* New York: Free Press, 1995.
Heath, Frederick M. "Mary Elizabeth Massey." *Southern Studies* 20 (1981): 116–21.
Helsley, Alexia Jones. "Mitchell King Builds His Dream Home." *Proceedings of the South Carolina Historical Association* (2004): 13–26.
Helsley, Alexia Jones, and George Alexander Jones. *A Guide to Historic Henderson County, North Carolina.* Charleston, S.C.: History Press, 2007.
Helton, Arthur. *The Price of Indifference: Refugees and Humanitarian Aid in the New Century.* New York: Oxford University Press, 2002.
Henry, James O. "The United States Christian Commission in the Civil War." *Civil War History* 12 (1960): 374–88.
Hess, Earl J. *Lee's Tar Heels.* Chapel Hill: University of North Carolina Press, 2002.
Hildebrand, Reginald F. *The Times Were Strange and Stirring: Methodist Preachers and the Crisis of Emancipation.* Durham, N.C.: Duke University Press, 1995.
Hixson, Ivy May. "Academic Requirement of Salem College, 1854–1909." *North Carolina Historical Review* 27 (1950): 419–29.
Hollow, Elizabeth Paton. "Development of the Brownsville Baptist Female College: An Example of Female Education in the South, 1850–1910." *West Tennessee Historical Society* 32 (1978): 48–59.
Holzer, Howard, Edna Greene Medford, and Frank J. Williams. *The Emancipation Proclamation: Three Views.* Baton Rouge: Louisiana State University Press, 2006.
Humphreys, Margaret. *Intensely Human: The Health of the Black Soldier in the American Civil War.* Baltimore: Johns Hopkins University Press, 2008.
———. *The Marrow of Tragedy: The Health Crisis of the American Civil War.* Baltimore: Johns Hopkins University Press, 2013.
Hunt, Judith Lee. "'High with Courage and Hope': The Middleton Family's Civil War." In *Southern Families at War*, edited by Catherine Clinton, 101–18. New York: Oxford University Press, 2000.
Inscoe, John C. "The Civil War's Empowerment of an Appalachian Woman: The 1864 Slave Purchases of Mary Bell." In *Discovering Women in Slavery: Emancipating Perspectives on the American Past*, edited by Patricia Morton, 61–81. Athens: University of Georgia Press, 1996.
———. "Mountain Masters as Confederate Opportunists: The Profitability of Slavery in Western North Carolina." *Slavery and Abolition* 16 (1995): 85–110.
Inscoe, John C., and Gordon B. McKinney. *The Heart of Confederate Appalachia: Western North Carolina in the Civil War.* Chapel Hill: University of North Carolina Press, 2000.
Jabour, Anya. *Scarlett's Sisters: Young Women in the Old South.* Chapel Hill: University of North Carolina Press, 2007.
Janney, Caroline E. *Burying the Dead but Not the Past: Ladies' Memorial Associations and the Lost Cause.* Chapel Hill: University of North Carolina Press, 2008.

Jasanoff, Maya. *Liberty's Exiles: American Loyalists in the Revolutionary World.* New York: Knopf, 2011.

Johnson, Clint. *Pursuit: The Chase, Capture, Persecution and Surprising Release of Jefferson Davis.* New York: Citadel Press, 2008.

Johnson, Walter. "A Nettlesome Classic Turns Twenty-Five." *Common-Place* 1:4 (2001).

Jones, James B. "A Tale of Two Cities: The Hidden Battle against Venereal Disease in Civil War Nashville and Memphis." *Civil War History* 31 (1985): 270–76.

Jordan, Laylon W. "Schemes of Usefulness: Christopher Gustavus Memminger." In *Intellectual Life in Antebellum Charleston*, edited by Michael O'Brien and David Moltke-Hansen, 211–29. Knoxville: University of Tennessee Press, 1986.

Jordan, Weymouth T., and Gerald W. Thomas. "Massacre at Plymouth: April 20, 1864." *North Carolina Historical Review* 72 (1995): 125–97.

Kenzer, Robert C. *Kinship and Neighborhood in a Southern Community: Orange County, North Carolina, 1849–1881.* Knoxville: University of Tennessee Press, 1987.

King-Owen, Scott. "Conditional Confederates: Absenteeism among Western North Carolina Soldiers, 1861–1865." *Civil War History* 57 (2011): 349–79.

Knight, Edward V., and Oscar Creech. *A History of Chowan College.* Murfreesboro, N.C.: Chowan University, 1964.

Kruman, Marc W. *Parties and Politics in North Carolina, 1836–1865.* Baton Rouge: Louisiana State University Press, 1983.

Leaming, Hugo Prosper. *Hidden Americans: Maroons of Virginia and the Carolinas.* New York: Garland, 1995.

Lelouids, James L. *Schooling in the New South.* Chapel Hill: University of North Carolina Press, 1996.

Levine, Bruce C. *The Fall of the House of Dixie: The Civil War and the Social Revolution That Transformed the South.* New York: Random House, 2013.

Lischer, Sarah Kenyon. *Dangerous Sanctuaries: Refugee Camps, Civil War, and the Dilemmas of Humanitarian Aid.* Ithaca, N.Y.: Cornell University Press, 2005.

Litwack, Leon. *Been in the Storm So Long: The Aftermath of Slavery.* New York: Vintage, 1980.

Long, Gretchen. *Doctoring Freedom: The Politics of African American Medical Care in Slavery and Emancipation.* Chapel Hill: University of North Carolina Press, 2012.

Manning, Chandra. "The Order of Nature Would Be Reversed: Soldiers, Slavery, and the North Carolina Gubernatorial Election of 1864." In *North Carolinians in the Era of the Civil War and Reconstruction*, edited by Paul D. Escott, 101–28. Chapel Hill: University of North Carolina Press, 2008.

———. *What This Cruel War Was Over.* New York: Knopf, 2007.

———. "Working for Citizenship in Civil War Contraband Camps." *Journal of the Civil War Era* 4 (2014): 172–204.

Marten, James. *The Children's Civil War.* Chapel Hill: University of North Carolina Press, 1998.

Martin, Jonathan D. *Divided Mastery: Slave Hiring in the American South.* Cambridge, Mass.: Harvard University Press, 2004.

Martin, Sandy Dwayne. *For God and Race: The Religious and Political Leadership of AMEZ Bishop James Walker Hood.* Columbia: University of South Carolina Press, 1999.

Martinez, Jaime Amanda. *Confederate Slave Impressment in the Upper South.* Chapel Hill: University of North Carolina Press, 2013.

———. "For the Defense of the State: Slave Impressment in Confederate Virginia and North Carolina." PhD diss., University of Virginia, 2008.

———. "The Slave Market in Civil War Virginia." In *Crucible of the Civil War: Virginia from Secession to Commemoration,* edited by Edward L. Ayers, Gary W. Gallagher, and Andrew J. Torget, 106–35. Charlottesville: University of Virginia Press, 2006.

Martis, Kenneth C. *The Historical Atlas of the Congresses of the Confederate States of America: 1861–1865.* New York: Simon & Schuster, 1994.

Massey, Mary Elizabeth. *Bonnet Brigades.* New York: Knopf, 1966.

———. *Ersatz in the Confederacy: Shortages and Substitutes on the Southern Homefront.* Columbia: University of South Carolina Press, 1952.

———. *Refugee Life in the Confederacy.* With a new introduction by George C. Rable. 1964. Reprint, Baton Rouge: Louisiana State University Press, 2001.

Masur, Kate. "'A Rare Phenomenon of Philological Vegetation': The Word 'Contraband' and the Meanings of Emancipation in the United States." *Journal of American History* 93 (2007): 1050–84.

McCallum, James. *Martin County during the Civil War.* Williamston, N.C.: Martin County Historical Society, 1971.

McCandless, Peter. *Slavery, Disease and Suffering in the Southern Lowcountry.* New York: Cambridge University Press, 2011.

McCurry, Stephanie. *Confederate Reckoning.* Cambridge, Mass.: Harvard University Press, 2010.

McFeely, William S. *Yankee Stepfather: General O. O. Howard and the Freedmen.* New Haven, Conn.: Yale University Press, 1968.

McGee, David Howell. "'On the Edge of the Crater': The Transformation of Raleigh, North Carolina, during the Civil War Era." PhD diss., University of Georgia, 1999.

McPherson, James M. *Battle Cry of Freedom.* New York: Oxford University Press, 1988.

———. *Marching toward Freedom: The Negro in the Civil War, 1861–1865.* New York: Knopf, 1967.

Meekins, Alex Christopher. *Elizabeth City, North Carolina and the Civil War.* Charleston, S.C.: History Press, 2007.

———. "Unionism and the Arcane Origin of 'Buffalo.'" *North Carolina Historical Review* 85 (2008): 282–316.

Meier, Kathryn Shively. *Nature's Civil War: Common Soldiers and the Environment in 1862 Virginia.* Chapel Hill: University of North Carolina Press, 2013.

Memminger, Edward Read. *An Historical Sketch of Flat Rock.* Flat Rock, N.C.: Norment, 1954.

Miles, Loyce Braswell. "Forgotten Scholars: Female Secondary Education in Three Antebellum Deep South States." PhD diss., Mississippi State University, 2003.

Mills, Cynthia, and Pamela H. Simpson, eds. *Monuments to the Lost Cause: Women, Art, and the Landscapes of Southern Memory.* Knoxville: University of Tennessee Press, 2003.

Mobley, Joe A. *James City: A Black Community in North Carolina, 1863–1900.* Raleigh: North Carolina Division of Archives and History, 1981.

———. *Weary of War: Life on the Confederate Home Front.* Westport, Conn.: Praeger, 2008.

———. "Zebulon B. Vance: A Confederate Nationalist in the North Carolina Gubernatorial Election of 1864." *North Carolina Historical Review* 77 (2000): 434–54.

Mohr, Clarence L. *On the Threshold of Freedom: Masters and Slaves in Civil War Georgia.* Athens: University of Georgia Press, 1986.

Moorehead, Caroline. *Human Cargo: A Journey among Refugees.* New York: Picador, 2005.

Moose, William. *A History of Mitchell Community College.* Statesville, N.C.: Mitchell Community College, 2005.

Morgan, Lynda J. *Emancipation in Virginia's Tobacco Belt.* Athens: University of Georgia Press, 1992.

Murray, Elizabeth Reid. *Wake: Capital County of North Carolina.* Vol. 1, *Prehistory through Centennial.* Raleigh, N.C.: Capital County Publishing, 1983.

Myers, Barton A. *Rebels against the Confederacy: North Carolina's Unionists.* New York: Cambridge University Press, 2014.

Myers, Constance Ashton. "Mary Elizabeth Massey: A Founder of Women's History in the South." In *South Carolina Women: The Lives and Times,* edited by Marjorie Julian Spruill, Valinda W. Littlefield, and Joan Marie Johnson, 3:262–86. Athens: University of Georgia Press, 2012.

Nash, Ann Strudwick. *Ladies in Making.* Hillsborough, N.C., 1964.

Nelson, B. H. "Some Aspects of Negro Life in North Carolina during the Civil War." *North Carolina Historical Review* 25 (1948): 143–66.

Nelson, Scott Reynolds. *Iron Confederacies: Southern Railways, Klan Violence, and Reconstruction.* Chapel Hill: University of North Carolina Press, 1999.

New Orleans Architecture. Vol. 5, *The Esplanade Ridge.* Grenta, La.: Friends of the Cabildo, 1977.

Noble, M. C. S. *A History of the Public Schools of North Carolina.* Chapel Hill: University of North Carolina Press, 1930.

North Carolina Troops. 18 vols. Raleigh: North Carolina Department of Archives and History, 1966–2011.

Oakes, James. *Freedom National: The Destruction of Slavery in the United States, 1861–1865.* New York: Norton, 2013.

Ott, Victoria E. *Confederate Daughters: Coming of Age during the Civil War.* Carbondale: Southern Illinois University Press, 2008.

Pace, Robert F. *Halls of Honor: College Men in the Old South.* Baton Rouge: Louisiana State University Press, 2004.

Paludan, Philip Shaw. *Victims: A True Story of the Civil War.* Knoxville: University of Tennessee Press, 1981.

Patton, Sally Smathers. *Flat Rock: Little Charleston of the Mountains.* Hickory, N.C., 1961.

Perry, Darlene M. "A Profitable, but Risky Business: Slave Hiring in Colonial and Antebellum Eastern North Carolina." M.A. thesis, East Carolina University, 2004.
Phillips, Jason. "The Grave Vine Telegraph: Rumors and Confederate Persistence." *Journal of Southern History* 72 (2006): 753–88.
Pope, Christie Farnham. "Preparation for Pedestals: North Carolina Antebellum Female Seminaries." PhD diss., University of Chicago, 1977.
Poteat, R. Matthew. *Henry Toole Clark.* Jefferson, N.C.: McFarlane, 2009.
Powell, William S. *Dictionary of North Carolina Biography.* 6 vols. Chapel Hill: University of North Carolina Press, 1979.
———. *Higher Education in North Carolina.* Raleigh, N.C.: State Department of Archives and History, 1970.
Price, Charles L. "John C. Barnett, a Freedmen's Bureau Agent in North Carolina." In *Of Tar Heel Towns, Shipbuilders, Reconstructionists and Alliancemen,* edited by Joseph F. Steelman, 51–74. Greenville, N.C.: East Carolina University Publications, 1981.
Pusey, William Webb. "Lexington Female Academy." *Virginia Cavalcade* 32 (1982): 40–47.
Pybus, Cassandra. *Epic Journeys of Freedom: Runaway Slaves of the American Revolution and Their Global Quest for Liberty.* Boston: Beacon Press, 2006.
Rable, George C. *Civil Wars: Women and the Crisis of Southern Nationalism.* Urbana: University of Illinois Press, 1989.
———. *The Confederate Republic.* Chapel Hill: University of North Carolina Press, 1994.
Raney, David. "In the Lord's Army: The United States Christian Commission in the Civil War." PhD diss., University of Illinois at Urbana-Champaign, 2001.
Raper, Horace W. "William W. Holden and the Peace Movement in North Carolina." *North Carolina Historical Review* 31 (1954): 493–526.
Redford, Dorothy Spruill. *Somerset Homecoming.* New York: Doubleday, 1988.
Reid, Richard M. *Freedom for Themselves: North Carolina's Black Soldiers in the Civil War Era.* Chapel Hill: University of North Carolina Press, 2008.
———. "A Test Case of 'Crying Evil': Desertion among North Carolina Troops during the Civil War." *North Carolina Historical Review* 58 (1981): 234–62.
Reilly, Stephen Edward. "Reconstruction through Regeneration: Horace James' Work with the Blacks for Social Reform in North Carolina, 1862–1867." PhD diss., Duke University, 1983.
Ripley, C. Peter. "The Black Family in Transition: Louisiana, 1860–1865." *Journal of Southern History* 41(1975): 369–80.
Roberts, Giselle. *The Confederate Belle.* Columbia: University of Missouri Press, 2003.
Robinson, Armstead L. *Bitter Fruits of Bondage.* Charlottesville: University of Virginia Press, 2005.
Rose, Willie Lee. *Rehearsal for Reconstruction: The Port Royal Experiment.* Indianapolis: Bobbs-Merrill, 1964.
Sandbeck, Peter B. *The Historic Architecture of New Bern and Craven County, North Carolina.* New Bern, N.C.: Tryon Palace Commission, 1988.
Savitt, Todd L. "Slave Life Insurance in Virginia and North Carolina." *Journal of Southern History* 43 (1977): 583–600.

Sayers, Daniel O., P. Brendan Burke, and Aaron M. Henry. "The Political Economy of Exile in the Great Dismal Swamp." *International Journal of Historical Archaeology* 11 (2007): 60–97.

Schama, Simon. *Rough Crossings: Britain, the Slaves, and the American Revolution.* New York: Ecco, 2006.

Schantz, Mark S. *Awaiting the Heavenly Country: The Civil War and America's Culture of Death.* Ithaca, N.Y.: Cornell University Press, 2008.

Schneider, Tracy Whittaker. "The Institution of Slavery in North Carolina, 1860–1865." PhD diss., Duke University, 1979.

Schultz, Jane E. *Women at the Front: Hospital Workers in Civil War America.* Chapel Hill: University of North Carolina Press, 2004.

Schwalm, Leslie A. "Between Slavery and Freedom: African American Women and Occupation in the Slave South." In *Occupied Women*, edited by LeeAnn Whites and Alecia P. Long, 137–53. Baton Rouge: Louisiana State University Press, 2009.

———. *A Hard Fight for We.* Urbana: University of Illinois Press, 1997.

Scott, Anne Firor. *The Southern Lady.* Chicago: University of Chicago Press, 1970.

Shurr, Nancy. "Inside the Confederate Hospital: Community and Conflict during the Civil War." PhD diss., University of Tennessee, 2004.

Siddali, Silvana R. *From Property to Person: Slavery and the Confiscation Acts, 1861–1862.* Baton Rouge: Louisiana State University Press, 2005.

Silkenat, David. "'In Good Hands, in a Safe Place': Female Academies in Confederate North Carolina." *North Carolina Historical Review* 83 (January 2011): 40–71.

———. *Moments of Despair: Suicide, Divorce, and Debt in Civil War Era North Carolina.* Chapel Hill: University of North Carolina Press, 2011.

———. "'A Typical Negro': Gordon, Peter, Vincent Colyer, and the Story behind Slavery's Most Famous Photograph." *American Nineteenth Century History* 15 (2014): 169–86.

Simkins, Francis B., and James W. Patton. *The Women of the Confederacy.* Richmond, Va.: Garrett and Massie, 1936.

Sims, Anastasia. *The Power of Femininity in the New South: Women's Organizations and Politics in North Carolina, 1880–1930.* Columbia: University of South Carolina Press, 1997.

Sinha, Manisha. "Eugene D. Genovese: The Mind of a Conservative Marxist." *Radical History Review* 88 (2004): 4–29.

Smith, Margaret Supplee, and Emily Herring Wilson. *North Carolina Women Making History.* Chapel Hill: University of North Carolina Press, 1999.

Sondley, Forster. *Asheville and Buncombe County.* Asheville, N.C.: Citizen, 1922.

Sprunt, James. *Chronicles of the Cape Fear River, 1660–1916.* Raleigh, N.C.: Edwards & Broughton, 1916.

Stanley, Amy Dru. "Beggars Can't Be Choosers: Compulsion and Contract in Postbellum America." *Journal of American History* 78 (1992): 1265–93.

Sternhell, Yael. *Routes of War.* Cambridge, Mass.: Harvard University Press, 2012.

Stewart, Rodney. *David Schenck and the Contours of Confederate Identity.* Knoxville: University of Tennessee Press, 2012.

Stillman, Rachel Bryan. "Education in the Confederate States of America, 1861–1865." PhD diss., University of Illinois–Champaign, 1971.
Stoops, Martha. *The Heritage: The Education of Women at St. Mary's College, Raleigh, North Carolina, 1842–1982*. Raleigh, N.C.: St. Mary's College, 1984.
Stowe, Steven M. "The Not-So-Cloistered Academy: Elite Women's Education and Family Feeling in the Old South." In *The Web of Southern Social Relations: Women, Family & Education*, edited by Walter J. Fraser Jr., R. Frank Saunders Jr., and Jon L. Wakelyn, 90–106. Athens: University of Georgia Press, 1985.
Sundquist, K., L. M. Johansson, V. DeMarinis, S. E. Johansson, and J. Sundquist. "Posttraumatic Stress Disorder and Psychiatric Co-morbidity: Symptoms in a Random Sample of Female Bosnian Refugees." *European Psychiatry* 20:2 (March 2005): 158–64.
Tarlton, William S. *Somerset Place and Its Restoration*. Raleigh, N.C.: Department of Conservation and Development, Division of State Parks, 1954.
Taylor, Alan. *The Internal Enemy: Slavery and War in Virginia, 1772–1832*. New York: Norton, 2013.
Thomas, William G. *The Iron Way: Railroads, the Civil War, and the Making of Modern America*. New Haven, Conn.: Yale University Press, 2011.
Tolley, Kim. "Science for Ladies, Classics for Gentlemen: A Comparative Analysis of Scientific Subjects in the Curricula of Boys' and Girls' Secondary Schools in the United States, 1794–1850." *History of Education Quarterly* 36 (1996): 129–53.
Trelease, Allen. "A Southern Railroad at War: The North Carolina Railroad and the Confederacy." *Railroad History* 164 (1991): 5–41.
Trotter, William R. *Bushwhackers*. Winston-Salem, N.C.: John F. Blair, 1988.
Van Noppen, Ina W. "The Significance of Stoneman's Last Raid." *North Carolina Historical Review* 38 (1961): 19–44, 149–72, 341–61, 500–526.
Walbert, Kathryn. "'Endeavor to Improve Yourself': The Education of White Women in the Antebellum South." In *Chartered Schools: Two Hundred Years of Independent Academies in the United States, 1727–1925*, edited by Nancy Beadie and Kim Tolley, 116–36. New York: Routledge, 2002.
Walls, William Jacob. *Joseph Charles Price: Educator and Race Leader*. Boston: Christopher Publishing, 1943.
Watson, Alan D. *A History of New Bern and Craven County*. New Bern: Tryon Palace Commission, 1987.
Webber, Mabel. "St. John's in the Wilderness, Flat Rock, N.C., Tombstone Inscriptions." *South Carolina Genealogical and Historical Magazine* 40 (1939): 52–57.
Weeks, Stephen B. *Confederate Textbooks: A Preliminary Biography*. Washington, D.C.: GPO, 1900.
Weiner, Marli F. *Mistresses and Slaves: Plantation Women in South Carolina, 1830–1880*. Urbana: University of Illinois Press, 1998.
West, Emily. *Chains of Love: Slave Couples in Antebellum South Carolina*. Urbana: University of Illinois Press, 2004.
———. "Surviving Separation: Cross-Plantation Marriages and the Slave Trade in Antebellum South Carolina." *Journal of Family History* 24 (1999): 212–31.

Wheaton, Thomas R., Jr. and Mary Beth Reed. *James City, North Carolina: Archeological and Historical Study of an African American Urban Village.* Stone Mountain, Ga.: New South Associates, 1990.

Wiley, Bell Irvin. *The Life of Johnny Reb.* Indianapolis: Bobbs-Merrill, 1943.

———. *Southern Negroes, 1861–1865.* New Haven, Conn.: Yale University Press, 1938.

Willard, George-Anne. *Louisburg College Echoes.* Louisburg, N.C.: Louisburg College, 1988.

Williams, David. *Bitterly Divided: The South's Inner Civil War.* New York: New Press, 2008.

Williams, Heather Andrea. *Help Me Find My People: The African American Search for Family Lost in Slavery.* Chapel Hill: University of North Carolina Press, 2012.

———. *Self Taught: African American Education in Slavery and Freedom.* Chapel Hill: University of North Carolina Press, 2005.

Williams, Timothy J. *Intellectual Manhood: University, Self, and Society in the Antebellum South.* Chapel Hill: University of North Carolina Press, 2015.

Wilson, Charles Reagan. *Baptized in Blood: The Religion of the Lost Cause, 1865–1920.* Athens: University of Georgia Press, 1980.

Wood, Peter H. *When the Roll Is Called Up Yonder: A Black History in Hillsborough, North Carolina.* Hillsborough, N.C.: P. H. Wood, 2005.

Wyatt-Brown, Bertram. *Southern Honor.* New York: Oxford University Press, 1983.

Yates, Richard E. "Governor Vance and the Peace Movement." *North Carolina Historical Review* 17 (1940): 1–25, 89–113.

Yearns, W. Buck. *The Confederate Congress.* Athens: University of Georgia Press, 1960.

Zuber, Richard L. "Conscientious Objectors in the Confederacy: The Quakers of North Carolina." *Quaker History* 67 (1978): 1–19.

INDEX

abolitionism, 11, 13, 28, 30–31, 57, 63–65, 220

African American refugees: ages of, 20–21; census of, 59–60; churches, 43–45, 48, 56, 78; employment, 26–28, 38–39, 75–76; escape from slavery, 16–19, 21–24; family and children, 20, 26, 38–39; free blacks, 19, 56; gender, 20, 67; housing and overcrowding, 41–43, 68, 73–74, 87–88, 92–96; from outside North Carolina, 16; politics, 76–79; postwar experience, 221–22, 224–31; poverty, 37–39, 92–96; schools, 45, 47–49, 51, 55–56, 58, 63–64, 68–69, 74, 83, 227–28; soldiers, 55–56, 58, 61–67, 71, 76–77; as spies and scouts, 28–30, 62; Union policy on, 24–26. *See also* slaves

American Missionary Association, 69, 74, 94

Andrews Chapel (New Bern), 56, 78

Asheville, N.C., 168, 178, 184–86, 198, 202, 205, 208, 214

Baltimore House (New Bern), 86–87

Barbour, Mary, 20

Barrett, John C., 225–26

Beaufort, N.C.: African American refugees in, 17, 21, 42, 55, 62, 67, 72–73, 78–80, 98–99; disease in, 91–92; refugees from, 106, 112, 145, 221; Unionist refugees in, 34–35, 61, 72, 82–83; Union occupation of, 15, 23, 30, 50

Bell, Mary, 202–3

Bellamy, Ellen, 220–21

Biddle, Rosa, 164

Big Bob, 18

blockade (Union), 107, 126–27, 131, 162, 172

Board of Councilors (Roanoke), 76

Boots, Edward N., 79

Boylan, William M., 128–29

Bray, Nicholas, 48–49

bread riots, 132

Bryan, Henry Ravenscroft, 100–103

Bryan, Lucy, 154

Bryan, Mary Norcott, 3, 100–106, 115, 118

Bryson, Joseph, 212–13

Buffaloes. *See* Unionist refugees

Buncombe Turnpike, 186, 203

Bureau of Refugees, Freedmen, and Abandoned Lands, 5, 7, 74, 96–99, 218, 224–30

Burnside, Ambrose: conflicts with Edward Stanly, 46–47, 49; invasion of North Carolina, 11, 63, 109, 130; leaves North Carolina, 38, 52; policy on African American refugees, 16, 18, 23–30, 40, 43, 62

Burwell, Margaret, 152, 163, 174–75

Burwell, Robert, 174

Butler, Benjamin, 24–26, 64, 67, 78, 88, 185, 204

Butler, Richard, 39

Cain, Bessie, 178–81

Cameron, Paul, 120, 143

Capehart, Sue, 154

Carolina Female College, 167

Chapel Hill, N.C., 108, 119, 123, 130, 143

charity. *See* free labor ideology

Charley (fugitive slave), 29

Charlotte, N.C., 35; Confederate refugees in, 5, 126, 132–33, 217, 222–23; freedpeople in, 225–26; housing in, 118–19; Jefferson Davis in, 157–59; railroads, 106, 116, 138; removed slaves, 109, 141, 145–46; Sherman's march and, 150–53, 155

Charlotte Female Institute, 152, 163, 174–75

Chesnut, Mary Boykin, 2, 134, 189, 195

Choiseul, Beatrix De, 208–9
Chowan Female Baptist Institute, 164, 176, 181
Christian Commission, 11, 27–28, 53, 74
Clapp, Henry, 20–21, 31, 56, 59–62
Clarke, Mary Bayard, 120
Clarke, R. R., 16
Clingman, Thomas, 30
Collier, Elizabeth, 153–54
Collier, Susan, 178–79
Collins, Josiah, 134, 139–40, 142–44
Colored Ladies Relief Association, 76–77
Columbia, S.C., 93, 150–53, 155, 186, 189, 199, 217
Colyer, Vincent: aids African American refugees, 11, 13, 16, 19, 37–38, 96; background, 27–28; conflicts with Edward Stanly, 47–54; employs African American refugees, 28–29; opens schools, 44; refugee crisis, 40–43; successors, 57, 63, 98
Company Shops (Burlington), N.C., 101–2, 118
Concord, N.C., 35, 132, 146, 155, 177, 179, 224
Concord Female College, 167, 175, 177, 179
Confederate refugees: from Columbia, 151–52; from eastern North Carolina, 15, 100–103, 105; financial problems, 130–42, 198–202; gender roles, 117–18, 132–33; homesickness, 104, 123, 203–5; hostility toward, 131–32; housing, 118–27; from Mississippi, 128–29, 184–85; number of, 130; in Piedmont, 100–159; politics, 147–49; postwar experience, 214–15, 217–24; relief for, 149–50; transportation, 115–18; from Virginia, 106–7; in western North Carolina, 184–215. See also slaves
Confederate soldiers, 14–15, 154, 221
conscription (Confederate), 19–20, 32–33, 39–40, 46, 70, 79–81, 148–49, 192–95, 197, 199, 211
contrabands. See African American refugees
Cooke, Homer A., 84
Cotten, Sallie Southall, 182–83

Creasey, William, 86
Creecy, Bettie, 166, 168, 170, 174
Creecy, Richard, 166, 168, 170
Cronly family, 108, 136–37, 155–56
Culling, Martha, 45
Curtis, Kate, 165, 167, 172, 175
Curtis, William, 14–15

Danville, Virginia, 24, 138, 157–58
Dargan, Clara, 217–18, 220
Davenport Female College, 165, 167, 169
Davis, Jefferson, 2, 65, 106, 131, 157–59, 166, 197, 210, 220
Davis, Sutton, 17
Davis, Varina, 2, 106, 119, 157–58, 166
Dennett, John, 224
DeRosset family, 108–9, 114, 119–20, 134, 136
desertion, 1, 46–47, 70–71, 80, 94, 105, 132, 148, 193–94, 205–14
disease, 88–92, 146–47. See also malaria; smallpox; typhoid fever; yellow fever
Dismal Swamp, 18–19
Doherty, William H., 27
Downs, Jim, 3, 12–13, 88

Earle, Thomas, 31
Eddins, William, 33
Edgeworth Female Seminary, 169
Edmondston, Catherine, 111–12, 114–16, 140
Elizabeth City, N.C., 19, 58, 61–62, 114, 168
Elliott, William, 188
Ellis, John W., 163
Emancipation Proclamation, 50–51, 55–61, 63, 77, 92, 103, 110
Emmerton, James, 31
Equal Rights League (North Carolina chapter), 79, 92. See also National Equal Rights League
Espy, Sarah, 113

Farmer, Henry T., 192, 196–97, 213
Fayetteville, N.C., 93, 107–8, 127, 153–54
Felton, Isaac K., 65, 77

female academies, 160–83; Confederate soldiers visit, 177–79; curriculum, 176–77; diet, 172–73; dress code, 172; isolation and safety of, 167–69; slaves at, 173–74; students as refugees, 165–67; teachers, 174–75; Union soldiers visit, 179–81; war news at, 169–71
Fenno, John, 47
First Confiscation Act, 25–26
Fitz, E. S., 98
Flat Rock, N.C., 186–214
Fort Fisher, 19, 115
Foster, John, 45, 49, 52, 57–58, 60–63
Fowle, Joseph, 90
Freedmen and Southern Society Project, 3
Freedman's Bureau. *See* Bureau of Refugees, Freedmen, and Abandoned Lands
Freedman's Convention, 78, 227
free labor ideology, 37, 68, 74–75, 97
Freeman, Sarah, 69

Gale, Katherine Polk, 2, 184–86, 198, 204
Gale, William, 185
Galloway, Abraham, 55, 63–65, 77, 79, 92
Glazier, James, 44
Goldsboro, N.C., 106, 118, 138, 141, 148, 153–54
Good, John, 78–79
Goodloe, Daniel Reeves, 58
Goss, Warren Lee, 71–72
Graham, William A., 122
Grant, Ulysses S., 185, 217
Greensboro, N.C.: Confederate refugees in, 106, 129; in 1865, 155–58, 217, 225; female academies in, 160–61, 167, 171, 175; overcrowding, 118–19, 132–33, 150, 152–53; removed slaves in, 111–12, 138, 140–41, 145, 203
Greensboro Female College, 160–61, 167, 171, 182

Hadley, George, 211–13
Hall, Rowland, 24, 39, 49
Hammill, William W., 50
Hand, D. W., 82

Hanks, Clarrisa Phelps, 14
Harriet (fugitive slave), 48–49
Harris, George W., 89
Hassell, Cushing, 106, 111
Hatteras Island, N.C., 15, 31, 33, 42, 105, 153, 170
Hawkins, Rush C., 26–27
Hawley, Joseph R., 94, 220
Hedrick, John A., 46–47, 50, 73, 80–83, 89
Hendersonville, N.C., 196, 208
Henrietta (enslaved cook), 143–44
Henry, Milly, 128–29, 136, 224
Herrington, William D., 1–3
Hill, D. H., 17, 30, 61
Hill, Edward, 77
Hill, Eliza, 108
Hill, Pauline, 165, 169, 171–72, 179–80
Hillsborough, N.C., 159, 174–75; Confederate refugees in, 106, 108–9, 127, 130–31, 154; housing in, 118–20, 122; removed slaves in, 114, 134, 139
Hogan, M. K., 226–27
Hoke, Robert F., 70–71
Holden, William Woods, 148–49
Homans, Amos, 23
Hood, James Walker, 55, 77–79
hospitals, 141–42
Howard, O. O., 97–99, 180
Hubbard, F. M., 143–44
Hurry Scurry plantation, 139, 143

James City, N.C. *See* Trent River settlement
Johnson, Andrew, 97, 228
Johnson, Samuel, 72
Johnston, Joseph E., 151, 157–58, 223
Johnston, Lydia, 151, 157
Johnstone, Andrew, 188, 194–99, 202, 206–10, 212–13, 215
Johnstone, Elliott, 207
Johnstone, Mary, 188, 193–210
Jones, Turner, 160–61
Jonkonnu, 45

King, Mitchell, 190, 196, 201, 204
Kinnegy, William, 18, 29
Kinsley, Edward, 64–65, 77, 96

Kinston, N.C., 14–15, 29–30, 33, 35, 61–62, 80–81, 110
Kirk, George, 194
Kuykendall gang, 208–9, 212–13

Lacy, Drury, 125–26, 156
Lacy, Mary, 124–26, 156
Larned, Daniel Reed, 49–50
Lee, Mildred, 166
Lee, Robert E., 125, 158, 166, 217
Lexington, N.C., 102, 106
Lincoln, Abraham, 27, 34, 45–46, 49–52, 55–56, 58, 62–63, 65, 77, 158, 164, 175, 180. *See also* Emancipation Proclamation
Loftin, William, 30, 62
Louisburg, N.C., 131
Louisburg Female College, 164–65, 167, 171–72, 176, 179–80
Lowery War, 20
loyalty oaths, 19–20, 47–49, 60–61, 94, 156–57

malaria, 89, 95, 187
Mallett, Susie, 105
Malone, Lucie, 162
Mangum, A. W., 116, 146, 152
Massey, Mary Elizabeth, 2–4, 7
McClellan, George, 25, 38, 52–53
McKimmon, Kate, 175–76, 182–83
Means, James, 57–60, 62–63
Means, Thomas, 198, 213
Meekins, Isaac, 228
Memminger, C. G., 187, 189, 191, 210–11, 214
Middleton, Harriott and Susan, 188–89, 195–96, 198–200, 203, 205–6
Middleton, Henry, 189, 198
Mix, Simon H., 29
Montgomery, Lizzie, 171
Morehead City, N.C., 13, 15, 23, 35, 70, 78, 90, 93
Myers, Barton, 32

National Equal Rights League, 55, 92. *See also* Equal Rights League (North Carolina chapter)

National Freedmen's Relief Association, 69, 74, 228
New Bern, N.C., 1–3, 5, 13–103, 106–7, 116–18, 122, 131, 137, 164, 218–19, 221–22
New Bern Academy, 13, 48
no-man's land, 23–24
Nonie Gran, 201–2
North Carolina Railroad, 102, 116, 118, 121, 138–40, 145

Oakes, James, 25–26
Outten, Macy, 131–32

Page, J. W., 82, 84
Pailin, Emily, 19
Parker, Allen, 17
passports, 34
peace movement, 148–49
Peninsula Campaign, 38, 106, 157, 166, 169
Pettigrew, Charles, 33, 113, 140–41
Pettigrew, William, 111, 113, 134–36, 145
Pickett, George E., 69–70, 80
Piedmont Railroad, 112, 138, 140–41, 203
Pierson, Clinton, 77–79
Pigott, Emmeline, 35–36
Pinckney, Charles, 196
Polk, Leonidas, 2, 166, 184–85, 198
Polk, Lucia, 166, 185
Pool, John, 33
poor relief, 149–50
Port Royal, S.C., 188, 203
Plymouth, N.C., 15, 21, 31–33, 39, 41, 47, 50, 57, 62, 67, 70–74, 82–85, 91, 126
prostitution, 84–87

Quaker Belt, 105, 148

railroads, 115–16, 137–41. *See also* North Carolina Railroad; Piedmont Railroad; Western North Carolina Railroad
Raleigh, N.C., 5, 13, 72, 100, 102, 105–8, 111, 118–22, 125–29, 138, 140, 144, 146–49, 153–54, 156–57, 164–68, 175, 178, 185, 217, 224–25, 227
Ramsey, James G. M., 132, 155, 222–24

Ramsey, Margaret, 155, 222–24
Randolph, John A., Jr., 65, 77–79
rape, 87
refugees: crisis, 7; historical antecedents, 6–8; number of, 7–8; terms for, 5. *See also* African American refugees; Confederate refugees; Unionist refugees
Reid, Whitelaw, 221–22, 224
Roanoke Island, N.C.: African American refugees on, 20, 24, 26, 28, 43, 45, 55, 78, 83, 99; colony on, 67–72, 76; housing, 41, 92–93; postwar development, 226–29; Unionist refugees on, 32–33, 83; Union occupation, 11, 15, 17, 106, 109–10, 116, 123, 135, 170
Roberts, Lavinia, 218–21
Robertson, George, 214
Rodman, William Blount, 112, 156
Roe, Alfred, 43
Rogers, Hattie, 16
Rumley, James, 30, 79–80, 91–92, 221

Salem Female Academy (Salem College), 162–63, 165–67, 173, 175, 178, 180–81
Salisbury, N.C., 106, 132, 138, 141, 152, 155, 217, 225
Sanitary Commission, 53, 82
Schenck, David, 105, 114, 130, 133
Schenck, Nicholas, 107
Schweinitz, Robert de, 163
Seward, William, 46, 49
Shelton Laurel Massacre, 194
Sherman, Thomas W., 26
Sherman, William Tecumseh, 93–97, 136–37, 150–58, 179, 181, 217, 219
Singleton, William Henry, 29–30, 61–62
slave patrols, 22–23, 142–43, 197–98
slaves: ads for runaway, 144–45; removal, 104–6, 109–15, 126–27, 130, 187–89; rental, 133–42, 202; resistance by, 143–46; sales, 133, 136–37, 202–3. *See also* African American refugees
smallpox, 42–43, 89, 146, 219
Smedes, Aldert, 162–63, 167, 170, 172–74
Smith, Henry, 133, 145
Smith, William, 36, 84–86

Somerset Plantation, 139
Spencer, Cornelia Phillips, 114, 119, 151
spies (Confederate), 35–36, 61
spiritualism, 171
Stacy, A. G., 165
Stanly, Edward, 45–52, 56, 58, 60–62
Stanton, Edwin, 18, 25, 27, 46–47, 49, 78
Starkey, Mary Ann, 64–65, 76–77, 96
Sternhell, Yael, 3–4
St. John in the Wilderness Episcopal Church, 187, 190, 196, 202, 205
St. Mary's School, 119, 162–76, 178–82, 185
Stoneman, George, 154–55, 158, 180
Stuart, Ann, 205
Sullivan, Lou, 166, 169, 173–74
Sumner, Charles, 30, 50–51
Swain, David L., 123

Thomas, William Holland, 110
Trent River settlement (James City), 60, 70, 73–74, 87–88, 90, 92–93, 98, 219, 221, 226, 228–29
typhoid fever, 60, 88–89, 146–47
Tyson, Bryan, 105, 148

Uncle Tom's Cabin (Stowe), 30
Unionist refugees, 4–6, 12, 32–37, 46–47, 58, 71, 80–87, 93, 218; housing and overcrowding, 42, 87; poverty, 39–40, 81–82, 84; segregation from black refugees, 82–84; as soldiers, 46–47, 71–72, 80–81
Union soldiers (northern): fugitive slaves and, 21–22, 29–30; hostility to Stanly, 49–50; occupation of eastern North Carolina, 12–16; occupation of the Piedmont, 154–57; opinions of Southern whites, 34–37, 79; racial attitudes of, 30–32, 50, 57
United Daughters of the Confederacy, 182–83

Vance, Zebulon B., 108, 110, 131–32, 143, 148–50, 193, 197, 200
Vance gang. *See* Kuykendall gang

wagons, 116–17
Ward, Giles, 35
Warren, Edward, 146
Warrenton, N.C., 39, 107, 124–26
Warrenton Female College, 161
Washington, D.C., 27, 46, 49–51
Washington, N.C.: African American refugees, 28, 31, 34, 60–62, 65–67, 78, 92; Confederate refugees from, 99, 106, 174; evacuation of, 70–73, 82, 91; overcrowding in, 42–43; Unionist refugees, 39, 61, 86; Union occupation, 15, 17, 126
Western North Carolina Railroad, 110, 138, 186

Whittlesey, Eliphalet, 97–98, 225, 227, 229
Wild, Edward Augustus, 63–64, 66–68
Williams, Mary Boykin, 189, 208–9
Wilmington, N.C., 5, 13, 64, 224; Confederate refugees from, 114, 136, 143, 155, 165, 220–22; conscripted laborers at, 19; Union occupation, 94, 153, 178; yellow fever epidemic, 107–9, 127
Wilson, N.C., 123, 125–26, 141

Yarborough House (Raleigh), 106, 119, 166
yellow fever, 19, 67, 85, 89–92, 102, 107–8, 127, 220
Yellowley, Harriet, 109, 123–24, 126
Yorke, Amos, 53–54

UnCivil Wars

Weirding the War: Tales from the Civil War's Ragged Edges
    edited by Stephen Berry
Ruin Nation: Destruction and the American Civil War
    by Megan Kate Nelson
America's Corporal: James Tanner in War and Peace
    by James Marten
The Blue, the Gray, and the Green: Toward an Environmental History of the Civil War
    edited by Brian Allen Drake
Empty Sleeves: Amputation in the Civil War South
    by Brian Craig Miller
Lens of War: Exploring Iconic Photographs of the Civil War
    edited by J. Matthew Gallman and Gary W. Gallagher
The Slave-Traders Letter-Book: Charles Lamar, the Wanderer, and Other Tales of the Slave Trade
    by Jim Jordan
Driven from Home: North Carolina's Civil War Refugee Crisis
    by David Silkenat
The Ghosts of Guerrilla Memory: How Bushwhackers Became Gunslingers in the American West
    by Matthew Christopher Hulbert
Beyond Freedom: Disrupting the History of Emancipation
    edited by David W. Blight and Jim Downs

www.ingramcontent.com/pod-product-compliance
Lightning Source LLC
Chambersburg PA
CBHW011749220426
43669CB00022B/2955